D1518215

FINDING SALVATION IN CHRIST

For Ethe,
In friendship,
Bill

Finding Salvation in Christ

Essays on Christology and Soteriology
in Honor of William P. Loewe

EDITED BY

Christopher D. Denny and
Christopher McMahon

☙PICKWICK *Publications* · Eugene, Oregon

FINDING SALVATION IN CHRIST
Essays on Christology and Soteriology in Honor of William P. Loewe

Pickwick Publications
An Imprint of Wipf and Stock Publishers
199 W. 8th Ave., Suite 3
Eugene, OR 97401

www.wipfandstock.com

ISBN 13: 978-1-60608-638-4

Cataloging-in-Publication data:

Finding salvation in Christ : essays on Christology and soteriology in honor of William P. Loewe / edited by Christopher D. Denny and Christopher McMahon.

xii + 332 p. ; 23 cm. Includes bibliographical references.

ISBN 13: 978-1-60608-638-4

1. Loewe, William P. 2. Salvation—Christianity—History of doctrines. 3. Jesus Christ—History of doctrines. I. Denny, Christopher D. II. McMahon, Christopher.

BT203 F35 2011

Manufactured in the U.S.A.

Contents

Acknowledgments *vii*

List of Contributors *ix*

Introduction: William Loewe, Bernard Lonergan, and the Salvific
Matrix (Christopher D. Denny) 1

PART 1: William Loewe and the Work of the Theologian

1   *Estote Firmi*: New York's Local Church under Cardinal Spellman's
    Watch—Some Foundations for an Intellectual Journey
    (Patrick J. Hayes) 23

2   Jesus Founding the Church: A Perspective Drawing upon
    Loewe and Lonergan (Dennis M. Doyle) 49

PART 2: Soteriological Narratives in the Christian Tradition

3   Schillebeeckx's Phenomenology of Experience and Resurrection
    Faith (Anthony J. Godzieba) 73

4   Narrating Salvation: Historical Jesus Research and Soteriology
    (Christopher McMahon) 107

5   Injustice at Ephesus (Gerard S. Sloyan) 128

6   *Propter Nostram Salutem*: The Cross and Our Salvation
    (Thomas J. Schärtl) 143

7   Anselm's *Cur Deus Homo?* Genres of Language and the Narrative
    of Salvation (Christopher D. Denny) 171

Contents

PART 3: Lonergan and Theological Method

8 The Law of the Cross and Emergent Probability
   (Cynthia S. W. Crysdale) 193

9 Finding the Ground: Method, Universality, and Ethical Discourse
   (David M. Hammond) 215

10 "Irrational Exuberance" at the Foot of the Cross: Redeeming the
   Rhythms of Economic Life (Stephen L. Martin) 238

PART 4: Finding Salvation in a Pluralistic World

11 Woundedness and Redemption in the Feminine Body of Christ
   (Kathleen A. McManus, OP) 265

12 Marriage Practices and the Redemption of the World
   (Jason E. King) 292

13 Christ in the Many and Diverse Religions: An Interreligious
   Christology (Peter C. Phan) 307

Epilogue: Continuing Conversations (William P. Loewe) 319

Acknowledgments

As editors of this volume we would like to express gratitude to all those who have helped make this book possible. Chris Spinks and Diane Farley at Wipf and Stock Publishers have provided encouragement and guidance from the very beginning of the project. The contributors to the volume have been generous with their time, and they have worked patiently with us to improve the quality of the final product. We would like to offer a special note of gratitude to William Loewe, to whom these essays are dedicated. As a teacher and mentor, Professor Loewe has challenged and encouraged us to think clearly and rigorously in the service of the gospel. He has offered advice and critiques for us as editors and for our contributors as well, all of which have made the volume stronger.

We would like to thank Saint Vincent College, especially the Faculty Development Committee; the Vice President of Academic Affairs, John Smetanka; the Dean of the School of Humanities and Fine Arts, Fr. Rene Kollar, OSB; and the chair of the Department of Theology, Jason King, whose support and encouragement were indispensable in seeing this project to completion. Additionally, we would like to thank Katherine Macioce, Claire Alessi, and Ashley Myers, the talented and resourceful student research assistants at Saint Vincent who helped with a variety of tasks associated with this volume. We also tip our hats to Barbara Sain from the Theology Department at the University of St. Thomas in Minnesota and to Cynthia Chambers at St. John's University for their help in tracking down references on short notice.

Our research and teaching endeavors have always had the support of our family members, which makes our final acknowledgments the most important. Chris Denny thanks the other members of his domestic church—wife Christina, and daughters Susanna and Beatrice—for their patience and support over the past few years. Christopher McMahon would like to thank his wife Debra for her faith and encouragement. We are truly blessed to be among such women.

Christopher D. Denny
Christopher McMahon
July 2010

List of Contributors

Cynthia S. W. Crysdale teaches in the School of Theology at the University of the South (Sewanee, TN). Some of her most recent publications include "Risk, Gratitude, and Love: Grounding Authentic Moral Deliberation," in *The Importance of Insight: Essays in Honour of Michael Vertin*, edited by David Liptay and John Liptay (Toronto: University of Toronto Press, 2007); and *Embracing Travail: Retrieving the Cross Today* (New York: Continuum, 1999). She is also the editor of *Lonergan and Feminism* (Toronto: University of Toronto Press, 1994).

Christopher D. Denny is Associate Professor in the Department of Theology and Religious Studies at St. John's University in New York City. His recent publications include articles in the *Journal of Ecumenical Studies, Communio, Logos*, and *Horizons*, as well as essays in the volumes *Vatican II: Forty Years Later* (Maryknoll, NY: Orbis, 2006) and *Making Peace in Our Time* (Weston, MA: Peace Press, 2008).

Dennis M. Doyle has taught in the Religious Studies program at the University of Dayton for twenty-six years. An expert in contemporary ecclesiology, he is the author of numerous essays, and two books: *The Church Emerging from Vatican II* (revised and updated; Mystic, CT: Twenty-Third, 2002) and *Communion Ecclesiology: Vision and Versions* (Maryknoll, NY: Orbis, 2000).

Anthony J. Godzieba teaches in the Department of Theology and Religious Studies at Villanova University and is the editor of the journal *Horizons: The Journal of the College Theology Society*. He has written dozens of essays for journals such as *Theological Studies, Louvain Studies*, and *The Heythrop Journal*. Some of his most recent publications include "Bodies and Persons, Resurrected and Postmodern: Towards a Relational Eschatology," in *Theology and Conversation: Toward a Relational Theology*, edited by Jacques Haers and Peter De Mey (Leuven: Peeters, 2003); and "Incarnation, Eschatology, and Theology's Sweet Predicament," *Theological Studies* 67/4 (December 2006).

David M. Hammond teaches Philosophy and Religious Studies at High Point University and has written on theological method, John Henry Newman, and the work of Bernard Lonergan. He is the editor of *Lived Christianity* (Mystic, CT: Twenty-Third, 2000) and his essays have appeared in *The Heythrop Journal, Thought, Method, Logos, Horizons*, and other journals.

Patrick J. Hayes has taught at Fordham University, St. John's University in New York, and the University of Makeni in Sierra Leone, West Africa. He is the author of numerous essays and reviews on American church history and has served as an editor for a number of publications, including *The Making of Modern Immigration: An Encyclopedia of People and Ideas* (forthcoming from ABC-CLIO), *The Living Light*, and the online journal *H-Catholic*. Hayes's monograph, *A Catholic Brain Trust: The History of the Catholic Commission on Intellectual and Cultural Affairs*, is forthcoming from the University of Notre Dame Press.

Jason E. King is the coauthor (with Donna Freitas) of *Save the Date* (New York: Crossroad, 2001) and *Killing the Imposter God* (San Francisco: Jossey-Bass, 2007), as well as the author of numerous essays on dating and marriage in journals such as the *Journal of Ecumenical Studies, Horizons*, and *Josephinum*. He is the chair of the Theology Department at Saint Vincent College in Latrobe, PA.

William P. Loewe is Associate Professor of Theology at The Catholic University of America. His work has appeared in journals such as *Anglican Theological Review, Theological Studies, Horizons*, and *Catholic Biblical Quarterly*. He is the author of *The College Student's Introduction to Christology* (Collegeville, MN: Liturgical, 1996), and coeditor (with Vernon Gregson) of *Jesus Crucified and Risen: Essays in Honor of Dom Sebastian Moore* (Liturgical, 1998) and (with Carol J. Dempsey) of *Theology and Sacred Scripture* (Maryknoll, NY: Orbis, 2001).

Stephen L. Martin is the author of *Healing and Creativity in Economic Ethics: The Contributions of Bernard Lonergan's Economic Thought to Catholic Social Teaching* (Lanham, MD: University Press of America, 2008). He serves as chair of the Theology Department at Immaculata University in Pennsylvania.

Christopher McMahon teaches in the Theology Department at St. Vincent College, Latrobe, PA. He is the author of *Jesus Our Salvation* (Winona, MN: Anselm Academic, 2007), *Called Together: An Introduction to Ecclesiology* (Anselm Academic, 2010), and essays for journals such as *Dialog, The Heythrop Journal,* and *American Benedictine Review.*

Kathleen A. McManus, OP, is the author of *Unbroken Communion: The Place and Meaning of Suffering in the Theology of Edward Schillebeeckx* (New York: Rowan and Littlefield, 2003). She is a member of the Blauvelt (NY) Dominican community and teaches in the Theology Department at the University of Portland.

Peter C. Phan is the Ignacio Ellacuria Chair of Catholic Social Thought at Georgetown University. He is a past president of the Catholic Theological Society of America and the author of numerous works including *Christianity with an Asian Face* (Maryknoll, NY: Orbis, 2003) and *Being Religious Interreligiously* (Orbis, 2004).

Thomas J. Schärtl serves on the faculty of Catholic Theology at the University of Augsburg, where he specializes in the intersection of philosophy and theology. He is the author of numerous books, including *Glaubens-Überzeugung: Philosophische Bemerkungen zu einer Erkenntnistheorie des christlichen Glauben* (*Faith and Conviction: Philosophical Remarks on an Epistemology of Christian Faith*; Münster: Aschendorff, 2007), as well as numerous essays in major international journals such as *Stimmen der Zeit, Concilium,* and *Catholica.*

Gerard S. Sloyan is Emeritus Professor of Religion at Temple University and is a Distinguished Lecturer at The Catholic University of America and at Georgetown University. His work on behalf of Catholic education and theological training in the United States over the past fifty years has left an indelible mark on the Christian community. He is the author of numerous books and essays. Among his most recent publications are *Jesus on Trial: A Study of the Gospels* (Minneapolis, MN: Fortress, 2006) and *Jesus: Word Made Flesh* (Collegeville, MN: Liturgical, 2008).

Introduction:
William Loewe, Bernard Lonergan, and the Salvific Matrix

CHRISTOPHER D. DENNY
ST. JOHN'S UNIVERSITY

The Work of William Loewe

According to the fourth-century Syriac document *The Doctrine of Addai,* in the reign of the Roman Emperor Tiberius there lived a king of Edessa who suffered from an incurable illness. This king, Abgar, received word from his royal messengers of a Palestinian man named Jesus who attracted crowds of followers and performed mighty deeds before astonished onlookers. Upon hearing these reports, Abgar told his courtiers: "These mighty works are not of men, but of God; because there is not anyone who can make the dead alive, but God only."[1] Unable to leave Edessa, Abgar decided to write a letter to Jesus requesting that Jesus come to Abgar to heal him. Entrusting his letter to his archivist Hannan, Abgar dispatched Hannan to Jerusalem, where the messenger found Jesus in the house of Gamaliel. After reading the letter, Jesus told Hannan,

> Go and say to your lord, who has sent you to me, "Blessed are you, who, although you have not seen me, believe in me, for it is written of me, those who see me will not believe in me, and those who see me not, will believe in me. But as to that which you have written to me, that I should come to you, that for which I was sent here is now finished, and I am going up to my Father, who sent me, and when I have gone up to Him, I will send to you one of my disciples, who will cure the disease which

1. *The Doctrine of Addai*, trans. George Phillips (London: Trubner, 1876) 3.

1

you have, and restore you to health; and all who are with you he
will convert to everlasting life. Your city shall be blessed, and no
enemy will again become master of it forever."[2]

After dutifully copying down Jesus' reply, Hannan, who also doubled
as Abgar's court painter, painted a portrait of Jesus, and brought both
the message and the picture back to Abgar. *The Doctrine of Addai* then
relates that after Jesus' ascension to heaven, Thomas the apostle sent
the disciple Addai to Abgar. When Addai was escorted into the king's
presence, Abgar joyfully proclaimed, "'Of a truth you are the disciple of
Jesus, that mighty one, the son of God, who sent to me saying I send
you one of my disciples for healing and for life,'" to which Addai responded, "'Because you so believe, I place my hand on you, in the name
of Him in whom you believe.'"[3] At the disciple's touch, Abgar was then
immediately cured of his illness.

This story is not only a tale about Abgar's personal salvation, but
also an instructive anecdote in introducing this current volume of essays. Abgar seeks a face-to-face encounter with Jesus, but has to wait for
a healing that is anticipated, both by a message from Jesus and also by
a portrait of Jesus' likeness. Abgar's cure is only subsequently delivered
by a disciple sent from one of Jesus' apostles. Biblical scholars will note
the earlier parallel in 2 Kings 5:1–14, where the prophet Elisha sends a
messenger to instruct the leprous Syrian general Naaman to wash in the
river Jordan, disappointing Naaman, who had been hoping for a cure
delivered in person from Elisha. Mediated salvation is a feature in both
of these stories, in which the presence of the healer is mediated through
other people.

William Loewe, PhD, the honoree of this festschrift, has spent
over thirty-five years insisting upon the inevitability of mediation, not
only in the subfields of Christology and soteriology, but in the enterprise of Christian systematic theology itself. Introduced to the thought
of Bernard Lonergan by Quentin Quesnell early in his academic career, Loewe has insisted that graduate students in his "Theological
Foundations" classes at The Catholic University of America take to
heart Lonergan's opening sentence in *Method in Theology*: "A theology
mediates between a cultural matrix and the significance and role of a

2. Ibid., 4–5, translation emended.
3. Ibid., translation emended.

religion in that matrix."[4] In his publications and in his teaching, Loewe demonstrates that Lonergan's statement is not an ingenious contrivance designed to make theology palatable to our modern sensibilities. Rather, Lonergan's definition is the product of historically informed study of the changing strategies that Christians have used to convey the meanings ascribed to Jesus throughout the centuries.

This theological mediation of Jesus' significance began in the first century with the oral preaching of the first disciples, and later with the gospels that early Christian communities committed to writing. In an early article from 1977, Loewe departed from positivistic assumptions of historical-critical immediacy in New Testament studies in calling attention to the link between symbol and psyche in the writing of the New Testament. "The Christian scriptures," Loewe wrote, "symbolize the realm of the transcendent by presenting Jesus as God's self-revelation. They thematize the significance of the central New Testament image, that of the crucified and risen Jesus, as redemptive. Thirdly, through the symbolic character of their imagery, they acquire and exercise symbolic force."[5] For Loewe, even in the first century of the Christian era there was no fundamentalist christological shortcut that would circumvent the need to mediate the intelligibility of Jesus' importance for the nascent communities of Christian believers. The lack of such a shortcut was for Loewe not a cause for consternation, but a call to recognize the importance of communal discernment among Jesus' disciples. "Christian communities," wrote Loewe, "trace their origin to the person of Jesus; the incarnate meaning borne by Jesus functions as an outer word which mediates their religious conversion, specifies it as Christian, and in this mediation renders community possible."[6]

In the early centuries of the patristic era, the writings of church fathers such as Irenaeus, Clement of Alexandria, and Origen served as a bridge between the religious world of first-century Palestine and the intellectual thought patterns of Greek philosophy. As Loewe has demonstrated in a series of articles, Irenaeus of Lyons wrote *Against Heresies* to forge diverse elements of the oral and written Christian

4. Bernard Lonergan, *Method in Theology* (Toronto: University of Toronto Press, 1994) xi.

5. William P. Loewe, "Lonergan and the Law of the Cross: A Universalist View of Salvation," *Anglican Theological Review* 59/2 (1977) 162–74, at 171.

6. Loewe, "Lonergan and the Law of the Cross," 169.

traditions into a unitary symbolic narrative, the comprehensive scope of which could match the emerging Gnostic myths of creation and salvation.[7] Augustine's writings mark another pivotal historical moment in Christian soteriological tradition, as book seven of the *Confessions* details how neoplatonic philosophy liberated Augustine from picture thinking. Examining the incorporeality of his own thought process induced Augustine to reject materialistic conceptions of God. Sight and knowledge are differentiated in Augustine's mature theology, as indicated in book one of *On Christian Doctrine*, in which Augustine presents human learning as a pedagogical journey towards God.

By the High Middle Ages, scholasticism had provided another challenge for Christology, as Christian discourse was once again transposed, this time from the symbolic narratives incorporated in patristic exegesis into the theoretical explanations characteristic within university settings. Innovative theologies differentiated intellectual experience from religious experience to a greater extent than the Fathers had. By fits and starts Christian scholasticism undertook systematic mediation of the founding narratives under the growing weight of the textual tradition. Loewe argues that Anselm's *Cur Deus Homo* marks a watershed moment in Christian theology, as Anselm rejects Boso's attempt to return to the safe comforts of patristic symbolic typology in the face of anonymous interlocutors who demand rational and necessary explanations of the Christian doctrine of atonement.[8] Anselm's rational en-

7. See Loewe, "Myth and Counter Myth: Irenaeus' Story of Salvation," in *Interpreting Tradition: The Art of Theological Reflection*, ed. Jane Kopas, The Annual Publication of the College Theology Society 29 (Chico, CA: Scholars, 1984) 39–54; "Irenaeus' Soteriology: *Christus Victor* Revisited," *Anglican Theological Review* 67/1 (1985) 1–15; "Irenaeus' Soteriology: Transposing the Question," in *Religion and Culture: Essays in Honor of Bernard Lonergan, S. J.*, ed. Timothy P. Fallon and Philip B. Riley (Albany: State University of New York Press, 1987) 167–79; "Jesus the Christ: Soteriology and the Stages of Meaning," in *Salvation in Christ: Comparative Christian Views*, ed. Roger R. Keller and Robert L. Millet (Provo, UT: Brigham Young University Press, 2005) 107–12.

8. See Loewe, "Method in the *Cur Deus Homo*: Concept, Performance, and the Question of Rationalism," in *Ethnicity, Nationality, and Religious Experience*, ed. Peter C. Phan, The Annual Publication of the College Theology Society 37 (Lanham, MD: University Press of America, 1995) 73–83; "By Way of Introduction: Anselm, Sebastian Moore, and Friends," in *Jesus Crucified and Risen: Essays in Spirituality and Theology in Honor of Dom Sebastian Moore*, ed. William P. Loewe and Vernon J. Gregson (Collegeville, MN: Liturgical, 1998) v–xiv; "Jesus the Christ: Soteriology and Stages of Meaning," 112–16.

terprise demands jettisoning longstanding soteriological assumptions such as the idea of the devil's rights over humanity in the postlapsarian era, a doctrine held by Augustine and other fathers. Irenaeus's soteriological mediation asked the question, "What is the story of Christian salvation?" "Anselm in turn," Loewe writes, "answered a further question: Within the world of the story, how does the death of Christ, the story's central figure, bring about our salvation?"[9]

In the next generation, Abelard continued Anselm's theoretic mediation in his *Sic et Non*, in which Abelard attempted to clarify Christian theology's primary narratives with the help of systematic rules employed to reconcile contradictions in the patristic tradition. In subsequent decades, theologians employed the *quaestio* to contrast and compare traditional authorities as disputation supplanted the *lectio* of monastic theology. Even among the advocates of scholastic mediation, however, theological diversity was present, as Abelard's commentary on Romans bypassed Anselm's emphasis on honor and justice in favor of a more subjective theory in which salvation was understood as a model of charity. As Christian theology becomes aware of itself as an academic discipline alongside other disciplines, Aquinas adapted both Aristotle's intellectual taxonomy and his realistic metaphysics and opened the *Summa Theologica* by presenting theology as an ordered *scientia* that mediated the articles of faith serving as theology's first principles.

The Protestant Reformation belies any interpretation of christological history as an unmitigated trajectory of progressive differentiation, as Luther sought to wrest soteriology from the clutches of theoretical disputes by recasting its mediating question as one of personal interiority: "How is the Christian narrative of salvation operative within *me*?" Loewe judges that true knowledge of Christ for Luther is experiential knowledge of Christ and his benefits, and the dramatic element within Luther's explanation of Christ's benefits emerges from Luther's own personal drama.[10] On one level, this marks a historical retreat from scholastic preoccupations with theory, as Luther is not critically interpreting the Christian story as Anselm was. Luther is op-

---

9. Loewe, "Jesus the Christ: Soteriology and Stages of Meaning," 120.

10. See Loewe, "Jesus the Christ: Soteriology and Stages of Meaning," 117–19. Loewe sides with Gustav Aulén, *pace* Paul Althaus and Robert Culpepper, in interpreting Luther's soteriology as anti-theoretical rather than as an example of a penal-substitution theory.

erating at the theological level of common sense rather than theory, and yet the mediating function of Christology is just as present as it had been in *Cur Deus Homo*, as the significance of Christianity's role within early modernity's cultural matrix is trending towards explicit personal transformation rather than doctrine. By the nineteenth century, this process accelerates after the Enlightenment's denigration of religious dogma, which the philosophes spurned as authoritarian-sponsored superstition. Schleiermacher responded to religion's cultured despisers by laying doctrine and empirical concerns aside in favor of the mediating function of a feeling of absolute dependence—*Gefühl*—presumably more accessible to the cultural matrix of modern subjectivity. Loewe writes:

> Schleiermacher had the merit of expressing a new question to define a further stage in the development of Christian understanding of the doctrine of the work of Christ. . . . What is the transformation of consciousness, evoked by Jesus first in His earthly ministry and now through the mediation of the life of the Christian community, that generated the story, that creates the horizon within which the intelligibility of the story can be determined, and that provides the criterion for judging the authenticity of conflicting interpretations of the story?[11]

Theology's task for Schleiermacher is to describe the Christian community's God-consciousness within history.

These shifting cultural mediations in Christian theology are of course not the product of a seamless process of historical determinism but rather of contrasting intellectual, moral, and religious frames of references that have been fiercely contested throughout the history of Christianity. Bernard of Clairvaux attacked what he considered Abelard's substitution of mere dialectics and judgment for the supposed immediacy of religious faith. Bernard insisted that scrutiny (*scrutinium*) had no place in theology, and instead appealed to wonder (*admiratio*) as Christianity's only proper foundation. During his time at the University of Paris, Aquinas was attacked for using Aristotelian philosophy to mediate the truths of Christian theology by those who favored continued use of the neoplatonic paradigm forged by Augustine and his heirs. In twentieth-century Catholic theology, neo-Thomism

11. Loewe, "Jesus the Christ: Soteriology and Stages of Meaning," 120.

was attacked by theologians who concluded that scholasticism's cognitive and systematic mediations desperately needed supplementing with a theology that was both critical and methodical. Bernard Lonergan's *Method in Theology* contributed to this enterprise, and readers familiar with Lonergan's work will recognize that the christological history sketched above is indebted to Lonergan's foundational methodology, insofar as Lonergan conceives of the various stages of human meaning, from common sense to theory to interiority, as products of human performance in search of authenticity. Indeed, with his explication of Lonergan's attempts to resituate the meaning of Chalcedonian dogma within the cultural matrix of mid-twentieth-century Catholic theology, Loewe demonstrated how Lonergan's own published oeuvre marked a journey towards greater theological authenticity, as the uneasy mixture of neo-scholastic form and historical-critical method in Lonergan's pre-Vatican II dogmatic writings gave way to a more directly psychological understanding of personhood.[12]

Loewe has devoted the bulk of his research and publications towards explicating the soteriological consequences of Lonergan's theology, and further developing Lonergan's "Law of the Cross" in pursuit of what Loewe calls "a responsible, contemporary soteriology."[13] Since historical and theological developments never cease, Christians in each new generation have to answer Jesus' question, "Who do you say that I am?" with answers wrested from the emergent cultural matrices in which they live. Against misinterpretations from those who may be suspicious that such creative fidelity is a mask for setting aside traditional affirmations about Christ no longer popular in contemporary contexts, Loewe urgently casts the need for soteriological renewal as a matter intrinsic to theology:

> The progress of the modern era has a shadow side. What is ultimately at stake is the fundamental objectivity of meaning and value, the elements which constitute any culture. In the present context we can only note that the problem of integration in its full scope signals a new stage in the development of hu-

---

12. See Loewe, "Jesus, Son of God," in *The Desires of the Human Heart*, ed. Vernon Gregson (Mahwah, NJ: Paulist, 1988) 184–90.

13. See Loewe, "Toward a Responsible Contemporary Soteriology," in *Creativity and Method: Essays in Honor of Bernard Lonergan, S. J.*, ed. Matthew L. Lamb (Milwaukee: Marquette University Press, 1981) 213–27.

man intelligence. . . . That context calls for a critically mediated soteriology. Such a soteriology cannot simply assume its basic terms. Those terms, namely sin and redemption, cannot be unquestioningly taken over from Scripture and tradition. Their meaningfulness must be secured.[14]

Theological meaning in this context is not a privatized fetish, but a constitutive element of human experience that mediates the worthy virtues of rationality and goodness. When shared among persons and cultures, meaning secures community as people adhere to what Lonergan called the transcendental precepts: be attentive, be intelligent, be reasonable, be responsible. The particular historical worlds in which Christians live are not characterized by mere contemplation but by active social engagement at economic, political, and technological levels. Sin and redemption are the opposing possibilities facing human beings, as they choose either the irrationality of individual and group bias, or the authenticity achieved by responding to unrestricted divine love that is mediated through human subjectivity. Concurring with the assessment of Robert Doran, Loewe judges that a praxis-oriented soteriology finds refined articulation in *Method in Theology*, in which Lonergan's analysis of human subjectivity moves beyond cognition to encompass intentionality:

> Sin finds embodiment in social, political, economic, and cultural institutions, and hence there devolves upon the community a task of discernment and criticism. If sinful structures and dehumanizing belief systems draw their plausibility from the myth of the way things are, the Christian community possesses in its own myth and ritual the imaginative resources with which to challenge the power of that myth in prophetic denunciation.[15]

In the decades since Loewe's characterization of Lonergan's anthropology, the claim that values and intentionality can mediate transcendence has been bluntly challenged and rejected by thinkers on separate fronts. On one hand, so-called postliberals have challenged the Lonerganian claim that differing cognitive and linguistic formulations can be judged to mediate a common core experience across religious

14. Loewe, "Lonergan and the Law of the Cross," 165.

15. Loewe, "Toward a Responsible Contemporary Soteriology," 225; see also 218–19.

traditions.[16] On the other hand, in common parlance the meaning of the term "value" is increasingly distant from the ontological and metaphysical context in which Lonergan placed the term, conjuring up fears that a consumerist understanding of value only serves to undermine objective morality in favor of a rank moral subjectivism.[17] Lonergan and Loewe, however, are innocent of such a restricted soteriological position. In response to the first charge, no theologian insisted upon the historicity of knowledge more than Lonergan in *Method in Theology*. To claim that there is a common core experience across religious and cultural divisions does not necessarily entail the claim that this experience can be detached from the linguistic media through which experience is conveyed. Indeed, Loewe has criticized Schleiermacher precisely on the charge of reducing doctrinal truth to personal experience.[18] In response to the second charge, Lonergan's Law of the Cross invokes the same taking up of one's cross of which Jesus spoke in Luke 9:23: "If anyone wishes to come after me, he must deny himself and take up his cross daily and follow me." This taking up of one's cross after all involves dying to self, not just through binding oneself through a rigorous physical asceticism, but through what Lonergan and Loewe describe as a interior transvaluation of one's values, the very opposite of a subjectivist position.[19]

16. George Lindbeck's 1984 book *The Nature of Doctrine* singles out Lonergan's definition of religious experience as the basis for criticizing what Lindbeck calls the "experiential-expressive" model of religious experience. Lindbeck's work has been influential for many of the Radical Orthodoxy theologians mentioned in this current festschrift. See Lindbeck, *The Nature of Doctrine: Religion and Theology in a Postliberal Age* (Louisville: Westminster John Knox, 1984) 30–45.

17. See for example Peter Kreeft's *Ecumenical Jihad*, in which the author writes: "Of course, objective morality, or the Natural Law, is not one among many moral options; it is the very definition of morality. 'Subjective morality' is an oxymoron; it is no morality at all; it is a mere game. If I (or we) make rules, I (or we) can change them. If I tie myself up, I am not really bound. And a nonbinding morality is not morality, only 'some good ideas.' It has no *laws*, nothing with teeth in it; only 'values': soft, squooshy things that feel like teddy bears." Peter Kreeft, *Ecumenical Jihad: Ecumenism and the Culture War* (San Francisco: Ignatius, 1996) 18.

18. See Loewe, "Two Revisionist Christologies of Presence: Piet Schoonenberg and Roger Haight," in *A Sacramental Life: A Festschrift Honoring Bernard Cooke*, ed. Michael H. Barnes and William P. Roberts, Marquette Studies in Theology 37 (Milwaukee: Marquette University Press, 2003) 113–14.

19. See Loewe, "Toward a Responsible Contemporary Soteriology," 220.

The stakes in contemporary christological developments were important enough for Loewe that he devoted a good portion of his work in the 1990s to composing a theological guide to benefit the many undergraduate students in his classes. Loewe introduced his 1996 textbook by informing students that in recent years Christology "has come to form a cottage industry," and *The College Student's Introduction to Christology* attempts to bring order to that burgeoning enterprise by framing its treatment of the subject around the crucial distinctions between historical statements about Jesus and statements of faith about the Christ, as well as the cultural shift brought about in Christology by historical consciousness and the natural sciences. [20] Rather than coddling students by sheltering them within an ahistorical and exclusively dogmatic Christology, Loewe helps students to understand that the allegedly shocking pronouncements breathlessly heralded by recent covers of *Time* and *Newsweek* have been bandied about since Hermann Reimarus and David Strauss shocked readers in the eighteenth and early nineteenth centuries with their heterodox conclusions. Introducing the final section of the text, subtitled "The Christological Process," Loewe invites interested students to help shape the Christologies of the future, from whatever cultural matrix in which they live. "The christological process," Loewe wrote, "is unfinished and open-ended. It will need to be performed anew in each generation for as long as people continue to discover in Jesus the meaning of ultimate reality and what human living is about."[21] Jesus is not a superhero sent from outside the universe to provide college students with an extrinicist escape from the business of living. Rather, in the faith of the church, Jesus meets the human need for fulfillment by answering questions that people already pose in their day-to-day existence. Loewe noted: "What is the character of ultimate reality, what is the purpose of human living? The scope of these questions renders them religious in character no matter what answer one provides to them."[22]

In recent years Loewe has entered into prominent christological debates within Catholic theology. With the collapse of neo-scholasticism after Vatican II, pluralism in the fields of Christology and soteriol-

20. Loewe, *The College Student's Introduction to Christology* (Collegeville, MN: Liturgical, 1996) 1.

21. Ibid., 176.

22. Ibid., 178.

ogy has been the order of the day in Catholic theology, and no subfields
in theology reach the heart of "transvaluation of values" more directly.
In 2000, Loewe built upon the analysis of his colleague at The Catholic
University of America, John Galvin, who several years earlier had noted
the shift in interest from the dogmatic belief in Christ's humanity to
a focus on the historicity of Jesus of Nazareth's life.[23] In keeping with
Lonergan's suspicion of historical positivism, Loewe proffered a question that he hoped would clarify the theological stakes emerging in
the wake of the publicity afforded to the Jesus Seminar by the popular
media: "What is the theological and christological relevance of the project and results of research on the historical Jesus?"[24] For Loewe, this is
neither a rhetorical nor a self-evident question, as the accumulation of
putative facts about Jesus of Nazareth is always selective, conditioned
by the subjectivity of the researcher involved, and subject to revision
and correction by subsequent historical research. Just as Lonergan argued in *Method in Theology* that knowing was more than seeing, Loewe
challenged christological positions from across the theological spectrum that aimed to draw a direct line between the tentative findings of
historical Jesus research and the theological consequences for dogmatic
and systematic Christology.

A few years later, Loewe weighed in on the christological implication of Roger Haight's important book, *Jesus, Symbol of God.*[25]
Questioning the ontological foundations of Haight's provocative thesis
that the salvation Christians experience in Jesus shares a foundation
with all religious experience, Loewe continued to rely upon the key
distinctions among experience, knowing, and doctrine in formulating
his response to Haight's book. While Loewe's earlier work expressed his
appreciation for attempts to reinterpret classic christological doctrine
in a modern context, his major concern with any reduction of religious
doctrine to experience is that such a move obscures the trinitarian

23. See John P. Galvin, "From the Humanity of Christ to the Jesus of History: A
Paradigm Shift in Catholic Christology," *Theological Studies* 55/2 (June 1994) 252–73.
The paradigm shift is also outlined by Loewe's former colleague Elizabeth A. Johnson;
see her *Consider Jesus: Waves of Renewal in Christology* (New York: Crossroad, 1990)
49–65.

24. Loewe, "From the Humanity of Christ to the Historical Jesus," *Theological
Studies* 61/2 (June 2000) 317.

25. See Loewe, "Two Revisionist Christologies of Presence," 93–115; Roger Haight,
Jesus, Symbol of God (Maryknoll, NY: Orbis, 1999).

reality of the Godhead, as a God who is experienced as utterly transcendent and completely ineffable may just as well be a unitarian deity
in which Father, Son, and Spirit have no ultimate reality. Both Haight
and Loewe judge that their respective christological approaches support soteriological universalism, meaning that God's offer of salvation
necessarily extends to the whole human race.[26] Their theological differences emerge in their contrasting understandings of religious meaning
and the implications of what human knowing and judgment entail in
matters of religion, and their disagreement provides support for Karl
Rahner's famous claim that "anthropology and Christology mutually
determine each other if they are both correctly understood."[27]

Not one to be pigeonholed and simplistically placed on either side
of the theological spectrum, Loewe in 2008 offered a sympathetic response to the work of Jon Sobrino, whose writings had been criticized
by the Congregation for the Doctrine of the Faith two years previously.[28]
For Loewe, works such as *Jesus the Liberator* and *Christ the Liberator*
are the products of a praxis-oriented Christology that deserves expression alongside the traditional scholastic Christologies rooted in metaphysical formulations of the person of Christ. In his assessment of the
Congregation's notification, Loewe continued Lonergan's call for seeing
the christological dogmas of the early church councils as a beginning
rather than as a terminus for reflection on the person of Christ:

> While scholastic Christology, fundamentally a metaphysically
> informed reflection on the dogmatic teaching of the Council
> of Chalcedon, once held the field, the past thirty years have
> been witnessing the emergence of a different paradigm among
> Catholic theologians. Christology from this more recent per-
> spective involves more than a systematic understanding of clas-
> sical conciliar dogma. That task remains, but as one moment
> within a broader project that seeks to shed the light of faith on a
> comprehensive genetic and dialectical account of the origin and

26. See Loewe, "Lonergan and the Law of the Cross."

27. See Karl Rahner, "Theology and Anthropology," in *Writings of 1965–67*, trans.
Graham Harrison, *Theological Investigations* 9 (New York: Herder, 1972) 28.

28. See Loewe, "Interpreting the Notification: Christological Issues," in *Hope
and Solidarity: Jon Sobrino's Challenge to Christian Theology*, ed. Stephen J. Pope
(Maryknoll, NY: Orbis, 2008) 143–52; Jon Sobrino, *Jesus the Liberator: A Historical-
Theological View*, trans. Paul Burns and Francis McDonagh (Maryknoll, NY: Orbis,
1993); Sobrino, *Christ the Liberator*, trans. Paul Burns (Maryknoll, NY: Orbis, 2001).

development of the church's beliefs about Jesus with a view to bringing his revelatory and redemptive significance to bear on the present. Sobrino's work finds its home within this context.[29]

The Essays in this Volume

The essays in this current volume follow in Loewe's theological wake and continue the project that he highlights above. Part 1, "William Loewe and the Work of the Theologian," features two essays that place the life and work of Loewe within a biographical and intellectual context. Patrick Hayes's opening piece, "New York's Local Church under Cardinal Spellman's Watch—Some Foundations for an Intellectual Journey," introduces readers to mid-twentieth-century New York City and the hierarch who dominated its Catholic Church for three decades. Controversial during his long tenure, Spellman shepherded the Church from World War II through Vatican II, and the far-reaching changes introduced during that time provided Loewe with a model demonstrating how the Church attempted to maintain its tradition during a period of complex social and religious changes. During his early years as bishop, Spellman maintained the autocratic style of ecclesiastical governance in favor during the early twentieth century, but he did so during a period in which a rapidly Americanizing Catholic Church enjoyed its newfound prestige among the wider American public. As bishop of the military ordinariate, Spellman's "muscular Christianity" during these years was put at the service of a common civil creed that he believed was essential to beat back the forces of fascism and communism threatening human civilization. Loewe grew up in the geographical and religious shadow of Spellman's New York City, amidst the growing suburbanization of Westchester County. Loewe's seminary education under the tutelage of the Jesuits in Shrub Oak, New York, typified the mixture of tradition and innovation characteristic of 1960s Catholicism, and his studies with Gerald McCool and Gilles Milhaven combined Aristotelian metaphysics with personalist philosophy and an emerging pluralism in moral philosophy. For Hayes, Loewe's intellectual formation in the mid to late 1960s can be set within a transitional age in which cultural upheavals and theological pluralism brought the

29. Loewe, "Interpreting the Notification," 150.

curtain down upon the autocratic style of religious uniformity present through most of Spellman's reign.

As Dennis Doyle demonstrates in his essay "Jesus Founding the Church: A Perspective Drawing upon Loewe and Lonergan," Loewe has passed along the fruits of his Jesuit education to succeeding generations of students. Building upon his dissertation research under Loewe, Doyle recounts the trajectory of his own intellectual development, in which he has employed a Lonerganian perspective to comprehend ecclesiological developments in the church's history. For Doyle, a proper delineation of theological specialties enables theologians and church historians to approach the question "Did Jesus found the church?" by properly differentiating the different levels of meaning on which that question can be answered. Just as Loewe has argued for distinguishing historical and theological levels of meaning in historical Jesus research and in Christology, Doyle believes that Jesus' presumed founding of the church can yield opposing answers, depending on whether that question is asked from within the framework of historical-critical methodology or from within dogmatic theology. Moreover, Doyle shows that the contemporary cultural matrix in which this question is asked is now shaped by ecumenical concerns that were not present in earlier eras.

Part 2 of this festschrift, "Soteriological Narratives in the Christian Tradition," features five essays in which the authors use a hermeneutic of retrieval to assess the contemporary value of classic formulations of the Christian understanding of salvation. Anthony Godzieba leads off the section with his essay "Schillebeeckx's Phenomenology of Experience and Resurrection Faith." Godzieba profiles one of the most noted expositors of theological reinterpretation of the late twentieth century. In challenging Loewe's assessment of how Schillebeeckx understands the first disciples' experience of Jesus' resurrection, Godzieba claims that Schillebeeckx's oeuvre provides readers with a distinctive understanding of the category of "experience," one that transcends objectivist and subjectivist understandings of the term. Drawing upon the phenomenologies of Martin Heidegger, Maurice Merleau-Ponty, and Hans Georg-Gadamer, Godzieba argues that Schillebeeckx's reconstruction of the resurrection experience cannot be shoehorned into any preexistent philosophical understanding of what the category of experience means. In its awesome singularity, Christ's resurrection presents him to his followers as a figure both familiar and strange, and this epiphany calls into question the theological adequacy of well-worn dualistic epistemological categories.

Like Doyle and Godzieba, Christopher McMahon protests against historical-critical naïveté in his contribution, "Narrating Salvation: Historical Jesus Research and Soteriology." Taking a cue from Loewe's 2000 article in *Theological Studies* and a recent article by Godzieba in *Louvain Studies*, McMahon attempts to steer a *via media* between the latent positivism of much historical Jesus research and theological endeavors that unacceptably minimize the religious significance of the Jesus of history.[30] With scholarly and popular reconstructions of Jesus' life and death jostling for the public's attention, McMahon turns to Lonergan's distinction of theological specialties for aid in making two contrasting points. First, in keeping with the critical subjectivity fostered by Loewe, McMahon argues that historical reconstructions of Jesus' ministry are never value free. Second, McMahon reminds readers that precritical or fictional narratives about Jesus, from the biblical Gospels to contemporary novels, can mediate religious values and so acquire a normative status irrespective of their shortcomings according to the criteria of modern academic history.

Moving from the first century to the fifth, Gerard Sloyan brings decades of his scholarly research and reflection to bear in his essay, "Injustice at Ephesus." After tracing the political context of imperially sanctioned Christology from the time of the Council of Nicaea, Sloyan moves beyond the bounds of a narrow interpretation of Chalcedonian dogma to rehabilitate the Christology of the Antiochene patriarch Nestorius. Like Doyle, Sloyan has ecumenical concerns in mind as he seeks to reinterpret Nestorius for a contemporary context in which members from different branches of the Christian communion are more inclined to dialogue across religious differences than to anathematize and excommunicate opponents.

Thomas Schärtl moves the historical focus to the medieval period in his essay, "*Propter Nostram Salutem:* The Cross and Our Salvation." Schärtl responds to Gianni Vattimo's soteriological indictment of Anselm of Canterbury's *Cur Deus Homo* ("Why God Became Human"). By using the work of Peter Hünermann and Loewe, Schärtl builds

30. See Loewe, "From the Humanity of Christ to the Historical Jesus"; Anthony J. Godzieba, "From 'Vita Christi' to 'Marginal Jew': The Life of Jesus as Criterion of Reform in Pre-Critical and Post-Critical Quests," *Louvain Studies* 32 (2007) 111–33.

his case that the debt-satisfaction theory of atonement that disturbs Vattimo and others is susceptible to an ethical interpretation more credible to modern audiences than the surface language of restitution present in Anselm's classic treatise. For Schärtl and Jürgen Werbick, a proper interpretation of *Cur Deus Homo* must place Anselm's juridical terminology within the covenant of salvation history. Such an interpretation shifts the emphasis from the supposed necessary bargain between Father and Son towards God's response to the human sinfulness that should not mar God's world. This divine response is at root not one of feudal justice but of forgiveness, and Schärtl takes a page from Jacques Derrida in asserting that like all acts of forgiveness Christ's cross reveals a paradox—the extralegal pardoning of the unpardonable.

Rounding out part 2, Christopher Denny also retrieves *Cur Deus Homo* in his essay, "Anselm's *Cur Deus Homo*? Genres of Language and the Narrative of Salvation." Denny employs Loewe's interpretation of Christian theological history to argue that interpreters' verdicts upon *Cur Deus Homo* correlate strongly with their identification of the genre of Anselm's treatise. Despite a long tradition of commentary on *Cur Deus Homo*, theologians have reached no consensus in ascribing a narrative or a theoretical genre to the work. Amidst the multifarious contemporary theological approaches to *Cur Deus Homo*, William Loewe's 1995 article, "Method in *Cur Deus Homo*: Concept, Performance, and the Question of Rationalism," sets forward a unique position.[31] While other interpreters have also claimed that Anselm's philosophical presuppositions are at odds with the manner in which *Cur Deus Homo*'s argument proceeds, Loewe uses Lonergan's differentiation of theological specializations to assert that the theoretical genre in the work is a postnarrative mode of discourse that mediates the gospel narratives without replacing them. Understood in this manner, *Cur Deus Homo* does not prove the necessity of the Incarnation by pitting a deterministic theory against the contingent narrative of salvation history in a zero-sum game. Denny concludes that if Anselm's treatise does indeed allow theory to coexist with narrative, rather than supplanting narrative, examination of selected contemporary expositions of *Cur Deus Homo* shatters any naïve illusion that textual exegesis of the work can

31. See Loewe, "Method in the *Cur Deus Homo*."

be divorced from the doctrinal assumptions with which Anselm's interpreters approach his text.

Part 3 of this volume, "Lonergan and Theological Method," contains three essays with a detailed focus on Bernard Lonergan, the man who has been the preeminent theological inspiration for Loewe throughout his career. In her essay, "The Law of the Cross and Emergent Probability," Cynthia Crysdale explicates the anthropological dynamism at work in Lonergan's Law of the Cross. In highlighting how the Law of the Cross transforms loving obedience to suffering into liberation, Crysdale explains how Lonergan's legal approach to soteriology escapes classicism in a contemporary world in which scientific laws are not Aristotelian but tentative and subject to revision in light of further evidence. In his essay, Dennis Doyle notes that Lonergan's mature theology had as its primary goal the transposition of neo-scholastic categories into a new cultural context. Crysdale's contribution follows up upon Doyle's by demonstrating how the transposed schemas that Lonergan identifies in the cognitive process yield insights and possibilities that cannot be predicted in advance. Just as Schärtl seeks to overcome deterministic interpretations of *Cur Deus Homo*, Crysdale finds that Lonergan overcomes the transactional and masochistic soteriologies that valorize either preordained justice on one hand, or a cult of suffering on the other.

David Hammond, in "Finding the Ground: Method, Universality, and Ethical Discourse," urgently defends the ideal of universal reason against postliberal and postmodern criticisms from the Radical Orthodoxy movement. Hammond finds in Lonergan's methodology an attempt to set forth a foundation for universal human reason that is yet socially and historically informed, and warns that theological perspectives that obscure what human beings have in common do not foster effective tools for global cooperation across religious divides. Lonergan's cognitive theory, contends Hammond, is not the "secular reason" denigrated by contemporary critics as an enervated theology scratching out an existence under the hegemonic empiricism of natural science. Along with Crysdale, Hammond defends the ideal of progressive integration in theology, and he believes that pressing global problems necessitate Christianity's common pursuit of rational, moral, and religious cooperation beyond the boundaries of the visible church. Against the religious particularism advocated by some postliberal theologians, Hammond claims that universalist understandings of human rationality do not necessarily entail religious indifferentism, nor does Hammond's advocacy of an interior ground for human rationality and value reduce religious commitments to mere personal preferences.

Stephen Martin also advocates the practical consequences of Lonergan's theology against Radical Orthodox alternatives in his essay, "'Irrational Exuberance' at the Foot of the Cross: Redeeming the Rhythms of Economic Life." For Martin, theology's engagement with the social sciences has become urgent in the face of recent economic policies that have concentrated wealth in the hands of the upper classes. Whereas some prominent Radical Orthodox theologians have rejected dialogue between economic theories and Christian theology to promote an exclusive reliance on anti-theoretical religious praxis, Martin believes that such a rejection is not morally viable on a widespread level. Providing the reader with a detailed explanation of Lonergan's lesser-known early works on macroeconomics, Martin commends Lonergan's economic theories, which advocate continued movement of wealth between the basic and surplus goods and circuits within an economy, as a superior alternative to the reigning orthodox economic policies promoted by Federal Reserve Chairman Alan Greenspan during the 1990s. Martin makes the case that while Lonergan's work allows for the relative autonomy of economics in relation to theology, Lonergan's economic principles are neither secularist nor divorced from religious principles. Like Hammond, Martin highlights the value of Lonerganian theories that do not depend upon a conversion to Christianity, and that can be used to facilitate justice in a religiously pluralist world.

The theme of Christian soteriological transposition into a contemporary world marked by biological, social, and religious pluralism is continued in part 4 of this volume, "Finding Salvation in a Pluralist World." Kathleen McManus offers an eco-feminist soteriological paradigm in her essay, "Woundedness and Redemption in the Feminine Body of Christ." McManus seeks to broaden the soteriological implications of classic phenomenology with a more explicit focus upon the embodied experience of women that constitutes the "Feminine Body of Christ." Distinguishing her approach from soteriologies that reject suffering's relevance for women's liberation, McManus surveys a range of ecological and social evils to demonstrate that suffering is part of women's experience and its importance cannot be minimized as theologians construct more inclusive soteriologies. Unlike colonial theologies that

seek to impose the model of the suffering Christ on indigenous popula-
tions with little regard for the suffering that colonialism and globalization have wrought, McManus correlates the suffering Body of Christ
with the suffering of the poor and marginalized victims of Christian
European colonialism. McManus challenges sanitized historiographies
of the church's history that turn away from the damage that the patriarchal church has inflicted on its feminine members. She reviews the
strategies by which saints such as Catherine of Siena, Teresa of Avila,
and Rose of Lima transformed self-emptying kenosis into spiritual solidarity with others who were suffering in their male-dominated societ-
ies, and presents them as hopeful models for contemporary wounded
women as they seek to create a more just society and a more inclusive
church.

Jason King's essay, "Marriage Practices and the Redemption of the
World," argues that the domestic church and the global church cannot be neatly segregated from each other, and that both these facets
of the Christian community mutually condition the salvation of their
members. Like Crysdale, King incorporates Lonergan's understanding
of schemes of recurrence, progress, and decline into his piece, as he explores how Lonergan's Law of the Cross elucidates the nuclear family's
quest for salvation amidst a consumer culture. Drawing upon the work
of John Kavanaugh and Vincent Miller, King discovers an urgent need
for families to break free of the competitive models of community that
dominate market economics and that lead to a cycle of decline in domestic and communal solidarity. The open household that King offers
as an alternative does not view persons outside the nuclear family as
strangers to be kept at bay, but instead expands hospitality towards others. The emergent "gift-economy" in this domestic model contributes to
a cycle of soteriological progress by extending the very definition of the
household and integrating strangers into it.

Peter Phan's article, "Christ in the Many and Diverse Religions:
An Interreligious Christology," surveys recent attempts by theologians
to develop a Christology in concert with members from religious
traditions other than Christianity. Phan does not promote a theology
of religions that ignores religious differences in favor of a presumed
common core, but rather indicates how appreciation of other salvific
paths enables Christians to understand Jesus Christ more fully. Phan's
article stands in continuity with the Lonerganian approach used by

several contributors to this volume, as he holds that the contemporary understanding of Jesus Christ cannot remain static, given the reality of religious pluralism. More adequate understandings of Jesus will emerge as Christians engage people from other religions. In Phan's analysis, Raimon Panikkar offers a helpful exposition of an interfaith Christology shorn of Western metaphysical assumptions.

At the volume's conclusion, William Loewe responds to the contributors. He challenges working assumptions, commends insights, and provides questions for further consideration, all in an attempt to, in his words, continue the conversation. Those who have learned from him over the decades would expect nothing less. Through his many years of scholarship and teaching in the fields of Christology and soteriology, Loewe has himself become a mediating icon of sorts. As King Abgar encountered the power of the risen Christ only through the mediation of Addai, so do we encounter this power through mentors and friends who understand the ways in which Christ is present in our midst and who are willing to guide us. We offer this festschrift to William Loewe in the happy conviction that Christians who walk by faith and not by sight can understand that mediation is not a sign of despair at the absence of Christ but rather the space within which a community of disciples is formed.

PART 1

William Loewe and the Work of the Theologian

1

Estote Firmi: New York's Local Church Under
Cardinal Spellman's Watch—Some Foundations
for an Intellectual Journey

PATRICK J. HAYES

UNIVERSITY OF MAKENI (SIERRA LEONE)

Catholic life in New York's archdiocese from the beginning of the
Second World War to the mid-1960s was marked by a sense of surety
and power that the Church in America had rarely seen. Catholics held
mayoral and other public offices throughout the archdiocese, were bar-
ons of commerce, and, with their wealth and prestige, began a gradual
migration from the city center to bedroom communities "up state," to
what one historian has called the "crabgrass frontier."[1] Catholic sprawl
had been advancing northward from Manhattan, the Bronx, and
Yonkers for at least two generations prior, but in the aftermath of World
War II, the numbers had climbed so high that most new parishes were
erected in Westchester and Duchess Counties. Many Catholics had
seen what was happening to their city of birth or point of entry into
America and found it wanting, both for themselves and their children.
"Getting out" meant "going up."

---

1. See Kenneth T. Jackson, *Crabgrass Frontier: The Suburbanization of the United
States* (New York: Oxford University Press, 1985).

This was a part of the story of William Loewe's youth, and insofar as it was formative for his theological interests and acumen it deserves some examination. He was born at a time and place that experienced rapid sociological change, witnessed unique political drama, coined particular cultural references and developed an attitude that I will argue shakes off an old apologetic Catholicism and finds strength in a new form. The Jesuit theologian Bernard Lonergan wrote in his classic work *Method in Theology*, "while in biography the 'times' are a subordinate clarification of the 'life,' in history this perspective is reversed."[2] An essential corollary to this, however, is that there is a fair amount of historical determinism at work in the creation of both the life and how it fits into history; the social is informed by the individual just as the personal must be measured against the popular. This essay will provide some historical background for Loewe's life prior to his graduate training as a professional theologian. These formative years are important for understanding why the Catholicism that beset Loewe's environment continued to hold his attention and, in fact, moved him to shape an ongoing Catholic narrative through his later work. In this the local Church is hardly a minor player, for the kind of Catholicism Loewe encountered in his youth, which I argue had a unique sense of purpose and vigor, constitutes the centripetal and centrifugal forces that made the man. This is where he hammered out both an intellectual self-understanding and a sense of place, and from which he launched his considerable contributions to the theological enterprise. It is important to understand the kinds of influences emergent at the time—by no means specific to Loewe or his immediate circle—that made Catholics both who they were and *how* they were.

To do so I will try to take a bird's-eye view of the social and ecclesial markers in the history of the Archdiocese of New York, the cradle that bore Loewe, so to speak. At the center lies its cardinal archbishop, Francis Spellman, who not only appreciated a strong will in his fellow man, he exhibited his own strength of character for causes he thought just. In doing so, Spellman left a legacy for New York's Catholics to be impassioned and creative and even daring in how they worked out their faith and grounded the principles used to support it. Though neither his style nor his ideas were permanently fixed, his perseverance later in

2. Bernard Lonergan, *Method in Theology* (New York: Seabury, 1972) 184.

life allowed a kind of Greek tragedy to play out: those with a new theological outlook would supplant the elders. By the time of the Second
Vatican Council, budding theologians like Loewe were beginning to see
how they could take the strength they inherited and fashion something
viable and fresh—they hoped to keep Tradition alive, but different.
After reviewing Spellman's life and times, I look at how Loewe cut this
new path.

Spellman's Leadership in the *Archidioecesis Neo-Eboracensis*

Loewe's early years coincided with a number of transition moments
within the local Church, ushered in by a savvy and internationally
recognized archbishop. He capitalized on his connections to transform
nearly every facet of ecclesial life in his see, right down to directing that
each rectory possess a telephone so the faithful (and His Grace) would
have ready access to their pastors. Though known colloquially today as
the "American Pope"—not so much as an alternative to papal authority
as much as an extension of it—Francis Cardinal Spellman wielded considerable control within the archdiocese.[3] He assumed responsibility
for the New York See in April 1939, nearly eight months after the death
of Patrick Cardinal Hayes, the deeply beloved "Cardinal of Charities,"
and was formally installed the next month. From the first, and though
small of stature, he put his new flock on notice that his ministry would
not be marked by fear, even in dark times. In his sermon at the instal-
lation Mass, Spellman told the congregation that he wore "the Cross
as my shield and my breastplate because I am set for the defense of

---

3. See John Cooney, *The American Pope: The Life and Times of Cardinal Spellman*
(New York: Times Books, 1984). See also Robert I. Gannon, *The Cardinal Spellman
Story* (Garden City, NY: Doubleday, 1962). Both of these biographies, as reviewers
have pointed out, are faulty insofar as they are factually erroneous, tendentious, or
conceive Spellman as an object more appropriate to hagiography. The definitive ac-
count has yet to be written. For critique, see e.g., Roger Van Allen, "Cardinal Spellman:
His Real Biography Is Still Needed," *Records of the American Catholic Historical
Society of Philadelphia* 96/1–4 (March–December 1985) 93–101. For overviews of the
man and his ministry, see especially Gerald P. Fogarty, "Francis Cardinal Spellman:
American and Catholic," in *Patterns of Episcopal Leadership*, ed. Gerald Fogarty (New
York: Macmillan, 1989) 216–24; and Florence D. Cohalan, *A Popular History of the
Archdiocese of New York* (Yonkers, NY: US Catholic Historical Society, 1999) 305–73.

the Gospel."[4] Hayes had enjoyed absolute discipline among his clergy, largely because he left them in life appointments, and Spellman did nothing to undermine that when he took over. Their filial devotion was matched by their ordinary's own loyalty to Pope Pius XII, who, as the Cardinal Secretary of State, had consecrated Spellman a bishop in 1932. There was a clear demarcation of roles in this chain of command. Bonded in this way to their Supreme Shepherd, the ranks of the clergy were solidified, forming a bedrock for institutional, doctrinal, and ethical uniformity. The confidence that this engendered put Spellman on a near equal par with the cardinals of Boston and Chicago, and it was well known that Spellman's links to the pope and the Roosevelts were but samples of his international standing as well. When Cardinal Mundelein of Chicago succumbed in October 1939, Spellman was poised to come into his glory, easily eclipsing the standing of Cardinals O'Connell of Boston and Dougherty of Philadelphia. Insofar as New York finally realized its centrality as the capital of Catholicism in North America, the Spellman years were exciting, even romantic in their domination of American Catholic culture, to say nothing of the episcopal appointments that were made in the United States owing to a word from 452 Madison Avenue.

New York City, too, had also arrived as the quintessential American urban center. World War II had insured a steady stream of manufacturing, which would not begin to see a decline until well into the 1960s. By the end of the Second World War, the Port of New York was the conduit for international shipping and trade and was a tightly controlled and lucrative entry point for food stuffs and machinery.[5] The city was the premier travel destination both for foreigners and those within the United States. It was the publication capital of the world, where, in addition to dozens of publishing houses, the city's streets were littered with scores of newspapers and magazines of every description and language. Though rivaled by Chicago for its impact on national commerce, in the aftermath of the Great Depression New York led the

4. Spellman's homily reprinted in *Conference Bulletin of the Archdiocese of New York* 34/2, supplement for the silver jubilee of the Cardinal's episcopal ordination (September 1957) 15–18, here at 17.

5. On the port, see James T. Fisher, *On the Irish Waterfront: The Crusader, the Movie, and the Soul of the Port of New York* (Ithaca, NY: Cornell University Press, 2009).

rebound and quickly outstripped the Windy City in the financial services sector—a position it has never relinquished either symbolically or in fact. It was not only the country's most populated city, it was lauded as the most vital. Media of various kinds parodied or romanticized its mayors. One knew that New York was cultural king if only by tuning into *Fibber McGee and Molly* during the 1940s, which made a comedy of life on "Wistful Vista" under the leadership of "Mayor LaTrivia," a clear reference to New York's colorful Mayor Fiorello "The Hat" LaGuardia.[6] In 1957, Bob Hope played the playboy Mayor Jimmy Walker in *Beau James*, a film that tended to celebrate Walker's moral laxity, but which more importantly kept attention on Gotham's many charms.[7] Art, music, theater, fashion—all came together in a merry dance, expressed by the most lavish displays, in the most spectacular venues, by the most beautiful people.

Today the concept of New York as grandiose metropolis quickly becomes prone to nostalgia, especially considering its more seamy side of life—continuous poverty, rampant diphtheria, pestilence (from lice to rats), and the constant battle for sanitation in highly concentrated neighborhoods, most of which lacked proper housing for its citizens.[8] The city's population surged to its peak by 1950 and the ghetto was becoming a more conspicuous and unhealthful blight on the urban landscape. The people of New York knew the costs of human filth. It

---

6. See Claire Schultz, *Fibber McGee and Molly, On the Air, 1935–1959* (Albany, GA: Bear Manor Media, 2008).

7. On Walker's dalliances and place in New York political history, see, e.g., Gerald Leinwand, *Mackerels in the Moonlight: Four Corrupt American Mayors* (Jefferson, NC: McFarland, 2004) 109–74; Herbert Mitgang, *Once upon a Time in New York: Jimmy Walker, Franklin Roosevelt, and the Last Great Battle of the Jazz Age* (New York: Free Press, 2000); George Walsh, *Gentleman Jimmy Walker: Mayor of the Jazz Age* (New York: Praeger, 1974).

8. See, e.g., Maxine Hammonds, *Childhood's Deadly Scourge: The Campaign to Control Diphtheria in New York City, 1880–1930* (Baltimore: Johns Hopkins University Press, 1999); and *The "Underclass" Debate: Views from History*, ed. Michael B. Katz (Princeton: Princeton University Press, 1993). In 1948, "in density of population, New York was five hundred times the national average," wrote historian George J. Lankevich, "But no one seemed aware of it. People preferred talking about the power of New York's economy: a fifth of America's wholesale transactions took place within its boundaries." Lankevich, *American Metropolis: A History of New York City* (New York: New York University Press, 1998) 184.

bred a mentality often accompanying the squalor of moral turpitude. Crime was a fact of life and no neighborhood was immune. Uptown in the Bronx, the sounds of kids playing stick ball were interrupted by their mothers calling them home to supper—in Italian and German and Yiddish—and blame for all manner of social ills was placed at the doorstep of these urchins. The grit of the city came out on screen, too, as the hardscrabble working class found itself portrayed in pictures like *On the Waterfront* (1954). Although shot in Hoboken, its blend of Catholicism and labor strife in the holes of stevedores resonated with anyone who ever strolled along the Chelsea piers. In this New York, one was never far from either the Ritz or Palookaville.

If New York set the tone for urban life in America, it also did yeoman work to tamp down the social negatives that could drag its reputation into the gutter. In this fight, the New York Archdiocese, with its numerous Catholic charities, was a leading exponent of human development, a champion of the New York that tendered itself ready for everything new and improved, and an ally in building up the best while not forgetting the least. The admixture of ecclesial significance and cultural location served to put Spellman's reign at least on par with that of Archbishops John Carroll in the eighteenth century or John Hughes in the nineteenth. Spellman ushered in what promised to be a hopeful era. His tenure began what the historian John Patrick Diggins has labeled "the proud decades."[9] There was an air of possibility about New York; the Depression seemed to be finally over. Two weeks after Spellman was installed, the New York World's Fair opened under the theme "Dawn of a New Day." In less than a year, however, Spellman was called upon to lead through a Second World War—a test of mettle for both the archbishop and the souls in his care.

Military Vicar of the Largest Archdiocese in the World

When Cardinal Hayes died, the administration of the archdiocese fell to his auxiliary, Bishop Stephen Donahue. A classmate of Spellman and on the short list to succeed Hayes, Donahue was among the first to send

---

9. John Patrick Diggins, *The Proud Decades: America in War and Peace, 1941–1960* (New York: Simon and Schuster, 1988).

congratulations to Boston, where Spellman was residing as pastor of Newton Center's Sacred Heart Parish. Donahue confirmed a standard pledge of loyalty by the clergy and faithful, but he also invoked the Almighty to grant the archbishop-elect strength to carry out the duties required by the burdens of his office.[10] It does not seem as though Spellman ever withered under pressure during the whole of his tenure in the See of New York, and, while it does not go without qualification, the theme of strength is a continual trope that emerges throughout his episcopate. One need not exploit the old saw about a person small in stature compensating by showing toughness or always itching to prove himself. Demonstrating strength was a hallmark of Spellman's service both to God and country—quite apart from his height. He did it through the people that he allowed to encircle him. These were men of formidable talents and strong personalities. Disagreement with His Eminence was not unknown—but it never became a matter that ruffled Spellman's own sense of self-assurance. One thinks, for instance, of the awkward letter of resignation placed before Spellman by then Monsignor J. Francis McIntyre, the chancellor of the archdiocese, upon Spellman's ascendency. McIntyre had embarrassed Spellman during Cardinal Pacelli's visit to the United States in 1936, keeping Spellman from important meetings arranged for Pacelli, but the new archbishop waved him off. "Retaliation is a luxury I have never been able to afford."[11] In fact, he relished having men around him that could speak freely and forcefully. It built trust and made his administration more effective. This can be seen in the bishops he assembled to assist him in his ministry, both in the archdiocese and in the military ordinariate.

Spellman was appointed the military ordinary in December 1939, taking over the Diocese *Castrensis* from Hayes, who occupied that see for most of his episcopal career—some twenty-one years. Spellman bested him by remaining in that post from late 1939 to his death on December 2, 1967. With war on the horizon, Spellman asked

10. Gannon cites the letter of Donahue in full. See Gannon, *Cardinal Spellman Story*, 136.

11. Ibid. Almost immediately, Spellman appointed McIntyre to the Archdiocesan Board of Consultors and the following year had him named his auxiliary, a role he did not assume until he was officially installed in 1941. McIntyre would go on to become the Cardinal Archbishop of Los Angeles. The events of 1936 are relayed in Cooney, *American Pope*, 70.

for and received help from Father John O'Hara, CSC, then president of the University of Notre Dame. Spellman ordained O'Hara a bishop in January 1940 and appointed him military vicar.[12] The following year he received further assistance from another religious order. The Redemptorist Fathers surrendered their Baltimore Provincial, Father William McCarty, CSsR, to become Spellman's military delegate. A burly, former semi-professional baseball player, he was also ordained to the episcopate by Spellman in St. Patrick's Cathedral in January 1943. Both O'Hara and McCarty were chosen for their abilities to govern, and so when Spellman repeated the words of the Pontifical, which he would do on thirty other occasions—"May thy hand be strengthened"—he was earnest but confident in his selections.[13] McCarty took up residence with Bishop O'Hara at St. Cecelia's Parish, run by the Redemptorists, at 105th Street in Spanish Harlem. In addition to the home diocese, there-fore, Spellman's work encompassed all the chaplain activities of priests enlisted in the war effort, which, by 1941, at the beginning of hostilities, numbered about 500 chaplains. By war's end, the number had risen to about 3,300 priests in the army and navy serving over sixteen million total troops, of whom nearly five million were Catholic. Wherever these men were, Spellman was their ordinary—making his the largest diocese on the planet. He recognized boldness and wished to reward it. Given the fact that the Congregation of the Holy Cross and the Congregation of the Most Holy Redeemer headed the roster of enlisted chaplains, it was seen as both a practicality and reward to these institutes to place their members as bishop delegates. There was no room for timidity dur-ing these times. It was important to project order and discipline, and both of Spellman's military delegates were robust and exacting leaders who lent themselves unselfishly to the task of administration.

12. A fulsome account is found in Thomas T. McAvoy, *Father O'Hara of Notre Dame: The Cardinal-Archbishop of Philadelphia* (Notre Dame, IN: University of Notre Dame Press, 1967) 195–267. O'Hara had collaborated with Spellman on a visit of then Cardinal Pacelli to the Notre Dame campus when the Holy See's Secretary of State toured the United States in October 1936. Although Pacelli was only there for an hour, the cordial relations struck in this meeting were memorable for all concerned.

13. *Pontificale Romanum: Summorum Pontificum iussu editum a Benedicto XIV et Leone XIII pontificibus maximis recognitum et castigatum* (Mechlin: H. Dessain, 1958) 127.

Moments after Bishop William McCarty's episcopal ordination: (L to R)
Bishop Thomas Molloy of Brooklyn, Bishop McCarty, Archbishop Spellman,
Bishop O'Hara. Molloy would later become an archbishop; McCarty would
go on to become bishop of Rapid City, South Dakota; Spellman and O'Hara
would become cardinals. (Photo courtesy of the Archives of the Baltimore
Province of the Redemptorists, Brooklyn, NY)

For Spellman, having such able assistants allowed for him to move
freely to make visits to the troops overseas. Between June and December
1942, he set out on a whirlwind tour of four continents where American
servicemen were stationed.[14] Whereas Hayes never flew to meet the
troops, Spellman gained a reputation for flying to be with the enlisted
in far away parts each Christmas—whether in the Atlantic or Pacific
theater; whether in World War II, the Korean War, or Vietnam. By
August and September 1944, Spellman was making his way comfort-
ably in the circles of the Allied Command, meeting with General Mark
Clark and King George VI in Italy that August (the three were nearly

---

14. See Spellman's travelogue in *Action This Day: Letters from the Fighting Fronts*
(New York: Charles Scribner's Sons, 1943).

blown up by a hidden mine) and touring the regions around Paris that had come into the control of the First Army three months earlier.

Already for several years prior to American engagement in the European conflict, Catholics were wary of fascism in Spain and Italy and communism in Mexico and Russia. These were real threats to the survival of Christianity in places that held deep, centuries-old religious sentiments. Coupling these with Hitler's ghastly racial policies meant that the Church, in Spellman's perspective, was one of the few civilizing forces left to save humanity. It meant that all of its might had to influence what historians have called the "civic national creed" whereby the wider public weal had to uphold a common set of ideals, subordinating difference, or else perish under the thumb of unbridled evil. The attack on Pearl Harbor was the last straw. It was clear who America's friends were, just as it was clear who the enemy was. After December 7, 1941, justice could only be served through force. After that dizzying day, America "began the fight to save her life," Spellman wrote. "Our prayer for 'Peace with Justice,' became a prayer for 'Peace with Justice after Victory,' for it was dismally clear that only through the predominance of American man-power and American arms could anything except death and enslavement ensue."[15] When America was tested, Spellman thought, Catholics could rise to the challenge. It had the will and it had the brawn, not merely to take physical possession of territory currently held by the enemy, but to annihilate the evil in their midst. Most importantly, America had the power of religious ideals to defeat those pernicious philosophies. "I believe this total victory can come only through religion, and I believe that through religious faith and religious life it can come and will come."[16]

The form in which Spellman addressed these matters has been aptly described as a kind of "muscular Christianity," that is, a working out of the Christian imperatives from a position of fearlessness and willfulness in using power to achieve moral ends. It does not mean bullying someone into believing the gospel, but it does suggest that, for the good

15. See Spellman's introduction to *The Road to Victory: The Second Front of Prayer* (New York: Charles Scribner's Sons, 1943) x. He penned these sentiments in October 1942. Elsewhere in this volume he would decry poorly formed instruments to secure peace. "I am a man of peace, but gone is my hope of building a world safe for democracy on such foundations as the Treaty of Versailles" (24).

16. Ibid., x.

of the individual or community, authority of office can be used to do combat in the arena of ideas. For those outside of the Catholic subculture this was a welcome contribution to the national defense. It showed the Church's leaders as substantial and willing to shed their own blood for the cause of freedom common to all decent citizens. In this effort, Spellman applied a straightforward theological claim, one that often set Catholics apart but which furnished the most appropriate framework for action. He simply looked at the world as a vast field imbued with God's immutable laws, which necessarily had to be applied in truth "to man in the political, social, educational, economic and cultural aspects of his daily life."[17] Law, in this neo-Thomistic sense, was for humanity's fulfillment.

For Spellman, observance of God's immutable law was not merely an intellectual proposition. Practical freedom was the *sine qua non* required for salvation and occasionally, when it was threatened, freedom required defense. Of course, the more that Spellman appeared, for instance, in the pages of *Life* magazine clothed in army fatigues or administering Communion to soldiers in battle gear, the more it gave the impression that the "Little General" was intimately linked to the machinery of war. This was not something that he would easily escape, and by the time of the Vietnam conflict he would be caricatured for his role in the promotion of military might. Monsignor (later Auxiliary Bishop) Patrick Ahern, Spellman's long-time secretary (1958–1967) and speechwriter, would try to counsel his ordinary against coming off as too hawkish. "There are those in America who feel your words are too violent," he said in an interview. "I tried to tell Spelly to tone it down." Would he listen? "Sometimes."[18] And yet even in 1966, on his twenty-first Christmas visit with the troops (this time in the company of General William Westmoreland, in Vietnam), there was no distinction between cross and flag in the Cardinal's mind. Evil had merely changed its spots and nothing short of an American victory was required. The jingoism this conjures belies the combination of pastoral solicitude for the troops, patriotic support of American foreign policy, and a lack of

---

17. Letter of Spellman to Father [Thurston] Davis, SJ, February 9, 1959, reprinted in *America* 101 (April 11, 1959) 80. The letter was written on the occasion of *America's* golden anniversary. The Cardinal praised the journal's articles as being consistent with this ideal.

18. Bishop Patrick Ahern, personal interview with the author, August 2009.

sensitivity to the peace movement, a fact typified by the arrest of two dozen anti-war protestors outside of his cathedral. It is also easy to view the Cardinal's actions as part of an effort to save civilization or a wider cabal to manipulate public opinion in support of a Vietnamese Catholic mandarin, Ngo Dien Diem.[19] The photo opportunity such visits created also presented a further example of how ensconced Catholics were in the American project, even playing their part in the military industrial complex (contra Paul VI's admonitions to sue for peace), and making concrete their claim for equal participation in the country's unparalleled prosperity at home and a global, moral superiority abroad.[20]

Citizen Spellman: Domestic Politics

The clout Spellman garnered both for the Church in America and himself is signaled by the cordial relations he carried on with the highest echelons of power. Although not entirely friendly with President Truman, the Cardinal never publically challenged him. Spellman carried on a much more intimate relation with Presidents Eisenhower and Nixon and was expeditious, if chilly, with President Kennedy. In the years of the Cold War especially, Spellman had multiple contacts with J. Edgar Hoover, whose FBI would routinely brief Spellman on alleged communistic activities and accept information conveyed through the Holy See's back channels. The Cold War presented numerous opportunities for Spellman to speak out or write on the encroachments of "Christ-hating Communists"—whether it was because of the arrest of

19. On the campaign to save civilization, see "Spellman Again Tells G.I.'s in Vietnam They Are Defending Civilization," *The New York Times* (December 27, 1966) 4; on the "Vietnam Lobby," see Joseph G. Morgan, *The Vietnam Lobby: The American Friends of Vietnam, 1955–1975* (Chapel Hill: University of North Carolina Press, 1977); and the review of this book by James T. Fisher, "With Friends Like These . . . ," *Reviews in American History* 25 (1997) 709–14. Fisher takes up the "Vietnam Lobby" in a separate article, "The Second Catholic President: Ngo Dinh Diem, John F. Kennedy, and the Vietnam Lobby, 1954–1963," *U.S. Catholic Historian* 15/3 (Summer 1997) 119–37. See also Joseph T. Morgan, "A Change in Course: American Catholic Anticommunism and the Vietnam War," *U. S. Catholic Historian* 22/3 (Fall 2004) 117–30; Seth Jacobs, *America's Miracle Man in Vietnam: Ngo Dinh Diem, Religion, Race, and U.S. Intervention in Southeast Asia* (Durham, NC: Duke University Press, 2004); and Jacobs, *Cold War Mandarin: Ngo Dinh Diem and the Origins of America's War in Vietnam* (Lanham, MD: Rowan and Littlefield, 2006).

20. See Diggins, *The Proud Decades*.

his friend, Hungarian Cardinal Joseph Mindszenty, to support Senator Joseph McCarthy, or to denounce events on the Korean Peninsula and later in Vietnam.[21]

While war presented itself as an all-too-opportune moment for Spellman to flex his muscle overseas, he did not lack for similar occasions on the home front. In his relationship with labor, he proved himself no friend of unions, which he suspected of being infiltrated with socialist elements. When he showed up at St. Joseph's Seminary one night in 1949 to tell his seminarians they were to be drafted into service the next day, no one expected it would be to bury the nearly 1,000 bodies then in storage owing to a protracted strike by archdiocesan cemetery workers. The gravediggers were dumbstruck when they saw His Eminence enter Calvary Cemetery in Queens accompanied by three bus loads of seminarians, but of course, this was precisely the effect that Spellman hoped for, spouting to the press that he was proud of his strike breaking.[22] No less a personality than Dorothy Day served notice to the Cardinal that what he really buried was Catholic social teaching.[23] Labor leaders were incensed and felt betrayed by an institution that had had their back over the previous decade, especially since so many of their members had been raised up through archdiocesan labor schools.[24]

Spellman's attitudes toward social problems within the archdiocese were frequently contrarian, but often for the right reasons. Censorship was a perennial favorite with the Cardinal—for the very

---

21. See Richard Gid Powers, "American Catholics and Catholic Americans: The Rise and Fall of Catholic Anticommunism," *U.S. Catholic Historian* 22/4 (Fall 2004) 17–35, here at 25; Donald F. Crosby, *God, Church, and Flag: Senator Joseph R. McCarthy and the Catholic Church, 1950–1957.* (Chapel Hill, NC: University of North Carolina Press, 1978) passim; and Vincent P. De Santis, "American Catholics and McCarthyism," *Catholic Historical Review* 51/2 (April 1965) 1–30.

22. See Will Lissner, "Cardinal Directs Seminarians Dig Ninety Graves, Spellman Leads 100 Past the Strikers at Calvary—Offer to Use Pick Declined," *The New York Times*, March 4, 1949, 1.

23. See Arnold Sparr, "'The Most Memorable Labor Dispute in the History of U.S. Church Related–Institutions': The 1949 Calvary Cemetery Workers' Strike against the Catholic Archdiocese of New York," *American Catholic Studies* 119/2 (Summer 2008) 1–33; William D. Miller, *Dorothy Day: A Biography* (San Francisco: Harper and Row, 1982) 404–5; and Dana Anderson, *Identities Strategy: Rhetorical Selves in Conversion* (Columbia: University of South Carolina Press, 2007) 58–61.

24. See further Thomas J. Shelley, "Cardinal Spellman and His Seminary at Dunwoodie," *Catholic Historical Review* 80/2 (April 1994) 282–98.

laudable objective of preserving good morals—though it played out in odd ways by pressuring the New York Licensing Commission to ban films like Roberto Rosselini's *The Miracle* (1950) and Elia Kazan's *Baby Doll* (1956), which not only found Spellman in the pulpit lambasting Hollywood for such trash, but cadres of parish priests in the theater lobbies taking down names of their parishioners.[25] History looks more kindly toward the Cardinal's views on the race question, a matter that was pivotal to understanding American Catholicism in the 1950s and 60s.[26] Already he had exhibited a certain pastoral solicitude toward the churches in Harlem, making some of his earliest confirmation stops at St. Charles Borromeo and the Church of St. Benedict the Moor, two of the city's historically Black Catholic parishes. Spellman's interest in the welfare of Black Catholics stemmed from a brief stint in the archives in the Archdiocese of Boston. It was there, as a newly ordained priest, that he had organized the papers of Bishop James Augustine Healy, the nation's first Black Catholic prelate. While hardly a crusader for equal rights, Spellman felt compelled to support those of his priests who marched on Selma, refused to denounce Martin Luther King Jr. when asked by J. Edgar Hoover, and lent his name to those working in the field of improving race relations.[27]

However, while it could be argued that it was his private wish to see full integration, Spellman nevertheless walked a tightrope on the

25. See Raymond J. Harberski, *Freedom to Offend: How New York Remade Movie Culture* (Lexington: University of Kentucky Press, 2007) esp. ch. 3, "Baby Doll and *Commonweal* Criticism."

26. On the role of race and American Catholicism, see especially John McGreevy, *Parish Boundaries: The Catholic Encounter with Race in the Twentieth Century Urban North* (Chicago: University of Chicago Press, 1996).

27. In August 1953 Father Albert S. Foley, SJ, was contacted by Spellman, who congratulated him on his articles on race that were appearing in the pages of *America*. Spellman asked whether he would be willing to ghostwrite a piece on race. When Foley delivered the draft text, the Cardinal then inquired what he could do for him and the Jesuit wondered whether Spellman had any influence with publishers. At the time, Foley was then shopping *Bishop Healy: The Beloved Outcaste* around the New York publishing circuit. Foley showed the Cardinal the manuscript and Spellman told him to go back to Farrar, Straus and Cudahy, from which the manuscript had been recently rejected, and to inform John Farrar "that he thought it was a good book to publish." On the strength of that endorsement, overriding the business office, the firm took what turned out to be a bestseller among Catholic literature. See Albert S. Foley, "Adventures in Black Catholic History: Research and Writing," *U.S. Catholic Historian* 5/1 (1986) 103–18.

question of minorities in schools. In the aftermath of *Brown v. Board of Education* (1954), Spellman's silence became deafening. Despite the hesitations of individual pastors and sisters superior to admit them, it had long been the policy of the Archdiocese of New York to open its schools (even under Cardinal Hayes) to African Americans. Just as there was push back in public school districts, parents of children in Catholic schools tended to prefer a segregated system, too. As one analyst of Catholic education has put it: "From all appearances, the re-sistance of the Catholic Church to welcoming African Americans into parish schools, the movement of Catholic parents to suburban areas after the Brown decision, and the negligence of the church in creating racially integrated parish schools seems to mimic the Caucasian public school community in its racially separatist attitude and action."[28]

The school question was a constant thorn in Spellman's side. At least since May 1949, after the so-called Barden Bill was introduced in Congress, he excoriated all who would deny federal aid to parochial schools. The heat was turned up when Eleanor Roosevelt wrote a column on restricting federal funds for public schools only, specifically attacking Spellman's argument. The Cardinal shot back that such opposition was too often born of ignorance and bigotry. He called Roosevelt's remarks "unworthy of an American mother" and only buried the hatchet with her by making a personal call on the former First Lady at Hyde Park that August.[29] With Presidents Truman and Eisenhower, he had to fight for every penny for Catholic education.[30] Perhaps Spellman's greatest chal-

28. Darlene Eleanor York, "The Academic Achievement of African Americans in Catholic Schools: A Review of the Literature," in *Growing Up African American in Catholic Schools*, ed. Jacqueline Jordan Irvine and Michèle Foster (New York: Teachers College Press, 1996) 19. "However," York continues, "the Church's seeming resistance to the harmonious integration of Catholic schools should be placed in a larger his-torical perspective. . . . By the middle 1950s, when the Brown decision was made, the Catholic Church in the United States had already had a long history of educating numerous cultural and ethnic groups. Throughout that history, never did the Catholic Church engineer the assimilation of any ethnic group in the United States. On the contrary, Catholic educational history—from a cultural perspective—has been toler-ant and supportive of separatist schooling."

29. See "Mrs. Roosevelt First Lady 12 Years, Often Called 'World's Most Admired Woman,'" *New York Times*, November 8, 1962, 35; and Gannon, *Cardinal Spellman Story*, 314–22. See also Seymour P. Lachman, "The Cardinal, the Congressmen, and the First Lady," *Journal of Church and State* 7/1 (Winter 1965) 35–66.

30. See George A. Kizer, "Federal Aid to Education: 1945–1963," *History of*

lenge was in dealing with President Kennedy. Both before and after his rise to the White House, Spellman subdued a personal distaste for the senator and sought to placate the first Catholic to hold the Oval Office. This was an odd dance, for Kennedy himself was often found having to give more importance to his faith than he was usually accustomed. This was as true before the election as it was after. In mid-September 1960, Kennedy was on the defensive, giving notice to Southern ministers that he did not speak for the Catholic Church in America, nor did the Church speak for him. These remarks did little to assuage an already prejudiced sector of the voting public. In October, Kennedy advisor Arthur Schlesinger recorded how the candidate was prepping for the Al Smith Dinner—an annual event founded by Cardinal Spellman to benefit New York's Catholic charities. Both Schlesinger and Ted Sorenson, Kennedy's speechwriter, were working on the future president's talk before the dinner. It was not going well. Kennedy kept getting the sense that the speech was "too Catholic" and suggested that the two keep at it. After the dinner, Schlesinger reported in his journal that "[Kennedy] was ironically entertained by the fact that this high Catholic audience had applauded Nixon a good deal more than it had applauded him. 'It all goes to show,' he said, 'that, when the chips are down, money counts more than faith.'"[31]

The worst episode for Kennedy came just two weeks before the election. The Catholic bishops of Puerto Rico, led by Bishop James McManus, insisted that the Island's Catholic faithful refrain from voting for the Puerto Rican governor Luis Muñez Marin because of his stance on birth control. With the bishops threatening excommunica-

---

Education Quarterly 10/1 (Spring 1970) 84–102. The National Defense of Education Act (1957) was perhaps the major windfall for parochial schools, though it came through intense lobbying of an Eisenhower White House hardly known for educational advocacy.

31. Arthur M. Schlesinger, Jr., *Journals, 1952–2000* (New York: Penguin, 2007) 90. Kennedy often ran into Catholic clergy who baited him by testing his orthodoxy on policy questions, and his replies were sometimes combative. One historian noted that "Kennedy would not accept the view that priests had any special competence in public matters. A cleric who was angered by his answer at a Catholic girls' school that 'recognition of Red China was not a moral issue,' queried, 'Senator Kennedy, do you not believe that all law comes from God?' The senator answered heatedly, 'I'm a Catholic so of course I believe it—but that has nothing to do with international law.'" Lawrence H. Fuchs, *John F. Kennedy and American Catholicism* (New York: Meredith Press, 1967) 208.

tion, Kennedy swallowed his pride and asked Cardinal Spellman to quell the feud. It did not take an overly astute reading of the national temperament to see that a church-state conflict in a US territory presented all the ammunition the Nixon camp would need to prove that a Catholic would have to show deference to the hierarchy in matters of public policy.[32] Sensing an opportunity, Spellman willingly intervened with the Holy See's secretariat of state, which promptly reigned in McManus. In yet another instance of Spellman's magnanimity (or political maneuvering), the Cardinal later drew McManus closer to himself, petitioning the nuncio to the Caribbean to take McManus out of Puerto Rico so that he might become one of Spellman's growing team of auxiliary bishops. Spellman again showed no inhibition. McManus was literally set out to pasture, minding "the back porch" of the archdiocese in Ulster and Sullivan Counties.

Let Them Be Strong

New Rochelle, New York, sits in the shadow of the hulking colossus to the south and siphons part of its identity as a bedroom community from the large percentage of daily commuters who travel to Manhattan for work. In 1906, George M. Cohan produced *Forty-Five Minutes from Broadway*, a play about New Rochelle, but even the title indicates that all about the town is measured against the Great White Way slicing through Manhattan. Residents did not seem to mind. There was something good and pure about retaining a close proximity to the city but avoiding its contaminants. When Phyllis McGinley penned her little ditty on the burg, she captured the sense of tranquility in suburban life mixed with *ennui*: "In New Rochelle, in New Rochelle / How placidly the people dwell / 'Mid lawn and tree and fringed gentian / And furnaces that need attention."[33] When one considers the Norman Rockwell portraits of an upscale middle-class that typically graced the covers of the *Saturday Evening Post*, it was because Rockwell found his subjects in New Rochelle, where he lived. The tonier set populated the New

32. See Shaun A. Casey, *The Making of a Catholic President: Kennedy vs. Nixon 1960* (New York: Oxford University Press, 2009).

33. Phyllis McGinley, "Musings aboard the Stamford Local (During an Expedition into Darkest Westchester)" *The New Yorker*, November 5, 1938, 22.

Rochelle Yacht Club and by the 1930s established the community as the wealthiest per capita in the state.[34] What was true of the postwar era is true even today. New York City dominates much of the pace and enterprise of town. It provides sanctuary and the creature comforts one could not enjoy in the five boroughs—space, cleanliness, decency. It was a preferred location for Westchester's Catholics.

Residents of New Rochelle enjoy the amenities of good local schools, including two Catholic colleges, fed in part by two high schools run by the same communities of women and men religious. In addition to Ursuline Academy and the College of New Rochelle, run by the Sisters of St. Ursula, Iona Preparatory School and Iona College are institutions with proud and storied histories written by their founders, the Irish Christian Brothers. The Gaels of Iona Prep, in particular, are a study in the theme examined here. Its very motto, *Estote Firmi* ("Let them be strong," from the pseudepigrahical Pauline *Letter to the Laodiceans*), typifies the expectations of the young men who passed through its halls, future captains of industry, as well as the Catholic culture they would one day inherit. If, as Andrew Greeley asserted in 1959, "Westchester County might be a seedbed for future prophets," New Rochelle stands at the cusp of producing a new kind of Christian witness—white-collar workers whose social conscience knew no horizon.[35] It is where William Loewe was nurtured.

Iona Prep's most famous alumnus is not William Loewe but Frank Abagnale. The subject of the film *Catch Me If You Can*, Abagnale was perhaps the premier check kiter in the world. The film portrays a boy straight from Iona Prep coming into caper after caper, tumbling into a life of crime. With the help of an earnest FBI agent, Abagnale realizes he has the power to affect his own redemption in the crucible of his own choices. Without Agent Hanratty, Abagnale's life would have ground to an ignoble end. This is a story that reverberates in Loewe's own work, particularly the lifting up of the sinner by the hand of God. If strength is found already within us, it often requires the divine instrumentality of Christ to awaken it and for the scales to fall from our eyes in acknowledging it.

34. It simultaneously became the third wealthiest community per capita in the nation. See http://www.newrochelleny.com/203.asp.

35. See further Barbara Davis, *New Rochelle* (Mount Pleasant, SC: Arcadia, 2009) 111.

So much of what is visible in the reign of Francis Spellman, whether internationally or locally, can be viewed as a touch point in William Loewe's life, too. Loewe was born November 28, 1941, and taken home from the hospital on December 7 as Pearl Harbor was under attack. The son of Jane and Herman Loewe, he drew his ethnic heritage from an Irish mother and German father. His paternal grandfather was an assimilated German Jewish professor who escaped Nazi Germany in 1934 and, predating the swelling exodus of Catholic New Yorkers to the suburbs, settled in New Rochelle. William Loewe had a standard parochial education at Holy Family School, just a few blocks up the hill from Iona College. Although parochial schools in New Rochelle were immune from the civil code, public schools in New Rochelle were not formally desegregated until 1961, and then only by court order. Loewe's parochial education was also far from being a model of integration. As he later recounted in a personal interview, "There were no black children in Holy Family and one at Iona Prep during my school years."

Since the parish community was a typical world-making vehicle for many Catholics, Loewe's early participation in parish life as a student and altar server allowed for certain kinds of influences to take hold. Holy Family is the youngest of all the parishes of New Rochelle, but the clergy who served it helped to sink deep roots. Built in 1913, the parish was run for years by Monsignor Charles E. Fitzgerald, PhD (among a solitary few New York clergy who held a non-pontifical terminal degree). Fathers John Coffey, Paul Haverty, and Raymond McNulty were curates in 1942 and these men, for the most part, were stationed there nearly in perpetuity. New Rochelle's population ballooned after the war. Holy Family School had over 300 boys and 250 girls in 1949. Within a decade the number climbed to over 700. A coterie of Sisters of St. Dominic of Newburgh was in charge, many of whom had taught Loewe's future colleague at Catholic University, Father Gerard Sloyan. The workload was brutal, with nearly two score to a classroom.

During his senior year at Iona Prep, at age sixteen, he decided on entering religious life, though not as an Irish Christian Brother. Instead, he was attracted to the Society of Jesus for their reputation as intellectuals, but because he did not know any Jesuit who could personally vouch for him, the vocation director asked that he attend the College of the Holy Cross for a year so that he might become acquainted with the life. He was drawn to their intellectual formation immediately. It was enough to prompt his entrance into Bellarmine College in Plattsburgh, New York, where the Jesuits had a house of formation in the old Hotel Champlain on Bluff Point. He then pursued philosophical studies at Loyola Jesuit Seminary at Shrub Oak, New York, obtaining his bachelor's, a master's degree in French, and a licentiate in philosophy from Fordham. In 1967 he left the Jesuits after a year of regency at St. Peter's Prep, Jersey City. Loewe taught high school in Queens, and by 1968 began doctoral studies at Marquette, where, even at this early stage, he began to turn seminar papers into publishable work.[36]

Without doubt, seminary life proved vital to Loewe's future direction. This was an area in which the Cardinal had little control and so formation was left to the respective religious houses. Unlike the archdiocesan seminary, in which Spellman had an abiding interest, Shrub Oak was an enclave for philosophical creativity among the faculty. At the time, Bill was exposed to some of the order's most fertile minds. Although the faculty typically reported using the standard required textbooks, what emerged in the classroom was exhilarating. Father John McCormack used phenomenological insights for the course in rational psychology. Father Gerald McCool led a critical examination of what he called "canonical Aristotelianism" in the course on metaphysics.[37] Father Robert Johann explored cosmology through personalism and Father John Giles Milhaven surveyed modern epistemology through primary text readings from Descartes to Maréchal.[38] It is here that Loewe learned to think, and to think with boldness, power, and strength—a style that pervades the intelligibility of his later work, which has closely examined the Church's christological doctrines and sought to make them relevant for contemporary Catholics.

What did he absorb? A brief survey of his professors' writings is revealing. McCool, for instance, was an expert on the *imago Dei* tradi-

36. Loewe's first article was a paper written originally for Quentin Quesnell's Luke seminar. See William P. Loewe, "Towards an Interpretation of Luke 19:1–10," *Catholic Biblical Quarterly* 36/3 (1974) 321–31.

37. Classical metaphysical categories such as potency and act, being and existence, substance and accident were delineated in the canon of Greek philosophy and brought into conversation with Christian writers such as Sts. Augustine and Thomas Aquinas.

38. For the faculty and curriculum at Shrub Oak, see *Kalendarium Collegii Shrub Oak S. Ignatii Loyolae, Facultas Philosophica, Collegii Maximi Woodstockiensis in annum scholarem 1964–1965* (Shrub Oak, NY: Loyola Seminary, 1964) 24–31, a copy of which is available in the Society of Jesus Archives, New York Province.

tion, particularly as it manifested itself in St. Augustine. McCool was able to trace this doctrine over the centuries and to lift up its anthropological and social implications. "The goal of man's spiritual striving is the Infinite Perfection of Being, pure *esse*," he once wrote. "As pure *esse*, God must be Spirit, the Pure Act of Knowledge and Love. The Infinite Spirit is the unitary source of both the dynamic intelligibility of nature and the dynamic intelligence of man. Furthermore, as the infinite, self-possessing identity of being, intelligibility, and goodness, God is a person."[39] How does one gain purchase on this realization? To answer, McCool borrows from fellow Jesuit Bernard Lonergan. In his *Philosophy of God and Theology*, Lonergan lays out three levels of "conscious dynamism." At the level of intelligence the grasp of a datum provokes a question: what is it? At the level of reflection the knower asks the question: is it so? At the final level of human understanding is the level of deliberation, in which what has become known is now assessed and picked out from a myriad of choices as the most authentic thing, the truest good.[40] What supplies the connective tissue between the knowing and the known? McCool further states that

> the real question about God, which the reflective human knower finds as a "given" in his concrete experience, is the lived question about the ground of intelligibility and value which man discovers as an undeniable prior "given" in his own experience. It is a lived question whose undeniable presence in man's experience would be unintelligible unless man already possessed—on the level of *intellectus* or *Vernunft*—an implicit awareness of truth and value and of their ground in the personal God. Man's dis-

---

39. Gerald A. McCool, "Duty and Reason in Thomistic Social Ethics," in *Freedom and Value*, ed. Robert O. Johann (New York: Fordham University Press, 1976) 137–59, at 139. That Being, especially God's Being, was made altogether personal was something McCool continued to trace out at 139: "At first there seems little new in this approach to God. It reads like a rehearsal of the transcendental Thomist natural theology whose origin goes back to Joseph Maréchal's *Le Point de depart de la métaphysique* [3rd ed., Paris: Desclée de Brouwer, 1944]. Many years ago Joseph de Fever's *La Preuve réelle de Dieu* [Paris: Desclée de Brouwer, 1953] and, more recently, Henri Bouillard's *The Knowledge of God* [New York: Herder and Herder, 1968] acquainted European and American Thomists with this type of natural theology; and, although Gilsonian and Maritainian Thomists have never taken kindly to it, a generation of American undergraduates has become familiar with its brief and lucid exposition in Joseph Donceel's *Natural Theology* [New York: Sheed and Ward, 1962]."

40. See McCool, "Duty and Reason in Thomistic Social Ethics," 140–42.

covery of God is linked to his discovery of a grounded "ought" which rules his conduct, an "ought" which tells him to "act intelligently" because intelligent action is a value which it is his duty to pursue.[41]

The reply to the moral ought is, in McCool's line of thinking, "a response to the loving God."[42]

We have to imagine that such claims made an impression on Loewe and were reinforced or stretched further in other of his classes. For many young Jesuits then in studies, the hunger for relationship tapped into the larger question of spiritual formation. Writing in *America*, the Jesuit scholastic Leo J. O'Donovan—future president of Georgetown University—wondered aloud about the existentialism of mediation, of how life in Christ is actually accomplished. He said it was principally through exchange in community. Exchange was based on a certain type of obedience, particularly to those who are wise. In community is found the sense of continuity whereby our own lives are made wise. This is a spiritual reality, he said, in which we plumb the depths of our own personhood.[43]

Loewe's formators were feeling much the same way. Whereas for McCool an acknowledgement of one's need to reply to the moral imperative remains internal to the individual, in Robert Johann's terms, this is done through a love relationship with another. *That* is where being is found—in the external manifestation. Insofar as it is an "absolute, unconditioned value, totally enveloping everything that exists," being is experienced in consciousness and so remains subjective and yet simultaneously open to the outside world.[44] There is no abstraction; encounter takes place in the concrete. Johann claimed that "whatever be the union effected by love, it cannot be one of fusion or identification, where the originality (in the line of value) of each of the terms is absorbed and lost in some common denominator. Loving the self in the

41. Ibid., 143.

42. Ibid., 144.

43. See Leo J. O'Donovan, "Mediating Our Life in Christ," *America* 105, April 8, 1961, 74–77.

44. See Robert O. Johann, *The Meaning of Love: An Essay towards a Metaphysics of Intersubjectivity* (Westminster, MD: Newman, 1959) 5. For his part, Johann insisted that openness to encounter with the Absolute has an eschatological dimension, insofar as this openness is a first step toward paradise (10).

other, I cherish his proper initiative, that by which he is radically distinct from me. Instead of eliminating this distinction, direct love will, if anything, maintain and intensify it."[45]

Among all of his teachers at Shrub Oak, however, it may be that Giles Milhaven provided the most intense intellectual ferment. For in Milhaven's challenges to see law as something non-absolute, riddled with exceptions, he forced his students to see their world in a radically different light. Law was authoritative because it rested on tradition, but it was not without blemish, owing to repeated misuse. As Milhaven parsed the implications of this, Loewe saw a system unfold. It was what came to be called "the new morality"—a movement steeped in a deep and abiding appreciation for all the tradition offered, but one that necessitated a practical openness to the vicissitudes of culture and its pluralistic whims.[46] Milhaven's approach preferred an application of law to realities as they were, and where a question emerged, the law of love would be primary. This law of love even possessed a certain relativity, unbridled by convention (or even divine command ethics), but was tethered to a logic as yet indeterminate and often obscure. This was probably one of the elements that attracted Loewe to Bernard Lonergan, who believed systematic theology to be less about certitude of propositions and more about "understanding of what one knew by faith to be true."[47]

Milhaven and the new morality were operating on the frontiers of Catholic theology and Loewe had a front row seat. This was not the catechism he had been taught in one of the archdiocesan schools. Yes, the demands of loving one's neighbor were generally accepted—though the weight of the particular actions or words (such as those vilifying "godless Communists" or watching the Catholic senator from Massachusetts

---

45. Ibid., 35.

46. Part of Milhaven's work in this regard, particularly in the mid to late 1960s, is collected in his book, *Toward a New Catholic Morality* (Garden City, NY: Image, 1970). Milhaven taught philosophy at Canisius and Fordham, theology at Woodstock College, and later, after having left the Society of Jesus, religious studies at Brown University. It may be noted that the situation ethics of Joseph Fichter is similar to Milhaven's system. See Charles Curran, *Catholic Moral Theology in the United States: A History* (Washington, DC: Georgetown University Press, 2008) 97.

47. William P. Loewe, "Jesus, Son of God," in *The Desires of the Human Heart: An Introduction to the Theology of Bernard Lonergan*, ed. Vernon Gregson (Mahwah, NJ: Paulist, 1988) 185–86.

have to defend his religion) often rubbed against the grain. Milhaven's claims were bold and severely critiqued. Gabriel Marcel, for instance, saw it as poisonous: "As a Christian, I deplore it. It is extremely dangerous and not easy to fight against."[48] Marcel asked that society turn away from the world to counteract the new morality, which he believed was an insidious new form of solipsism. "Men tend more and more to think of the world around them, and finally also of themselves, in technical and mechanical terms," he said, and warned against a resultant "manipulation of life." The consequences of the new morality extended to the wider theological community, too, and threw in with progressive currents that sought to revise seemingly established doctrines. Prompted both by the Second Vatican Council as well as the social and political transformations occurring around the world, people like Milhaven were shaking the foundations of belief itself. This era ushered in fresh ways of approaching sacred Scripture, the very idea of revelation, faith, and the role of reason.[49] New perspectives on classical themes allowed for, if not encouraged, wholly novel methodologies for doing theology, such as liberationist or feminist methods, and helped open the way for biblical theologians to postulate all manner of theories lying at the heart

48. "'New Morality' Rejected," undated news clipping (c. 1966) in Francis Connell, CSsR Papers, Archives of the Baltimore Province of the Redemptorists, Brooklyn, NY, folder "Morality." See further Gabriel Marcel, *The Existential Background of Human Dignity* (Cambridge: Harvard University Press, 1963); *Philosophy in a Technological Culture*, ed. George F. McLean (Washington, DC: The Catholic University of America Press, 1964).

49. There are historical moments that may be traced in order to account for this new outlook. Loewe's own writings suggest that the fifteen hundredth anniversary of the dogmatic definitions issuing from Chalcedon in 1951 were determinative of a new course for Christology among Catholic theologians. See e.g., "Jesus Christ (In Theology)," *New Catholic Encyclopedia*, 2nd ed. (Detroit: Gale, 2003) 7:810–12, where he suggests the anniversary marks a paradigm shift. Others see events such as the departure of Charles Davis from the Catholic priesthood in late 1966 as putting the classical categories of theology, about which Davis had written widely, into doubt. The ensuing analysis was typified by exchanges like that between Fathers Richard McBrien and Francis Connell, CSsR, in the winter of 1966–67. See McBrien "The New Apologetics" *The Pilot*, November 18, 1966; idem., "Loss of 'Faith' . . ." *The Pilot*, December 31, 1966. 14; Francis J. Connell, "Letter to the Editor: Theologians Differ over Reason's Role in Act of Faith," *The Pilot*, January 28, 1967, 8; and McBrien, "PILOT Columnist Answers C.U. Dean's Critique of 'Contemporary Theology," *The Pilot*, January 28, 1967, 8.

of Christian consciousness, not least of which was the study of christological doctrines and their continued relevance.

In the New York Archdiocese, too, there were winds of change
blowing. During Vatican II, in the debate on the draft of the document
that became *Gaudium et spes*, Cardinal Spellman rose up to call for a
"genuine religious obedience" to the Church's magisterium even while
the Church engaged more fully with the modern world. Only in such
a spirit could authentic dialogue take place, he suggested. But that is
not how these words were perceived; in fact, they suggested a heavy-
handed use of office. Spellman was so insistent on the point that he sent
the text of his speech to all the communities of religious functioning in
the archdiocese. Many regarded it as an "early Christmas card," but one
did not need to be a savant to understand the Cardinal's message: "don't
get carried away by all this talk of modernization and step out of line."[50]
Spellman came home to face the music he was trying to drown out. In
the aftermath of Vatican II, the American hierarchy elected a young
archbishop from Detroit, the future Cardinal John Francis Deardon, to
lead a newly constituted conference of bishops, effectively supplanting
Spellman and the old guard. In 1967, after several years and close to a
million dollars of trying to defeat the Blaine Amendment from with-
holding tax money from New York's parochial schools, Spellman was
forced to throw in the towel. And 1967 marked the first time since the
end of World War II that the archdiocese did not build a new Catholic
school.[51] There were fewer cornerstones to lay. Beleaguered by twenty-
eight years in office and already past the mandatory retirement age for
bishops, the Cardinal died on December 2, 1967.

William Loewe is a witness to these developments. And as any
good witness does, he tells of these transformative years and ideas and
exposes their (de)merits in light of the gospel. This is why Loewe's words

---

50. Edward Wakin and Joseph Scheuer, *The De-Romanization of the American
Catholic Church* (New York: New American Library, 1970) 185–86. Spellman's inter-
vention, October 20, 1964, is blunted by the following characterization of his remarks:
"Frequently when ecclesiastical directives are wanting the faithful must act on their
own responsibility. The essential condition of all fruitful dialogue is fidelity to the
Church and to its authority." *Council Daybook, Vatican II, Session 3/September 14 to
November 21, 1964* (Washington, DC: National Catholic Welfare Conference, 1965)
165.

51. See Wakin and Scheuer, *De-Romanization of the American Catholic Church*,
134.

have meant so much to us, his students and colleagues. In recognizing his influence in this festschrift it seems fitting to invoke another passage from the *Letter to the Laodiceans*: *salutant vos sancti*, "The saints salute you."

2

Jesus Founding the Church: A Perspective Drawing upon Loewe and Lonergan

DENNIS M. DOYLE

UNIVERSITY OF DAYTON

William Loewe, who directed my dissertation over twenty-five years ago, has influenced my own work deeply. My dissertation compared the positions of Wilfred Cantwell Smith and Bernard Lonergan on the relationship between religious belief and truth. In this essay I will try to express some of what I have learned from my director, both while writing my dissertation and in the decades since, about Lonergan and about theology. Taking up the issue of Jesus' founding of the church, I will focus especially on how Loewe's approach to Christology has influenced my own approach to an important issue in ecclesiology.

Loewe is one of several people who encouraged me to move beyond an explicit concentration in Lonergan studies and to make use of what I had learned in other areas. As he wrote, "the real demonstration of the value of Fr. Lonergan's work consists not in its exposition but in the creative, collaborative performance of the manifold tasks to which it so clearly urges."[1] Such tasks include not only intellectual activities but extend to the practical tasks needed to unfold the work of salvation in

---

1. William P. Loewe, "Toward a Responsible Contemporary Soteriology," in *Creativity and Method: Essays in Honor of Bernard Lonergan, S.J*, ed. Matthew L. Lamb (Milwaukee: Marquette University Press, 1981) 213–27, at 227.

concrete ways. There is Lonergan-inspired work that needs to be done in theology as well as in Christian living, in political science as well as in political action, in economics as well as in business leadership.

Loewe's own work is recognizably Lonerganian in a way that involves more application than exposition of Lonergan's work. In some places the influence of Lonergan may be evident only to other Lonerganians. For example, in his 1984 article, "Myth and Counter-Myth: Irenaeus' Story of Salvation," Loewe does not cite a single work by Lonergan. Yet the second sentence begins, "Once theology recognizes its task to be one of mediating between the Christian religion and the world of human culture . . ."[2] Thus an identifiably Lonerganian starting point can be located in the essay. But it is even more evident to anyone connected with Lonergan studies that the entire essay, in which Loewe explores how Irenaeus's pretheoretical contribution to christological tradition reflects a mythic form of consciousness that battles against the Gnostic myths, finds its background in Lonergan's discussion of the ongoing discovery of mind in the chapter "Doctrines" in *Method in Theology*. Finally, the climactic point of the essay, that "For Irenaeus the cross of Christ provides the key which unlocks the treasure hidden in scripture," can be connected to a Lonerganian Christology and soteriology that focus on the law of the cross.[3]

This is not to say that Loewe is in any way concealing the influence of Lonergan in his work. In the article on Irenaeus he cites his own previous article on soteriology that explicitly explains and documents the Lonerganian background of his operating terms and concepts. These two articles can be read together as part of a larger project in soteriology so that the Irenaeus article is really not so cordoned off from its roots as it might first appear to the reader who simply encounters it as a freestanding article in an annual volume of the College Theology Society.

---

2. William P. Loewe, "Myth and Counter-Myth: Irenaeus' Story of Salvation," in *Interpreting Tradition: The Art of Theological Reflection*, ed. Jane Kopas, The Annual Publication of the College Theology Society 29 (Chico, CA: Scholars, 1984) 39–53, at 39.

3. Loewe, "Myth and Counter-Myth," 52.

Dissertation Lessons

My dissertation was a study of Wilfred Cantwell Smith and Bernard Lonergan comparing their treatment of the question of religious truth.[4] The specific focus was on how their differences on religious truth were reflected in the contrasting ways in which they fashioned a distinction between faith and belief. Smith found religious truth to emerge from interreligious dialogue within a context of a shared faith generating a corporate critical consciousness that transcended particular beliefs. Lonergan found the attainment of religious truth to be linked with faith, understood as seeing through the eyes of love, as it issues in belief. Belief is based upon a judgment of value by which one accepts the judgments of fact and the judgments of value that are handed on through a religious tradition. Smith's position was avant-garde if not trendy. Lonergan's position, itself future-looking and ingenious, remained a way by which theologians could help to guide the faithful transmission of what they themselves had received.

The third of four sections of my dissertation was devoted to explicating Lonergan's understanding of the relationship between faith, belief, and truth. It was in this section that I had to do the most rewriting and recasting. It was not just a matter of writing clearer sentences and paragraphs with fewer typos and grammatical errors. It was more a matter of responding to Loewe's criticisms concerning my rudimentary grasp of what Lonergan was about. Loewe had me perform two major rounds of revision of this segment. I had to move from my semantic and conceptual entry point into Lonergan's definitions and their immediate interconnections to a fuller understanding of how these meanings and concepts played out within the framework of Lonergan's overall project.

Both major revisions of my third section involved returning to the texts and trying to achieve a deeper grasp of what Lonergan was about. Lonergan himself had written of the years that he had spent reaching up to the mind of Aquinas. I had to spend a couple of years reaching up to the mind of Lonergan. I am not claiming to have attained the heights; I am claiming that after two major revisions in response to Loewe's criticisms I had a respectable grasp of what Lonergan was about.

4. See Dennis Doyle, "The Distinction between Faith and Belief and the Question of Religious Truth: The Contributions of Wilfred Cantwell Smith and Bernard Lonergan" (PhD diss., The Catholic University of America, 1984).

Loewe led me to the insight that for Lonergan the current task of theology was the performance of a transposition of truths grasped within one context into a new dynamic context. The prior context was one in which a particular culture had been understood as normative. The new context is one of cultural pluralism. In the prior context, theoretical formulations had come to be taken as absolute and permanent. In the new context, the relationship between the realms of theory and common sense had to be grasped from an examination of the realm of interiority. The permanence of meaning as well as the truth of prior understandings had to be distinguished from the particular ways in which they had been expressed.

The ability to transpose the meanings understood in the prior context into the new, dynamic context depended upon the authenticity of one's religious, moral, and intellectual conversion. One's own religious, moral, and intellectual conversion remained connected to the religious, moral, and intellectual conversion of one's community. As grounded in conversion, the attainment of objectivity is the fruit of authentic subjectivity.

In *Method in Theology* Lonergan gave only one explicit example of transposing a theological concept from the prior context to the new context.[5] What had been labeled in a rather objectified manner as "sanctifying grace" in the prior context needed to be appropriated in the new context as the dynamic state of being in love with God. This transposition was central to Lonergan's overall project. Grasping this allowed me to see that both Lonergan's definition of faith (the knowledge born of religious love) and his definition of religious belief (the acceptance of the judgments of fact and judgments of value of a religious tradition) involved a transposition of earlier theological categories whose definitions had tended to become reified.

In the prior context faith had been the supernatural virtue by which one believes. Belief had been the act of faith. In the new, dynamic context, faith takes on an explicitly existential element. Faith sees through the eyes of love. Belief, which entails the acceptance of what is objectively true, requires a judgment of value rooted in authenticity. Communities of people who are authentically converted live out their experience of being in love with God. These people see through the eyes

---

5. See Bernard Lonergan, *Method in Theology* (New York: Seabury, 1972) 288–90.

of love. Such sight leads them not only to accept as true the judgments of fact and the judgments of value upon which their religious tradition is based, but also to appropriate the meanings of these judgments with proper understanding.

Many contemporary thinkers, including some theologians, tend to regard a reliance on religious belief as uncritical because one must accept what one has not arrived at for oneself in an immanently generated manner. Lonergan, however, treated belief as a form of knowledge. Although belief is not immanently generated knowledge, it is still a legitimate form of knowledge that is rooted in a judgment of value. One makes a reasonable judgment to believe. In the case of religious belief, the underlying judgment of value flows from the faith that is itself rooted in love. Religious belief requires more than "pure" reason, but it is by no means unreasonable or uncritical. Vigilance against the irrational continues to purify the religious believer's understanding.

Lonergan described how in the usual process of coming to know something, understanding precedes judgment. In this regard, questions of meaning precede questions of truth. When it comes to belief, however, the reverse is the case. One accepts as true something that one does not know for oneself. Lonergan emphasized that belief, including religious belief, constitutes a kind of knowledge. But it is a kind of knowledge in which the embrace of truth is basically prior to achieving a fuller understanding. One accepts the doctrine of the Trinity without comprehending it, yet Christians can grow in their understanding of this truth.[6]

A consideration of the eight functional specialties into which Lonergan categorized theological tasks can offer further exploration of how knowledge can precede understanding in matters of belief.[7] The first four specialties constitute what Lonergan called the mediating phase of theology, the pursuit of knowledge prior to conversion and prior to an embrace of an explicit tradition as revelatory. These four are Research, Interpretation, History, and Dialectics. The second four functional specialties constitute the mediated phase, the phase that is based in conversion and the embrace of a tradition. These are Foundations, Doctrines, Systematics, and Communications. The first four functional

6. See ibid., esp. 115–19, 347–51.
7. See ibid., 125–45.

specialties correspond with the Lonerganian levels of conscious operations labeled experience, understanding, judgment, and decision. The second four functional specialties also correspond with these levels of conscious operations, but in reverse order: Foundations is linked with decision, Doctrines with judgment, Systematics with understanding, and Communications with experience.

This reversal of ordering explains why in Lonergan's *Method in Theology* the seventh functional specialty of Systematics, which corresponds with meaning and understanding, comes after the sixth functional specialty, Doctrines, which corresponds with truth and judgment. This ordering is in contrast to the second and third functional specialties of Interpretation and History, in which what corresponds with understanding and meaning precedes judgment and truth. In the first four functional specialties, coming to grasp a range of possible understandings comes before making judgments concerning truth and prior to a deeper grasp of meaning through further understanding. In these second four functional specialties, the acceptance of revealed truth expressed as doctrine precedes further attempts to achieve systematic understanding.

The second four functional specialties are not thereby uncritical or fideistic, for at least three reasons. First, each functional specialty remains interconnected with the tasks and standards of all the functional specialties, including the earlier ones that are explicitly critical. Systematic understanding of doctrine remains dependent upon what is arrived at in interpretation and in history. Theologians are not licensed to ignore history or science because they are operating in a different functional specialty. Second, systematic understanding of doctrine is further critically linked with the authenticity of the religious, moral, and intellectual conversion of the individuals and communities within which the meaning of doctrines are appropriated and lived out. Third, belief, when grounded in an authentic judgment of value, is not uncritical.

One embraces or remains within a particular religious tradition because of a judgment of value, in this case, a belief. This belief is possible because one sees with the eyes of love. One sees with the eyes of love because one is in the dynamic state of being in love. One can engage in belief because it is good to believe. One can believe in a religious tradition because through one's eyes of love one sees that it is good to believe in that tradition. Religious beliefs constitute a world of meaning in which believers live. The initial judgment of the truth of a tradition's beliefs is a judgment about the way of life in which the tradition issues, the visions it inspires, the institutions it engenders, the good it brings about, and the love that it manifests. Surely one is also attracted by an initial sense of the truth of the basic judgments of fact and judgments of value that constitute the tradition's world of meaning. One can spend the rest of one's life coming to a fuller lived realization of the truth and meaning of these basic beliefs.

Loewe challenged me to move my understanding of Lonergan from the level of the semantic and the conceptual to the level of method. What took me to this more sophisticated understanding was the insight that the theological task being called for by Lonergan was basically one of transposition of beliefs from the prior context to the new context of cultural pluralism, and that the ability to perform such a transposition was the fruit of religious, moral, and intellectual conversion. Religious beliefs remain claims to truth. The subjective, existential, and communal dimensions of making religious truth claims are brought to the fore.

Lonergan's approach to theology is to be contrasted with approaches that begin with an antipathy between theology on the one hand, and history, the human sciences, and the natural sciences on the other hand. The best of human knowledge obtained through the most critical of academic methods has its place in the larger theological enterprise. The first four of Lonergan's functional specialties are dedicated to the pursuit of knowledge in an academic and critical manner.

Lonergan's approach to theology is equally to be contrasted, however, with approaches that would take a so-called purely academic point of view, such as an historical reconstruction of religious events, as the starting point for all theological tasks. On the contrary, once a theologian moves into Lonergan's final four functional specialties, those four that correspond with the tasks that have usually been thought to constitute "theology," the most basic task that the theologian performs is the appropriation of a religious tradition as it informs the life of a religious community. Academic integrity as well as authentic conversion serve as necessary prerequisites and ongoing guides and supports for this most fundamental task of appropriation.

Post-Dissertation Lessons

Earlier I made the claim that Loewe's work is Lonergan-saturated in a particular way that moves more in the direction of application than in the direction of exposition. In the years since writing my dissertation, I have been influenced by the way in which Loewe's application of Lonergan goes beyond the transposition of neo-scholastic categories to a more thoroughly reconstructive approach to Christology and soteriology. If Lonerganian theology were to be mostly about the transposition of neo-scholastic categories into the new context of cultural pluralism, then Loewe would be engaging in sideshows. The law of the cross was not a major operative category in the neo-scholastic manuals. The retrieval of Irenaeus's soteriology would not be of immediate relevance.

In recent decades it has become ever clearer that theology's contemporary tasks involve more than simple transposition. As Loewe put it in an article about the theological use of historical Jesus studies, "The rapid collapse and near disappearance of neo-scholastic manual theology after Vatican II left Roman Catholic theologians with a massive task of reconstruction."[8] Loewe draws upon the work of John Galvin to describe how an older paradigm in Christology, one in which the neo-scholastics drew upon Chalcedon for their basic starting point, has given way to a newer paradigm that, starting with Jesus' ministry, seeks to recapitulate the entire tradition with a view toward mediating that tradition within the contemporary context.[9]

Lonergan's *Method in Theology* offers theologians support for the massive task of reconstruction that the present context calls for. What I have come to see more clearly in the decades since I wrote my dissertation is that Lonergan's identification of this task with the transposition of neo-scholastic categories in the new context of cultural pluralism was itself a very time-bound connection. It made sense when the bulk of existing theology existed in neo-scholastic texts. It made sense when Lonergan was addressing himself mainly to priests and seminarians who had been steeped in neo-scholasticism. The focus on transposition

8. William P. Loewe, "From the Humanity of Christ to the Historical Jesus," *Theological Studies* 61/2 (June 2000) 314–31, at 314.

9. See ibid., 314–15. See also John P. Galvin, "From the Humanity of Christ to the Jesus of History: A Paradigm Shift in Catholic Christology," *Theological Studies* 55/2 (June 1994) 252–73.

was a way of assuring that basic truths would remain true even as they were being appropriated into the new context. Through the 1960s and early 70s, when Lonergan was writing *Method in Theology*, such a transposition was the main task of the day for Roman Catholic theology.

Even by the time I was writing my dissertation in the early 80s, however, the theological scene had shifted dramatically. The neo-scholastic synthesis had basically collapsed. There were rapidly fewer and fewer theologians who had been formed in that mould. How could theology most basically consist in a transposition of what was known and lived out in a neo-scholastic context if that context itself had come to exist only in relatively rare pockets of the theological world?

I want to be clear that I am speaking here of my own growth in perception and not of some lack of foresight in Lonergan. It was I, and not Lonergan, who still needed to come to grasp that method as transposition was more his way of explaining the theological project to a significant particular group at a particular point in time than it was the eternal way to carry out that project. My focus on transposition in my dissertation was legitimate because I concentrated on what Lonergan was doing when he developed his position on the relationship between faith and belief. Theology today, however, by continuing to take seriously a much wider range of sources, is indeed about a more thorough task of reconstruction.

Reading Loewe's work has helped me to grasp and articulate this difference. Loewe's acknowledgement of a fundamental theological shift gives the results of historical Jesus research a legitimate place but does not pivot around such results. In summing up this particular point, Loewe relies upon the Lonerganian-influenced work of David Tracy. Loewe states:

> Faith, as Tracy argued, is response to Jesus encountered through the mediation of community and tradition as God's self-communication in the present, and what norms the tradition is the apostolic witness to Jesus in his religious significance as the Christ. Hence, given both the nature of historical-Jesus constructs and the nature of Christian faith, appeals such as those of the Jesus Seminar to the "historical Jesus" as the real Jesus that should norm Christian faith are misguided. "The historical Jesus" constitutes neither the ground nor basis for Christian faith, nor is it the norm of Christian faith. Certainly

> no historical reconstruction can prove the appropriateness of
> Christian response to Jesus as God's self-presence, although, as
> Tracy, Galvin, and Dulles concur, the results of research on the
> historical Jesus can serve to clarify and perhaps confirm certain
> presuppositions of the confession of Jesus as the Christ.[10]

Loewe's work here gives me a model by which I can acknowledge more
fully the radicality of the contemporary shift in theology and still raise
critical questions, from a Lonerganian perspective, concerning how
that shift is carried out.

Jesus' Founding of the Church

Loewe's appreciation of both the theological usefulness and the limitations of historical Jesus research in Christology inspires my own approach to an important question in ecclesiology.

I had lunch with a couple of young theologians recently at a theology conference in England. I mentioned to them something about Jesus
founding the church. One of them said flatly that one cannot say that
Jesus founded the church. As we started to disagree about this point,
he invoked Lonergan. He said that Lonergan shows us that theology
must be grounded in historical consciousness. Historical scholarship
has shown us that Jesus did not really intend to found a church. What
we call the church actually developed decades after the life of Jesus.[11]
The other young scholar explained to me that Lonergan gave theology
an empirical starting point, and that the taking seriously of historical
research was called for by that empirical starting point.

---

10. Loewe, "From the Humanity," 329–30. For Loewe's fuller explanation of Tracy's
position, see 319–21.

11. In his theological writings before becoming Pope Benedict XVI, Joseph
Ratzinger identified the rejection of Jesus' founding of the church as a key element
in what he labeled "ecclesiological relativism." See Joseph Cardinal Ratzinger, "The
Ecclesiology of the Constitution *Lumen Gentium*," in *Pilgrim Fellowship of Faith: The
Church as Communion*, trans. Henry Taylor (San Francisco: Ignatius, 2005 [German
original, 2002]) 123–52, at 144–49. At that time Ratzinger explicitly identified
Leonardo Boff's *Church: Charism and Power: Liberation Theology and the Institutional
Church*, trans. John W. Diercksmeier (Maryknoll, NY: Orbis, 1985 [Portuguese origi-
nal 1981]), as an example of "ecclesiological relativism" linked with a faulty interpretation of the "subsists in" passage in number 8 of *Lumen Gentium*.

I objected strongly on two counts. First, I argued, one can indeed say that Jesus founded the church. To be critically minded is to be careful about what one means and does not mean by such a statement. One needs to clarify that one does not mean things that would contradict the best in historical-critical scholarship.

Second, I declared (remember that this was a lunchtime conversation) that Lonergan would agree with me. For Lonergan the shift to an empirically based method in theology still included an appropriation of classic doctrines. The Catholic theologian as a converted subject operating in the final four functional specialties will articulate the basic doctrines of Catholic Christianity and attempt to understand them systematically and to communicate them within the context of Catholic and other communities. The articulation and understanding of doctrines will be critical, ecumenical, and faithful in accordance both with the rational standards that apply to all functional specialties and with the religious, moral, and intellectual conversion lived out by the individual theologian within that theologian's community. I argued that any attempt at a full-scale historical reconstruction represented an effort limited to the first four functional specialties. A fuller theological approach must include also an appropriation of a tradition's faith claims, with an eye toward legitimate doctrinal development, which includes an explanation of what those claims mean if they are not to contradict either reason or faith.

Jesus Christ's founding of the church is obviously an issue that can evoke a deeply felt response from me. I still agree with the basics of what I had blurted out, but I wish now in a calmer moment to recognize more of the complexities of the matter, to be more explicit about what a historical approach has to offer theology, to acknowledge the ecumenical concerns of those who dismiss the idea of Jesus founding a church, and finally to present my own position in a more persuasive manner.

Even those who emphasize the limitations of what historical Jesus research can contribute to theology might think that Jesus' founding of the church is precisely the type of issue that historical research can help to clarify. One is even tempted to see the question as one that is more properly historical than theological—did he or didn't he? There is a scholarly consensus that Jesus foresaw his own death as ushering in the kingdom of God as the end of days, but Jesus is not thought to have intentionally laid the groundwork for a particular church organization to develop.

Some theologians take the claim that Jesus founded the church as especially problematic because of what they take to be its implications for ecumenism. Accompanied by polemically shaped versions of the marks of the church, the claim about the church's founding became prominent and hotly contested during the time of the Reformation. The debate was all tied in with the arguments about which church is the one true church. On the Catholic side, these claims were linked with exaggerated and unverifiable assertions about direct links between the apostles and the historical lines of bishops and popes. To continue to affirm the truth of a phrase whose meaning has altered substantially carries an awkwardness at best; at worst it appears to be misleading and obfuscating. If for centuries the primary meaning given to the claim was that Jesus built his church upon the rock of Peter, and that the lines of bishops and popes can be directly traced back to the apostles, and if those understandings have now become historically problematic even for Catholics themselves, should not the claim itself be acknowledged to be problematic? In our times, the Congregation for the Doctrine of the Faith's *Dominus Iesus* (2000), with its strict interpretation of the *subsistit in* passage of Vatican II's *Lumen Gentium*, appeared to some Catholics as well as to a number of other Christians to indicate that contemporary Catholic teaching still misuses the concept of the church that Christ founded in a way that is exclusionary to non-Roman Catholic Christians. For this reason some theologians prefer to say that one can talk about various traditions and their connections with Jesus through the Holy Spirit, but on the matter of Jesus founding the church, it would be better to take one's cues from historical research and admit that, in the most basic ways that such a concept has been imagined, he did not.

Addressing Historical Concerns

My own position is that it remains important to Catholic teaching to proclaim that Jesus Christ founded the church and that Catholic theology should seek further understanding of what that proclamation means (and does not mean). At the same time, I concede that the semantic and conceptual terrain is messy. For example, in non-theological educational and academic contexts, it can be appropriate first to acknowledge that the answer to the question of whether Jesus founded the church depends on what one intends to mean by the phrase.[12] In Catholic theological contexts, too, the affirmation that Jesus founded the church still needs to be followed by an exploration of what one means by the basic teaching. For example, if one means that Jesus envisioned the offices of pope and bishop in the structured ways that they developed in history, such a position runs counter to the evidence. If, however, one means that the community that Jesus formed around himself developed into what we know as the church, such a position is tenable.

I find the objection that Catholic claims surrounding Jesus' founding of the church should be dismissed because they represent a counter-reformational agenda somewhat ironically to have a flaw similar to that of my own tendency to focus on transposing neo-scholastic categories. Instead of privileging such categories in order to transpose them, however, this objection highlights such categories in the interest of rejecting them. In either case, neo-scholastic categories are given more attention than what they are due in the present context. One dimension of my response to this objection is to move to a fuller *ressourcement* that can go beyond neo-scholasticism and beyond the counter-reformational tendencies of early modern Catholicism and beyond even the great treatises of the Middle Ages to include also Scripture and the patristic witness. Another dimension of my response, beyond simply the number and range of sources, is to highlight that sources need to be interpreted by the theologian in accordance with an intellectual conversion that allows one to identify different forms of expression linked with various operations of human consciousness. This is a process that we observed in Loewe's Lonergan-inspired approach to the soteriological vision of Irenaeus.

---

12. This is the approach of Daniel Harrington, SJ, in *The Church according to the New Testament: What the Wisdom and Witness of Early Christianity Teach Us Today* (Franklin, WI: Sheed and Ward, 2001) 20–22. Harrington expressly clarifies, however, that he writes "primarily as a New Testament specialist. . . . While I am a Roman Catholic priest, I see my task here not as promoting or defending distinctively Catholic positions but rather as helping Christians (and their friends) appreciate better what the New Testament says and does not say about the Church." Harrington is aware that there also exist further tasks designed to pursue a fuller theological understanding of what the Church teaches.

In the patristic reception of Scripture the church is envisioned as having many birth moments.[13] Jesus' founding of the church needs to be understood within the context of various highly symbolic claims that both connect the church with and distinguish the church from Israel. The church as part of God's eternal plan is preexistent.[14] It is prefigured in the ark, in the covenant, and in the temple. It has its beginning in the annunciation; the incarnation; the baptism of Jesus; Jesus' various proclamations of the reign of God; the calling of the disciples; the leadership of Peter; the power of the keys; the call to lift up one's cross; the institution of the Eucharist; the designation of the disciples as friends and not slaves along with Jesus' prayer for their unity; the blood and water that flow from the side of Christ; Mary and John at the foot of the cross; various elements of the post-resurrection appearance stories; and the disciples inspired by the Holy Spirit at Pentecost. Such a list can be easily and greatly expanded.

Such religious statements and claims represent various forms of expression related to what human beings are doing when they are understanding and judging and intending. Any theological consideration of the various points of origin attributed to the church calls for an exercise in symbolic consciousness. The various proposed birth moments of the church are not competing in a zero-sum game such that the naming of one rules out the legitimacy of all others. The way in which Spirit-filled Christians wrote and interpreted Scripture in the early Christian centuries connected the church with the will of God, be it through the Father, the Son, the Holy Spirit, the Spirit-filled apostolic witness, or Mary's "let it be." The divine origin of the church is related with Jesus Christ in various ways.

---

13. Jean-Marie R. Tillard explains that even though the event of Pentecost dominates the thought of the patristic authors when addressing the origin of the church, that origin is identified also at other moments in New Testament witness and that in outline it goes back to Abraham when he was chosen to be the father of believers. See Tillard, *Church of Churches: The Ecclesiology of Communion*, trans. R.C. de Peaux (Collegeville, MN: Liturgical, 1992 [French original 1987]) esp. 3 and 105.

14. For this point and for the points that follow in this paragraph I rely on Thomas Halton, *The Church*, Message of the Fathers of the Church 4 (Wilmington, DE: M. Glazier, 1985) 31–32, 35. Halton references Romans 8:29 as well as passages in Ignatius of Antioch and in Clement of Alexandria. Another good source for scriptural and patristic references can be found in the original footnotes to *Lumen Gentium*.

Ancient claims that Jesus founded the church can be linked with particular concerns that arose in particular situations. Such is likely the case with Matthew as well as with Irenaeus. Such concerns appear to be apologetic in nature. In Matthew, they protect against attacks on the God-given identity of the collective followers of Christ. In Irenaeus, they protect against the Gnostic threat to the apostolic heritage. As such, claims that Jesus founded the church are part of the apostolic witness in Scripture and tradition. Such claims cannot simply be limited to the Reformation and to the counter-reformational tendencies of early modern Catholicism.

Has contemporary historical research overturned such claims? We can approach this question in a way that parallels Loewe's approach to the issue of Jesus' intentionality in regard to his own consciousness of his divinity. Loewe holds that Christian faith is based first of all in "Jesus as he is known through the witness of Scripture and the life of the community of his followers."[15] Speculative historical reconstructions are not the basis of faith, but within limits they can be helpful to theology. There is no clear historical consensus concerning how Jesus understood his own identity. There is a wide range of speculation, some of it honestly a challenge to traditional Christian doctrine. Loewe does not attempt a surefire historical reconstruction of what Jesus actually thought. In the face of sensationalist reconstructions that paint a picture of Jesus diametrically opposed to traditional understandings, Loewe is one among numerous scholars who argue for the more likely possibility of the following scenario: Jesus had a very intimate experience of God as Father or Abba.[16] He saw himself in a very special way as God's representative and he foresaw his own death and even his resurrection as being tied to the ushering in of the reign of God. He envisioned the apostles as judges over the twelve tribes of Israel and himself as over the

15. Loewe, *The College Student's Introduction to Christology* (Collegeville, MN: Liturgical, 1996) 206.

16. See, for example, E. P. Sanders, *The Historical Figure of Jesus* (London: A. Lane, Penguin, 1993) 238–81; N. T. Wright, *Who Was Jesus?* (Grand Rapids: Eerdmans, 1993) 97–103; Raymond E. Brown, *An Introduction to New Testament Christology* (New York: Paulist, 1994); and Gerald O'Collins, *Christology: A Biblical, Historical, and Systematic Study of Jesus* (Oxford: Oxford University Press, 1995). In his *College Student's Introduction to Christology*, 82–85, Loewe gives a theoretical yet brief and accessible explanatory account of how Jesus' self-awareness could be continuous with later Christian doctrine.

apostles. He spoke in a way that placed his own authority above the Law of Moses. It is a credible position to hold that Jesus' self-understanding was very likely in continuity with the ways in which Christians came to understand and express his identity and mission in Scripture and in tradition as the decades and centuries passed.

Taking seriously what historical studies have to offer theology, Loewe's approach avoids exaggerated claims about Jesus' self-consciousness of his divinity while offering an understanding of Jesus that can arguably fit with both theological and historical concerns. Jesus' own self-understanding is not eliminated entirely, but neither is a historical reconstruction placed over against traditional witness concerning him. On a commonsense faith level, Jesus' self-understanding is taken to be in harmony with what tradition says about him. On a theoretical level, the theologian recognizes that access to Jesus is mediated through centuries of faith-based witness up through the present.

Can the will of Jesus remain at the foundation of the church even as challenges to exaggerated claims about Jesus' explicit intentions are addressed?[17] Avery Dulles emphasized that Jesus formed around himself a community of disciples, and from this community the church developed.[18] This emphasis is in line with scriptural and patristic witness without including problematic claims about Jesus explicitly intending to designate particular offices and functions. It is an approach that takes seriously historical criticism yet can still take its place within a symbolic consciousness that recognizes a large number of "birth moments" of the church throughout the Old and New Testaments. It can explicitly link baptism and the Eucharist to Jesus' formation of this community. It allows for the connection between later, Spirit-led developments and

17. Francis Schüssler Fiorenza offers what is likely the most comprehensive study of the question of Jesus and the founding of the church in *Foundational Theology: Jesus and the Church* (New York: Crossroad, 1985). He points out weaknesses in developmental approaches that rely upon a reconstruction of Jesus' consciousness and instead offers a hermeneutical approach that explores the connections that early Christians made between the church and its understanding of Jesus. I find Loewe's attention to Jesus' self-consciousness to be not in contradiction with Fiorenza but rather to be a careful claim concerning what can be plausibly held on a commonsense level worked out within a hermeneutical framework compatible with that of Fiorenza. I intend my use of the phrase "the will of Christ" not to suggest a psychological reconstruction of exactly what Jesus thought but also to be in harmony with the approach of Fiorenza.

18. See Avery Dulles, *A Church to Believe In: Discipleship and the Dynamics of Freedom* (New York: Crossroad, 1982) 8.

the will of Christ. It connects with the contemporary emphasis on the church as a community of disciples. It is a more than credible position to hold that the church that emerged in the early Christian centuries is the continuation of the community that Jesus himself formed.[19]

Historical studies can and legitimately have influenced the formulation of Catholic theology and official Catholic teaching concerning Jesus' founding of the church. Francis Sullivan, for example, traces significant lines of continuity in the transmission of apostolic authority. He recognizes, however, that historical evidence simply does not allow one to conclude definitively that the episcopacy understood as a differentiated office consolidating various powers exercised by presbyters had emerged within the time of the writing of the New Testament.[20] Rather, Sullivan finds that various forms of authority were present in the early church. By the second half of the second Christian century, there had emerged a church-wide system of bishops of local churches in communion with one another. In the face of the Gnostic threat, the relatively quick emergence of this church-wide authoritative structure was received by Christians as God-given with deep gratitude. The survival of the church depended upon it. Sullivan argues that this Spirit-guided development is an integral dimension of the maturing of the church that is comparable to the determination of the canon of Scripture, and in that sense remains valid today.[21]

Roger Haight agrees with Sullivan to a point. Haight accepts that the development of the monoepiscopacy can rightly be claimed to have been necessary as well as to have been divinely inspired. He disagrees with Sullivan, however, that the episcopal structure of the church is

---

19. One of the best books developing this position is Gerhard Lohfink, *Jesus and Community: The Social Dimensions of Christian Faith*, trans. John Galvin (Philadelphia: Fortress, 1984 [German original 1982]). The substance of Lohfink's extensive study is in harmony with Dulles's position as briefly outlined above. Still, Lohfink's rhetorical strategy is somewhat different. He finds the question as to whether Jesus really founded a church to be posed in the wrong way (p. xi). I can sympathize with his approach, but I still find that as a theologian I must ask: how can Catholic teaching about Jesus' founding of the church best be understood? Lohfink's book provides a comprehensive answer to this question.

20. See Francis Sullivan, *From Apostles to Bishops: The Development of the Episcopacy in the Early Church* (New York: Newman, 2001) 217–30.

21. See ibid., 230.

binding on all Christians of all times.[22] Haight makes a distinction between a structure being divinely willed and a structure being historically necessary. He finds Sullivan's argument to justify the episcopacy as a legitimate structure but not as a necessary structure.

Haight's language about Jesus' founding of the church needs to be sifted through carefully. Haight is explicitly developing what he calls a transdenominational ecclesiology from below.[23] He is able to say that once historical qualifications are made, "Jesus remains the founder of the church."[24] Yet Haight also distinguishes between, on the one hand, the Christian movement and the ecclesial existence it constitutes and, on the other hand, various particular church structures and denominations. The Christian church with an organized structure does not emerge until sometime after AD 100.[25] For Haight, what Jesus founded was the Christian movement or the church understood in a broad, transdenominational sense. Various structures or patterns of organization can lay claim to being divinely willed and even in particular cases historically necessary, but not in an exclusive manner that would rule out other divinely willed structures and patterns of organization. Haight uses the phrase "subsists in" in a manner that is directly in tension with the use of that phrase in *Lumen Gentium*. Whereas *Lumen Gentium* uses the phrase to speak of a special connection between the church that Christ founded and the Catholic Church, Haight speaks of the ecclesial existence that "subsists in" the many institutional forms of the various churches.

Haight insists that denominational ecclesiologies remain necessary and denies that his pursuit of a transdenominational ecclesiology in any way undermines that need.[26] His difference from Sullivan, however, suggests that he expects future denominational ecclesiologies to be built upon transdenominational presuppositions. Haight admits that his transdenominational approach is not grounded in a concrete, historical community. What is it, then, that does ground his approach?

---

22. See Roger Haight, *Christian Community in History*, 3 vols. (New York: Continuum, 2004–8) 1:193n104; 3:45.

23. See ibid., 3:3–27.

24. Ibid., 3:74.

25. See ibid., 1:74.

26. See ibid., 3:viii.

I suggest that Haight's approach from below builds primarily upon an historical reconstruction of the emergence of early Christianity. There is no distinction within Haight's approach between a mediating phase of theology that relies upon common academic methods and a mediated phase that calls also for the appropriation of the faith of a concrete, particular community in accordance with its religious, moral, and intellectual conversion. Rather Haight describes the theological dimension of his study as bringing a level of perception and a type of language to his historically grounded approach that recognizes the activity of God and the effects of God's grace. Haight claims to dismiss any type of reductionism, whether that be a historical reductionism that ignores the divine dimension of the church or a theological reductionism that ignores the historical dimension. Haight does not sufficiently include, however, the perspective of the religious insider as insider, the perspective of the converted subject appropriating the doctrines of a particular community within the lived context of that particular community.

Haight's groundbreaking and challenging work has performed a service by raising many important questions for contemporary theology. I cannot pretend that more traditionally minded theological approaches have adequately addressed these questions, particularly those about the church founded by Jesus, in any final way. With Lonergan in mind, however, I would like to see more inquiry into these questions that takes seriously the role of the theologian as a faith-based appropriator of a lived tradition. With Loewe in mind, I would like to see more reliance on the faith witness of the church and less reliance on historical reconstruction as the basis for theological work. Haight's attempt to use two languages, those of history and theology, to gain a range of insights into what is basically a historical reconstruction, falls short of being a theologically adequate method.

Interpreting *Lumen Gentium*

A question remains about how to interpret the treatment of Jesus' founding of the church in *Lumen Gentium* (*LG*). This question takes us right back to the question of the extent to which historical reconstruction can serve either as a basis or as a corrective for faith claims. The founding of the church appears in *LG* in five places. According to paragraph 5 of *LG*, the church is inaugurated when Jesus preaches the coming of the kingdom of God, and the mission of inaugurating the church throughout the world is given when the risen Lord pours out his Spirit upon the disciples. In *LG* 8, the church that Christ founded is said to "subsist in" the Catholic Church, governed by the successor of Peter and the bishops in communion with him, though elements of sanctification and of truth can be found outside its visible structure. *LG* 9 speaks of Jesus' founding of the new Israel that is the church. Paragraphs 18–20 of *LG* portray Jesus Christ as instituting a variety of offices in the church and willing that the successors of the apostles shepherd the church for all time. *LG* 48 speaks of the founding of the church in terms of the risen Christ establishing his Body which is the church by pouring out his Spirit upon his disciples.

Lumen Gentium 18–20 may appear on the surface to stand in contradiction with the results of contemporary historical research concerning whether Jesus envisioned a church with the particular offices that gradually emerged. I read these sections as offering a kind of first-order narrative, not an academic treatise, that draws upon Scripture and tradition to emphasize the continuity between the church that develops in history and the will of Christ. Still, however, the wording is careful:

> . . . [*apostolorum*] *successores, videlicet episcopos, in ecclesia sua—usque ad consummationem saeculi pastores esse voluit* [18].[27] . . . he willed the successors [of the apostles], which one can understand as bishops, in his church—to be shepherds until the end of the world [18].[28]

The use of *voluit*—"he willed"—can be read as being directly in reference to the successors of the apostles, whatever shape that succession might have taken. The phrase, "which one can understand as bishops," should be read as a parenthetical clarification concerning what shape the succession indeed took, rather than as a description of precisely what Jesus had envisioned.

27. Norman Tanner, ed., *Decrees of the Ecumenical Councils*, vol. 2: *Trent to Vatican II* (London: Sheed and Ward, 1990) 863.

28. This is my own translation. Tanner translates *videlicet* as "namely." My own translation, "which one can understand as," draws on an etymological meaning of *videlicet* as "permitted to see." Even the word "namely," however, can be read as connoting something similar to my translation.

Still, this sentence and the ones that follow do suggest more about the intentions of Jesus than a strictly historically based approach could arrive at. Historical reconstruction, however, is not the basis of Christian faith. It is to be hoped that most educated people of faith realize that first-order narrative accounts are not intended to be police reports of what actually happened. Few Catholics today hear stories about Adam and Eve as if they were eyewitness testimony. Catholics believe that the Gospels faithfully tell us what Jesus said and what he did, but they also realize that variety in the accounts can reflect differences in the situations of the communities that produced them. I find it best to read *LG* 18–20 in the light of *LG* 5 and in conjunction with various other passages that link the church not only with Christ but also with the Father and the Holy Spirit. I read the "subsists in" language in the light of all of these others and tend to favor interpretations of the passage that recognize a real and significant but not entirely unrestricted ecumenical openness.

I make these hermeneutical maneuvers because I find the claim that Jesus founded the church to belong to contemporary Catholic teaching as well as to Scripture and tradition. For all of the many qualifications that need to be made, it still makes a difference whether Christians believe that the church is something willed by Jesus Christ himself. If sometime in the future Christian churches and communities by the grace of God reach more palpable forms of full visible communion, the founding of the church by Jesus will remain an important part of the church's heritage. It can be hoped that future claims about Jesus founding the church can be based on research that is significantly less polemical and more ecumenical than in the past.

What Would Lonergan Do?

So, what would Lonergan or, for that matter, Loewe, do?

I have discussed things that I have learned from Loewe and Lonergan both during and after writing my dissertation. Lonergan's first four functional specialties take an empirically based starting point and develop positions based on the best that human reason and interpretation can offer. Religious, moral, and intellectual conversion provides a bridge to the final four functional specialties. The empirical, the rational, and the hermeneutical are never left behind but rather continue to operate at full blast. Once one begins to speak in an explicitly theological manner, however, one appropriates the teachings that have been handed down within one's religious tradition. One attains a horizon within which one can understand what the basic claims of one's tradition mean. One can articulate these doctrines in a manner that acknowledges legitimate doctrinal development. One can seek a fuller understanding of how they fit together with each other and with the world in which one lives. And one can live out these truths within the context of a community whose basic meanings and values are constituted by the realities to which the community gives witness. Loewe has helped me to read Lonergan in a way that calls me to be open to radical change and radical action even as I strive to appropriate faithfully the truths handed down in tradition. Most often the intellectual dimensions of these changes, I find, are in the form of new formulations and new understandings rather than in the casting off of inconvenient truths.

I am still a bit bothered, however, about the way I had responded with a defensive outburst to those two young theologians at the conference in England. I must take most seriously what Lonergan said about the way in which conflicts should be worked out within the fourth functional specialty, Dialectics. He wrote:

> Now the task of dealing with these conflicts pertains, not to the methodologies, but to theologians occupied in the fourth functional specialty. Moreover, the theologian's strategy will be, not to prove his own position, not to refute counter-positions, but to exhibit diversity and to point to the evidence for its roots. In this manner he will be attractive to those who appreciate full human authenticity and he will convince those that attain it. Indeed, the basic idea of the method we are trying to develop takes its stand on discovering what human authenticity is and showing how to appeal to it.[29]

This passage reminds me of how my attempts to refute the position of my young theologian friends, as well as my current approach, do not display sufficient appeals to human authenticity. I need to get in touch with Professor Loewe, the facilitator of deep and authentic intellectual conversions, and see if he can help me with this.

29. Lonergan, *Method in Theology*, 253–54.

PART 2

Soteriological Narratives in the Christian Tradition

3

Schillebeeckx's Phenomenology of Experience and Resurrection Faith

ANTHONY J. GODZIEBA
VILLANOVA UNIVERSITY

Interpretations of the New Testament Easter Evidence

Edward Schillebeeckx's treatment of Christ's resurrection in his *Jesus: An Experiment in Christology* (1974/1979), while controversial, remains a potent hermeneutical reflection on the original Easter experience as well as on resurrection faith today.[1] By closely examining Schillebeeckx's theory in its original existential-phenomenological context, I wish to highlight here its continuing explanatory force regarding the origin and meaning of belief in the resurrection of Jesus.

The catalyst for this analysis is William P. Loewe's discussion of the origins of resurrection faith in *The College Student's Introduction to Christology*, a work valuable for its clarity in presenting some of the knottiest christological problems. Loewe approaches the New Testament evidence for the resurrection—particularly Paul's *kerygma* in 1 Corinthians 15 and the Gospel narratives of the empty tomb and Jesus' appearances to the disciples—through a series of four questions designed to elicit the meaning and implications of resurrection faith.

---

1. See Edward Schillebeeckx, *Jesus: An Experiment in Christology*, trans. Hubert Hoskins (New York: Crossroad, 1979) 320–650. Hereafter, page references to this work will be noted by parenthetical citations in the text.

The questions cover the temporal gamut of past, present, and future: the first ("what are the data?") deals with the textual evidence as we encounter it now; the second and third ("why are the data the way they are?" and "why are there any data at all?) probe the "world behind the text," inquiring into the experiences that gave rise to the existence and the form of the textual witness as it has come down to us; and the fourth question ("what difference does it make if Jesus was raised from the dead?") is a pointedly hermeneutical one that attempts to discern the "world in front of" the text, the evidence's "applicative" moment—how the texts provoke new possibilities for present and future Christian existence that transform the lives of believers and bring them into deeper participation in divine life.[2] Although Loewe's method is not explicitly labeled "phenomenological" or "hermeneutical," it most definitely shares with those methods a concern both for meaning and for the structure and origins of experience.

This concern for structure and origins is appropriate to the discipline of Christology because the Christian tradition is best viewed as a "history of effects," a *Wirkungsgeschichte* (to use Hans-Georg Gadamer's term).[3] That is, the tradition, as an ensemble of practices and reflections, functions as the ongoing, developing reception and realization of the salvific truth of Jesus Christ that was first experienced by Jesus' disciples in their personal encounters with him. As Schillebeeckx puts it, "this astonishing and overwhelming encounter with the man Jesus became the starting-point for the New Testament view of salvation. To put it plainly, 'grace' has to be expressed in terms of encounter and experience; it can never be isolated from the specific encounter which brought about liberation."[4] In the light of Christianity's foundational

2. See William P. Loewe, *The College Student's Introduction to Christology* (Collegeville, MN: Liturgical, 1996) 98.

3. See Hans-Georg Gadamer, *Wahrheit und Methode: Grundzüge einer philosophischen Hermeneutik*, vol. 1, *Hermeneutik*, Gesammelte Werke 1 (Tübingen: Mohr Siebeck, 1990) 305–12; ET: *Truth and Method*, 2d rev. ed., trans. Joel Weinsheimer and Donald G. Marshall (New York: Continuum, 2004) 300–07. For the Christian tradition interpreted as a *Wirkungsgeschichte*, see Anthony J. Godzieba, "Method and Interpretation: The New Testament's Heretical Hermeneutic (Prelude and Fugue)," *The Heythrop Journal* 36/3 (July 1995): 286–306.

4. Edward Schillebeeckx, *Christ: The Experience of Jesus as Lord*, trans. John Bowden (New York: Crossroad, 1981[Dutch orig., 1977]) 19. Hereafter, page references to this work will be noted by parenthetical citations in the text.

incarnational and sacramental commitments, it makes no sense to separate the historical event of Jesus of Nazareth—the initial contextual-
ized impulse of the Christian tradition—from the tradition itself, as did
the earliest "quest for the historical Jesus." One of the necessary tasks
of christological reflection is to use the diverse methods available to
probe, as far as possible, the events and experiences that have provided
the initial impetus for both the tradition and our present activity of
belief. Loewe himself, while insisting that research into the "historical
Jesus" has its limits and that "no historical reconstruction can prove the
appropriateness of Christian response to Jesus as God's self-presence,"
has argued that there is indeed continuity between the historical reconstructions and the Christ of faith: they "differ as epistemological categories, not substantively." And "when historical-Jesus constructs are
drawn into the horizon of faith and illumined by the light of faith, the
coherence of these historical images and narratives with the transformative values appropriated in the tradition's confession of Jesus as the
Christ may be grasped."[5] Walter Kasper makes a similar point regarding
the need for a genetic analysis when he takes up the central issue of the
continuation of Jesus' "cause" after his crucifixion and the aftereffects of
the events that constitute the Paschal Mystery.

> There was continuity after Good Friday; indeed in some senses
> it was then that movement really began. . . . The powerful his-
> torical dynamism of this revival can only be made comprehen-
> sible, even in purely historical terms, by positing a sort of "initial
> ignition." Religious, psychological, political and social elements
> in the situation, as it was at the time, can be cited in explanation.
> Yet, seen from the point of view of historical circumstances,
> Jesus' "cause" has very slender chances of surviving. Jesus' end
> on the cross was not only his private failure but a public ca-
> tastrophe for his "mission," and its religious discrediting. The
> renewal must therefore be seen as strong enough not only to
> "explain" the unnatural dynamism of early Christianity, but to
> "come to terms with" that problem of the cross.[6]

The search for this "initial ignition" leads most Christologies to the
Gospels' resurrection accounts, especially to the post-resurrection ap-

5. Loewe, "From the Humanity of Christ to the Historical Jesus," *Theological Studies* 61/2 (June 2000): 314–31, at 330.

6. Walter Kasper, *Jesus the Christ*, trans. V. Green (New York: Paulist, 1977), 124.

pearance narratives rather than the empty tomb narratives. Loewe is no exception.[7] In emphasizing the appearance accounts, he outlines three basic interpretive positions. The first holds that the disciples had "a real encounter with the risen Jesus" that includes a visual component stemming from "an initiative of the risen Jesus" and "involves an experience of seeing him that, though unique and mysterious, is also real" and not a "psychologically induced visionary experience." References to "sight" (e.g., 1 Corinthians 15:3: "he appeared [*ōphthē*] to Kephas . . .") are to be taken literally. The second position also holds that the disciples had a real encounter with Jesus that was "an occasion on which the recipients of the risen Jesus' self-manifestation underwent an experience with a visual component." However, this position's definition of "real" includes the possibility of a visionary experience "explicable by the discipline of psychology." This is an attempt to account for the New Testament evidence that the risen Jesus is encountered ("seen") only by those who had a prior involvement with him and subsequently preached his presence and his message.[8] The two positions, while agreeing that there was a "real encounter with the risen Jesus" and a "visual component" to that encounter, differ with regard to what they are willing to include in their definitions of objectivity—a difference at the deeper level of philosophical presuppositions as to what counts as "real."[9]

As position three, situated between the first two, Loewe proposes Schillebeeckx's theology of resurrection faith. He focuses specifically on Schillebeeckx's original argument that the disciples did indeed have a real encounter with Jesus that resulted in their experience of grace

---

7. As Loewe notes, "scholars do not propose that the empty tomb tradition accounts for the rise of belief in Jesus' resurrection" (*College Student's Introduction*, 132). This is so because, as Raymond Brown noted over a quarter of a century ago, "the fact that the tomb was found empty allows several explanations. . . . Of itself, then, the empty tomb was probably not at first a sign of the resurrection, and the emptiness of the tomb was not formally a part of Christian faith in the risen Jesus. Modern fundamentalist statements such as 'our faith depends on the empty tomb' or 'We believe in the empty tomb' . . . misplace the emphasis in resurrection faith. Christians believe in Jesus, not in a tomb" (*The Virginal Conception and Bodily Resurrection of Jesus* [New York: Paulist, 1973] 126–27).

8. Loewe, *College Student's Introduction*, 134.

9. "Position One requires the objectivity of miracles and of appearances of the risen Jesus to be the kind that is certified by the empirical natural sciences. Position Two distinguishes that kind of objectivity from the objectivity that belongs to the truth of faith" (ibid., 135).

and forgiveness for having forsaken Jesus at the hour of his death. In that earlier argument, Schillebeeckx grounds the appearance tradition in the conversion experience of Peter who subsequently reunited the remaining disciples, who in turn had had their own conversion experiences. These experiences of forgiveness, coupled with the disciples' memory of Jesus' life and praxis, "became the matrix in which faith in Jesus as the risen One was brought to birth. They all of a sudden 'saw' it."[10] The disciples subsequently expressed their experience of conversion and their real encounter with Jesus, the catalyst of this conversion, in terms of a "'visual' model" meant to convey the historical reality of "an event engendered by grace, a divine salvific initiative."[11] This was their testimony to the fact that "a dead man does not proffer forgiveness" but rather the living Jesus.[12]

> The objective, sovereignly free initiative of Jesus that led them on to a Christological faith—an initiative independent of any belief on the part of Peter and his companions—is a gracious act of Christ, which as regards their "enlightenment" is of course revelation—not a construct of men's minds, but revelation within a disclosure experience, in this case given verbal embodiment later on in the "appearances" model. What it signifies is no model but a living reality. Understood thus, the ground of Christian belief is indubitably Jesus of Nazareth in his earthly proffer of salvation, renewed after his death, now experienced and enunciated by Peter and the Twelve.[13]

Loewe mentions the criticism leveled at this theory by Schillebeeckx's theological colleagues and by the Vatican's Congregation for the Doctrine of the Faith (CDF). However, he does not discuss in any detail Schillebeeckx's clarifications and substantive additions to the third Dutch edition of *Jesus* nor his important discussion of "experience" in both the 1977 *Christ* and the 1978 *Interim Report*, all of which formed part of Schillebeeckx's ongoing response to these various

---

10. Schillebeeckx, *Jesus*, 391.

11. Ibid., 390.

12. Ibid., 391.

13. Ibid., 390. For the details of this portion of Schillebeeckx's argument, including his discussion of the first century A.D. Jewish eschatological and apocalyptic background for the "Easter experience," see *Jesus*, 390–97.

critiques.[14] This is unfortunate because it is precisely in the amplification (indeed the fine-tuning) of his earlier argument that Schillebeeckx tackles the very issues that Loewe deems decisive in the formulation of the various "positions," namely the philosophical issues surrounding the issues of experience, objectivity, and "the real." In the remainder of this essay, I want to make the case that Schillebeeckx's phenomenological approach to the appearance narratives, as a sophisticated sorting out of the notions of "objective" and "subjective" in a theological setting, fundamentally advances our ability to articulate the objectivity that structures the New Testament accounts while also accounting for the disciples' experience of faith steeped in first-century Palestinian Jewish eschatology.

"Experience" and Its Phenomenological Context

Schillebeeckx summarizes his basic view of revelation this way: "Of course revelation—the sheer initiative of God's loving freedom—transcends any human experience; in other words, it does not emerge from subjective human experience and thinking; it can, however, only be perceived in and through human experiences. There is no revelation without experience."[15] This claim is not new; it is a common starting point for Roman Catholic theology after Vatican II. But whereas a more transcendental position such as Karl Rahner's considered God's self-disclosure in revelation as the fulfillment of the possibilities of human ontological structures (reworked from the *existentialia*, the existential structures of Martin Heidegger's *Being and Time*), Schillebeeckx professed to see revelation both rooted in and contrasting with experience:

14. For the additions, see *Jezus, het verhaal van een levende*, 3rd ed. (Bloemendaal: Nelissen, 1975) 528 a–e; *Jesus*, 644–50. See also Edward Schillebeeckx, *Interim Report on the Books "Jesus" and "Christ,"* trans. John Bowden (New York: Crossroad, 1981 [Dutch orig., 1978]) 3–19. For a translation of documents relating to the CDF's investigation of Schillebeeckx, along with Schillebeeckx's responses, see *The Schillebeeckx Case: Official Exchange of Letters and Documents in the Investigation of Fr. Edward Schillebeeckx, O.P. by the Sacred Congregation for the Doctrine of the Faith, 1976–1980,* ed. Ted Schoof, trans. Matthew J. O'Connell (Ramsey, NJ: Paulist, 1984). See also the commentary by Herwi Rikhof, "Of Shadows and Substance: Analysis and Evaluation of the Documents in the Schillebeeckx Case," in *Authority in the Church and the Schillebeeckx Case,* ed. Leonard Swidler and Piet F. Fransen (New York: Crossroad, 1982) 244–67.

15. Schillebeeckx, *Interim Report*, 11.

"God's revelation is the opposite of our achievements or plans, but this contrast in no way excludes the fact that revelation also includes human plans and experiences and thus in no way suggests that revelation should fall outside our experience."[16] But if I am rooted in my experience, how do I appropriate these new elements of "contrast"? If my experience is transcended, how can I know at all?[17]

For Schillebeeckx, experience means "learning through 'direct' contact with people and things," and what is perceived is simultaneously integrated into our field of experiences:

> In this way they become the framework within which we interpret new experiences, while at the same time this already given framework of interpretation is exposed to criticism and corrected, changed or renewed by new experiences. *Experience is gained in a dialectical fashion:* through an interplay between perception and thought, thought and perception.[18]

This dialectical framework guides integration of new experiences in the element of interpretation. It opens up the person to "contrast experiences" that confound our expectations and yet can be appropriated within this expanding framework.[19] Experience and interpretation thus occur simultaneously: "we experience in the act of interpreting, without being able to draw a neat distinction between the element of experience and the element of interpretation."[20] By means of this interpretative dimension, a person can admit experiences that transcend the fund of experiences already present. In this way, Schillebeeckx grounds his theory of revelation in a basic epistemological structure of human subjectivity.

Although sparing with his references, it can be shown that the main influences on Schillebeeckx's view of experience are those philosophical analyses that come out of phenomenology, specifically those of Heidegger and Maurice Merleau-Ponty (who are not cited in either *Christ* or the *Interim Report*) and Gadamer (whose lengthy section on

16. Ibid.

17. This is akin to Kant's noumenon/phenomenon problem, to which Schillebeeckx alludes (see *Christ*, 56).

18. Schillebeeckx, *Christ*, 31–32; my emphasis.

19. Schillebeeckx, *Interim Report*, 13.

20. Schillebeeckx, *Christ*, 33.

experience in *Truth and Method* is cited).[21] In fact, his position has much in common with the existential phenomenology popularized in the 1960s by the Dutch philosopher William Luijpen, among others.[22] If Schillebeeckx's argument is to have its full impact, we must make his presuppositions clear.

Secondly, if phenomenology is truly the unspoken presupposition to his fundamental notion of experience, then we should emphasize that Schillebeeckx employs a method that, in its philosophical manifestation, critiques the subject-object distinction and seeks to surpass metaphysical dualism. This is especially important in the contemporary context. Over the past quarter-century Western theologians have become almost painfully aware of how modern theology's indebtedness to both the postmedieval rationalist heritage (coming after nominalism) and modern metaphysics (the Suarezian influence which was destabilized only with Heidegger) has caused what Joseph O'Leary terms a "lack of fit" between the Christian experience of God and the rationalist-metaphysical categories that promised a comprehensive explanation of that experience. This mismatch stifled theology's ability to carry out its task as *fides quaerens intellectum* and take into account the transformation in being provoked by the unprecedented givenness of God in the incarnation (and, by extension, the relationality that we now regard as central to any theology of the Trinity). As O'Leary puts it, "There is a complex topology of the world of faith that can never be fitted into the horizons of metaphysical theology, which rather act as a screen against it. A creative retrieval of the tradition today works toward a clearing of the fundamental horizons of faith, and subordinates the quest for metaphysical intelligibility to this prior openness."[23]

It is precisely this retrieval of the original experience of the Easter revelation event that Schillebeeckx attempts by employing a phenomenological theory of experience to analyze the testimony passed down

---

21. Ibid., 855n17.

22. E.g., see William Luijpen, *Existential Phenomenology*, trans. Henry J. Koren (Pittsburgh, PA: Duquesne University Press, 1969). Schillebeeckx cites other works by Luijpen in *Christ*, 41.

23. Joseph Stephen O'Leary, *Religious Pluralism and Christian Truth* (Edinburgh: Edinburgh University Press, 1996) x. See also O'Leary's comment that theology today "must be phenomenological," that is, "theology must constantly question back to the primary level of faith, the original concrete contours of the revelation-event, the 'matter itself' that is apprehended by a contemplative thinking" (ibid., ix).

to us in the New Testament. Rather than "raid" phenomenology for its insights, he seems to follow the insights of phenomenological analysis to their conclusions and uses them to craft a responsive and responsible fundamental theology, convinced that these insights truly illuminate the character of what it means to be human in the grip of grace. And so, in my view, Schillebeeckx not only uses phenomenology, he *proceeds phenomenologically in doing theology*, and specifically in his discussion of the post-resurrection appearance narratives. The result, I want to argue, is a more adequate treatment of the issues of objectivity, subjectivity, and corporeality in the appearance narratives than can be derived from the two positions identified by Loewe.

To test this thesis, we will probe the phenomenological background to Schillebeeckx's theory of experience and its application to resurrection faith. My discussion focuses on specific aspects of the works of Merleau-Ponty, Gadamer, and Heidegger that have clear echoes in Schillebeeckx's own discussion.

Maurice Merleau-Ponty

Merleau-Ponty's original project sought to work out a phenomenological analysis of the encounter between the subject and the world by using Edmund Husserl's "phenomenological reduction"—the suspension of the "natural attitude" of belief in the reality of things in order to achieve a transcendental point of view from which to reflect "on the intentions at work in the natural attitude and on the objective correlates of those intentions."[24] He attempted to "correct" Husserl's idealistic bias (phenomenology as the search for "pure essences") by investigating perception, thereby building a phenomenology "from the ground up." This project was stimulated by Heidegger's "existential analytic" of Dasein

---

24. Richard Cobb-Stevens, "The Beginnings of Phenomenology: Husserl and His Predecessors," in *Continental Philosophy in the 20th Century*, ed. Richard Kearney, Routledge History of Philosophy 8 (New York: Routledge, 1994) 5–37, at 19. For Husserl's own (complex) explanation of his "discovery," see his 1907 lectures *The Idea of Phenomenology*, trans. William P. Alston and George Nakhnikian (The Hague: Nijhoff, 1970); *Ideas Pertaining to a Pure Phenomenology and to a Phenomenological Philosophy, First Book: General Introduction to a Pure Phenomenology*, trans. F. Kersten, Edmund Husserl, vol. 2, Collected Works (The Hague: Nijhoff, 1983[Ger. orig., 1913]) 131–43 (§§ 56–62). See also Dermot Moran, *Introduction to Phenomenology* (2000; reprint, New York: Routledge, 2006) 124–63.

(Being-in-the-world) in *Being and Time*. Merleau-Ponty's conclusion is that there is no radical separation of the human subject and the world. Rather, there is an effective involvement of subject and world—the human person is an incarnate spirit, and through the interaction of the person (through the modes of the body-subject [perception] and the *cogito* [thought]) and the world, the true human world we inhabit, a "world of meaning," is disclosed, indeed built up. Within that ambiguous region of openness the "text" of the human world is composed, the network of meanings around me and connected to me is constituted in my everyday involvement with my world.[25] Speaking of perception, he says that "normal functioning must be understood as a process of integration in which the text of the external world is not so much copied, as composed."[26] Merleau-Ponty subsequently widened his field of phenomenological investigation beyond the analysis of behavior and perception, and attempted to develop an ontology that would not only account for the nature of perception but would also include politics and art, and eventually put him in touch with the source of the "perceived world," namely "brute or wild Being"[27] seen as a *Gestalt*, the ground/background of the world and man.[28]

A text from this later stage, "The Metaphysical in Man" (1947), contains a passage that sums up much of his investigation of human experience.

> It is our very difference, the uniqueness of our experience, which attests to our strange ability to enter into others and re-enact their deeds. . . . From the moment I recognize that my experience, precisely insofar as it is my own, makes me accessible to what is not myself, that I am sensitive to the world and to others, all the beings which objective thought placed at a distance draw singularly nearer to me. Or, conversely, I recognize my

25. See Maurice Merleau-Ponty, *Phenomenology of Perception*, trans. Colin Smith (London: Routledge and Kegan Paul, 1962) 453: "To be born is both to be born of the world and to be born into the world. The world is already constituted, but also never completely constituted; in the first case we are acted upon, in the second we are open to an infinite number of possibilities. But this analysis is still abstract, for we exist in both ways *at once*."

26. Ibid., 9.

27. Maurice Merleau-Ponty, *The Visible and the Invisible*, trans. Alphonso Lingis (Evanston, IL: Northwestern University Press, 1968) 170.

28. See ibid., 170, 227–28.

affinity with them; I am nothing but an ability to echo them, to understand them, to respond to them. My life seems absolutely individual and absolutely universal to me.[29]

My openness is now interpreted even more precisely: my experience is the horizon against which universal structures appear, but universality appears only through my immersion in a world where I am in contact with individual persons and things. There is no "metaphysical consciousness" (i.e., consciousness of the being-structures of "world" precisely as being-for-me) without objects of experience.[30] Consciousness only gets "filled out," as it were, only grasps meaning in its very openness to "what is not myself." It is thus radically situated and never drifts off to some pure realm of abstract universals through which I might know others and the world. The retreat to some detached knowledge of essences in order to know—a retreat that realism and Cartesianism both undertake—is a false step.

> All knowledge of man by man, far from being pure contemplation, is the taking up by each, *as best he can*, of the acts of others, reactivating from ambiguous signs an experience which is not his own, appropriating a structure . . . of which he forms no distinct concept but which he puts together as an experienced pianist deciphers an unknown piece of music: without himself grasping the motives of each gesture or each operation, without being able to bring to the surface of consciousness all the sediment of knowledge which he is using at that moment. Here we no longer have the positing of an object, but rather we have communication with a way of being.[31]

All my knowledge comes from lived experience, which, like the playing of the pianist, ferrets out and discloses meaning as I am involved in experiencing, and never apart from that involvement. But that involvement precisely does not close me off, but rather opens me to the other, to things, and to the totality of meanings we call "world." The

---

29. Maurice Merleau-Ponty, *Sense and Non-Sense*, trans. Hubert Dreyfus and Patricia Allen Dreyfus (Evanston, IL: Northwestern University Press, 1964) 83–98, at 94.

30. See Merleau-Ponty, *Sense and Non-Sense*, 94: "This world, other people, human history, truth, culture . . . [indeed,] metaphysical consciousness has no other objects than those of experience."

31. Ibid., 93; emphasis in original.

totality and its "structure" only get known by means of my involvement with what is "not my own." Meanings are not constituted by consciousness fabricating them on its own, but by consciousness' interaction with the "stuff" of the world, primarily through the body, and then through the *cogito*. My immersion in the world through perception already automatically insures that from the start my existence is double-edged: it is *absolutely individual* because of my own perspective, rooted in the perceived world by my body; at the same time it is *absolutely universal*, since the interplay between my subjectivity and the world opens me to the *whole world*. This accessibility to what is not myself—to the world and to others—through my standpoint serves to ground my appropriation of meaning or structure. Even though consciousness accomplishes constitution of meaning, it can do so only along the lines of the direction or hint provided by the world that is "found ahead of us, in the thing where our perception places us, in the dialogue into which our experience of other people throws us by means of a movement not all of whose sources are known to us."[32]

Thus, it is not only sense perception that is a product of the dialogue between subjectivity and world, but also every level of human existence that is dependent on human experience. Meaning is essentially a blending of foreground and background: human experience is the horizon against which the *sens* of the world appears. My experience is both perspectival and open, individual yet universal. Because of my radical situatedness, the "absolute standpoint" is impossible. "[If] I have understood that truth and value can be for us nothing but the result of the verifications or evaluations which we make in contact with the world . . . that even these notions lose all meaning outside of human perspectives, then the world recovers its texture . . . and knowledge and action, true and false, good and evil have something unquestionable about them precisely because I do not claim to find in them absolute evidence."[33]

Merleau-Ponty thus insists on the contextual situatedness of human existence: all knowledge is founded on experience, and indeed every human act is rooted in the structure of present experience. In the course of his refutation of the absolute standpoint, Merleau-Ponty

32. Ibid.
33. Ibid., 95.

also implicitly refutes subjectivism by showing that the very workings of experience necessarily include the world, "the other", what is not-myself, alongside subjectivity. This phenomenological analysis of experience reveals experience's double edge (individuality/universality) and also asserts its primacy, points which are crucial to Schillebeeckx's own analysis of experience.

Hans-Georg Gadamer

Gadamer's analysis of experience can be seen as supplying what is lacking in Merleau-Ponty, namely, a more critical examination of the concept of experience as it relates to thought.

The concept of experience is, for Gadamer, "one of the most obscure we have."[34] That obscurity is not cleared up by the prevailing notions of experience governed by the scientific model, which aims for certainty and strips experience of its historicity in order to objectify it, make it verifiable by anyone, and assure its universality.[35] This reveals a bias akin to the bias of the absolute standpoint criticized by Merleau-Ponty. The authentic character of experience becomes obscured when it is defined not in terms of its own characteristics but in terms of the supposed "result," an absolute that is presupposed and known "absolutely." In its true character, experience is neither a straight-line process nor does it lead consciousness away from its historical rootedness. Rather, experience is a process involving starts, stops, and reversals. It is, paradoxically, a process of negation which leads to development. Even the everyday use of the word manifests this paradoxical character:

> We use the word "experience" in two different senses: the experiences that conform to our expectation and confirm it and the new experiences that occur to us. This latter—"experience" in the genuine sense—is always negative. If a new experience of an object occurs to us, this means that hitherto we have not seen the thing correctly and now know it better. Thus the negativity of experience has a curiously productive meaning. It is not simply that we see through a deception and hence make a correction, but we acquire a comprehensive knowledge.[36]

34. Gadamer, *Truth and Method*, 346.

35. See ibid., 347.

36. Ibid., 353.

The negation that we experience is our expectations being con-
founded, even shattered: this object is *not* as I expected, this situation is
not as I predicted. My thinking has a certain "fit," and the clash with the
world forces thinking to adjust its "fit," to expand in order to comprehend.[37] Consciousness does not control meaning; rather, constitution
of meaning takes place when our previous appropriation of meaning
and the expectations that have thereby been generated are in turn shattered by an unexpected twist in the manifestation of being. Experience
thus leads to a deeper understanding of the world and being, but this
occurs only in the process of experiencing, in historical consciousness.
The clash between expectation and novelty leads Gadamer to term experience "dialectical." After an experience, nothing remains the same:
"In view of the experience that we have of another object, both things
change—our knowledge and its object. We know better now, and that
means that the object itself 'does not pass the test.' The new object contains the truth about the old one."[38]

Gadamer credits Hegel with revealing the fundamentally dialectical character of experience and asserting its historicity. But, contrary
to Hegel's assertion that the primary direction of experience is inward,
Gadamer contends that experience's dialectical character first thrusts
me outward: by its very nature it forces me to come to grips with the
not-I that surpasses my expectations. Once that object/situation/con-
cept is dealt with—that is, once consciousness expands in order to comprehend—the process is repeated, endlessly. Experience, like Husserl's
intentionality, always implies both the subject and object poles of the
encounter (or, in Husserl's more exacting terms, *noesis* and *noema*).
Like intentionality, it is a dynamism that constantly drives subjectivity
outward. On this point, Gadamer should be quoted in full:

> The truth of experience always implies an orientation toward
> new experience. That is why a person who is called experienced
> has become so not only *through* experiences but is also open
> *to* new experiences. The consummation of his experience, the

---

37. "Seeing the thing" should be taken here in the sense of the encounter between
Dasein and the world that Heidegger works out in *Being and Time* [44], trans. John
Macquarrie and Edward Robinson (New York: Harper and Row, 1962) 256–73;
through Dasein's encounter with things, things are freed in their being—they show
themselves from themselves in the clearing opened up by Dasein.

38. Gadamer, *Truth and Method*, 354.

> perfection that we call "being experienced," does not consist in
> the fact that someone already knows everything and knows bet-
> ter than anyone else. Rather, the experienced person proves to
> be, on the contrary, someone who is radically undogmatic; who,
> because of the many experiences he has had and the knowledge
> he has drawn from them, is particularly well equipped to have
> new experiences and to learn from them. The dialectic of expe-
> rience has its proper fulfillment not in definitive knowledge but
> in the openness to experience that is made possible by experi-
> ence itself.[39]

There is nothing here that can get boiled down to a predictable "re-
peatable objectivity," since experience by its very nature confounds
predictability.

Besides uncovering the primordial openness of experience to new
experiences, Gadamer's phenomenological analysis reveals something
still deeper, a fundamental structure of human existence itself. By always
including "a qualitatively new element," experience "inevitably involves
many disappointments of one's expectations and only thus is experience
acquired."[40] Experience also encompasses pain and disillusionment.
These descriptions hint at the reality of human limitation and the essential role that the shattering of expectations plays in every experience.
"Only through negative instances do we acquire new experiences. . . .
Every experience worthy of the name thwarts an expectation. Thus the
historical nature of man essentially implies a fundamental negativity
that emerges in the relation between experience and insight."[41] We are
continually brought up short by our own finitude, by the limits of the
power of reason, and by "the limited degree to which the future is still
open to expectation and planning. . . . Genuine experience is experience of one's own historicity."[42] Thus openness to new experiences is at
once a spectrum of infinite possibilities and the cause of suffering. In
every experience the totality of existence comes into play; it causes me
disappointment, yet at the same time it engenders hope by remaining
open to new experiences, which break the predictability and deception
that enslave consciousness.

39. Ibid., 355.
40. Ibid., 356.
41. Ibid.
42. Ibid., 357.

Schillebeeckx specifically cites this section of *Truth and Method*, and it is easy to see the main outline of his theory of experience in Gadamer's argument: the historical nature of consciousness, the absolute dependence of consciousness on present experience, the limitation of my perspective, and experience's radical openness to new experiences. While Schillebeeckx goes his own way in crafting a theology of revelation, it is instructive to see how far he is willing to follow Gadamer in formulating his theological appropriation of Gadamer's analysis.

Martin Heidegger

Even though both Merleau-Ponty's and Gadamer's arguments presuppose Heidegger's work, Heidegger is considered last here because his overall philosophical project was a consideration of the meaning of Being rather than a consideration of the structure of consciousness and experience. His analysis of human experience (the "existential analytic" in *Being and Time*) provides a wider focus for a theory of experience and, when appropriated, a theology of revelation, and expands the narrower concerns of Merleau-Ponty and Gadamer.

Heidegger's contributions to the discussion are numerous. Here we will deal only with three of the most basic points.

TRUTH

The basic ontological structure of the person is *to be in the world*. Thus human existence (Dasein) is radically historical and temporal. Dasein works out its being-in-the-world as "care," a circumspective orientation toward the world. In being-towards-the-world, Dasein frees entities to be what they are, providing a "clearing" for beings to be disclosed as *phenomena*. This process of *dis-closure* is the primordial meaning of "truth," *a-lētheia* (uncovering, revealing, "bringing out of darkness [*lēthē*]"). "Truth" is primarily an *event of manifestation*. Only derivatively can the word be applied to what is traditionally referred to as *adequatio*, the agreement between the knowing subject and the known object; any such assertion of agreement is a confirmation of the prior event of "dis-closure" in the encounter between the person and the world in experience.⁴³ In other words, meaning—the Being-structure of the world and the complex of intertwined meanings that make up "world"—is dependent upon Dasein, the "clearing" that it provides through its circumspective "care," and its act of constitution.⁴⁴ There is no independent "world" without Dasein, since "world" is a network or structure of referential meanings both revealed and constituted in the encounter between person and entities. Without the clearing provided by Dasein's experience, there "is" no Being, since the dis-closure of the truth of beings and Being is radically dependent for its constitution on the interplay of person and world in experience.⁴⁵ But this does not mean that truth is "left to the subject's discretion," because in the experience of dis-closure the person comes "face to face with the entities themselves"—that is, the uncovering of ontological structures is a cooperative venture between the person and entities in the encounter.⁴⁶ Entities reveal a sense of Being that does not originate with Dasein.

PRE-UNDERSTANDING (*VORGRIFF*)

"Every inquiry is a seeking. Every seeking gets guided beforehand by what is sought."⁴⁷ Every approach to an encounter, every action of disclosure and understanding, is already guided by a *Vorgriff*, a pre-

---

43. "Being-true as Being-uncovered is in turn ontologically possible only on the basis of Being-in-the-World. This latter phenomenon, which we have known as a basic state of Dasein, is the *foundation* for the primordial phenomenon of truth" (*Being and Time*, 261).

44. "Of course only as long as Dasein *is* (that is, only as long as an understanding of Being is ontically possible), 'is there' [*gibt es*] Being. When Dasein does not exist, 'independence' 'is' not either, nor 'is' the 'in-itself'" (ibid., 255). Heidegger famously revised the meaning of "*es gibt*" in his later writings; see, e.g., his *Letter on Humanism*, trans. Frank A. Capuzzi and J. Glenn Gray, in *Basic Writings*, ed. David Farrell Krell, rev. ed. (San Francisco: HarperCollins, 1993), 217–65, esp. at 238.

45. "'*There is*' truth only in so far as Dasein is and so long as Dasein is. Entities are uncovered only *when* Dasein *is*; and only as long as Dasein *is*, are they disclosed. . . . Before there was any Dasein, there was no truth; nor will there be any after Dasein is no more" (*Being and Time*, 269); emphasis in original.

46. Ibid., 270.

47. Ibid., 44.

conceptual understanding or "fore-structure" of understanding.[48] For example, the question of the meaning of Being is ontologically prior to all other questions because Dasein is the being for whom Being is an issue. To ask the question means that understanding is incomplete. But Dasein must already have some pre-understanding of Being, or else the question would never have been known in order to have been posed.[49] We somehow "see beforehand," dimly, the goal of the inquiry, and it guides the direction of the inquiry and the direction of the progressive understanding. Heidegger terms this development of understanding "interpretation" (*Auslegung*), the articulation and realization of the possibilities grasped by understanding—in other words, the "laying out" (*auslegen*) of the elements of pre-understanding engendered in the earlier stage of the experiential encounter.[50] The *Vorgriff* is not a product of consciousness, but rather the product of the interplay between person and world; once gained, it sets up definite directions for interpretation. While interpretation can either disclose an entity/situation (act positively in revealing its meaning) or close it off (work against what we are interpreting), it is the *Vorgriff* that guides the process and somehow sets standards as to whether a particular interpretation is "revelatory" or successful. But this guiding act of the pre-understanding only comes into play in the experience itself; there is no *Vorgriff* outside experience. The situation set up by the *Vorgriff* is a circular one: "all interpretation . . . operates in the fore-structure. . . . Any interpretation which is to contribute understanding, must already have understood what is to be interpreted."[51] This is the hermeneutic circle, the fundamental nature of understanding.

48. Ibid., 191.

49. Ibid., 40.

50. "In interpreting, we do not, so to speak, throw a 'signification' over some naked thing which is present-at-hand, we do not stick a value on it; but when something within-the-world is encountered as such, the thing in question already has an involvement which is disclosed in our understanding of the world, and this involvement is one which gets laid out by the interpretation[*durch die Auslegung herausgelegt wird*]" (ibid., 190–91; *Sein und Zeit*, 12th ed. [Tübingen: Niemeyer, 1972] 150).

51. Ibid., 194.

"ALETHEIOLOGY" OF BEING

This earlier focus on the existential analytic of Dasein as the most appropriate way to get at the meaning of Being gives way in Heidegger's later works to a concentration on Being itself as it manifests itself as language, as art, as history, and as temporality. His main concern is the retrieval of the original experience of Being, which can be discerned in the pre-Socratic Greek philosophers but which has fallen into oblivion and been covered over in the subsequent history of philosophy by a thinking that is "calculative"—that is, it treats Being as an object (thus leading to an objectifying metaphysics) and represents "it" as *ousia*, *idea*, substance, will-to-power, and so on, all of which representations have kept the original experience of Being hidden from view.[52]

What Heidegger advocates instead is "meditative" thinking, a non-representational thinking that thinks Being from "within" the experience of Being as presencing. He finds three words key to his retrieval of the original Greek experience: *physis* (not "nature" but "blossoming forth into presencing"), *alētheia* ("dis-closure," as discussed above), and *logos* (originally not "word" but "laying-together-in-collectedness").[53] The original experience of Being is the experience of presencing and withdrawing—Being coming to presence as *physis* but at the same time withdrawing into *lēthē*, hiddenness. As Being comes to presence as beings, Being in its true character hides behind beings. The true experience of Being, therefore, and the structure of the whole of reality, is presence/absence, *alētheia/lēthē*, a movement that is the root of the experience behind the philosophical fragments of Anaximander, Heraclitus, and Parmenides. Heidegger calls this relationship between Being and beings the "ontological difference," a keystone of his later thought. He explains it this way:

> The Being of beings means Being which is beings. The "is" here speaks transitively, in transition. Being here becomes present in

52. For the difference between "calculative" and "meditative" thought, see Heidegger's *Gelassenheit* (Pfullingen: Neske, 1959); ET: *Discourse on Thinking*, trans. John M. Anderson and E. Hans Freund (New York: Harper and Row, 1966).

53. See *Being and Time* [44], 256–73; "The Anaximander Fragment," "Logos (Heraclitus, Fragment B 50)," and "Aletheia (Heraclitus, Fragment B 16)," in *Early Greek Thinking*, trans. David Farrell Krell and Frank A. Capuzzi (New York: Harper and Row, 1975) 13–78, 102–23.

the manner of a transition to beings. But Being does not leave its own place and go over to beings, as though beings were first without Being and could be approached by Being subsequently. Being transits (that), comes unconcealingly over (that) [*Sein geht über (das) hin, kommt entbergend über (das)*] which arrives as something of itself unconcealed only by that coming-over [*Überkommnis*]. Arrival means: to keep concealed in unconcealedness—to abide present in this keeping—to be a being. . . . Being in the sense of unconcealing overwhelming [*der entbergenden Überkommnis*] and beings in the sense of arrival that keeps itself concealed, are present, and thus differentiated, by virtue of the Same, the differentiation [*dem Unter-schied*].[54]

Being, in coming over to/as beings, renders itself manifest—beings thus arrive in presence. However, in this very coming-over Being itself is concealed—beings announce the arrival of Being, but Being manifests itself only through beings, never as Being. Thus the arrival-into-unconcealment (*alētheia*) is simultaneous with the withdrawal-into-unconcealment (*lēthē*). Being is the source of this transition to and fro and of the difference (*Unterschied*, the "cutting") between Being and beings that separates them and in the separating (dif-ferring) holds them together. Thus Being's basic structure is presencing-and-absencing ("aletheiological") and never pure presence. This structure is manifested differently in different epochs: Being sends itself (*schicken*) as history (*Geschichte*) and as temporality.

While Heidegger focuses on ontological questions rather than "experience" per se, the three "moments" of his project that we have discussed nevertheless serve an important function for our topic. They demonstrate that the primacy of experience has an ontological basis, that the encounter within experience between subjectivity and the world is the primary mode of knowing, that the subject-object distinction fostered by specifically modern approaches to reason is derivative, and that all meaning is radically human in the sense that, without the experience that thrusts human subjectivity outward, there is no meaning, no disclosure of truth. This confirms in a phenomenological (and even more radical) way the basic scholastic principle of knowledge elaborated in various ways by Thomas Aquinas: *Cognitum autem est*

54. Martin Heidegger, *Identity and Difference* [bilingual edition], trans. Joan Stambaugh (New York: Harper and Row, 1969) 64–65 (English), 132 (German).

in cognoscente secundum modum cognoscentis ("whatever is known is known according to the mode of the knower").[55] Here, however, there are never absolute meanings, only meanings engendered in the event of disclosure which is properly present in experience. The insistence of Merleau-Ponty and Gadamer on the primacy of experience and on the a priori openness of experience to what is new and unprecedented thus finds ontological legitimation in Heidegger.

Schillebeeckx's Concept of Experience

Schillebeeckx's insistence on experience as the starting point for his theological reflection on revelation is incomprehensible without this phenomenological background. The "authority" with which he invests experience, and the transcendent element of revelation which Schillebeeckx sees being mediated through human experience, would not be credible outside a phenomenological framework, since this account of consciousness and subjectivity gives full weight to experience. If Schillebeeckx were employing a realist epistemology, his theology would have the tendency to ground revelation in rational certainty and his characterization of salvation would wind up in some version of extrinsicism akin to that of neo-scholasticism.[56] He repudiates this position, however: "The experience of ourselves and the world cannot be completely analysed in terms of a difference between objective and subjective. There 'to find salvation in Jesus' is not either a subjective experience or an objective fact."[57] On the other hand, he also rejects

---

55. Thomas Aquinas, *Summa theologiae* [*ST*] Ia, q. 12, a. 4, resp., in *Summa theologiae*, vol. 3 [Ia. 12–13]: *Knowing and Naming God*, trans. Herbert McCabe (London: Eyre & Spottiswoode; New York: McGraw-Hill, 1964) 14–15. See also *ST* Ia, q. 75, a. 5, resp.: "*Manifestum est enim quod omne quod recipitur in aliquo recipitur in eo per modum recipientis*" ["Obviously the way anything is received depends on how the receiver is fitted to receive it"] (vol. 11, trans. Timothy Suttor[1970], 22–23). The scholastic dictum *quidquid recipitur per modum recipientis recipitur* goes back at least to Boethius' *Consolation of Philosophy* 5.4.

56. For a discussion of Neo-scholastic extrinsicism, see Francis Schüssler Fiorenza, *Foundational Theology: Jesus and the Church* (New York: Crossroad, 1984), 266–75; Anthony J. Godzieba, *Bernhard Welte's Fundamental Theological Approach to Christology*, American University Studies, Series 7, vol. 160 (New York/Bern: Peter Lang, 1994) 18–34.

57. Schillebeeckx, *Christ*, 36.

the view of experience that can be characterized as purely affective. The problem with these alternatives is that they are extremes: realism uses experience only as a launching point that points toward the goal of absolute essences, while any emphasis on experience as a set of emotional states—undoubtedly an essential element of experience—tends to rob experience of "the particular cognitive, critical and productive force"[58] that Schillebeeckx believes are its crucial elements.

Schillebeeckx's position echoes Gadamer's description of dialectical experience. Experience is "direct contact with people and things" that touches off a dialectical process:

> The discoveries about reality that we have already made and put into words open up new perspectives: they direct perception in our experience to something particular. . . . In this way they become the framework within which we interpret new experiences, while at the same time this already given framework of interpretation is exposed to criticism and corrected, changed or renewed by new experiences. Experience is gained in a dialectical fashion: through an interplay between perception and thought, thought and perception.[59]

While calling experience the "ability to assimilate perceptions," Schillebeeckx really treats experience in a wider way. Reality is "discovered" and frameworks are altered in many ways, not only sensibly. In this context he raises the problem of objectivity more trenchantly.

> Our real experiences are neither purely objective nor purely subjective. On the one hand, they are not purely subjective; for we cannot simply make something out of something at our whim. At least partially, there is something which is "given," which we cannot completely manipulate or change; in experience we have an offer of reality. On the other hand, it is not purely objective; for the experience is filled out and coloured by the reminiscences and sensibilities, concepts and longings of the person who has the experience. Thus the irreducible elements of our experiences form a totality which already contains interpretation.[60]

58. Ibid., 29.
59. Ibid., 31–32.
60. Ibid., 33.

A phenomenological viewpoint holds that meanings are constituted—that is, in Merleau-Ponty's terms, that knowledge comes from lived experience, the intersection of subjectivity and world. In Schillebeeckx's terms, that constitution includes the intersection of past experiences ("reminiscences and sensibilities") with the present, where the past functions as an interpretive framework that both structures what is "new" but also is "corrected, changed or renewed" by the "new." But that constitution of meaning is driven by a prior moment of disclosure, a grappling with reality that is "given" and that resists our expectations. There are two aspects to note. First, Schillebeeckx rejects the realist *adequatio* foundation of truth in favor of the Heideggerian formulation: reality gets disclosed through experience. Second, Schillebeeckx agrees with Merleau-Ponty and Gadamer as to what gets revealed in experience: the not-I, what is different, alien—what shatters my expectations.

> The permanent resistance of reality to our rational inventions forces us to constantly new and untried models of thought. Truth comes near to us by the alienation and disorientation of what we have already achieved and planned. This shatters the so-called normativeness or the dogmatism of the factual, of what is "simply given." The hermeneutical principle for the disclosure of reality is not the self-evident, but the scandal, the stumbling block of the refractoriness of reality.[61]

A number of phenomenological insights are at work here in this argument. First of all, Schillebeeckx assumes both Merleau-Ponty's and Gadamer's analyses of experience that make appropriation of the not-I, openness to what is not part of my subjectivity, part of the nature of experience. Then, there is the assumption of truth as the event of *alētheia*: since disclosure is the primary meaning of truth, the assumption is that disclosures are never at an end, that truth is always operative in constituting meaning, and thus we are "constantly" working out interpretations.

Finally, this resistance of reality to experience and expectation is the source of the contrast of "negativity." Gadamer's remarks should be recalled: in experience I feel the sting of my own finitude and painfully learn that I am radically historical. A comparison of two passages is instructive:

61. Ibid., 35.

Gadamer	Schillebeeckx
Experience . . . inevitably involves many disappointments of one's expectations and only thus is experience acquired. . . . Only through negative instances do we acquire new experiences. . . . Every experience worthy of the name thwarts an expectation. Thus the historical nature of man essentially implies a fundamental negativity that emerges in the relation between experience and insight. . . .[Aeschylus witnesses to this with his phrase "learning through suffering."]He refers to the reason why this is so. What a man has to learn through suffering is not this or that particular thing, but insight into the limitations of humanity, into the absoluteness of the barrier that separates man from the divine. It is ultimately a religious insight—the kind of insight that gave birth to Greek tragedy.[62]	The "negativity" which makes us revise earlier insights as a result of the resistance offered by reality is productive; it has a quite special positive significance as a "revelation of reality," even though it may be dialectically negative and critical. People learn from failures—where their projects are blocked and they make a new attempt, in sensitive reverence for the resistance and thus for the orientation of reality. This demonstrates that human experience is finite, that man is not lord of reality, for all his plans, though without them experiences would be impossible.[63]

Both thinkers attempt to articulate what happens at the limit of human experience and the productive force such experiences of negativity and "shattering" have. And both thinkers eventually resort to metaphors suggesting that experience has a fundamentally "religious" structure that is disclosed whenever we encounter what exceeds the limits of expectation.

The real point in showing these parallels is not to demonstrate that Schillebeeckx is beholden to philosophical analyses of human experience, but to show how he uses such a phenomenological framework creatively in a theological context to get at the intrinsic relationship

62. Gadamer, *Truth and Method*, 356–57.

63. Schillebeeckx, *Christ*, 35.

between revelation and experience. By combining the accumulative nature of experience (already implying a thrust outward from subjectivity) with its concomitant critical negativity, Schillebeeckx makes the case for the essential "gift" nature of reality and the fact that reality *exceeds* our experience and our expectations but nonetheless can only be encountered *through* our experience.

> Reality is always more than and different from what we imagine it to be. From a negative, critical point of view this is because of our experience that man cannot ground the possibilities of his own existence. . . . This raises the *question* whether he may not and cannot experience reality, to the degree to which it escapes human planning, as a *gift* which frees man from the impossible attempt to find his basis in himself, and makes it possible for him to think and plan endlessly, although this reality which is independent of him is for its part the basis and source of responsible human action in reason, freedom, and planning.[64]

What differentiates Schillebeeckx's position from a transcendental argument such as Karl Rahner's is that he does not find the divine-human point of intersection *within* experience but sees it *as* experience. Every human experience, and thus humanity's historical nature, is shot through with the frustration of finitude. The person's very historicity is the point of contact with God. This assertion is the basis for Schillebeeckx's entire Christology: that Jesus is the humanity of God, God's pledge to give a saving contrast to present experiences of evil, God's aligning himself on the side of the suffering. For Rahner, the process of divinization is relatively smooth: God supplies the condition for the possibility of existence and fills those needs that the person feels when the person experiences limitation in relatively rare limit-situations. In Schillebeeckx's analysis, limit-situations are constantly present: my constant flow of experiences confronts me with my finitude and hence with suffering in some form. In every situation I feel the ache of frustration as I experience limitless possibilities given to me as well as my inability to match them with limitless response.[65] In every experi-

---

64. Ibid., 47.

65. While Schillebeeckx does not cite Maurice Blondel, his analysis demonstrates a close affinity with Blondel's "method of immanence." See Maurice Blondel, *The Letter on Apologetics*, in *The Letter on Apologetics and History and Dogma*, trans. Alexander Dru and Illtyd Trethowan (Grand Rapids, MI: Eerdmans, 1994 [Fr. orig., 1896]).

ence, I realize that I am not in control, that my reason is not capable of accounting for every aspect of reality. "Man is not master of reality, but only its steward. From this it emerges in turn that this talk of God and his revelation is indissolubly bound up with our interpretative experience, as believers, of the reality of man and the world."[66]

Schillebeeckx's concept of interpretation, the guiding element that is part of every experience, looks much like Heidegger's *Vorgriff* as read through Gadamer. Interpretation is previous experience which has sedimented in consciousness and thereby becomes a guiding framework that influences the structure of future experiences.[67] However, Schillebeeckx again goes further than his models:

> Interpretative identification is already an intrinsic element of the experience itself, first unexpressed and then deliberately reflected on. However, there are interpretative elements in our experiences which find their foundation and source directly in what is actually experienced, as the content of a conscious and thus to some degree transparent experience, and there are also interpretative elements which come to us from elsewhere, at least from outside this experience, though it is never possible to draw a clear distinction.[68]

If I read him correctly here, what he is attempting is to account phenomenologically for the directionality which is given to experience by what is experienced—a directionality that is first grasped preconceptually, then articulated. Merleau-Ponty makes the same point in asserting the universal aspect of experience when he argues that understanding picks up a "hint" from the world as to what direction to follow in the constitution of meaning.[69] The content of experience is never totally divorced from the subject, and yet Schillebeeckx can avoid the charge of subjectivism because of his emphasis on the givenness of "the real": "Reality constantly directs our planning and reflection like a hidden magnet. . . . Experience is supported and constrained by a

---

66. Schillebeeckx, *Christ*, 56.

67. See ibid., 31.

68. Schillebeeckx, *Interim Report*, 13.

69. "The germ of universality or the 'natural light' without which there could be no knowledge is to be found ahead of is, in the thing where our perception places us" (*Sense and Non-Sense*, 93).

permanent reference to the inexhaustibility of the real."[70] Schillebeeckx is certainly committed to the meaning-constituting action of the interplay between experience and interpretation, and committed as well to highlighting the resistance of reality which always confronts us with its "refractoriness" and opacity. But the constitution of meaning is not rudderless; rather, it is anchored in the fundamental givenness and "resistance" of reality that directs experience's constituting operations toward an authentic-though-always-inadequate grasp of the world of our experience. In fact, Schillebeeckx's appropriation of the aletheiological structure serves as the foundation for his theory of revelation.

> For the believer, the very existence of man and the world is a symbol or a manifestation of the divine, but always in such a way that there is a necessary identity between the revelation and the concealment of the divine. For when confronted with any manifestation of the divine, God's essential reserve is always experienced: God can never be reduced to one of the forms in which he is manifested. Reality continues to surprise us.[71]

A Phenomenology of the Easter Appearance Narratives

How does this phenomenological theory of experience play out when employed in the discussion of the Gospels' post-resurrection appearance narratives? Schillebeeckx employs it to retrieve, as far at it is possible at this historical distance, the original experiences that were the catalyst for those narratives and the precise linguistic form that they take. In other words, he is after a particular moment in the transforming experience of grace that Jesus' disciples had in their encounter with their Lord and that eventually gave rise to the New Testament's message of salvation for all.[72]

Elsewhere I have characterized this as a "strong" theory of the resurrection that is found in a place where many might least expect it (precisely because of the criticism raised against Schillebeeckx's earlier

70. Schillebeeckx, *Christ*, 36–37.

71. Ibid., 55.

72. "As a non-empirical event of and with Jesus himself after his death, the resurrection is *per se* trans-historical, but belief in Jesus' resurrection is an event of and in our history, and as such is in principle accessible to a historical and genetic analysis" (*Interim Report*, 75); see also ibid., 10.

formulation of this theory). By a "strong theory," I mean that it does three things: (1) affirms the resurrection as an event that happens both to Jesus himself and to his disciples; (2) sees the empty tomb narratives and the appearance narratives as interlocking evidence not to be separated; and (3) affirms the true bodily resurrection of Jesus, the eschatological transformation of his corporeal identity.[73] With his employment of a specifically phenomenological theory of experience, I believe that Schillebeeckx has provided such a theory. It puts Schillebeeckx's theology of the resurrection on a different part of Loewe's three-position grid and answers Loewe's questions about the role of objectivity in a much more adequate way.

I believe that one can prescind from Schillebeeckx's specific starting point, the narrative of conversion occasioned by the forgiveness experienced by Peter and the other disciples. This is the aspect of Schillebeeckx's retrieval upon which Loewe and many other commentators have focused. But the quite speculative nature of this reconstructed narrative derails an adequate evaluation of his theology and shunts the critics too quickly into a judgment that the "subjective" aspects of the retrieval overwhelm the "objective." Schillebeeckx, in fact, strongly argues for their equal force, and did so even before his revisions (which, in fact, add much-needed precision to his argument).[74]

The more central affirmation of the fundamental structure of the resurrection experience of both Jesus and the disciples can be retrieved from Schillebeeckx's revised argument if we keep his phenomenological epistemology in mind. Let me quote two passages to illustrate this.

> It is evident from that analysis of the Easter experience that *the objective cannot be separated from the subjective aspect of the apostolic belief in the resurrection.* Apart from the faith-motivated experience it is not possible to speak meaningfully about Jesus'

73. See Anthony J. Godzieba, "Bodies and Persons, Resurrected and Postmodern: Towards a Relational Eschatology," in *Theology and Conversation: Toward a Relational Theology*, ed. Jacques Haers and Peter De Mey, vol. 172, Bibliotheca Ephemeridum Theologicarum Lovaniensium (Leuven: Peeters, 2003) 211–25, at 215.

74. See, e.g., Schillebeeckx, *Jesus*, 391, and especially *Interim Report*, 79: "It is the aim of my book to stress both the objective and the subjective aspects of resurrection faith over against all objectivistic and subjectivistic one-sidedness in such a way that the 'object'—Jesus' personal and corporeal resurrection and exaltation with God—and the 'subject'—the experience of faith which is expressed in scripture in the story of the appearances—cannot be separated."

resurrection. . . . Without being identical with it, the resurrection of Jesus—that is, what happened to him, personally, after his death—is inseparable from the Easter experience, or faith-motivated experience, of the disciples. . . . Besides this subjective aspect it is equally apparent that . . . *no Easter experience of renewed life was possible without the personal resurrection of Jesus—in the sense that Jesus' personal-cum-bodily resurrection [Jezus' persoonlijk-lichamelijke verrijzenis]. . . "precedes" any faith-motivated experience.*[75]

I am concerned . . . with a theological clarification for modern men[and women]which will make it understandable why the first Christians seized on the model of the appearances of God and angels in the Old Testament in order to express their Easter experience. *Here I will concede that this need not be a pure model; it can also imply a historical event.*[76]

These are key passages illustrating Schillebeeckx's hermeneutic retrieval of the disciples' experience and his attempt to clarify its fundamental structure. In this retrieval there are two key phenomenological elements wound tightly together, dealing with the "subjective" and "objective" elements of the constitution of Easter faith.[77] First, there is the emphasis on the meaning-giving role played by "faith-motivated" human subjectivity: truth as an event of manifestation needs the mediation of experience, interpretation, and constitution in order for it to be disclosed in a humanly graspable way (the phenomenological version of *quidquid recipitur per modum recipientis recipitur*). This is the insight behind Schillebeeckx's claim that "the resurrection of Jesus . . . is inseparable from the . . . faith-motivated experience of the disciples" without it being made identical with or reduced to that faith-motivated experience. Schillebeeckx makes it clear that this experience would never have occurred without the non-I catalyst, the "objective" element of the disciples' experience that directed their constitution of the evidence in the direction of the claim that Jesus is personally alive; "He is risen." Schillebeeckx, in a somewhat clumsy expression, emphasizes

---

75. Schillebeeckx, *Jesus*, 645 (*Jezus*, 528b); my emphasis.

76. Schillebeeckx, *Interim Report*, 147n43; my emphasis.

77. What Schillebeeckx also demonstrates is the inadequacy of the traditional post-Cartesian understandings of "subjective" and "objective" in dealing with the Resurrection.

the objective element—the risen Jesus' transformed corporeality—by saying that Easter faith is impossible without being preceded by "*Jezus' persoonlijk-lichamelijke verrijzenis*" ("Jesus' personal-cum-bodily resurrection"). This clumsiness, though, is performatively productive: it signals the inadequacies of language for dealing with an eschatological event that nonetheless crosses over into materiality and history, akin to Merleau-Ponty's analogue for the act of knowing, the pianist "who deciphers an unknown piece of music: without himself grasping the motives of each gesture or each operation, without being able to bring to the surface of consciousness all the sediment of knowledge which he is using at that moment."[78]

The structure of the experience that Schillebeeckx retrieves is composed of two aspects. There is (for lack of better terminology) the "subjective" aspect: the disciples' Judaism and their immersion in the traditions of Second Temple Judaism and its prevailing eschatological mindset;[79] their fundamentally holistic understanding of person;[80] and their memories of Jesus, including his Kingdom proclamations, his parables, his lifestyle, and his horrific death. These function as the disciples' already appropriated fund of culturally and religiously situated expectations—an interpretive framework—within which they will understand any act of God that touches their experience.

There is also the non-negotiable "objective" aspect (what I would term the "not-I catalyst"), which serves to shatter the disciples' expectations and take their understanding of Jewish eschatology, personhood, and Jesus himself in an unexpected direction. This objective aspect is

---

78. Merleau-Ponty, *Sense and Non-Sense*, 93.

79. On the pervasive eschatological background, see James D. G. Dunn, *Christianity in the Making*, vol. 1, *Jesus Remembered* (Grand Rapids, MI: Eerdmans, 2003) 393–406; John P. Meier, *A Marginal Jew: Rethinking the Historical Jesus*, vol. 2, *Mentor, Message, and Miracles*, The Anchor Bible Reference Library (New York, Anchor/Doubleday, 1994) 237–70; John Riches, *The World of Jesus: First-Century Judaism in Crisis*, Understanding Jesus Today (Cambridge: Cambridge University Press, 1990) 87–107; E. P. Sanders, *Judaism: Practice and Belief, 63 BCE–66 CE* (London: SCM, 1992) 279–303; N. T. Wright, *Christian Origins and the Question of God*, vol. 3: *The Resurrection of the Son of God* (Minneapolis, MN: Fortress, 2003) 85–206.

80. See John L. McKenzie, "Aspects of Old Testament Thought," in *The New Jerome Biblical Commentary*, ed. Raymond E. Brown, Joseph A. Fitzmyer, and Roland E. Murphy (Englewood Cliffs, NJ: Prentice-Hall, 1990) 1284–1315; Hans Walter Wolff, *Anthropology of the Old Testament* (Philadelphia: Fortress, 1974).

(to use Kasper's phrase) the "initial ignition" that forces the disciples in the midst of their constitution of this experience to stretch all the categories of Second Temple Judaism in which they have been steeped to fit a new, unprecedented experience. The fact that the Gospel narratives (and Paul in 1 Corinthians) consciously choose the language of vision and body for their testimony, that they "misuse" apocalyptic language (e.g., alongside the belief that *all* will rise at the end of time, they make the claim that *one* has risen before all), that Jesus is both frighteningly unfamiliar and eventually recognized as "good old Jesus" (e.g., Luke 24:36–49; John 21:1–14), forces one to ask what kind of an experience it would have to be to act as a catalyst for *this particular kind* of consistent testimony *in this particular form*, rather than, say, the language of the martyred prophet, or the claim that the cause or the memory of Jesus continues.[81] This is the quintessential phenomenological question. And the answer is that this experience must be one that can *only* be constituted and expressed in this way, that is, an experience of the "real" that is given/disclosed and that gives "direction" or hints for interpretation, for which only the language of person, vision, body, unfamiliarity, familiarity, and "Jesus" is relatively appropriate. It is the experience of the "body as a symbol" of Jesus' self, the self-consistent in its identity throughout the transformation.[82] That self's corporeality, which bore the developed constitution of Jesus' self-identity through his human actions, still communicates his unified individuality and provokes continued relationships with his disciples, so much so that the narratives insist that *only* corporeal and visual language are up to the task of conveying the reality and the personal unity of Jesus as experienced within his continued relationships with his disciples. The disciples' experience of the risen Jesus is indeed a constituted experience of a personal relationship with him occurring within their history and ours.[83] But that constitution of meaning has resulted from the interpretive interplay of Second Temple Jewish anthropological and eschatological expectations challenged (and in some cases shattered) by

81. See Schillebeeckx, *Jesus*, 395–96.

82. See Sandra Schneiders, "The Resurrection of Jesus and Christian Spirituality," in *Christian Resources of Hope*, ed. Maureen Junker-Kenny (Collegeville, MN: Liturgical, 1995) 81–114, at 97.

83. As Schillebeeckx insists, the Easter experience "can also imply a historical event" (*Interim Report*, 147n43).

the clues of the transformed personal reality and unity of Jesus, which, according to the textual evidence, can be knit together in a meaningful way (as the intentional object of the disciples' experience) only when one takes the visual and corporeal clues seriously. It is the implicit judgment of the tradition as transmitted in the Gospels' appearance narratives that any talk of "the martyred prophet," "remembering the impact of Jesus' teaching," or other Jewish apocalyptic expectations is simply not adequate to the task.

What is important is that the New Testament texts witness to a crucial *experienced difference*, one that quite obviously provokes a shattering of expectations. At the root of the Easter experience is not simply the familiar Jesus (which would not be an "experience" but simply repetition of already sedimented interpreted experiences) but an identity that has been transformed: he frightens some, goes unrecognized by others, and walks through closed doors. So the narratives want to have it both ways—unfamiliar presence *and* good old Jesus—in order to communicate that this is indeed Jesus who is encountered, but somehow different from the pre-Easter Jesus. The narratives, across the various Gospel traditions, assume that only the use and the conscious misuse of the language of corporeality can get a handle on this experience. This must make us pause and ask: What kind of experience is this? What kind of bodiliness is this? How can corporeality support such a transformation, the ultimate possibility promised to those who commit themselves to the values of the kingdom of God? Again, these are quintessential phenomenological questions about the experiences behind the textual expressions, questions that any theological exploration of the Easter experience must ask.

One seriously misreads Schillebeeckx's analysis of Easter faith if one downplays the "objective" aspect, as many commentators have. Such a reading would force the events surrounding Easter into an order that contradicts the New Testament evidence. To overemphasize the subjective or "visionary" aspect is to say that God the Father has an effect on the disciples who in turn have an effect on the way that Jesus is perceived. The New Testament, on the other hand, insists that "the Easter event is primarily what God did with Jesus, not something that God did with the disciples. What he did with the disciples was only secondary."[84]

84. Reginald H. Fuller and Pheme Perkins, *Who Is This Christ? Gospel Christology and Contemporary Faith* (Philadelphia: Fortress, 1983) 36.

Schillebeeckx subscribes to this latter order of events wholeheartedly. His strong emphasis on the not-I catalyst of resurrection faith leads me to disagree with Loewe's conclusion that Schillebeeckx's argument "shows that positions two and three are not incompatible."[85] I would argue that Schillebeeckx's strong insistence on the equal force exerted both by the objective element (what the Father did for Jesus himself) that shatters expectations and by the constituting and the interpretive subjective element is his attempt to account for the claim of realism (position one) without resorting to an impossible realist epistemology. This renders Schillebeeckx's argument more inclusive than portrayed by Loewe.

One would also miss the full force of Schillebeeckx's analysis if one did not notice that, under the "pressure" of the resurrection experience, he is implicitly judging as inadequate the use of the traditional modern (i.e., post-Cartesian) definitions of "objectivity" and "subjectivity" to deal with the reality of revelation in general and the resurrection in particular. As Loewe suggests, this is the crux of the matter. Schillebeeckx, for his part, redefines these terms in the direction of a phenomenological epistemology of constituted knowing that is capacious enough to acknowledge both the participation of subjectivity in knowing reality and also that "reality is always more than and different from what we imagine it to be."[86] The "objective" can only be accessed through the constitution of meaning effected from the point of view of subjectivity, while the experience gained by subjectivity can only truly be "experience" when it encounters the new, the different, the unprecedented—when its comfortable expectations are shattered by the not-I element of experience. From the negativity and limitation under which subjectivity labors, Schillebeeckx draws two positive results. The first is an anthropological insight: reality can thus be experienced "as a *gift* which frees man from the impossible attempt to find his basis in himself . . ."[87] The second is the aletheiological insight applied to God: "When confronted with any manifestation of the divine, God's essential reserve is always experienced; God can never be reduced to one of the forms in which he is manifested. Reality continues to surprise

---

85. Loewe, *College Student's Introduction*, 138.

86. Schillebeeckx, *Christ*, 47.

87. Ibid.; emphasis in original.

us."[88] Schillebeeckx's analysis of Easter faith—his strong theology of the resurrection—guarantees that we will see the reality of Christ's resurrection, along with the resurrection faith that it continually provokes, as perhaps the biggest surprise of all.

88. Ibid., 55.

4

Narrating Salvation: Historical Jesus Research and Soteriology

CHRISTOPHER McMAHON
SAINT VINCENT COLLEGE

Few issues have beset the modern theological community more persistently than the debate concerning the theological relevance of the historical Jesus. Within the community of Roman Catholic theologians, the debate was epitomized by the positions David Tracy and Elizabeth Johnson articulated in the early 1980s. Yet, as historical Jesus research continued to proliferate in the late 1980s and throughout the 1990s, William Loewe revisited the debate in 2000 and concluded that the current state of historical Jesus research, particularly the epistemological issues it raises, had essentially vindicated Tracy's position against any normative claims. Appeals to the historical Jesus, however, continue unabated and have proliferated beyond the boundaries of the academy with a noticeable impact within the life of the church, particularly through the agency of various media outlets (print media, film, and cyberspace).[1] Amidst these developments, the attempts by John

---

1. Some examples include Mel Gibson's film *The Passion of the Christ* (Icon, 2004) as well as the series of books and films based on Dan Brown's *The Da Vinci Code* (New York: Anchor, 2003), all of which provoke the reader's religious imagination with appeals to the historical Jesus behind the Gospels and behind the Christian tradition. Even highly respected scholars like John Dominic Crossan have popularized their work with the conviction that reaching a more general and wider audience by tapping

Meier and N. T. Wright to "rethink" the historical Jesus have tended, in various ways, to highlight the import of historical Jesus research for the church as well as its inherent limitations. This essay explores the relevance of historical Jesus research, particularly as evidenced by Meier and Wright, when understood not as a purely historical project, but as an act of theological narration and proclamation constitutive of the church's evangelical and redemptive mission in a historically conscious world. The act of narrating, whether it takes the form of precritical exhortation or the form of a methodologically rigorous "quest," represents the perennial desire to enflesh the claims of the gospel in contemporary living, and it cannot be domesticated by the academy or confined to narrow questions of fact. Rather, narrating the historical Jesus remains inevitably elusive and conflicted, though it is still a powerful dimension of the church's mission.

Revisiting a Perennial Debate

The 1980s saw the rebirth of historical Jesus research. Although it is debatable to what extent this rebirth may actually be called a "third quest," renewed interest in the quest for the historical Jesus was spurred by the emergence of the Jesus Seminar and by projects such as E. P. Sanders's book *Jesus and Judaism*.[2] Roughly concurrent with these developments was the publication of the provocative essay from Elizabeth Johnson, "The Theological Relevance of the Historical Jesus: A Debate and a Thesis," which sets forth what might be fairly called a "liberationist" position on historical Jesus research.[3] Arguing against the position made

---

their imagination is essential to the success of their projects; see, Crossan, *Who Is Jesus?: Answers to Your Questions about the Historical Jesus* (Louisville: Westminster John Knox, 1999).

2. See E. P. Sanders, *Jesus and Judaism* (Philadelphia: Fortress, 1985).

3. See Elizabeth Johnson, "The Theological Relevance of the Historical Jesus: A Debate and a Thesis," *Thomist* 48/1 (January 1984) 1–43. While Johnson's position has developed in the past twenty-five years, the basic outline of the liberationist position on the theological relevance of the historical Jesus set forth in this essay is still influential. It is a "liberationist position" insofar as it uses the results of historical research in the service of a hermeneutics of suspicion, identifying and critiquing elements of the Christian tradition that obscure the liberating power of the Jesus story. Furthermore, historical research also provides for a hermeneutics of retrieval, reshaping or resymbolizing the tradition as a force for the liberation of the marginalized and powerless.

famous by Rudolf Bultmann and reiterated, although from a far more Catholic perspective, by David Tracy, Johnson insisted that a critically assured minimum of knowledge about the historical Jesus can be obtained through historical research. This basic knowledge can then be cast into a particular interpretive mold or framework, which can then yield multiple Christologies given the particular sets of concerns or locations of the theologian. Johnson goes on in her essay to emphasize the theological necessity of the historical Jesus as the "memory image" by which the church and the tradition have always referred to a prior reality.[4] As such, even though the historical Jesus is the product of modern historical research, it still functions as the symbol that mediates the reality of God's saving activity. In this way, Johnson contends that a sketch of the historical Jesus can provide necessary content for Christian faith and can also be used to test competing representations of Jesus.

In the pages of *Theological Studies*, William Loewe revisited and updated the parameters of the Tracy-Johnson debate concerning the theological relevance of historical Jesus research and challenged those who would argue for the normative value of the products of historical research.[5] Loewe concluded that the recent emphasis on historical Jesus studies in contemporary Christology has significant limits, and among the most important of these is the provisional character of such research.[6] After all, the affirmations (or negations for that matter) of historians and biblical scholars in one decade may have to be

The position of David Tracy can be found in *The Analogical Imagination* (New York: Crossroad, 1981), 233–41. Like Tracy, Loewe himself has been a staunch defender of liberationist theologies, though from a more Lonerganian perspective. Of particular interest is Loewe's essay "Dialectics of Sin: Lonergan's *Insight* and the Critical Theory of Max Horkheimer," *Anglican Theological Review* 61 (1979) 224–45; and "Interpreting the Notification," in *Hope and Solidarity: Jon Sobrino's Challenge to Christian Theology*, ed. Stephen Pope (Maryknoll, NY: Orbis, 2008) 143–52.

4. Johnson develops the notion of "memory image" from Van A. Harvey, *The Historian and the Believer: The Morality of Historical Knowledge and Christian Belief* (New York: Macmillan, 1966) 264–81.

5. See William P. Loewe, "From the Humanity of Christ to the Historical Jesus," *Theological Studies* 61/2 (June 2000) 314–31. It should be noted that Loewe's essay was originally titled "From the Humanity of Christ to the Historical Jesus: The Limits of the Paradigm Shift." The essay was a response to John Galvin, "From the Humanity of Christ to the Jesus of History: A Paradigm Shift in Catholic Christology," *Theological Studies* 55/2 (June 1994) 252–73.

6. See Bernard Lonergan, *Method in Theology* (New York: Seabury, 1972) 185–96.

revised significantly in the next. Additionally, there seems to be less and less consensus among scholars concerning what one can affirm of the historical Jesus. This lack of consensus among scholars, therefore, challenges the assumption that there is one established account of *the* historical Jesus, or even that there is agreement among scholars on a minimal sketch of the historical Jesus. The current state of historical Jesus research, therefore, compromises any claim of historical Jesus research as normative for the discipline of Christology or for Christian faith in general.

Loewe, however, does not dismiss the theological import of historical Jesus research. In fact, he affirms that such research has played an important role in recent years. In the first place, Loewe argues, historical Jesus research has played an important role in overcoming the abstract metaphysical discussions of the human nature of Jesus common within Roman Catholic Christologies.[7] Secondly, historical Jesus research has provided an important theological resource by helping to sketch a historical and genetic account of the christological tradition itself. In other words, by enabling one to get a sense of Jesus as a historical figure, and how he interacted with the world of the first century and came to challenge it, one gains a better understanding of the dynamics of his ministry and more fully understands why and how the earliest Christians came to believe that this human being, Jesus, was God's own perfect self-expression in the world, conquering sin and evil. Loewe thus frames the discussion of the theological relevance of historical Jesus research by siding, to a large degree, with the position of David Tracy.

A recent essay by Anthony Godzieba, however, has complicated the question of the theological relevance of the historical Jesus by questioning the notion that the historical Jesus is a purely modern construct. In his essay, Godzieba draws out the similarities that exist between the critical "quests" for the historical Jesus and the precritical readings of

---

7. Loewe notes the seminal contribution of Edward Schillebeeckx, *Jesus: An Experiment in Christology*, trans. Hubert Hoskins (New York: Seabury, 1979); see Loewe, "From the Humanity of Christ to the Historical Jesus," 315n3. For an example of the old style of dogmatic Christology, see Ludwig Ott, *Fundamentals of Catholic Dogma* (Cork: Mercier, 1963) 125–74; see also Galvin, "From the Humanity of Christ to the Jesus of History," 252.

the Gospels in which the "historical life of Jesus" was often used as a criterion for critique and reform of the Christian church.[8]

Godzieba examines two exemplary medieval texts to support his thesis, Jacobus de Voragine's *Legenda Aurea* and Ludolf of Saxony's *Vita Jesu Christi*. He discerns within these precritical accounts of the life of Jesus consistent attempts to identify trustworthy sources and to dismiss fanciful or unreliable sources, much in the same way Luke justifies his work in the opening lines of his Gospel. These precritical authors adopted the rhetoric of historical veracity in an effort to ground Christology in what they regarded as the actual events of Jesus' life. In the case of both authors discussed by Godzieba, the imitation of the details of Christ's life provided the unique means to salvation and, therefore, a corresponding effort to offer a more detailed and reliable account of the events reported in the Gospels became a soteriological imperative rather than a curiosity of sequestered academics. As such, the detailed account of how Christ suffered in the face of persecution and the way Christ related to his troubled disciples in the boat during the storm (Matthew 8:23–27) provide each of the medieval authors Godzieba examines the opportunity to exhort Christians to imitate Christ in their own lives more perfectly.

Godzieba argues that these precritical readings of the historical Jesus are in line with the critical work of modern and contemporary scholars like Hermann Samuel Reimarus, Robert Funk, and even John Meier, each of whom admits that his historical research carries within it the power to chasten or correct various distortions of the tradition. These modern scholars perform this task, however, without emphasizing the religiously redemptive value of the *imitatio Christi*, a prominent feature of the medieval spirituality cultivated by Francis of Assisi and by members of the Franciscan order such as Ludolf.

Godzieba concludes that one must recognize what he calls the "criteriological" function of the historical life of Jesus as a non-negotiable element of the tradition (i.e., the historical life of Jesus is used as a criterion of critique and reform) regardless of how the term "historical" might be construed. Such recognition, he suggests, should help contemporary theologians more accurately reassess the value of precritical

8. See Anthony J. Godzieba, "From '*Vita Christi*' to 'Marginal Jew': The Life of Jesus as Criterion of Reform in Pre-Critical and Post-Critical Quests," *Louvain Studies* 32 (2007) 111–33.

Christology.[9] Godzieba also provocatively concludes, however, that the medieval writers more accurately grasp the truth about Jesus because they uniquely stress the priority of practice, the *imitatio Christi*. Such imitation may be termed "kerygmatic" since it represents a response to the demands of the gospel and the need to enflesh the salvation made available in Christ. This project is not the domain of the isolated individual; rather, imitation requires the participation and resources of the church and its tradition.

Godzieba's insight may help to further nuance the debate, neatly framed by Loewe, by suggesting that the quest for the historical Jesus is less novel than many might assume, even if "the quest for the historical Jesus" is also a modern construct. For his part, Loewe rightly moves away from Elizabeth Johnson's account of the historical Jesus as the norm for contemporary Christology given, among other factors, the limitations inherent in historical research. Yet Godzieba's claims, regarding the continuity between the contemporary quests for the historical Jesus on the one hand, and the manner in which historical memory (i.e., the memory of past events) operated within precritical Christologies on the other hand, actually bolster Johnson's notion of the historical Jesus as the contemporary form of the church's "memory image" of him. Loewe's statement regarding the limitations of historical Jesus research in theology remains well founded, so long as one does not ignore the criteriological role of the historical life of Jesus, for there is something operative in the construction of the historical Jesus that ties it to the church's kerygmatic tradition and the concrete exercise of discipleship in the world. Thus, the actual life of Jesus remains at the heart of the church's proclamation and its redemptive work, whether it is approached methodologically as in modern historical research or approached as something else within precritical Christologies. The criteriological function and ecclesial-kerygmatic dimensions of historical Jesus research are even operative within the work of two of the most prominent and critical contemporary historical Jesus scholars.

9. See ibid., 132. See also Clive Marsh, "Why the Quest for Jesus Can Never Only be Historical: Explorations in Cultural Christology," *Louvain Studies* 32 (2007) 164–81, for a discussion of the role of the historical Jesus within contemporary depictions of Jesus. Marsh argues that the narrative of Jesus, however it is construed, represents an effort to interpret Jesus and to persuade an audience.

Meier and Wright and the Practice of Historical Jesus Research

Among those who have embarked on the quest for the historical Jesus, two stand out for the rigor of their methodological commitments and the force of their arguments. Both John P. Meier and N. T. Wright have attempted to "rethink" the historical Jesus in an effort to overcome the weaknesses that caused earlier attempts to falter.[10] Yet their approaches to the methodological issues and their performance of historical Jesus research differ markedly. Meier may perhaps be identified with Tracy's position on the historical Jesus insofar as Meier seems to be concerned about the manner in which popularized scholarship has distorted and misused historical Jesus research, freighting it with non-historical elements and making it normative among the guild of theologians. Meier, however, fails to take account of the epistemological issues involved in both historical investigation and in theology, issues that anchor Tracy's position by, among other things, distinguishing a variety of interrelated yet distinct questions the answers to which ultimately require distinct functional specialties within theology.[11] Although Wright shares Meier's concerns about both the popular and the academic distortion of historical Jesus research, Wright believes that historical Jesus research holds out promise for the revitalization of Christian discipleship. This belief then aligns closely with Johnson's position, and it echoes Godzieba's point about the criteriological function of the historical Jesus. Even though Meier and Wright differ so markedly in some respects, their respective performances of historical Jesus research suggests they are both keenly aware that their efforts have discernible and powerful implications for theology and for the life of the church.

Meier insists throughout his meticulously researched volumes that whether one affirms or denies the historicity of a particular episode recorded in the Gospels, one must account for that judgment. In other words, one must know precisely why the particular judgment is

10. See John P. Meier, *A Marginal Jew: Rethinking the Historical Jesus*, 4 vols., Anchor/Yale Bible Reference Library (New York: Doubleday, 1991–2009) [hereafter abbreviated as *AMJ*]; Nicholas T. Wright, *The New Testament and the People of God*, Christian Origins and the Question of God 1 (Minneapolis: Fortress, 1992) [hereafter *NTPG*]; idem, *Jesus and the Victory of God* Christian Origins and the Question of God 2 (Minneapolis: Fortress, 1996) [hereafter *JVG*].

11. For an overview of functional specialties in theology see Lonergan, *Method in Theology*, 125–45.

made. Historical inquiry proceeds by means of a rigorous and commonly accepted methodology and finds confirmation in the emergence of a consensus among historians irrespective of their personal religious commitments. Using the analogy of a papal conclave, Meier suggests that historical Jesus research is akin to locking a group of diverse historians in the basement of the Harvard Divinity School library and forcing them to come up with a consensus document on the historical Jesus.[12] Obviously, no individual scholar would get what she wanted; the document, therefore, would contain only a fairly pale profile of Jesus' ministry and death. Meier characterizes this profile as a compilation of various pieces of an inherently incomplete puzzle, one that falls far short of the "real" historical human being. As a hypothetical reconstruction, Meier's academic sketch of the historical Jesus is not the object of Christian faith, though it does serve as a restraint against flights of theological fancy and preserves the autonomy of the historian (or the historical-critical exegete) against the encroachment of theology, or ideology. In trying to clarify and distinguish theology from historical reconstruction, Meier has highlighted the epistemological issues inherent in the discussion of the historical Jesus. Many, including N. T. Wright, have suggested that Meier does this without carefully considering the implications for his own project.

One of Wright's favorite sources for the methodological discussion of historical Jesus research is the late Ben Meyer, who took exception to John Meier's characterization of the historical Jesus as a "modern abstraction" and a "hypothetical reconstruction" because of its propensity to underwrite neo-Kantian idealism.[13] For Ben Meyer, true judgments about the historical Jesus affirm something *real* about Jesus, and these affirmations are not mere "abstractions." Wright and Meyer are both joined by Roch Kereszty in rejecting Meier's repudiation of the historian's subjectivity as the necessary precondition for authentic historical inquiry.[14] Meier's use of the scholarly conclave image seems to under-

12. See Meier, *AMJ* 1:1–2.

13. See Ben F. Meyer, "The Relevance of Horizon," *Downside Review* 112 (1994) 1–15. Others have followed in this line of criticism including Tony Kelly, "The Historical Jesus and Human Subjectivity: A Response to John Meier," *Pacifica* 4 (1991) 202–28; Wright, *JVG*, 54–55; *NTPG*, 34–35, among others.

14. See Roch Kereszty, "Historical Research, Theological Inquiry, and the Reality of Jesus: Reflections on the Method of J. P. Meier," *Communio* 19 (Winter 1992) 576–

write a naïve realist epistemology—the act of knowing is akin to the act of seeing—where the subjectivity of the knower remains an obstacle rather than the precondition for knowledge.[15] Other lines of criticism suggest that Meier has succumbed to the naturalism endemic to the Enlightenment and its own metaphysical presuppositions.[16] Although Meier remains wedded to a methodology that sounds rather like the "scissors and paste" history derided by R. G. Collingwood, Meier's performance as a historian belies his formal statements on method.[17] His results exceed the methodology and confirm some of the critiques just mentioned: (1) the historical Jesus is more than an abstraction or an idea, and (2) the location, commitments, and context (i.e., the subjectivity) of the historian are crucial to the historian's project.

Meier's characterization of the historical Jesus as a pale sketch, a "hypothetical reconstruction," is contravened at several key points in his presentation. Perhaps the most obvious example is Meier's very fine discussion of the message of Jesus in volume 2 of *A Marginal Jew*, where Luke Timothy Johnson identified Meier's "creeping certitude" about his reconstruction of Jesus.[18] Meier situates himself into the very mind of Jesus in order to discern the origin and meaning of Jesus' message. Meier does this by consistently appealing to his primary criteria of historicity, especially the criterion of multiple attestations of forms and sources. Yet, while the criteria help to isolate data (i.e., the image of God's kingdom in the words and practices of Jesus), the meaning of this data is not entirely clear. Meier pulls together the available data in order to discern its meaning, and thereby reconstructs the myth that

600. In addition to the reviews mentioned above, see Larry W. Hurtado, "A Taxonomy of Recent Historical Jesus Research," in *Whose Historical Jesus?* ed. William E. Arnal and Michel Desjardins, Studies in Christianity and Judaism 7 (Waterloo, ON: Wilfrid Laurier University Press, 1997) 281–83.

15. Meier has leveled the charge of "rampant subjectivism" in response to such criticism from Lonerganians such as Ben Meyer. See Meier, "*A Marginal Jew*—Retrospect and Prospect," Archbishop Gerety Lecture at Seton Hall University, February 18, 1993, p. 4, available online at http://www.shu.edu/academics/theology/upload/marginal-jew.pdf.

16. For example, see William Lane Craig, "'*Noli Me Tangere*': Why John Meier Won't Touch the Risen Lord," *Heythrop Journal* 50/1 (January 2009) 91–97.

17. See Robin G. Collingwood, *The Idea of History*, rev. ed. (Oxford: Oxford University Press, 1994) 257–61.

18. Luke Timothy Johnson, "Testing the Gospel Story: What We Know about Jesus and How We Know It," *Commonweal* (November 18, 1994) 33–35.

informed the ministry of Jesus and even Jesus' own understanding and utilization of that myth.[19] And it is on the basis of this understanding that Meier interprets and argues for the basic historicity of the miracle tradition as well. Meier's concluding statements on this aspect of the historical Jesus are telling.

> Jesus not only presented himself as the Elijah-like miracle-worker who made the future kingdom already effective and palpable for his followers, but at the same time presented himself as a teacher who could tell the Israelites how to observe the Law of Moses. . . . The stance of this eschatological prophet, herald of the future-yet present kingdom, and Elijah-like miracle worker to the Mosaic Law, . . . will make all the more pressing the central question: Who does this man think he is?[20]

Meier does not limit his practice to the mechanical application of criteria to sources. Rather, he reconstructs the narrative world of Jesus by sympathetically and intelligently extending himself into the world of first-century Palestine in an effort to better understand the words and deeds of Jesus that might be culled from the canonical Gospels. In all of this, Meier's intelligence, experience, and commitments (i.e., his subjectivity) play an indispensible role in his work as a historian. For Meier, the christological question hovers like a specter in the selection and interpretation of the data he presents in the form of a historical narrative, even while he continues to insist that the criteria are doing all the work and the results he offers are nothing more than a pale and hypothetical sketch of Jesus. But Meier's pale sketch has more robust sinews, more tissue, than he is willing to concede in his methodological discussions.

Meier's comparison of the historical Jesus to Frankenstein's monster is instructive and somewhat ironic.[21] Meier evokes the literary image of a monster assembled from the limbs of various corpses in order to convey to the reader the severe limitations of historical research which proceeds in piecemeal fashion. Additionally, the image

19. See Meier, *AMJ* 2:241, 252.

20. Meier, *AMJ* 2:1046.

21. See Meier, *Christ and His Mission: Essays in Christology and Ecclesiology*, Good News Studies 30 (Wilmington, DE: M. Glazer, 1990) 34; see also Christopher McMahon, "The Historical Jesus and Frankenstein's Monster: The Historical Jesus According to John Meier," *New Blackfriars* 83/981 (November 2002) 505–13.

of Frankenstein's monster also pokes fun at those historians who, as George Tyrell observed over a century ago, attempt to create the historical Jesus in their own image and likeness.[22] The image of Frankenstein's monster is ironic because, in the original novel, Mary Shelley famously avoids describing the "secret" of animation that brings the assembled pieces to life. In fact, Victor Frankenstein refuses to disclose the secret to his trusted associate, Walton, because it was thought that this secret would surely corrupt whoever possessed it.[23] As Meier constructs the historical Jesus and occasionally discerns the "*Gestalt*" of Jesus' life and ministry, he paints a convincing and lively portrait of Jesus. Yet, the portrait exceeds the limitations of the criteria he employs with such rigor. The secret of life behind Meier's historical Jesus is the result of Meier's own commitment to historical investigation and the disciplined extension of himself into the world of Jesus—the world of first-century Palestinian Judaism. Meier's Jesus is hardly an abstraction. Moreover, the judgments Meier makes in constructing his portrait of the historical Jesus are offered up as a corrective to various distortions of the historical Jesus—particularly distortions that are viewed by Meier as contributing to the distortion of theology and history within the church and the academy. As such, Meier's project, though subject to some criticism for its methodological assumptions, stands as a powerful example of the complexities and the theological character of historical Jesus research even as it also points to its criteriological function.

In contrast to Meier, N. T. Wright has taken a position similar to that of Elizabeth Johnson and other liberationist theologians on historical Jesus research, which ostensibly subverts its critical character by insisting, through his adaptation of a critical realist and narrative epistemology, that such research is essential and even quasi-normative for Christian theological reflection.[24] While Wright refuses to tether

---

22. See George Tyrrell, *Christianity at the Crossroads* (London: Longmans, Green, 1909; repr. 1963) 49.

23. See Mary Shelley, *Frankenstein* (Oxford: Oxford University Press, 1993) chap. 4.

24. Wright distinguishes between history as an event (history-E) and history as a written account of events (history-W). He argues that theology must not "conform to every last hypothetical reconstruction ('history-W'), an impossible task in any case. Rather, as historians approximate to 'history-E', that history itself—Jesus himself, in other words, as a figure of 'history-E' and *not* simply of the historians' approximations—confronts, disturbs and beckons us in new ways" (Wright, "In Grateful

Christian theology to discrete historical judgments of fact, he nonetheless expresses a fundamental commitment to the historical character of Christian faith. For Wright, to the extent that history makes true judgments about what actually happened, Christian faith must bow towards the claims of history. In other words, historians make claims about reality, and to the extent that these claims are true theologians must take account, or else risk losing the ability to make any truth claims whatsoever.

> [H]istory and theology function well together; in fact they are distorted when one functions without the other. History, then, prevents faith from becoming fantasy. Faith prevents history from becoming mere antiquarianism. Historical research, being always provisional, cannot ultimately veto faith, though it can pose hard questions that faith, in order to retain its integrity precisely as Christian faith, must struggle to answer, and may well grow strong through answering. Faith, being subject to the vagaries of personality and culture, cannot veto the historical enterprise . . . but it can put hard questions to history, not least on the large topic of the origins of Christianity, and history may be all the better for trying to answer them.[25]

Wright seems to privilege the process of historical investigation, while maintaining a degree of caution about the capacity of discrete historical judgments to "veto" Christian faith. His narrative approach to history and human knowledge in general may have shortcomings, but this move allows him to overcome naïve historical positivism while at the same time avoiding the temptation of reducing Christian faith to "what it means for me."[26] Wright's focus on narrative and community is becoming more influential among many evangelical and neo-orthodox theologians who seek to emphasize the centrality of tradition and community in human living and knowing, thus placing the artifacts of the tradition and the community's interpretation of them at the center of any historical reconstruction of those communities and the worldviews

Dialogue," in *Jesus and the Restoration of Israel: A Critical Assessment of N. T. Wright's "Jesus and the Victory of God"*, ed. Carey Newman (Downers Grove, IL: InterVarsity, 1999) 251.

25. Wright, "Knowing Jesus: Faith and History," in Marcus Borg and N. T. Wright, *The Meaning of Jesus* (San Francisco: HarperCollins, 1999) 26–27.

26. Wright, *JVG*, 661.

that sustained them. It is in the reconstruction of these narrative world-views, however, that Wright has suffered his most persistent criticisms.

Many scholars have criticized Wright for his distortion of both the early Jewish and the early Christian worldviews and the narratives that inform those worldviews through his use of large-scale hypotheses that attempt to fit the data into a larger explanatory framework.[27] For Wright, the full story of Jesus (what he calls the "inside" of the Jesus event) comes to be known through the tradition he generated—the church.[28] Wright's concern for coherence, however, is seen by some as a covert attempt to allow Christian doctrine to control Wright's recon-struction of the historical Jesus, a charge that is echoed among many of John Meier's critics as well.[29] Wright's performance as a historian has left many critics with the impression that Wright's conclusions, while not simply a repackaging of traditional Christian dogma, nonetheless are comforting for mainline Christianity. Such criticisms, however, thinly mask the subversive, even iconoclastic, presuppositions of mod-ern historical Jesus research, even when it is employed in the defense of an "orthodox" theology.

In their performance of historical Jesus research, both Meier and Wright understand that there is something more to the historical Jesus than just assembling a set of historical facts. Meier intimates as much in his careful and almost restricted methodology and in his suggestion that historical Jesus research can serve as a "restraint" against flights of fancy. Wright, on the other hand, makes the connection between the-ology and history the explicit centerpiece of his project, even though many critics think that some of the historical judgments he expresses are overstated. Whether their work on the historical Jesus is performa-tively overstated or methodologically understated, Meier and Wright appear to be in substantial agreement: there is something at stake in

27. See Wright, *NTPG*, 100.

28. See Wright, *NTPG*, 117; *JVG*, 132.

29. See, e.g., Clive Marsh, "Theological History? N. T. Wright's *Jesus and the Victory of God*," *Journal for the Study of the New Testament* 69 (1998) 77–94; and in a more sympathetic direction see Tim Stafford, "N. T. Wright: Making Scholarship a Tool for the Church," *Christianity Today* 43/2 (February 8, 1999) 42–46. The charge against Meier has been less forthrightly stated, but it is mentioned by Mark Allan Powell (*Jesus as a Figure in History: How Modern Historians View the Man from Galilee* [Louisville: Westminster John Knox, 1998] 145) and implied in the methodological critiques men-tioned above by Luke Timothy Johnson, Tony Kelly, and Roch Kereszty.

their research, something that lays claim to the church's understanding and proclamation of the gospel. While the goal of establishing "what actually happened (*wie es eigentlich gewesen*)" remains the centerpiece of their respective efforts, and efforts of even the precritical work discussed by Godzieba, the quest for the historical Jesus is always *someone's* quest. Loewe has made the implications of this matter of fact pivotal for those who would make historical Jesus research normative for Christology. Moreover, the contemporary quest for the historical Jesus has been the occasion for debate rather than consensus, with the results of the research often proving ambiguous and unwieldy. How might these two conclusions inform an understanding of the theological relevance of historical Jesus research in light of Godzieba's claims regarding the criteriological function it has played in both precritical and modern Christologies?

Narrating Salvation

The Gospel of Luke begins with a literary preface in which the author makes a claim concerning the reliability and "orderliness" of the narrative that follows in comparison to other attempts to narrate "the things that have been fulfilled."[30] Thus, at the very heart of the Christian tradition, there stands an explicit attempt to construct a narrative of Jesus and his saving work that is grounded in some form of historical recon-

30. See Joseph Fitzmyer, *The Gospel According to Luke*, Anchor Bible 1 (New York: Doubleday, 1981) 287–99, for a discussion of the details of Luke's prologue. Of particular interest is the use of the Greek word διήγησις ("narrative") in 1:1 (i.e., "Since many have undertaken to compile a narrative of the things which have been accomplished among us," RSV). In 1:2 Luke contends that his narrative is based on the testimony of the "eyewitnesses" (οἱ αὐτόπται) and ministers of the word; see Joel Green, *The Gospel of Luke*, New International Commentary on the New Testament (Grand Rapids Eerdmans, 1997) 40–41. The testimony of these eyewitnesses then provides the basis for Luke's claim to write an orderly account of the events of Jesus' life and ministry (εὔδοξε κἀμοί . . . καθεξῆς σοι γράψαι). This orderly account will provide Theophilus with assurance (ἀσφάλεια) that is perhaps both historical (e.g., François Bovon, *Luke: A Commentary on the Gospel of Luke 1:1—9:50*, Hermenia [Minneapolis: Fortress, 2002]) as well as logical and rhetorical (see Rick Strela, "A Note on ἀσφάλεια [Luke 1:4]," *Journal for the Study of the New Testament* 30/2 [December 2007] 163–71). For a full study of the rhetorical dimensions of Luke's historical narrative, see Clare K. Rothschild, *Luke-Acts and the Rhetoric of History: An Investigation of Early Christian Historiography* (Tübingen: Mohr/Siebeck, 2004).

struction, and this reconstruction functions as a criterion of Christian living. Yet, the attempt to narrate (proclaim) the life of Jesus has taken many forms. The canonical Gospels have been paralleled throughout history by other narratives, and these narratives have been alternately complimentary and expansive, spiritual and mundane, heterodox and orthodox. As Godzieba has noted, appeals to the historical life of Jesus have exercised a criteriological function within the Christian community from the very earliest days. As the church continually struggles to articulate the saving significance of Christ to the world, it does so through the construction of narratives—narratives that credibly connected the story of Jesus with the experience of sin and the need for redemption. Even the question of the historical Jesus raises questions as to the adequacy of the tradition, the canonical Gospels, and the faithfulness of the church's witness. As seen above, John Meier and N. T. Wright (as well as countless other critical and precritical "questers" over the centuries) have pursued historical Jesus research in order to exercise influence over the Christian tradition through the construction of a saving narrative—one that overcomes the perceived shortcomings of previous "quests" and the flourishing of inadequate methodologies within the academy itself.

Increasingly, historical consciousness and a media-driven obsession with novelty have created a culture in which the academic reconstruction of the historical Jesus is made suspect in the eyes of the general population. Popularized accounts of Jesus, understood and accepted as the historical Jesus, even when they lack the historical rigor commonly recognized within the academy, have been highly influential within both the Christian church and the general population. Mel Gibson's film *The Passion of the Christ* and the narrative of Jesus that stands behind Dan Brown's books (which have helped fuel the popularity of "alternative" gospels) stand out as the most financially lucrative examples of this phenomenon. While such popularized accounts often bastardize both critical history and the Christian tradition, they nonetheless demonstrate both the criteriological function of historical reconstructions of the life of Jesus as well as the fluidity of such reconstructions.

The creations of Gibson and Brown are fine examples of the criteriological function of popularized accounts of the historical Jesus. While Gibson's *oeuvre* seems to reflect a conservative and pious religious sentiment, it also reflects a high degree of creativity—the director was obviously unobstructed in the film's production. For example, consider the ostensible historicity of the film. Through its use of ancient languages, its graphic depiction of the violence inherent in Roman executions, and the vivid portrayal of the disciples' despair, the film provoked extreme reactions in audiences worldwide—including the reported reaction of John Paul II ("It is as it was"). This type of reaction, echoed in the words of other Christian leaders, has given the film unique currency within contemporary culture.[31] Gibson's film gave its audience a sense of witnessing the execution of Jesus, but not as mere spectators; rather, the film was designed to function as a proclamation, a summons to conversion and a life of penance and thanksgiving. It did not matter that the film relied more on the writings of a nineteenth century mystic (Anne Catherine Emmerich) than on the work of historical scholars or even the canonical Gospels themselves.[32] The film retained a certain historical plausibility that went behind the Gospels, and that is where the film gained its power over its audience.

The Dan Brown phenomenon has taken the popularization of the historical Jesus in the opposite direction. Even though he works as a writer of fiction, he also incorporates pieces of legitimate historical research with his imagination as a writer and adds a sharp polemical edge to the story. In all of this, Brown seeks to play with his audience as he displays just enough historical plausibility to capture them with his narrative. Like Robert Funk and many other historical Jesus scholars, Brown takes as his starting point modernity's suspicion of religious authority and uses it to his advantage. For Brown, there is a Jesus behind the gospel that the church wants to hide in order to perpetuate its

---

31. See John Allen, "The Word from Rome," *National Catholic Reporter* 3/17 (December 19, 2003), online: http://nationalcatholicreporter.org/word/pfw121903. htm.

32. Among the many notable reviews of the film are those by Paula Fredriksen. She had been part of a group of advisors who read and commented on the film script and responded to the filmmakers regarding the historicity of the film and the theological issues raised by the film, including the film's alleged anti-Semitism. See Paula Fredriksen, "Mad Mel: The Gospel According to Gibson," *The New Republic*, July 28 and August 4, 2003, 25–29; and "Gospel Truths: Hollywood, History, and Christianity," in *Perspectives on 'The Passion of the Christ': Religious Thinkers and Writers Explore the Issues Raised by the Controversial Movie*, rev. ed., ed. Paula Fredriksen (Berkeley: University of California Press, 2005) 31–48.

deceptions, and by exposing this Jesus people are freed from a blind allegiance to a dysfunctional and dangerous faith.

The popularization of non-academic and dubious appeals to the historical Jesus is maddening to both historical Jesus scholars and to theologians alike. Many are tempted to simply dismiss or ignore the phenomenon. Rather than despising or dismissing these popularized fictions, however, Clive Marsh argues that such popularized reconstructions help to remind us that Jesus, even the historical Jesus, does not belong to the academy, or to anyone else for that matter, and cannot be controlled.[33] After all, the academics in John Meier's hypothetical historical Jesus conclave in the bowels of the Harvard Divinity School library may reach a consensus among themselves, but that consensus is not universal. The consensus developed among this select group of historians reflects the merging of perspectives (or horizons) made possible by a shared objective. But, in keeping with Meier's metaphor, we might add that others have bypassed (or escaped) the Harvard library (Gibson, Brown, and others), and their accounts of Jesus are immediately disseminated via electronic media of every kind. The effort to control the historical reconstruction of Jesus is doomed to failure, as Loewe and others have noted. Even the meticulous and balanced efforts of John Meier fail to generate any consensus among historians, despite the fact that this is the defining aspect of his methodology. Those who would despair and forsake historical Jesus research, however, need to come to terms with the *de facto* role played by reconstructions of the historical Jesus (or, "the actual life of Jesus" in precritical Christologies) in the history of the church and within contemporary culture. For although these reconstructions have never generated consensus, they remain a concern for theologians even as they proliferate in a variety of forms within contemporary culture. What is required is a way forward amidst the seemingly endless competing and contradictory narratives (some historical and others fictitious) with which we are beset.

While tempting to many academicians, the way forward cannot rest in the differentiation between history and fiction. While the two are certainly different, their differentiation must also acknowledge some basic similarities as well. In fact, Hayden White and Frank Kermode famously argued that there is, in some examples of historical writing and

33. See Clive Marsh, "Why the Quest for Jesus Can Never Only Be Historical," 169.

fiction, little or no difference.[34] But history has always been understood to represent the effort to determine "what actually happened," and thus to narrate a story, and yet this narration of discrete events requires the creativity, imagination, and intelligence of the historian. When the historical data are contested, how much more like fiction does history become? The academic discipline of history must, however, be afforded its due, and the goal of determining "what actually happened," though it remains a somewhat asymptotic goal, demands rigorous attention. Yet, as Benedict XVI suggests in his book *Jesus of Nazareth*, "we can never go beyond the domain of hypothesis, because we simply cannot bring the past into the present."[35] The end result is always some integration of the past, as understood with the present and the future, and this result requires an assessment that goes beyond the mere identification of genre.

Lonergan's account of the functional specialties provides a way forward here. In essence, what is required is a move to incorporate more explicitly what Lonergan called dialectics and foundations into any account of history and its role in narrating the saving story of Jesus. In his reading of Irenaeus' *Adversus Haereses*, William Loewe made good use of Lonergan's notion of dialectics, foundations, and soteriology to understand and appropriate Irenaeus's mythic narrative. Although the narrative was, in so many ways, controlled by the anti-Gnostic polemics of his time, Irenaeus's narrative remains valuable and a truthful account of God's saving work, so long as the genre of writing is mitigated by more foundational questions, which Loewe identifies as follows: "What values are mediated by acceptance of [story x] as the true story of God and humanity? What commitments shape the world in which his story invites us to dwell? That is, how does acceptance in faith render [story x] a saving story?"[36]

34. See Hayden White, "The Historical Text as Literary Artifact," *Clio* 3/3 (June 1974) 277–303. See also Frank Kermode, *The Genesis of Secrecy: On the Interpretation of Narrative* (Cambridge, MA: Harvard University Press, 1979); and T. R. Wright, "Regenerating Narrative: The Gospels as Fiction," *Religious Studies* 20/3 (September 1984) 389–400.

35. Joseph Ratzinger (Pope Benedict XVI), *Jesus of Nazareth: From Baptism in the Jordan to the Transfiguration* (New York: Doubleday, 2007), xvii.

36. William P. Loewe, "Irenaeus' Soteriology: Transposing the Question," in *Religion and Culture: Essays in Honor of Bernard Lonergan*, ed. Timothy Fallon and Philip Boo Reilly (Albany, NY: SUNY Press, 1987) 167–80.

The difference in genre between historical writing and the symbolic narrative of Irenaeus, the imaginative fiction of many contemporary writers, and the disciplined research of contemporary historians cannot be downplayed without gross oversimplification and distortion. Yet the foundational questions posed by Loewe may prove helpful in understanding and in appropriating the ecclesial-kerygmatic dimensions of historical Jesus research even as contemporary readers are faced with the myriad representations of the historical Jesus. Certainly there is a wide range of philosophical, hermeneutical, and methodological questions that will emerge among historians as they move from gathering data, to interpretation, to the establishment of historical facts. Yet Godzieba has rightly identified the role played by the historical Jesus in precritical Christologies, apart from the critical methodological questions raised by Lonergan's account of the historian's work. [37] The ultimate question regarding the construction and narration of the life of Jesus (or the historical Jesus) centers not on the identification of the role the historian's subjectivity has played in a given narrative, as important as that is; rather, the issue centers on the values that the narrative itself embodies and the extent to which those values resonate within the community of faith across time to make the story of Jesus a saving story. It is, however, within the theological movement known as Latin American liberation theology that the criteriological function of historical Jesus research has found its most persistent and passionate proponents.

Within liberation theology, the concern with the history of Jesus does not simply center on the question, "What actually happened?" Rather, a further question must always be addressed, namely, "Why does it matter?" It is this second question that opens up to the criteriological concerns identified by Godzieba, and it brings us back to the liberationist concerns with historical Jesus research (against which Meier famously argued) and the explicitly criteriological role it continues to play therein.[38] It is this criteriological role that directs historical Jesus research to an appropriate ecclesial-kerygmatic *telos*: the proclamation of God's saving work in history.

The classic statement on the historical Jesus and soteriology is offered by the Salvadoran Jesuit martyr Ignacio Ellacuría, for whom the

37. See Lonergan, *Method in Theology*, 197–234.

38. See Meier, "The Bible as a Source for Theology," *CTSA Proceedings* 43 (1988) 1–14.

task of contemporary theology is that of locating soteriology in history and in the suffering resistance to the forces of evil and oppression.[39] Research into the historical Jesus has the power to illuminate contemporary history and the possibility of redemption therein, yet it does so not through the isolation of discrete facts about Jesus. Rather, this illumination has its source in the desire to experience God's saving work in history. It is the job of theology to historicize salvation, and the quest for the historical Jesus represents one aspect of the Christian church's mission to continually historicize the grace of God in history and to make salvation historically operative.[40] In this context, with the goal of the historicization of Christian soteriology in mind, research and writing on the historical Jesus may serve as an important means by which the church lives out its redemptive mission.[41]

Conclusion

William Loewe has appropriately cautioned against the facile assumptions of those theologians who would use historical Jesus research as a *norma normans non normata* (an ultimate norm or standard) for Christology, and John Meier (along with others) is correct to point out the limitations of historical Jesus research within the confines of historical-critical methodology. The historical Jesus, however, eludes the confines of the methodology; and as Loewe rightly asks, *whose* historical Jesus are we talking about? This essay suggests that contemporary historical Jesus research, even as iconoclastic or positivistic as it might be at times, nonetheless stands within the broad parameters

39. See Ignacio Ellacuría, "Jesus and the Crucified Peoples," in *Systematic Theology: Perspectives from Liberation Theology*, eds. Jon Sobrino and Ignacio Ellacuria (Maryknoll, NY: Orbis, 1996) 257–78.

40. See Kevin Burke, "Reflections on Ignatian Soteriology: The Contribution of Ignacio Ellacuría," *Lonergan Workshop* 19 (2006) 37–50.

41. Robert Lassalle-Klein has edited a recent issue of the journal *Theological Studies* on "'The Galilean Jesus" (70/2 [June 2009]), which effectively demonstrates the ecclesial-kerygmatic dimensions of historical Jesus research. The essay by Sean Freyne ("The Galilean Jesus and Contemporary Christology," 281–97) nicely draws upon the available information on Galilee in the first century and emplots Jesus therein, making reference to the available scholarship on the historical Jesus. Freyne, however, consciously raises the question of the significance of such an imaginative emplottment for understanding the contemporary demands of discipleship.

of the Christian tradition and serves the church's redemptive mission. Narrating the historical Jesus, then, is not solely concerned with naïvely asking, "What did Jesus do or say?" Rather, narrating the historical Jesus represents the desire to imitate Christ, to enflesh the claims of the gospel in a way that brings together the concrete experience of sin and the corresponding hope for salvation. In a historically conscious and iconoclastic culture, the form that historical Jesus research takes cannot be domesticated by the academy and cannot be confined to narrow questions of fact. Rather, historical Jesus research will inevitably remain elusive, frustrating, imprecise, and conflicted even while it remains vibrant and powerful.

5

Injustice at Ephesus[1]

GERARD S. SLOYAN
TEMPLE UNIVERSITY (EMERITUS)

From Arius to Ephesus

In the year 318 a presbyter and powerful preacher of Alexandria named Arius was summoned by his bishop Alexander (313–28) to a council, at which his teaching on the mystery of Christ was condemned as errone-ous. Alexander was himself no mean theologian. Like all engaged in the christological debates of his age, he relied on Greek philosophical cate-gories without acknowledging a debt to pagan thinkers as he attempted to make explicit the apostolic tradition on this mystery. He insisted on the unity of the divine Triad while considering the Word to be an ὑπό-στασις or φύσις ("subsistence" or "nature," terms virtually identical for him), who was at the same time both the eternal Λόγος and human being in every respect. Chosen by God to be the mediator between God and creation, the human Jesus as Word of God enfleshed was not a crea-ture only. Such was the church's faith in who he was. Concurrent with Alexander's long familiar apostolic teaching, there was a report abroad that Arius was presenting the Word as "the firstborn [πρωτοτόκος] of all creation" in the sense of the first creature through whom all else was

1. This essay is dedicated to William P. Loewe, whose writings in the field of formal Christology have always derived from patristic thought.

made. [2] He was helped in maintaining this position by taking the second-century word ἀγέννητος (ingenerate or unbegotten) as applied to God the Creator to mean that only God should be so described. Arius was convinced that γεννητός, "begotten," as applied to Jesus, could not mean "eternally begotten." It had to mean "created." So subtle was he in his thinking and writing that he could go from God the unoriginate source of all, alone immortal, true, and wise, to God the indivisible, which had as its necessary corollary that whatever else exists must exist not by any communication of God's being but by creation, coming to be out of nothing. This theological opinion was the development of a previous theory termed the divine μοναρχία, which saw God as the sole ἀρχή or origin of all that is. Whatever else came to be, including the Λόγος that was in Christ, had to come from previous nothingness. Arius, it should be noted, was quite at ease with employing traditional vocabulary, with its words "holy Triad," "God," and "Son of God," to apply to Jesus Christ by way of courtesy of speech with respect to the primordially created Word.

Arius's condemnation by a council in his home city and diocese was followed by one in the same year, 318, at Antioch, and then by an imperial council presided over by Constantine I in his palace at Nicaea. The creed hammered out by the bishops assembled was relatively brief and Trinitarian in form, and after affirming faith in the Holy Spirit it said no more. Earlier, it expressed belief in "one God, the Father All-Sovereign, maker of all things visible and invisible," and proceeded in much greater detail to enunciate belief in

> one Lord, Jesus Christ, the Son of God, begotten of the Father, only-begotten, that is, of the substance of the Father, God of God, Light of Light, true God of true God, begotten not made, of

2. Colossians 1:15. The quoted hymn in which this word is found says of Christ, "He is the image of the invisible God the firstborn of/over all creation. ... And he is the head of the body, the church. He is the beginning [ἀρχή], the firstborn from the dead, that in all things he might have the primacy [αὐτὸς πρωτεύων]. For in him all the fullness [πᾶν τὸ πλήρωμα] was pleased to dwell" (1:15, 18–19). Arius was unmoved in his position on the createdness of the Λόγος or Υἱός (Son) when absolute firstness or precedence to all creation was being claimed for such a One. He acknowledged all the NT language that connoted divinity by saying that it referred to titles requiring utter devotion but no adoration of this first and greatest of God's creatures (see Athanasius's quotations from Arius's *Thalia* in *De Synodis* 15; see also Rowan Williams, *Arius: Heresy and Tradition*, rev. ed. (Grand Rapids: Eerdmans, 2001) 101–3.

one substance with the Father [ὁμοούσιον τῷ πατρί] through whom all things were made, things in heaven and things on the earth, who for us men and for our salvation came down and was made flesh, and became man [ἐνανθρωπήσαντα, the incorporated ἄνθρωπος, meaning a human, not ἄνηρ, a male] suffered, and rose on the third day, ascended into the heavens, is coming to judge the living and the dead. And in the Holy Spirit.[3]

There follows immediately upon the creedal formula a series of Arian propositions that are denied to make abundantly clear what should already be clear: "And those who say, 'There was when he was not,' and 'Before he was begotten he was not,' and that, 'He came into being from what was not,' or those who allege that the Son of God is 'Of another substance [ὑποστάσεως] or essence [οὐσίας]' or 'created' or 'changeable' or 'alterable,' these the Catholic Church anathematizes."[4] The final text had made numerous additions to the creed of Caesarea that its Arian-leaning bishop, Eusebius, the emperor's close confidant, had proposed for adoption, all in the matter of the deity of the Son. It also eliminated "Firstborn of all creation," the phrase favored by Arius to underscore the limited character of the Son. In place of the Caesarean text for Christ, "He lived among men," Nicaea substituted the Johannine-redolent "came down" (κατελθόντα)[5] and "was made flesh" (σαρκωθέντα).[6] No other attention was paid to Jesus' humanity at Nicaea because it was not in question, only his possession of the fullness of deity.

The emperor Constantine had summoned the council because he did not wish to have an ever-growing Christian population in his empire squabbling over what exactly was the faith they held. He named Ossius, bishop of Córdoba, leader of the few Western bishops who attended, to preside at the sessions. Constantine relied on him for theological counsel more than on Eusebius who was his chief political supporter among the Eastern bishops. Pope Sylvester declined to at-

---

3. *Enchiridion Symbolorum*, 23rd ed., ed. Heinrich Denzinger and Adolf Schönmetzer, (Freiburg: Herder, 1953) 125 [hereafter ES]; *Documents of the Christian Church*, 3rd ed., ed. Henry Bettenson and Chris Maunder (Oxford: Oxford University Press, 1999) 28–29.

4. *ES*, 126.

5. See John 6:41, 51, 58.

6. See John 1:14.

tend, pleading his advanced years, but sent two bishops to represent him. An important presence was that of the thirty-year-old deacon of Alexandria, Athanasius. It was his theological acumen that provided Alexander guidance in the wording of the creed and the repudiated positions of Arius. In the event, Constantine made the Catholic faith expressed by the council his own, even though he remained a catechumen and deferred his baptism until shortly before his death.

Authority in the empire was at that point, in 337, divided among his three sons. Constans (d. 350) remained a faithful Catholic but Constantius II (d. 360) went the Arian route. He spent his quarter-century in power harassing the Catholics and pagans alike. His cousin Julian, who had served as his Caesar in Gaul, revolted against Constantius and succeeded him upon his natural death, to live only thirty months and die in a war with the Persians. Orphaned at an early age and raised as a Catholic, the studious Julian is better remembered for turning his back on his boyhood faith than for his espousal of paganism as the empire's religion, which paradoxically helped effect its demise. Arianism met such a fate in the reigns of Valens and Theodosius I, who in 380 made Catholic Christianity the religion of his far-reaching Roman rule. The heresy of Arius, however, made steady headway via missionaries from Constantinople and Venice to the Germanic and other peoples north and east of the Alps. Attila was the most famed of these warrior chieftains who came south in military conquest, but he and his Huns were of Mongol stock and did not come as Christians. It was otherwise with the peoples known as Vandals, East Goths, and West Goths. Alaric, chief of the latter tribe, came as an Arian Christian, as his father had been before him while the Visigothic conversion of Christianity under Theodoric the Great came a century later. These tribesmen were considered "barbarians" by the conquered European south despite their baptized status.

Three years after the Nicaean settlement the youthful Athanasius was elected bishop of Alexandria. Over his long episcopate (328–70) he was exiled from his see no less than five times, the first of these by Constantine toward the end of his reign, and later by Constantius, Julian, and Valens in succession. Recalled to Alexandria by popular appeal in the days of the last named, he lived out his last seven years in relative peace.

The anti-Arian struggle persisted well after Athanasius's death, taking the form as might be expected of major stress on the divinity of Christ. Only in the Syrian East with Antioch as its chief bishopric was there a comparable effort to keep the humanity of Jesus Christ to the fore. Origen of Alexandria (ca. 185–253/4) was the master in both biblical scholarship and speculative theology of all who came after him. In a dispute with his bishop, Demetrius, who demanded his return from Caesarea in Roman Palestine where he had gone to teach, and much later in his acceptance of presbyteral ordination there against his bishop's wishes, he lived out his life of scholarship in that Mediterranean seacoast city. Although he speculated on many matters, the union of deity and humanity in Christ was not one of them. He taught vigorously the eternal coming forth of the Son of God from the Father ("the only-begotten Son of God is God's wisdom hypostatically existing"), and taught that this Son in very recent times took upon himself a human nature.[7]

Two men who came under Origen's intellectual influence, as it was impossible not to do, were a native of Antioch, Theodore, and a man of Alexandria, Cyril. The first of these became the bishop of Mopsuestia in Cilicia in 392 and lived out his life of pastoral leadership, study, and writing until his death in 428. Known in life and ever after as "The Exegete," he produced a steady stream of sermons, biblical commentaries, and theological treatises. An important one, *On the Incarnation*, was long lost, then recovered, but disappeared again in World War II. From the totality of his other extant writings it can be concluded that he taught the complete human nature of Christ, not only as a man of flesh and blood but, by dint of an analysis of what we would call Jesus' person (πρόσωπον), a man united to the Godhead at the roots of his being ("a man assumed"). In one place he called his unity a union of εὐδοκία, divine favor or approval, the word in the angels' song at Christ's nativity.[8] Overall, he favored the term "Word and assumed man" united

---

7. Origen, *On First Principles* 1.2, trans. G. W. Butterworth (Gloucester, MA: Peter Smith, 1973) 15. See ibid. 1.1: "He took to himself a body like our body . . . was born and suffered in truth . . . and truly died our common death" (3).

8. PG 66:976: "The Word inhabits the man as in a Son by good pleasure." See also 66:981: "the prosopon is brought about by the union." See also PL 67:587, 753. On the Syrians' Christology in full, see Francis A. Sullivan, *The Theology of Theodore of Mopsuestia*, Analecta Gregoriana 82 (Rome: University Gregorian, 1956) 260, where he finds Theodore in the main not identifying this πρόσωπον with the divine ὑπόστασις.

in one "person," who in his human soul acted freely in accomplishing the work of human redemption. The one person is the proper object of adoration, as God alone is.

At the midpoint of Theodore's long episcopate the presbyter Cyril, a man of keen intellect, holy zeal, and aggressive temperament, succeeded his uncle Theophilos as patriarch of Alexandria. The year was 412. He was to die in 444, which means that he did not participate in the council at Chalcedon, nor would even have agreed to the necessity of such a gathering. Upon becoming bishop Cyril immediately fell afoul of Alexandria's city government by pressing on it the claims of doctrinal orthodoxy. He closed down the church of a century-old sect, the disciples of Novatian, who was a rigorist in opposing the reconciliation of Roman Christians who had denied their faith in the Decian persecution. At the same time, he began to make the case strongly for the Egyptian church's understanding of the Nicaean settlement, at least his understanding of that statement. His target was the Syrian church, which at the time was in the ascendant, chiefly through two natives of Antioch who successively occupied the patriarchal chair of Constantinople—John, known as Chrysostom, and Nestorius. John, like Theodore, was trained in theology by his contact with Bishop Diodoros of Tarsus. Nestorius, a man of Persian stock, was probably a student under Theodore in his early period as a monk. His eminence as a preacher moved Emperor Theodosius II to nominate him in 428 to the chief Eastern see of the empire. He entertained in common with Cyril and Chrysostom a tragic antagonism to the Jews for their unbelief, namely in Christ and the church. Cyril and Nestorius, however, had nothing whatever in common in their understanding and verbal expression of the mystery of Christ. The attack of the Alexandrian incumbent on the Antiochene, moreover, was ethnic and political as much as it was religious.

Nestorius at Ephesus

The years after Nicaea had been taken up with the struggle in East and West between the Catholics, or orthodox, and the Arians. It took the form of attempting to achieve a suitable vocabulary for the impenetrable mystery of the triune God from the slim word-hoard provided by the apostolic tradition: "Father," "Son," and "Holy Spirit," and, with respect to Christ, words and phrases found largely in John but a few in hymns quoted by Paul in Philippians and Colossians: "begetting," "proceeding," "coming," "above," "below," "before," "flesh," "spirit," "are one," and "is greater than." Up to the year 250 or so, this meager but adequate vocabulary from biblical sources served the needs of intellectually oriented believers in the mystery of the incarnation of the Word and the resultantly revealed triune life of God. It was the continued fending off of the Arian challenge that brought renewed theological activity some seventy-five years later.

The proper business of theology is speculation on revealed mystery for purposes of the defense and spread of the gospel. The speculation in this case was based on the vocabulary of Greek philosophy in which all the mutual antagonists had been trained. The Alexandrian champion was by all odds Athanasius. Elected bishop of that city three years after Nicaea, his enforced exile from his see five times over the next thirty years was chiefly at the hands of Arian emperors but also of polemicists of that sect and even of his own church. Origen, a fellow townsman, would have been Athanasius's master in theology, writing about the incarnation traditionally and almost never speculatively. Athanasius's opposite number as a bishop teacher, although born twenty years after Origen's death, was the Antiochene native Theodore. These were the two on whose theology the litigants Cyril and Nestorius based themselves.

Cyril seized the opportunity for condemnation of the Antiochenes, whom he designated the "Word-man" party, while Cyril himself gravitated to a "Word-flesh" persuasion, advocating only a divine nature. Nestorius was baited into expressing his opinion of the title θεοτόκος (God-bearer) as applied to Mary, which he thought inadequate. It was not a question of the honor due to our Lady, as later centuries took it to be, but about the identity of her Son. Nestorius incautiously responded that it bespoke divine motherhood, to be sure, but was defective in the matter of the child she bore. Ἀνθρωποτόκος, "human being-bearer," would have been equally insufficient, whereas Χριστοτόκος would be the proper term, since in Catholic tradition "Christ" had always been the designation of the one person, Jesus, both human and divine. That was all the ammunition Cyril needed to have the Syrians unmasked as the two-persons party, one human and one divine. Nestorius believed no such thing. He was concerned only to keep the human Jesus, as all twenty-seven New Testament books portray him, to the fore in Christian consciousness. Nestorius's view had been censured at a Roman synod summoned by Pope Celestine I in 430 and another of Cyril's convening at Alexandria in the same year. Emperor Theodosius II had meantime convoked a council for early June in Ephesus.

The key to Cyril's argument by which he hoped to show Nestorius's views as heretical was his use of the non-biblical term ὑπόστασις univocally, that is, as properly applied to the Word and to a human being on equal terms. It had in previous debate been used interchangeably with οὐσία meaning "essence" or "individual existence," and used by some, like Theodore, as at times equivalent to πρόσωπον, "person." In Cyril's use the Word of God possessed subsistency or was a divine Subsistent; so too was every human a subsistent human being. Nestorius's claim that Mary was the mother of a human infant who was at the same time a divine child meant for Cyril two ὑποστασεῖς, two individuals, one divine and one human. Cyril's own explanation of the mystery of the incarnation was that the union of the two natures was καθ᾽ ὑπόστασιν, which translated into English means a hypostatic union in the one hypostasis of the Word—in the vernacular languages, this phrase means one divine person in two natures. On the basis of that verbally couched argument, Cyril had no problem in declaring Nestorius's refusal to accept θεοτόκος a clear statement of his belief in two persons in her womb, one human and one divine.

When Nestorius arrived at the tiny church that was to be the scene of the Council of Ephesus, he encountered Cyril already there armed with *Twelve Anathemas* of his position ready for signature.[9] Four days later, John of Antioch arrived at the head of the delegation of Eastern bishops. The proceedings came to a complete halt when the Syrians learned on June 26 that Nestorius had been excommunicated four days earlier. They promptly excommunicated Cyril from

9. J. N. D. Kelly tells the story in detail, complete with calendar dates of occurrences, in *Early Christian Doctrines*, 2nd ed. (London: A. & C. Black, 1960) 310–30. He cites as his primary sources letters of Cyril, Nestorius, and Celestine. See also his entry under Celestine's name in *The Oxford Dictionary of Popes* (Oxford: Oxford University Press, 1986) 41–42, referencing *Patrologiae Cursus, Series Latina* 50:417–558 and *Patrologiae Cursus, Series Latina—Supplement* 3:18–21; *Acta Conciliorum Oecumenicorum*, ed. Eduard Schwartz [1.1.7] 125–37; and *Liber Pontificalis*, ed. Louis Duchesne, vol. 1 (Paris: Thorin, 1886) ccxi, 230f. For a more complex calendar of events see G. R. Driver and Leonard Hodgson, "History of the Controversy," in Nestorius, *The Bazaar of Heracleides* (Oxford: Clarendon, 1925) xvii–xxix.

his see of Alexandria, likewise Memnon, the bishop of Ephesus, and rejected the *Twelve Anathemas*. When the legates of Pope Celestine I reached Ephesus on July 10 they examined Cyril's *Twelve Anathemas* and his second letter to Nestorius condemning his views. These had been read out to sixty like-minded bishops at the opening session of June 22, which Nestorius refused to attend. These documents had been heard but not acted on. The papal delegation on Celestine's previous pro-Cyril instructions approved them, thus creating the *Acta* of the Third Ecumenical Council.[10] At that point the Eastern bishops abandoned Nestorius for the sake of peace, allowing the condemnation of Nestorius's views *as defined by Cyril* to stand. Cyril had chosen the council as the site of the resolution of the argument and *his* version of what Nestorius believed as the object of condemnation, although the *Twelve Anathemas* were never made part of the *Acta* of the council.

After Ephesus: Nestorius's Defense

But things did not end with the council's adjournment, which had given satisfaction to neither party. Much debate and discussion followed it over the next two years, chiefly by letter. When in November 430 Nestorius had received the *Twelve Anathemas* from Cyril, Nestorius passed them on to John of Antioch, who in turn submitted them to two Eastern theologians, Theodoret of Cyrrhus and Andrew of Samosata, for refutation. Their critique was incorporated into a *Formulary* (σύμ-βολον) *of Union* probably drafted by Theodoret, which John then sent by letter to Cyril, to Sixtus III, the new bishop of Rome, and to Maximian, Nestorius's successor in Constantinople.[11] When it was pondered by Cyril well after the council, we know from a letter of his (Letter 39, *Laetentur Caeli*) that he received it with surprising enthusiasm,

---

10. See excerpts from the *Letter of Cyril to Nestorius* (*ES*, 250) containing the word θεοτόκος, *The Twelve Anathemas* (*ES*, 252–63), and *The Condemnation of Nestorius* (*ES*, 265). The latter document declares the Lord Jesus Christ to have been "blasphemed by him" while the *Anathemas* use the phrase καθ᾽ ὑπόστασιν three times, and "two persons or even subsistences," "only a divine habitation [ἐνοίκησις]," and an "assumed" or "God-bearing human being" once, all of which are denied. A "nature" of "flesh and blood like ours" and the possession "of the Spirit" by Jesus are affirmed.

11. See Driver and Hodgson, "History of the Controversy," xxii–xxiv; Kelly, *Early Christian Doctrines*, 328–29. The *Formulary of Union* contained no mention of *The Twelve Anathemas*, the deposed Nestorius, or the controversy.

since it did not contain his favored terms "one nature" or "hypostatic union." What it did affirm was a union of two natures in a unity of person (ἑνὸς πρόσωπον), by which was meant an individual; whether a divine individual or a human individual is left unspecified. The union "that has been accomplished" is "between perfect God and perfect man composed of a rational soul and a body, begotten before the ages from his Father in respect to his divinity but likewise . . . from the Virgin Mary in respect to his manhood, consubstantial with the Father in respect to his divinity and at the same time consubstantial with us in respect of his manhood."[12] The wording of this creedal statement in its totality made concessions to both sides and obviously paved the way for the acceptance of the Chalcedonian formula of 451 based on Leo's *Tome*—but also on the previous work of an Oriental genius unnamed.

Nestorius, a disgraced and vilified but never a broken man, wrote *The Bazaar of Heraclides* in his defense and using a pen name, in which he says that he had always held that Jesus Christ was one who had both a divine and a human nature "in the person of the union."[13] That is a way of saying that no one can know the exact terms of the union between perfect Godhood and perfect manhood in one person (πρόσωπον). It is by all means not a fusion of two natures into God-manhood. The liturgy of the Church of East Syria that survives Nestorius, which could well be the formula in which he presided at the Eucharist in Antioch before coming to Constantinople, may provide a clue. He prayed to God,

> Holy . . . and glorious. . . . Holy also is your only-begotten Son, our Lord Jesus Christ, with the Holy Spirit, who is with you eternally and who is from your nature and the maker of all creation. . . . It was not robbery that he regarded himself to be your equal but emptied himself and took the form of a servant, perfect man, who from a reasonable, intelligent and immortal soul and from a mortal human body and [the Lord God] conjoined it to him[self] and united it with him[self] in glory, power, and honour, to the son [who was] of a passible nature . . .[14]

12. Kelly, *Early Christian Doctrines*, 329.

13. See note 9. The Greek text is no longer extant. Paul Bedjan, in 1910, edited an early sixth-century Syriac translation of a work previously unfamiliar to the West, *The 'Book of Heraclides of Damascus': The Theological Apologia of Mar Nestorius* (Piscataway, NJ: Gorgias, 2007).

14. Text of *Mar Nestorius* [ll. 20–30] in Bryan D. Spinks, *Mar Nestorius and Mar*

The *anaphora* of Theodore, long-term bishop of a Cilician see, declared that "the only-begotten God the Logos who being in the likeness of God, it was not robbery that he regarded this, that he is the equal of God; but he emptied himself and took the form of a servant when he descended from heaven and put on our humanity, a mortal body and a reasonable, intelligent, and immortal soul from the Virgin Mary by the power of the Holy Spirit."[15] Theodosius's prayer had not included, as Nestorius's would later do, the Pauline phrase of the birth of Jesus from a woman and under the Law, so that he might redeem those under the Law and "enliven all those who were dead in Adam."[16] Taken together, the two Eucharistic Prayers engage in much multiplication of words to put beyond all doubt the conviction in faith that the Creator and creature are "conjoined" in "the one Lord Jesus Christ," without any attempt to explain in non-biblical vocabulary how that conjunction might have been effected. The conjunction simply was. The eternal and the temporal became the One who was known by the name Jesus and the twofold title Lord and Christ.

Nestorius's output was prodigious in letters, sermons, and treatises, but it is impossible to know what part of it was available to Cyril in the framing of his *Twelve Anathemas*. The Alexandrian may have possessed much of Theodore's writings and felt confident that the *assumptus homo*, in whom the Word dwelt in incomprehensible depth and intimacy, was the concept shared by the whole Antiochene school—hence, Word-man, a divine ὑπόστασις and a human πρόσωπον joined in a moral but not a true union (ἕνωσις) of two natures in the person of the Λόγος.

Nestorius wrote his defense in exile in Libya in 451 or 452, shortly before his death. In it he refers to the triumph of orthodox faith through Pope Leo's *Tome*, sent to Patriarch Flavian of Constantinople condemning Eutyches's monophysite doctrine, but did not mention the outcome of the Council of Chalcedon (451). At one point he spoke of "the bishop of Rome" (Celestine I, d. 432) as "exercising the direction of

---

Theodore the Interpreter: The Forgotten Eucharistic Prayers of East Syria: Introduction, Translation and Commentary, Alcuin/Grow Joint Liturgical Studies 45 (Cambridge: Groove, 1999) 29.

15. *Mar Nestorius*, ll. 17–22 (ibid., 35).
16. *Mar Nestorius*, ll. 31–33 (ibid., 29).

the plotting of the Council in Ephesus against me."[17] Paul Bedjan, the French Lazarist (Vincentian), tells how many dozens of pages of the Syriac translation of Nestorius's Greek original were missing from the manuscript available to him. He hazards numerous guesses as to what the words or phrases in the Greek might have been, starting with the Syriac word *Bazaar* (*tegurtâ*), a commercial term for business or merchandise. Bedjan thinks *bazaar* is a rendering of πραγματεία meaning a treatise, business, or affair. Despite the textual state of the Syriac version, Bedjan's 1910 editing of it was followed in 1911 by the serviceable French translation of François Nicolas Nau, a diocesan priest of Paris and prolific Syriac scholar. There has been no problem whatever in understanding Nestorius's defense of his writings, as taken by Cyril to be heretical and so understood by the Ephesian Council. Nestorius's *apologia* is dense, diffuse, and maddeningly repetitive but totally clear as to its main contention: that he has never held or taught any of the positions on the mystery of the incarnation repudiated by Cyril as not consonant with Catholic faith.

Nestorius's first book is devoted to a summary of all the christological errors the church has experienced up to his day, then to a heated denial that he has held or taught any of them, above all that in Christ there are two sons, the Son of God and the son of Mary. [18] Toward the end of that book he takes on Cyril's theory of a hypostatic union, saying that since Cyril conceives it to be a natural union, namely of a human nature with the divine hypostasis, it deprives that nature of the capacity to accept sufferings freely. As a result of that union, Christ was constrained to act as he did. Moreover, Cyril's hypostatic union is open to the charge of the possibility of the eternal Logos's, namely, Deity's, suffering on the cross.

The exiled patriarch devotes the remainder of his defense to what he did and does hold on the incomprehensible mystery of the incarnation. He rejects Cyril's vocabulary and argument as inadequate, as he had Mary's title θεοτόκος to account for her bearing the human infant Jesus as well as the eternal Λόγος. Adopting a term he thinks satisfactory, not to explain the mystery but to avoid error in speaking of it, he turns to πρόσωπον. Literally the word for "face," it connoted in

17. Nestorius, *Bazaar of Heracleides*, 375.
18. See ibid., 7–185.

ordinary Greek parlance a human person and, *faute de mieux*, the eternal Logos—in both cases one to whom one's acts must be attributed. Thus equipped verbally, Nestorius holds that two πρόσωπα became one πρόσωπον of the union. How that could be or in what the union consisted Nestorius did not presume to explain, since no human can know the workings of the eternal Word. That would require an intimate knowledge of deity, which no creature possesses. But Nestorius was sure that a prosoponic union fit the revealed facts of faith better than the theory of a hypostatic union, which did not retain the fullness of human personhood. To the obvious charge, which Cyril made stick at Ephesus, of Nestorius's belief that Mary bore two πρόσωπα, in effect Nestorius's answer was, "By no means, one, the πρόσωπον of the union." To Cyril's more obvious charge, "You believe in the fusion of two natures into one nature, anticipating Eutyches' error," Nestorius's response would have been, "I never held with one theandric nature in Christ, while my opponent drifts dangerously toward it."

On every page of the first and second parts of book 2 of *The Bazaar*, the Antiochene argues for the prosoponic union of a divine and a human πρόσωπον, not a hypostatic union, denying heatedly that it is a merely moral union of two persons.[19] Deserting the word φύσις as unsatisfactory to describe that which is proper to deity in God and humanity in man, he writes:

> Let it not be said that God is in the body metaphorically [the Syriac *bash'ilū* for the Greek θέσει, "in verbal figure"] but [that he is] . . . God the Word, who . . . exists eternally and came to be in the bodily frame and exists in the bodily frame, without having come forth out of his own οὐσία into the οὐσία of the flesh, or having undergone birth in the flesh from our οὐσία only . . ."

Two οὐσίαι inhabiting one human body? But that was already the faith of the church, deity and humanity conjoined in one person. It is Nestorius's faith, he maintains.

> For human is the nature which issued from Mary . . . and truly it belonged to our Saviour. For [as regards] the οὐσία of God the Word and as regards the οὐσία of man, I dissociate myself from you [Cyril], and not only as regards the term; for I have said, "I object not to the appellation of the Virgin, the Mother of Christ,

19. See ibid., 186–335.

for I know that she is to be honoured who received God, from whom the Lord of all [ὁ τῶν ὅλων] came forth."[20]

A careful study of *The Bazaar* reveals that Nestorius was no Nestorian heretic, as Western scholarship has long supposed and a limited number of Eastern Orthodox churchmen have also done more recently.[21]

But is the Nestorian (East Syrian, Persian) church a heretical communion? The West, and many Eastern Orthodox, all of whom define themselves as orthodox on the basis of the Chalcedonian definition, have been pleased to think so. They have based their view on statements in the introduction to the definition of the church's faith at Chalcedon:

> Those who try to deny the proclamation of the truth through the heresies they have devised [οἰκείων] have resorted to a useless vocabulary [κενοφωνίας]. . . . others by denying the Virgin the title God-bearer [θεοτόκος] by which she is designated create confusion and compounding, introducing one nature of flesh and then stupidly conjuring up a passible divine nature of the Sole-begotten. . . . Some try to corrupt the mystery of the divine dispensation by declaring in their imprudent madness that the one Begotten of the holy virgin Mary was a man and no more, dealt with in the synodal letters of the blessed Cyril sometime head of the church at Alexandria to crush the craziness [φρενοβλαβείας] of Nestorius and his ilk.[22]

Talk about giving a dog a bad name!

The damaged reputation of the "Antiochene Shepherd," the title accorded to Nestorius in the midst of that vitriol, is unlikely to be restored. But continuing scholarship into Nestorius's true position and the force of each term used by both litigants in the context of the times may pave the way for the Catholic West and the Orthodox East to acknowledge that the East Syrian or Persian church was not then and is not now a heretical communion. That church has such a marvelous record of the spread of the gospel and of fidelity to the apostolic faith that the stigma long attached to it can and should be removed by the church

20. Ibid., 192–93.

21. For a corrective to older scholarship, see John Meyendorff, *Imperial Unity and Christian Divisions: The Church from 450–680 A.D.* (Crestwood, NY: St. Vladimir's Seminary Press, 1989).

22. *ES*, 300.

of the West, which imposed it through its Roman bishop Celestine I. This stigma remained in the Chalcedonian prose of the papacy of Leo I before the church experienced an East-West division.

6

Propter Nostram Salutem: The Cross and Our Salvation

THOMAS J. SCHÄRTL

UNIVERSITY OF AUGSBURG

St. Anselm's Violence?

A rather vulgarized version of St. Anselm's *Cur Deus Homo* looks at the death of Jesus Christ as a juridical means to a certain end, that is, as a necessary punishment that eventually leads to the justification of the sinner. The impact of St. Anselm's soteriology in Latin Christianity was incredibly heavy. And it is therefore not surprising that Gianni Vattimo pointed to two highly problematic aspects that seem to be part of Christian soteriology: violence and economy.[1] Taken at face value both accusations seem to have some validity since the bloodiness of the cross traditionally appeared to be the cause of our salvation and the quantity of Christ's suffering appeared to be the currency and exchange rate of God's grace. If we read a key passage in St. Anselm's *Cur Deus Homo* with a theologically unbiased mind the economic connotations of spiritual facts literally jump at us:

> The substance of the question was: why God became man, so that he might save mankind through his death, when it appears that he could have done this in another way. You have respond-

1. See Gianni Vattimo, *Jenseits des Christentums. Gibt es eine Welt ohne Gott?* (Munich: Hanser, 2004) 155–66.

ed to this question with many cogent lines of reasoning, and
have thereby shown that it was not right that the restoration of
human nature should be left undone, and that it could not have
been brought about unless man repaid what he owed to God.
This debt was so large that, although no one but man owed it,
only God was capable of repaying it, assuming that there should
be a man identical with God. Hence it was a necessity that God
should take man into the unity of his person, so that one who
ought, by virtue of his nature, to make the repayment and was
not capable of doing so, should be one who, by virtue of his
person, was capable of it. . . . You have furthermore proved that
the life of this man is so sublime and so precious that it can suffice to repay the debt owed for the sins of the whole world, and
infinitely more besides.[2]

If we examine St. Anselm's vocabulary and his train of thought the
following line of argument might result:

1. On the side of humanity there is a *debt* caused by sin. Based on
   that debt humanity owes something to God.

2. Ultimate (divine) justice requires the *payment* of the *debt* in
   question.

3. Since humanity is not in a position to *pay off* the *debt* a substitute
   is required who is able to cover the magnitude of the *debt* and, in
   humanity's stead, take on the responsibility.

4. Only Christ, as the God-man, is in a position to cover the magnitude of the *debt* and to come up with an almost unlimited magnitude of grace.

5. Christ's suffering on the cross is the *price* that *pays off* humanity's
   debt and, furthermore, by overachievement, opens the way to have
   forgiveness for any further *debt*.

To Vattimo it is the equation of suffering and grace that undermines
the supreme benevolence of the Christian God as well as the unconditioned character of salvation. In other words, God's forgiveness—according to a standard theory of salvation—has a price tag attached to it.
The price is the suffering of a completely innocent man (the God-man

2. Anselm, *Cur Deus Homo* 2.18; quoted from *Anselm of Canterbury: The Major
Works*, ed. Brian Davies and G. R. Evans, trans. Janet Fairweather, Oxford World's
Classics (New York: Oxford University Press, 1998) 348.

Jesus Christ); and this rather brutal act is the only way to achieve God's mercy. But can the suffering of an innocent human being pay any price of whatever needs to be paid off? And doesn't negotiated and acquired mercy threaten one important aspect of mercy—its being an unsolicited gift that is freely given?[3]

A thought experiment, of the kind that is used in contemporary philosophical and ethical discussions, might help us to see the main point Vattimo was alluding to.[4] Just imagine that the President of the United States manages to imprison some of the most dangerous terrorists on the planet. Let us agree, for the time being, that all of those terrorists deserve serious punishment. It might be within the framework of our concept of justice to set most of these terrorists free when the head of the group is willing to reveal crucial information and to undergo serious punishment in exchange for the liberty of the rest of the group. But how would we react if the son of the President of the United States under the described circumstances stepped up and said, "Father, let these men go; punish me instead"? And what would we say if the president agreed to follow that advice and to set the terrorists free while having the life of his son taken away under the most brutal form of death penalty? Wouldn't such a procedure spit in the face of justice (any kind of justice we can think of)?

One might ask whether this analogy is truly accurate. But why should it be inaccurate? It is precisely modeled according to the above-mentioned Anselmian line of argument. But, from its rather critical undertone, it also brings to light that the notion of responsibility includes a first-person perspective—at least from a modern point of view: Nobody else can take away my responsibility. Paying off my debt might be a wonderful thing for somebody who is eager to help me within a strictly *economic* framework (and even within such a framework the idea remains highly problematic). But within the framework of moral

<hr/>

3. For a comparable assessment based on a purely biblical notion of forgiveness see Wilfried Härle, *Dogmatik*, 2nd ed. (New York: de Gruyter, 2000), 323–24.

4. A comparable thought experiment has been developed by the famous philosopher David Lewis; see his "Do We Believe in Penal Substitution?," in *Trinity, Incarnation, and Atonement*, ed. Michael Rea, Oxford Readings in Philosophical Theology 1 (Oxford: Oxford University Press, 2009) 308–13, esp. 308: "It is unheard of that a burglar's devoted friend serves the burglar's prison sentence while the burglar himself goes free; or that a murderer's still-more-devoted friend serves the murderer's death sentence."

responsibility the whole idea of a surrogate responsibility becomes dubious if not unjust in the most straightforward sense of the word.[5]

How significantly the connection of "debt," "payment," and "suffering" (with all the violence included) has shaped soteriological patterns in everyday piety can be seen when we take a look at Paul Gerhardt's (1607–76) congregational song (used in everyday service) quoted by famous theologian Dorothee Sölle. The song alludes to the Trinitarian Father who puts the burden of redemption and atonement on the shoulders of his Son:

> Go, my child, and take to yourself / the children whom I shut out / for punishment and the chastisement of wrath. / The punishment is severe, the wrath is great; / You can and shall release them, / through dying and through blood.[6]

Sölle admits that the whole concept looks rather strange if not totally incomprehensible from a modern point of view. Nevertheless, to a certain extent the idea of being in community and showing solidarity with the sufferings of other people—introducing liberation theology to some aspects of St. Anselm's grammar—might give us some theological reason, according to Sölle, to stick to the idea that the cross is indeed the means of our salvation.[7] In Sölle's own theological viewpoint the cross becomes *the* symbol of political protest, thus an entirely dangerous symbol:

> Love has its price. The cross expresses love to the endangered, threatened life of God in our world. It is no longer a question of a biophilic embracing of life which spares itself the cross. The more we love God, the threatened, endangered, crucified God, the nearer we are to him, the more endangered we are ourselves. The message of Jesus is that the more you grow in love, the more vulnerable you make yourself.[8]

5. For a critical reassessment of St. Anselm's soteriology see Hans Kessler, *Die Theologische Bedeutung des Todes Jesu: Eine Traditionsgeschichtliche Untersuchung* (Düsseldorf: Patmos, 1970).

6. Quoted in Dorothee Sölle, *Thinking about God: An Introduction to Theology*, trans. John Bowden (Philadelphia: Trinity, 1990) 121; *Gott Denken: Einführung in die Theologie* (Stuttgart: Kreuz, 1990) 160.

7. See Sölle, *Thinking about God*, 121–34; *Gott Denken*, 161–75.

8. Sölle, *Thinking about God*, 134; *Gott Denken*, 175.

In other words: The cross appears to be a symbol of love. But, how so? Isn't it—once we strip off all the economic vocabulary in order to over-come this business-related idea of salvation—reduced to a mere symbol of passion and virtue? How could such a symbol be the true source and cause of our salvation? Aren't there better role models of supra-human compassion and virtuous suffering in the world (one might think of Socrates's death or Mahatma Ghandi or Martin Luther King) that reveal the basic act of being compassionate and documenting solidarity with other human beings (especially with the marginalized and suppressed ones) in human history? If the bloodiness and violence of the cross is a necessary part of Jesus' heroism, one is tempted to ask: Heroism to what end? Is it sound to picture Jesus as social revolutionary or a lead-ing humanist?[9] If we reject the theological message of the Gospels in favour of a substantially political message in Jesus' teachings, it is clear that such a political program was watered down and spiritualized by the Gospels. Or, to phrase it differently, the cross cannot be explained by human heroism, if we take the Gospels' core messages seriously. There remains a *theo*logical core which requires further consideration.

A "Legal" Grammar of Salvation

Some interpretations of St. Anselm have tried to point to a different direction.[10] For example, Peter Hünermann, as did William Loewe[11] in the English-speaking world, offers a variety of remarkable insights that reveal a deeper ethical theory in St. Anselm's soteriology. What we call "debt" and "payment" has to be seen as a circumscription of what should be called "order" and "restitution." The guiding principle in all of this is, according to Hünermann's closer reading of St. Anselm's

9. For this kind of picture see John Dominic Crossan, *Jesus: A Revolutionary Biography* (San Francisco: HarperCollins, 1994).

10. For a ground-breaking new direction that has influenced a fresh look at St. Anselm's soteriology in the German-speaking world, see Gisbert Greshake, "Erlösung und Freiheit: Zur Neuinterpretation der Erlösungslehre Anselms von Canterbury," *Theologische Quartalschrift* 153 (1973) 323–45; and Raymund Schwager, "Logik der Freiheit und des Natur-Wollens. Zur Erlösungslehre Anselms von Canterbury," *Zeitschrift für Katholische Theologie* 105 (1983) 125–55.

11. See William P. Loewe, *The College Student's Introduction to Christology* (Collegeville, MN: Liturgical, 1996) 166.

basic notions, not divine wrath but divine honor.[12] And this is, literally, crucial since for St. Anselm the participation in divine honor as well as the aiming of all deeds at God's honor is the very essence of human action as such. Phrased that way, the restitution of divine honor is the ultimate condition for moral agency (based on order, goodness, and, as astonishing as it may sound in this context, beauty under the burden of original sin).[13] An ultimately dishonored and disgraced God would be an entirely inaccessible goal of moral agency for human beings[14]—so that any further disgrace would threaten the very destiny of human agency *tout court*:

> Thus, the honor of God is the measurement for the free agency of God and man. From this twofold premise the inner logic of salvation in Christ follows, according to Anselm, as a result. Along the way of his argument St. Anselm excludes a variety of possible solutions that would contradict the nature of divine as well as human freedom. Thus, God cannot simply respond to original sin with his mercy. He would overlook sin in such a case. There would be no restitution of the essential order of creation and its relation to God. On the one side, the honor of God would not be acknowledged as a constitutive moment for human freedom; moreover it would be placed as something external to man. Man as man would not be taken seriously; he would remain enslaved to himself. On the other side, God would not be faithful to himself either.[15]

---

12. See Peter Hünermann, *Jesus Christus: Gottes Wort in der Zeit. Eine Systematische Christologie* (Münster: Aschendorff, 1994) 199–202.

13. See Anselm, *Cur Deus Homo* 1.12–15.

14. See ibid., 1.24.

15. Hünermann, *Jesus Christus*, 201; "Somit ist die Ehre Gottes das Maß für das freie Handeln Gottes und des Menschen. Aus dieser doppelten Prämisse resultiert nach Anselm die innere Sachlogik der Erlösung durch Jesus Christus. Im Verlauf seiner Argumentation schließt Anselm eine Reihe von Lösungsmöglichkeiten aus, die der Freiheitsstruktur Gottes wie des Menschen widersprechen. So kann Gott auf den Sündenfall nicht einfach mit seiner Barmherzigkeit reagieren. Er würde damit über die Sünde hinwegsehen. Es fände keine Wiederherstellung der wesensgemäßen Ordnung der Schöpfung und ihrer Beziehung zu Gott statt. Die Ehre Gottes wäre einerseits nicht als konstitutives Moment der menschlichen Freiheit anerkannt, vielmehr lediglich als etwas Äußeres für den Menschen gesetzt. Der Mensch wäre als Mensch nicht ernstgenommen, er bliebe sich selbst versklavt. Andererseits wäre Gott sich selbst ebensowenig treu." All translations from Hünermann's work in this essay are by Thomas Schärtl.

Hünermann points to the fact that God's dignity requires his divine (and therefore unbreakable) faithfulness towards himself as an outcome of divinely immutable necessity (a necessity being the outcome of dignity). [16] Therefore, a simple act of mercy—in St. Anselm's very own concept—would not have resolved the problem of a dishonored and disgraced God. A human act of restitution (including a surplus of meaning based on the fact that the human agent in this case is simultaneously a divine agent) was required to do justice to divine dignity and honor as well as to human dignity and morality.

Maybe this line of thought becomes more digestible and approachable once we think of *debt* and *payment* as *mere metaphors* that, for the time being, should be crossed out and replaced by variables we might fill with different metaphors or—if accessible—with ethically significant concepts:

1. On the side of humanity there is an x caused by sin. Based on that x humanity owes something to God.

2. Ultimate (divine) justice requires the y-ment of the x in question.

3. Since humanity is not in a position to y the x a substitute is required who is able to cover the magnitude of the x and, in humanity's stead, take on the responsibility.

4. Only Christ, as the God-man, is in a position to cover the magnitude of the x and to come up with an almost unlimited magnitude of grace.

5. Christ's suffering on the cross is the *price* that ys humanity's x and, furthermore, by overachievement, opens the way to have forgiveness for any further x.

It might be another thought experiment to fill the blanks with phrases that stem from more modern ethical considerations. It might be noteworthy that Peter Abelard (amongst others) has pioneered this kind of different, ethically more sensitive approach—seeing Christ's death as the role model of love (not just a requested human love but, moreover, a divine love that is so great a gift that no human being can

---

16. See Anselm, *Cur Deus Homo* 2.17.

afford to deny it).[17] Nevertheless, for the time being, let us try a rather Kantian approach circling around the concept of *virtue* and *paradigm*:

1. On the side of humanity there is a *lack of virtue* caused by sin. Based on that *lack of virtue* humanity owes something to God.

2. Ultimate (divine) justice requires the *replacement* of the *lack of virtue* in question.

3. Since humanity is not in a position to *replace* the *lack of virtue* a substitute is required who is able to cover the magnitude of the *lack of virtue* and, in humanity's stead, take on the responsibility.

4. Only Christ, as the God-man, is in a position to cover the magnitude of the *lack of virtue* and to come up with an almost unlimited magnitude of grace.

5. Christ's suffering on the cross is the *paradigm of virtue* that *replaces* humanity's *lack of virtue* and, furthermore, by overachievement, opens the way to have forgiveness for any further *lack of virtue*.[18]

It is noteworthy that the reformulation keeps the Anselmian logic to a certain extent.[19] Still, we are dealing with the notion of *replacement*, which silently points to a certain understanding of justice and the no-

17. See Peter Abelard, *In Rom.* 3.26 (Lib. II, solutio) [*Fontes Christiani*, Zweite Reihe, 26/2:288]: "Nobis autem videtur, quod in hoc iustificati sumus in sanguine Christi et Deo reconciliati, quod per hanc singularem gratiam nobis exhibitam, quod Filius suus nostrum susceperit naturam et in ipsa nos tam verbo quam exemplo instituendo usque ad mortem persistit, nos sibi amplius per amorem adstrinxit, ut tanto divniae gratiae accensi beneficio nihil iam tolerare propter ipsum vera reformidet caritas."

18. For the role of these ideas within the concept of religion, see Immanuel Kant, *Die Religion innerhalb der Grenzen der Blossen Vernunft* (*Religion within the Limits of Reason Alone*), B 106–16.

19. This is an important result since some magisterial remarks on contemporary soteriology are eager to underline that the cross must not serve as a role model of compassion and virtue only; it has to be seen as a true "cause" of our salvation. For a closer examination of magisterial propositions concerning matters of soteriology, see Hünermann's comment on Jon Sobrino's so-called "notification" in Hünermann, "Moderne Qualitätssicherung? Der Fall Jon Sobrino ist eine Anfrage an die Arbeit der Glaubenskongregation," *Herder Korrespondenz* 61/4 (2007) 184–88. See also Knut Wenzel, *Die Freiheit der Theologie. Die Debatte um die Notifikation gegen Jon Sobrino* (Ostfildern: Grünewald, 2008). My point here is that a salvation theology that is wrapped around the idea of virtue and obedience (and presupposes the notion of paradigm) still requires, to a certain extent, the Anselmian grammar.

tion of duty, which is expressed in the fact that humanity owes God something. Furthermore, there is the idea of a vicarious representation still in place—a representation that is necessary to perform what cannot be done by any other human being. Although in St. Anselm's view vicarious representation is a very sophisticated concept, theological tradition (especially after the Reformation) reveals a slippery slope that turns vicarious representation into some sort of penal substitute.

The experimentally illustrated, somewhat Kantian transformation of Anselm's grammar, however, seems to be more appealing to a modern audience since the concepts of virtue and paradigm are able to include a morally significant first-person perspective that does not simply objectify Christ's achievements and demote them to a mere currency in the bargain of grace and justification. But can this transformation help us to improve the staurocentric logic of Latin soteriology?

Hünermann, although rather sympathetic with St. Anselm's soteriological grammar, is willing to admit the almost inevitable limitations of Anselmian concepts:

> The specific characteristics as well as the limitations of the Anselmian line of argument consist of the fact that the relationship of divine and human freedom has been developed on the basis of legal terms. Within a legal grammar it is about a mutual and unhindered acknowledgement of those subjects that freely take part in it. Man's sin is the refusal of acknowledging God and not just a particular event which relates to one moment within a basically legal relationship. Therefore, the restitution requires an unconditioned, infinite acknowledgement. This kind of acknowledgment of the Father which is exercised in Christ's death on the cross can be a benefit to the sinners because it is all about a legal relationship.[20]

---

20. Hünermann, *Jesus Christus*, 203; "Die Eigentümlichkeit und damit zugleich auch die Grenzen der Anselmschen Argumentation liegen darin, daß das Freiheitsverhältnis Gottes und der Menschen auf der Ebene des Rechts entfaltet wird. Im Bereich des Rechts geht es um die gegenseitige und vorbehaltlose Anerkennung der beteiligten Subjekte als freier. Die Sünde des Menschen ist Verweigerung der Anerkennung Gottes und nicht ein partikulares Geschehen, das sich auf ein Moment innerhalb des fundamentalen Rechtsverhältnisses bezieht. Deswegen fordert die Wiederherstellung auch eine unbedingte, unendliche Anerkenntnis. Diese von Jesus Christus in seinem Kreuzestod vollbrachte Anerkennung des Vaters aber kann den Sündern zugute kommen, da es im wesentlichen um ein Rechtsverhältnis geht."

To put it in a nutshell: St. Anselm's theory is spelled out in legal terms that, in one way or the other, are determined by rules of contract and, to a certain extent, by rules of honor and dignity. It needs to be added, nevertheless, that for St. Anselm a legal grammar is nothing less than a meta-ethical concept based on a theistic framework. Still, this legal grammar needs translation so that it is not misunderstood by a world-view that has separated the (public-related) purely legal sphere from an (subject-related) ethical area. So even with the best theological inter-pretation at hand, through the lenses of modernity a *vulgarized* version of St. Anselm's God still—pardon the following expression—looks like the chairman of Cosa Nostra in rural Sicily (even if this is exactly not what St. Anselm's meta-ethical point of view wanted to say).[21] Within such a framework it can be explained why the "acknowledgement of divine honor and the restitution of God's dignity" require the bloody cross of Christ as a key instrument. Only if we are willing to look at the cross as the implication of Christ's life and virtue, message, and self-understanding, which is an accidental but nonetheless relevant and important implication, could we serve the Anselmian meal with lots of Kantian gravy to modern sensibilities. Otherwise, we are stuck with the problem of violence again, and this very problem is ultimately caused by the legal grammar that serves as the basis of St. Anselm's soteriology itself.

Thomas Pröpper, whose own soteriological concept tries to com-bine a modern idea of moral liberty with a genuinely theological notion of salvation, points to the specific problems in St. Anselm's grammar—problems that won't go away even in the light of the kindest interpreta-tion of *Cur Deus Homo*:

> Despite the justified corrections of certain interpretive clichés, one should admit I think a certain automatism with respect to the idea of atonement in St. Anselm's concepts. For why else, if not for the difficult-to-comprehend reason that God's very honor demanded it, did the re-acknowledgment of God (which nevertheless belongs to human responsibility and is part of hu-

21. This is, at the end of the day, the heart of the feminist critique of Latin soteriol-ogy. See for example Joanne Carlson Brown and Carole R. Bohn, eds., *Christianity, Patriarchy and Abuse: A Feminist Critique* (New York City: Pilgrim, 1989). For a defence of the so-called penal substitution view see Thomas R. Schreiner, "Penal Substitution View," in *The Nature of Atonement: Four Views*, ed. James Beilby and Paul R. Eddy (Downers Grove, IL: InterVarsity, 2006) 67–98.

man dignity) not only require a previous divine revelation that puts human sin on trial and restitutes freedom, but also an act of atonement performed by the sacrifice of life to repay this debt? The act of atonement demanded furthermore is not adequately performed by guilty man but only by the sinless God-man. It is still only the initiative of the merciful God that opens the possibility of just reconciliation, but the death of Jesus is not conceived as the effective expression of forgiveness, but as satisfaction, as the condition for the abatement of sin.[22]

The restitution of divine dignity and honor could have been performed, as Pröpper underlines, by a divine act of revelation alone. Why would God need the bloodiness of the cross and the suffering of the innocent? How is the cross— as an event of redemption, punishment and payment—in any way related to such an understanding of dignity that preserves and re-establishes this revelation? Is there any way of understanding the specific impact of the cross on God's restored honor once we set the legal grammar of deed, deviation, and punishment aside? German theologian Jürgen Werbick comes to a similar conclusion: Although one needs to re-detect the often underestimated moral theory and "legal" logic in Anselm's "rational" soteriology, the result looks rather ambiguous: On the one side its medieval legal theory of mediation conflicts on a contract basis, which stabilizes Anselm's grammar and makes it rationally accessible.[23] On the other side it is the suffering of the innocent—seen as a substitute and surrogate suffering—which

---

22. Thomas Pröpper, *Erlösungsglaube und Freiheitsgeschichte: Eine Skizze zur Soteriologie*, 2nd ed. (Munich: Kösel, 1988) 78–79; "Trotz dieser begründeten Korrektur an den Klischees mancher Interpreten läßt sich, meine ich, nun doch eine gewisse Verselbständigung des Sühnemotivs in Anselms Gedankengang nicht übersehen. Denn warum sonst eigentlich, wenn nicht aus dem schwer vollziehbaren Grund, daß es Gottes eigene Ehre verlangte, bedarf die Wiederanerkennung Gottes, die allerdings in die Verantwortung des Menschen fällt und seine Würde ausmacht, zuvor nicht etwa nur der die Sünde des Menschen richtenden und seine Freiheit aufrichtenden Offenbarung, sondern eben auch seines die frühre Schuld begleichenden Sühneaktes durch das Opfer des Lebens? Eines Sühneaktes zudem, der als solcher dann doch nicht vom schuldigen Menschen, sondern einzig vom sündelosen Gottmenschen hinreichend geleistet werden konnte. Wohl ist es allein die Initiative des barmherzigen Gottes, welche die Möglichkeit der 'gerechten' Versöhnung eröffnet – aber Jesu Tod wird nicht als wirksame Gestalt der Vergebung, sondern als Genugtuung: als Bedingung des Sündennachlasses gedacht." Translation by Thomas Schärtl.

23. See Jürgen Werbick, *Den Glauben Verantworten: Eine Fundamentaltheologie* (Freiburg: Herder, 2000) 474–76.

threatens the true notion of divine justice. Contract theory allows for the idea that the cross of Jesus serves as a basis to domesticate God's justified wrath and to preserve humanity from being completely erased and dumped as a foul and rotten outcome of sin. Still, the unjustified suffering of the only innocent man objectifies the idea of redemption and transforms its very core into some kind of divine-human business transaction that balances an invisible spiritual bank account without taking visible care of what needs reconciliation and restitution in human existence and history.

Prerequisites for a Theology of Salvation

Instead of discussing what St. Anselm truly wanted to say about salvation—in other words, whether St. Anselm's "grammar of salvation" (as illustrated while using variables) is more important than the metaphors (the notions of debt and payment he is using)—let us take a look at what is generally required by a theologically sound theory of salvation:[24]

1. The cross has to be seen as a "cause" of salvation. However, the idea of cause cannot and must not be understood as a physical cause or as a quasi-physical means toward a certain end (i.e., the cross seen as some sort of currency). Furthermore, the cross must not be separated from Jesus' life and teachings although it may have a unique role that makes it irreplaceable eventually.[25]

---

24. It is legitimate to ask where these prerequisites may come from. To put it in a nutshell, they are a part of and a burden of the tradition, seen from a rather meta-theological and meta-doctrinal point of view. Prerequisites like these were expressively elaborated whenever the Magisterium had to deal with certain challenges in soteriology such as those presented by the Reformation and, lately, by liberation theology. Further challenges have appeared with modernity and modern moral theory. See Jürgen Werbick, *Von Gott sprechen an der Grenze zum Verstummen* (Münster: Lit-Verlag 2004) 339; for a meta-theological perspective, see 343–45. "Meta-theological" in this context indicates a reflection of theological concept formation and the conceptual and axiomatic prerequisites of theological consideration. From this perspective I would regard the above-mentioned soteriological theorems as the axiomatic constituents of any Christian soteriology. As always, however, axiomatic constituents still leave some room for their application.

25. See Hans Kessler, *Erlösung als Befreiung* (Düsseldorf: Patmos, 1972); Karl Lehmann, "'Er wurde für uns gekreuzigt': Eine Skizze zur Neubesinnung in der Soteriologie," *Theologische Quartalschrift* 162 (1982) 298–317.

2. The cross has to be seen as an essential token of what is a more general type that may serve as a headline to Jesus' life as such—to be the revelation and self-mediation of the one God as the triune identity. It is thought provoking to consider the cross—as Hans Urs von Balthasar does—as a revelation that depicts the inner-Trinitarian relationship between Father and Son. [26] Even if we may not fully agree with him, it is of utmost importance to respect the cross as a token of divine revelation.

3. The value of the cross is not the magnitude of suffering implied by it but—as Joseph Ratzinger for the German-speaking and Bernard Lonergan for the English-speaking worlds have underlined clearly—the greatness of love revealed through it.[27] If we talk about love in a christological context, we are confronted with the need to keep a double aspect intact: The cross needs to be interpreted as a sign of love between Father and Son, and it must be seen as a symbol of love between God and humanity.

It is not at all easy to keep all of these requirements intact and to stick to the indicated rules expressed in this set of soteriological prerequisites. Furthermore, it is easy to see that we are faced with a number of dangers: If we shouldn't take the cross as a somewhat "robust" cause of our salvation, what will remain of its theological relevance and impact beyond the fact that it expresses Jesus' admirable conviction to stick to his message until the very bitter end of the story?

And if we think of the cross as a revelation of the triune God how could we avoid the rather questionable idea that there is a drama going

---

26. See Pröpper, *Erlösungsglaube und Freiheitsgeschichte*, 197–98; Eberhard Jüngel, *Gott als Geheimnis der Welt: Zur Begründung der Theologie des Gekreuzigten im Streit zwischen Theismus und Atheismus*, 6th ed. (Tübingen: Mohr, 1992) 470–505; *God as the Mystery of the World: On the Foundation of the Theology of the Crucified in the Dispute between Theism and Atheism*, trans. Darrell L. Guder (Grand Rapids: Eerdmans, 1983) 343–68; Hans Urs von Balthasar, *Die Handlung, Theodramatik* 3 (Einsiedeln: Johannes, 1980) 297–305; *The Action*, trans. Graham Harrison, vol. 4 of *Theo-Drama: Theological Dramatic Theory* (San Francisco: Ignatius, 1994) 319–28.

27. See Joseph Ratzinger, *Einführung in das Christentum* (Munich: Kösel, 1968), 231–35; *Introduction to Christianity*, trans. J. R. Foster (San Francisco: Ignatius, 2004) 213–23. See also Bernard Lonergan, "The Redemption," in *Philosophical and Theological Papers 1958–1964*, ed. Robert C. Croken and Frederick E. Crowe, vol. 6 of *Collected Works of Bernard Lonergan*, ed. Frederick E. Crowe and Robert M. Doran (Toronto: University of Toronto Press 1996) 3–28.

on between Father and Son that is unloaded on the Son and finalized
by his very surrender to the authority of the Father?[28] Despite the psychologically revealing subtext of this idea—a subtext that would make
Nietzsche and Freud rather happy and would fuel the engine of their
standard criticism of Christianity—it confronts us with a rather problematic concept of God that can hardly be defended in the light of contemporary atheism. Or in other, simpler terms: Is a vengeful, wrathful,
uncontrollably angry and bloodthirsty God worthy of worship? Is there
anything like eternal wisdom and infinite goodness in the unloading of
the Father's wrath onto the innocent Son? Christopher Hitchens, who
offers an outsider's perspective, can serve as an incentive to question
the whole idea of a wrathful God who is pleased by the sacrifice of his
own innocent Son:

> However, the idea of a *vicarious* atonement . . . is a further re-
> finement of the ancient superstition. Once again we have a fa-
> ther demonstrating love by subjecting a son to death by torture,
> but this time the father is not trying to impress god. He *is* god,
> and he is trying to impress humans. Ask yourself the question:
> how moral is the following? I am told of a human sacrifice that
> took place two thousand years ago, without my wishing it and
> in circumstance so ghastly that, had I been present and in pos-
> session of any influence, I would have been duty-bound to try
> and stop it. In consequence of this murder, my own manifold
> sins are forgiven me, and I may hope to enjoy everlasting life.[29]

As we see, the trinitarian logic of the cross has to be spelled out carefully; the idea of divine wrath has to be reinterpreted in terms of relational
divine attributes so that we have to state that anger is not a genuinely
divine attribute but a circumscription of a relation humans experience
given the reality of sin.

28. See Balthasar, *Die Handlung*, 322–27; *The Action*, 332–38. Of course, there is
still the possibility to take Balthasar's comments on divine wrath and anger as considerations about rather metaphorical expressions that speak about the human experience of sin as the experience of divine absence. But this still leaves us with the question
why the only innocent human being (Jesus of Nazareth) has to be put into this situation of divine absence. Why would this make anything better for the human situation?
It is still the Anselmian grammar that can be found between the lines of Balthasar's approach and that puts comparable limitations on Balthasar's soteriology. For Balthasar's
critical evaluation of St. Anselm, see *Die Handlung*, 345–51; *The Action*, 255–61.

29. Christopher Hitchens, *God Is Not Great: How Religion Poisons Everything* (New
York: Twelve, 2007) 209.

In the light of comparable coping with the underlying concepts of St. Anselm's grammar, Jürgen Werbick argues for the need of a benevolent and sophisticated translation of soteriological models into the modern horizon of human self-understanding.[30] Otherwise, a petrified Anselmian theory would lead to a vulgarized economic and legalistic idea of salvation, which at the very end of the day would take away Christianity's credit in a modern and postmodern world. Christopher Hitchens's eloquently elaborated bashing of staurocentric soteriology is, seen from a wider perspective, just the peak of the iceberg and documents very vividly the effects a vulgarized Anselmian soteriology may have—a frightening chill and a bitter taste that can only be answered by sheer disgust. Werbick's vote can be read, in terms of contemporary discussions, as a kaleidoscopic view on the cross, which means that we have to be very careful in applying a single formula to our soteriological question.[31] This is exactly what Bernard Lonergan has recommended—embracing the variety of biblical motives that try to "explain" the cross theologically.[32] Lonergan's vote echoes the famous and sophisticated multilayered soteriology we can find in Thomas Aquinas, who, as it stands, does not abandon Anselm's grammar but tries to enrich it significantly.[33]

But this leads us to the third prerequisite: The idea of the cross being the symbol of divine love appears to be somewhat cynical given the brutality of Jesus' suffering and the loneliness (a theologically bitter loneliness) of his death. If the cross is meant to reveal anything this has to be circumscribed in the context of Jesus' life and mission, which are as such symbols of God' ultimate presence. As stunning as it may sound for the moment, the cross has to be explained as a sign of God's presence, once we follow the inner logic of the concept of revelation. But

30. See Werbick, *Von Gott Sprechen*, 338–43.

31. See Joel B. Green, "Kaleidoscopic View," in *The Nature of Atonement*, 157–85.

32. See Lonergan, "Redemption," 12–24.

33. See Thomas Aquinas, *Summa Theologiae* 3, q. 46–48. On this point I disagree with Eleonore Stump, who believes that Aquinas subsumes Christ's passion under two functions, namely "satisfaction and meriting grace"; see Stump, "Atonement According to Aquinas," in *Trinity, Incarnation, and Atonement*, 267–93, esp. 270. In contrast, I would underline that Aquinas offers, as Lonergan has pointed out, a variety of models circling around the concepts of vicarious representation, paradigm of virtue and love, etc. Among other models we find the ideas of sacrifice and meriting grace as well, but Thomas would shy away from offering a one-way formula for soteriology.

how can we claim something like that without neglecting the apparent fact that the cross is the ultimate moment of divine absence? What is revealed through the cross is, by all means, the impact, magnitude, omnipresence, depth, and harmfulness of violence as an almost transcendental given. In René Girard's "mimetic theory," the cross of Christ reveals the horror of violence, the burden of the mimetic mechanism, and a necessary interruption of the mimetic processes:

> Christ does not achieve this victory [i.e., the cross and resurrection] through violence. He obtains it through the renunciation of violence so complete that violence can rage to its heart's content without realizing that by so doing, it reveals what it must conceal, without suspecting that its fury will turn back against it this time because it will be recorded and represented with exactness in the Passion narratives.
>
> If we do not detect the role of mimetic contagion in the genesis of social orders, the idea that the principalities and powers are disarmed and exposed by the Cross will appear absurd, a pure and simple inversion of the truth. But our text [i.e. the letter to the Colossians] affirms that the Crucifixion produces just the contrary of this standard wisdom. This wisdom says that the principalities and powers nailed Christ to the Cross and stripped him of everything without any damage at all to themselves, without endangering themselves. Our text thus boldly contradicts everything so-called common sense regards as the hard and sad truth about the Passion. The powers are not invisible; they are dazzling presences in our world. They hold the first rank. They never stop strutting and flaunting their power and riches. There's no need to make an exhibition of them: they put themselves on permanent exhibition.[34]

But it is still questionable whether this "revelation" of violence (through the so-called scapegoat mechanism) carries a divine message and furthermore causes whatever we call "salvation."

As we try to do justice to the above-mentioned prerequisites we need to develop a notion of salvation before we can say something more specific about the impact of the cross. Let us therefore start with the very foundation of an appropriate theory of salvation as expressed in the first prerequisite. A possible way to a more appropriate understanding of salvation has to face the fact that the whole life of Jesus Christ

---

34. René Girard, *I See Satan Fall Like Lightning* (Maryknoll: Orbis, 2001) 140.

is relevant to understand and to bring about what we mean by salvation. So the life of Jesus becomes the hermeneutical tool to understand
the cross.[35] Christologically speaking, Jesus' life is the ultimate way to
participate in God's life.[36] The cross has to be seen as a key instrument
in enabling our participation in God. From a modern perspective this
newly regained participation must have an effect on our human self-
understanding: In the end God's act of grace must be an act that leads
to a new autonomy and freedom—a re-established, morally oriented
and internally dignified and justified freedom which can be the source
to overcome the many dimensions of sinful divisiveness.[37]

Now what would this kind of dignified and justified freedom look
like? Wouldn't it look like a truly liberated freedom that acts autono-
mously in accordance with God's will and not against it? This makes
obedience the guarantee of a truly liberated freedom that is secure and
safe enough—thanks to obedience—not to fall prey to sin and its temp-
tations. Jesus' life and death may be seen as an anchor point for a new
history of human obedience. His life and death establish a new relation
of acknowledgement between God and human beings (and this is, as
the benign reader may want to notice, in accordance with the very basis
of an Anselmian grammar of salvation): The life of Jesus documents,
as a paradigm, how humans acknowledge God as the true Lord and
the basis of all life and grace. And on the other side, God gets affected
by the human condition and by the human life through the life and

---

35. See Werbick, *Soteriologie* (Düsseldorf: Patmos, 1990) 174–225.

36. Of course, the idea of participation can be more easily established within the
framework of Greek (especially Platonic) metaphysics, in which humanity can be seen
as one certain property that exists as a whole and that gets affected by what is done by
any individual being who is part of that whole. In these coordinates the participation
of Christ in God leads to the participation of humans in God through Christ. It is more
complicated to spell out these ideas within a modern framework, for which humanity
exists as an abstract entity only (humanity appears to be something like a set). In this
context it becomes crucial to spell out participation in terms of relations between those
individuals that "form" the whole (humanity) in question. Hansjürgen Verweyen's idea
of salvation as "mutually becoming each other's icon and image" can be a way to meet
the needs of modern metaphysics and to translate the notion of participation into a
modern system of metaphysical coordinates; see Verweyen, "Gibt es einen Stringenten
Begriff von Inkarnation?," in *Incarnation*, ed. Marco Olivetti (Padua: CEDAM, 1999)
481–89; Verweyen, *Gottes letztes Wort: Grundriss der Fundamentaltheologie*, 3rd ed.
(Regensburg: Pustet, 2000) 233–55.

37. See Pröpper, *Erlösungsglaube und Freiheitsgeschichte*, 199–220.

death of Jesus Christ. God's way becomes irrevocably connected to a human life. In the middle of sin and sinfully manifested violence God himself establishes a new space to overcome the distance between God and human beings because he identifies himself with one human being. The death *and* resurrection of Jesus Christ are signs to indicate that violence and destruction are not the very last things we have to face in this world. As we see, the resurrection of Christ becomes another equally important hermeneutical instrument to understand the Cross.[38] Would the cross have any relevance for us without resurrection? In St. Anselm's logic one might be inclined to say "yes"; but this reveals the very limitations of that logic. Theologically speaking, without resurrection the cross must be a rather empty symbol, pointing nowhere, remaining entirely ambiguous.

Using the idea of participation we may also be in a position to make sense of more classic concepts and metaphors of salvation. In his writings Jürgen Werbick, one of the most subtle and most outspoken critics of any vulgarized Anselmian logic, points to the richness of New Testament interpretations of Holy Friday.[39] There is not only the idea of sacrifice, and where we find it this notion has to be put into the context of a rich Jewish theology of sacrifice as a means of covenant-based reconciliation. Furthermore the New Testament talks about a variety of other models and metaphors to illustrate the impact of the cross (of course, looked at through the lenses of Easter Sunday). In addition to the notion of sacrifice we will find the idea of covenant, liberation, transformation etc. Jesus is the substitute of humanity in all these respects; he is the pillar stone of a New Covenant, the ultimate and final sacrifice, the gate to our liberation from all evil, the New Adam who anticipates humanity's entire transformation. All of these ideas are guided by the New Testament concept of reconciliation and participation. Once we take reconciliation and participation to be the fundamental grammar of what New Testament theology wants to say about salvation we are in a position to reread all the other models of salvation we may have encountered. So, for instance, when we say that Jesus is the *sacrifice* to wash away our sins then we have to use the context of a strong theory of God's *covenant*: Jesus' cross is God's signature under a new "contract"

---

38. See Werbick, *Soteriologie*, 116–30.

39. See for example Werbick, *Den Glauben Verantworten*, 427–627.

with human beings; God expresses his irrevocable "yes" to human beings—neither sin nor violence can destroy this "New Deal." A new contract is established on the basis of Jesus' dedication and obedience.[40] He has dedicated his whole life and fate to the mystery of God whom he calls "Father." When we say that the death and resurrection of Jesus Christ are *liberation* then we have to express that the power of sin and the power of violence get deprived through the life, death, and resurrection of Jesus:[41] Jesus anticipates a common future in which sin, violence, and death will be overcome totally. When we say that Jesus is a *substitute* for humankind then we want to express that the history of violence and sin finds a counter-history in Jesus Christ: substitution starts with the fact that "Adam's disobedience" gets ultimately replaced and overridden by a true model of obedience. [42] Thus, the distance between God and humankind gets completely transformed through the life and death of Jesus Christ. His life is the first true life that meets God's standards. This life is like a new color on the sinfully dark paintings of humankind. And so this unique life has an impact on every life. The cross is the last consequence of Jesus' life, a true life of dedication and obedience to the only one who is worth dedication and worship—God.

At this point we are able to determine the very core of any theology of salvation that we cannot abandon without destroying the idea of salvation as such, regardless of its Anselmian phrasing: in the first place God demands acknowledgement, and God can demand obedience on the basis of his initial offer. God's creational love is the basic initiative to bring about the creaturely world. So it is neither surprising nor a problematic misrepresentation of basic insights when St. Anselm used legal terms to spell out the grammar of acknowledgment. The one-sidedness of legal logic, however, carried the danger of further misunderstanding of the truly inner logic of salvation, which consists of a mutuality of acknowledgment between God and the created reality.

---

40. See Werbick, *Soteriologie*, 248–59.

41. See ibid., 137–46.

42. See ibid., 259–75.

The Paradox of Forgiveness: Truly Divine Forgiveness

If we look back on what we have said about the prerequisites of a theology of salvation and about participation in God as the ultimate idea of salvation, it becomes clear that salvation is not anything like a business and not an object (in the most "objectifying" meaning of the word) that can be bought by paying a certain price. In this context, it is entirely misconceived to think of the cross as a price or a necessary punishment somebody has to undergo in order to cheer up God's bad mood. But what is the meaning and the impact of the cross? To interpret the resurrection of Christ as a symbol of our full participation in God is one thing—and it is a very accessible idea, nevertheless. To see the cross as a means of participation and reconciliation (and, in one way or the other, as a sign of divine revelation) is another, rather mind-boggling issue. How can we truly make sense of the cross without falling prey to the archaic idea of bloody sacrifice and necessary punishment?

To arrive at an acceptable conclusion we have to introduce our premises—premises that are somewhat different from Anselm's legal logic. Among others, the famous theologian Romano Guardini claimed in his epochal book *The Lord* that the cross should not have happened. Initially, Christ came to proclaim the kingdom of God.[43] The cross took place as part of the drama of revelation. It was, so to speak, the divine detour of salvation as an answer to sin itself. The cross was, in other words, God's loving embrace of nothingness, which was (and is) the brutal and unavoidable consequence of sin:

> The plunge from God towards the void which man in his revolt had begun (chute in which the creature can only despair or break) Christ undertook in love. Knowingly, voluntarily, he experienced it with all the sensitiveness of his divinely human heart. The greater the victim, the more terrible the blow that fells him. No one ever died as Jesus died, who was life itself. No one was ever punished for sin as he was, the Sinless One.[44]

Although Guardini still bows his head before St. Anselm, at least verbally, the above-mentioned quotation underlines that there is no drama between the eternal Father and the eternal Son but rather a drama be-

43. See Romano Guardini, *The Lord*, trans. Elinor Castendyk Briefs (Washington, DC: Regnery, 1982) 36–37.

44. Ibid., 466.

tween God and sin. Father and Son are "on the same side as well as on the same page." The cross had to happen because of God's patient response to sin. In a similar way Raymund Schwager underlines that the cross is the result of a drama—a drama caused by sin and violence.[45] The cross had to happen because of the rejection of the original message and the divine messenger; its occurrence is a result of dramatic necessity (rather than the result of an a-temporal divine law that requires brutal punishment). The cross is God's non-violent response to violence, his powerfully powerless willingness not to step aside when confronted with the violent forces of sin. But, still, what exactly makes the cross a dramatically necessary part of divine revelation? And why is the cross the utmost symbol and "cause" of salvation? Schwager recalls the core of true obedience which offers a counter-paradigm to sin:

> Whoever no longer determines himself by his own spirit, but entrusts this to the heavenly Father in order to allow himself to be totally determined by him, achieves a sort of openness and availability which go beyond our earthly experience and can only be hinted at by parables. The image of the clay with which the potter works can give a clue to this readiness to be shaped, and yet the one dying on the cross was much more than clay, for it was with his whole being and above all with his free will that he became a totally available "material." What at first appeared only negative in the "victim situation" was transformed with his death into a limitless opening of himself and making himself available, and abandonment of himself and total trust. His dying as total act of handing over already contains agreement in advance to that imminent sovereign action of the Father, which was realized in the resurrection of the crucified one. His will allowed itself to open up through obedience in suffering to a complete uniting in love with the will of the Father.[46]

The cross reveals God's "no" to sin (and what sin consists in); the cross reveals infinite obedience. But, still, what would this have to do with reconciliation? Doesn't the appraisal of obedience sound like God's ultimate judgment over sin and over the sinner?

---

45. See Raymund Schwager, *Jesus im Heilsdrama: Entwurf einer biblischen Erlösungslehre* (Innsbruck: Tyrolia, 1990) 77–87, 232–42; ET *Jesus in the Drama of Salvation: Toward a Biblical Doctrine of Redemption*, trans. James G. Williams and Paul Haddon (New York: Crossroad, 1999) 45–53, 182–91.

46. Schwager, *Jesus im Heilsdrama*, 239; *Jesus in the Drama of Salvation*, 188–89.

To introduce the premises we are looking for so desperately we need to take a step back and start over using Guardini's initial idea: The cross should not have happened; the death of the ultimate divine messenger, the brutal extinction of the Son of God, is a second "original sin." The cross is the symbol of a holocaust that should not have happened. The cross reveals what is unforgivable in itself—and so reveals the limitations of forgiveness within the logic of a human concept of justice. The fact that the cross happened reveals something absolutely divine. It reveals God's greatness: the greatness of his patience. His patience leads to a radical acknowledgment that is the basis of all reconciliation: the acknowledgment of the sinner. So the cross is not a way to satisfy a sovereign God, but quite the opposite: the cross is the way to express God's patience and mercy. Of course divine patience and mercy both require the infinity of divine love. Through the lens of a grammar of forgiveness, and the infinity of forgiveness that is required to forgive the unforgivable, the cross expresses—and this is not just some sort of theological euphemism—the infinity of divine love.

But to really understand the significant impact of the cross we have to focus on what can be called according to Jacques Derrida the *paradox of forgiveness*. Forgiveness seems to be necessary whenever something occurs that cannot be forgiven in the literal sense common to everyday understanding:

> In order to approach now the very concept of forgiveness, logic and common sense agree for once with the paradox: it is necessary, it seems to me, to begin from the fact that, yes, there is the unforgivable. Is this not, in truth, the only thing to forgive? The only thing that *calls* for forgiveness? If one is only prepared to forgive what appears forgivable . . . , then the very idea of forgiveness would disappear. If there is something to forgive, it would be what in religious language is called mortal sin, the worst, the unforgivable crime or harm. From which comes the aporia, which can be described in its dry and implacable formality, without mercy: forgiveness forgives only the unforgivable. One cannot, or should not, forgive; there is only forgiveness, if there is any, where there is the unforgivable. That is to say that forgiveness must announce itself as impossibility itself. It can only be possible in doing the impossible.[47]

47. Jacques Derrida, *On Cosmopolitanism and Forgiveness*, trans. Mark Dooley and Michael Hughes, Thinking in Action (New York: Routledge 2001) 32–33; emphasis

Within a purely legal logic forgiveness becomes necessary when we encounter the absolutely unforgivable (by standards of law). Vladimir Jankélévitch inspired Jacques Derrida's view on forgiveness. Focusing on the unforgivable, Jankélévitch writes:

> Besides, there is no reason for the oscillation to stop: the misfortune of this radical wickedness can, in turn, be the object of an exponential forgiveness; and the wickedness of this misfortune becomes a hyperbolic Unforgivable. If in becoming petrified this unforgivable were to remain ultimate and definite, then it would be nothing other than Hell: the Hell of despair. Is not the idea of an irremediable evil and one that would have the last word literally an "impossible supposition"? Fortunately, nothing ever has the last word! Fortunately, the last word is always the penultimate word ... so that the debate between forgiveness and the unforgivable will never have an end. The moral dilemma that ensues is insoluble, for if the imperative of love is unconditional and does not have any restrictions, then the obligation to annihilate evil, and if not to hate it (for it is never necessary to hate anyone), at least to reject its negating force, to put it out of action or to damage its destructive rage, such an obligation is no less imperious than the duty of love ...[48]

Jankélévitch is absolutely right in pointing to the dilemma: without forgiveness the basis of morality is lost, the ultimate good is out of sight. But with forgiveness the idea of justice seems to be threatened. Can there be infinite forgiveness for infinite wickedness (or sin, to phrase it theologically) within a finite framework? And, between the lines this is also expressed as another problem: if the oscillation between forgiveness and wickedness is endless, if there is no last word of forgiveness, what would happen to forgiveness as such? Aren't we in need of an

in original. In his creative discussion and modification of the inner logic of forgiveness Derrida refers predominantly to Vladimir Jankélévitch, *L'Imprescriptible* (Paris: Éditions du Seuil, 1987) and Jankélévitch, *Le Pardon*, Les Grands Problèmes Moraux 2 (Paris: Aubier-Montaigne, 1967); ET *Forgiveness*, trans. Andrew Kelley (Chicago: University of Chicago Press, 2005).

48. Jankélévitch, *Forgiveness*, 162. It is noteworthy that Jankélévitch takes a step back in his book *L'Imprescriptible*. With regard to the Holocaust and to the role of Germany (and with the prosperity of postwar Germany, which seems to have nothing to do with the repentance of the wicked) Jankélévitch assumes that there might be something absolutely unforgivable. For a further discussion see Derrida, *On Cosmopolitanism and Forgiveness*, 37–38.

ultimate last word of forgiveness to keep the victory of unconditional forgiveness once and for all? But doesn't this very need long for a transcendent forgiveness that surpasses the boundaries of any human, legal logic—of economy, taxonomy, and currency? Isn't this the reason why *true forgiveness* is *truly divine*? This divinity is also, to a certain extent, a sign of madness:

> Imagine, then, that I forgive on the condition that the guilty one repents, mends his ways, asks forgiveness, and thus would be changed by a new obligation, and that from then on he would no longer be exactly the same as the one who was found to be culpable. In this case, can one still speak of forgiveness? This would be too simple on both sides: one forgives someone other than the guilty one. In order for there to be forgiveness, must one not on the contrary forgive both the fault and the guilty *as such*, where the one and the other remain as irreversible as the evil, as evil itself, and being capable of repeating itself, unforgivably, without transformation, without amelioration, without repentance or promise? Must one not maintain that an act of forgiveness worthy of its name, if there ever is such a thing, must forgive the unforgivable, and without condition? . . . Even if this radical purity can seem excessive, hyperbolic, mad? Because if I say, as I think, that forgiveness is mad, and that it must remain a madness of the impossible, this is certainly not to exclude or disqualify it. It is even, perhaps, the only thing that arrives, that surprises, like a revolution, the ordinary course of history, politics, and law. Because that means that it remains heterogeneous to the order of politics or of the juridical as they are ordinarily understood.[49]

The paradox of forgiveness is mirrored in the paradox of the cross. In delivering the Son to the violence of the sinners God the Father reveals the truly unforgivable core of sin *and* forgives it, unconditionally. There is the risk that the sinner will be without any remorse or amelioration and that he remains without repentance and transformation, but this is precisely the madness of the cross, which reflects the madness of forgiveness.

If we take forgiveness as the backbone of whatever happened on the cross, we can appreciate the Lonerganian way in which William Loewe describes the cross's impact on salvation:

49. Derrida, *On Cosmopolitanism and Forgiveness*, 38–39; emphasis in original.

> Rather than continue the expanding process of sin, Jesus short-circuits it in his own person. Jesus, it seems, accepted dying out of love for the one he called Abba and out of a responsible love for all his fellow human beings. By this active refusal to play the normal game, Jesus' dying was transformed. Instead of being one more instance of the tired tale of sin and death his dying became an affirmation that some things are more important than saving one's skin. His dying became a statement that faithfulness to God and to other human beings is more important even than physical survival. His dying became an act of love for the God he called Abba and for the family into which all human beings are bound.[50]

Loewe's statement sheds new light to the Anselmian grammar—transforming the grammar of honor into the grammar of love. Within the direction of mankind to God this is absolutely the best way to understand the impact of the cross. But there is still the other way round: the direction from God to mankind that entails that we look at the cross as an event of divine revelation. We can do this once we apply the paradox of forgiveness to what happened on the cross. With this in mind we can, therefore, say: Forgiveness *transcends* the economic grammar of lawful punishment, which is meant to offer something like reimbursement, restitution, or anything that sounds like a payback for any harm that is done to others.

But what if no restitution will ever pay off the harm in question? This is the case when the idea of economic exchange and taxation of punishment literally breaks down. What cannot be restituted cannot be forgiven—this is true within the framework of a purely legal logic. What cannot be restituted can only be forgiven. The latter is true within the logic of grace. Once we apply this insight to what happened on the cross, we can say: The cross reveals the brutal and cruel depth of sin. There is no adequate punishment for the ultimate "no" to God and his message. Under the cross the Roman powers, the soldiers, the local authorities in Jerusalem, and the disciples are revealed as sinners; they are revealed as brutal executioners of violence, as sophisticated justifiers of injustice, as cowards and traitors. And with all of these people humanity is revealed as an accumulation of violence, injustice, cowardice etc. The core of their sin is revealed as the unforgivable. But simultaneously with

---

50. Loewe, *College Student's Introduction to Christology*, 170.

Christ's words, "Father, forgive them . . . ," the unforgivable is forgiven. The paradox of forgiveness is nothing that can be handled by human powers or agents. Only a truly divine agent can mediate the forgiving of the unforgivable. Forgiveness is required whenever something occurs that is beyond compensation; in this case the only way of "compensation" is forgiveness. Whenever it makes no sense anymore to claim compensation, forgiveness is the only response that remains. Forgiveness is beyond the forgivable since forgiving, in a human context, is still a way of compensation without getting compensation. So true forgiveness is divine forgiveness since it is beyond human standards of forgiving: it goes beyond the idea of compensation. It is, therefore, truly divine.

The crucifixion of the Son of God is a sin that cannot be forgiven within the human coordinates of forgiveness. There is no compensation for the crucifixion of the Son of God—it is an ultimate act performed by human beings, an ultimate act of violence. But Jesus' prayer, asking for forgiveness and revealing forgiveness, becomes a truly divine act: it offers forgiveness to something that cannot be forgiven by human standards. That God is willing and, furthermore, able (he is, actually, the only one capable of it) to forgive the unforgivable is what the cross of Jesus Christ has revealed to us. In this sense the cross was "necessary" to reveal the transcending dimensions of God's ability to forgive the unforgivable. Seeing and becoming aware of the impact of a forgiveness that transcends any human concept of forgiveness requires that the cross be put into a defining hermeneutical perspective—Easter. Whatever we may have to say about the resurrection of Christ theologically, there is one important aspect Easter adds to the cross. The resurrection of Christ is the ultimate word of forgiveness; it puts an end to ambiguity on God's side. It is, together with the cross, God's Last Word.[51] This ultimately Last Word had to become concrete, historically visible, symbolized by a divine act under the conditions of human existence to forgive the unforgivable and to reveal what God is and (only) God can do.

But let us, again, return to the question whether and how the cross is the *cause* of our salvation. The word "cause" is a burden to us since causality is a rather complicated concept that has a very objectivistic side to it. It is too easy to understand it, especially in the context of so-

51. In this regard see the theological concept of Hansjürgen Verweyen in *Gottes letztes Wort*.

teriology, in a quasi-physical but supernatural way so that we fall back into the economic taxonomy of salvation. If we want Gianni Vattimo and the divine dialectics of forgiving the unforgivable to meet halfway, we need to find a slightly different, maybe a more open, understanding of cause. So cause can be understood (in a very broad sense) as an event that brings about or triggers another event. Cause can also be something like an initial act that triggers a series of events or even a perspective that enlightens our interpretation. What happened at the cross? René Girard jumps into a mythological pattern to explain the event of the Cross: God tricked Satan—this is, although an archaic form of soteriology, a mythological representation of Jesus' death. Carefully using his grammar of mimetic theory, Girard gives us some hint to translate this mythological pattern when he writes:

> Medieval and modern theories of redemption all look in the direction of God for the causes of the Crucifixion: God's honor, God's justice, even God's anger, must be satisfied. These theories don't succeed because they don't seriously look in the direction where the answer must lie: sinful humanity, human relations, mimetic contagion, which is the same thing as Satan. They speak much of original sin, but they fail to make the idea concrete. That is why they give an impression of being arbitrary and unjust to human beings, even if they are theologically sound.
>
> Once we identify the bad contagion, the idea of Satan duped by the Cross acquires a precise meaning that the Greeks obviously sensed without succeeding in articulating it in a completely satisfying fashion. To be a "child of the devil" in the sense of the Gospel of John . . . is to be locked into a deceptive system of mimetic contagion that can only lead into systems of myth and ritual. Or, in our time, it leads into those more recent forms of idolatry . . .[52]

Girard invites us to turn our heads and to embrace some aspects, as he sees them, of Greek soteriology in contrast to a Latin tradition that finds itself trapped in the ideas of divine wrath, honor, and justice. But once we abandon the taxonomic idea of satisfaction (paying back a debt that, if we give it a close enough look, can never be paid off) we are free to see what is really initiated on the cross:

52. Girard, *I See Satan Fall*, 150–51.

The idea of Satan duped by the Cross is therefore not magical at all and in no way offends the dignity of God. The trick that traps Satan does not include the least bit of either violence or dishonesty on God's part. It is not really a ruse or trick; it is rather the inability of the prince of this world to understand divine love. If Satan does not see God, it is because he *is* violent contagion itself. The devil is extremely clever concerning everything having to do with rivalistic conflicts, with scandals and their outcome in persecution, but he is blind to all reality other than that.[53]

Jesus' cross reveals the depth of sin and violence in this world and ultimately responds to it with forgiveness. The "logic of love" Girard is alluding to fits perfectly with the paradox of forgiveness since forgiving the unforgivable presupposes the infinity of love, which is not accessible within the framework of this world. Only a transcendent source of love can, literally, carry the burden of forgiveness. Evil is a concrete, socially visible, and perceptible reality. Therefore infinite divine forgiveness has to become a similarly concrete perceptible reality. The cross is an initial act that causes this reality to become part of human history. Although human history is entirely obstructed and compromised by sin and the violence it contains, the cross and Easter Sunday initiate a counter-history to what the "prince of this world" has initiated—the miracle of forgiving the unforgivable. Simultaneously this is also the peak of divine revelation. The cross reveals God as the *One who is willing and capable of forgiving the unforgivable.*

53. Ibid., 152.

7

Anselm's *Cur Deus Homo?*
Genres of Language and the Narrative of Salvation

CHRISTOPHER D. DENNY
ST. JOHN'S UNIVERSITY

While Adolf von Harnack, Gustaf Aulén, and John McIntyre spent much of their energies investigating Anselm's place in the history of doctrine, more recent studies of *Cur Deus Homo* have brought a new set of concerns to the fore.[1] Contemporary Christian theologians have examined the relationship between the soteriological narrative of the New Testament and Anselm of Canterbury's theoretical transformation of this narrative in his *Cur Deus Homo (Why God Became a Human Being)*. This present review essay examines selected contrasting positions regarding both Anselm's rhetorical strategy in *Cur Deus Homo* and also the manner in which Anselm's text negotiates the boundaries between exegesis and theory. Reviewing contemporary interpretations of *Cur Deus Homo* demonstrates what should be obvious but is often frustratingly obscured—differing evaluations of *Cur Deus Homo* can-

---

1. See Adolph von Harnack, *History of Dogma*, trans. Neil Buchanan, 3rd ed. (New York: Dover, 1961) 6:54–79; Gustaf Aulén, *Christus Victor: An Historical Study of the Three Main Types of the Idea of the Atonement*, trans. A. G. Hebert (London: SPCK, 1931); John McIntyre, *St. Anselm and His Critics* (Edinburgh: Oliver and Boyd, 1954). The historical background for *Cur Deus Homo* is provided by Richard W. Southern in *St. Anselm: A Portrait in a Landscape* (New York: Cambridge University Press, 1992) 197–205.

not be separated from the doctrinal and soteriological positions with which interpreters approach Anselm's classic work.

Specifically, I will pursue two major goals in this essay. First, I will elucidate contrasting positions in the dispute as to whether Anselm's hypothetical soteriology uses language that is theoretical, narrative, or a mixture of both these literary genres. Second, I will show that, once differing positions on this issue have been set out, interpreters of *Cur Deus Homo* dispute whether or not Anselm has properly fixed the boundary between theory and narrative in his work properly. A dispute on this latter issue often reveals as much about the interpreter's own theological commitments and expectations as it does about Anselm's soteriological effort. William Loewe, to whom the present volume of essays is dedicated, is one of the few contemporary theologians who has paid requisite attention to this topic.

The Literary Genres of *Cur Deus Homo*—Narrative vs. Theory?

No one would reasonably deny that Anselm attempts to prove the necessity of the incarnation in *Cur Deus Homo*. The crucial question one should address is that of the means that Anselm employs in his attempted proof. Is Anselm's proof compatible with the Christian narrative? Does it draw upon the narrative of specifically Christian revelation in ways that are unacceptable for a theory?

In chapter 3 of the first book, Anselm (in his role as a character in the dialogue with Boso) notes that the classic patristic typological contrasts in soteriology, such as Adam/Jesus, death/life, sin/righteousness, tree of life/tree of Calvary, are not convincing to unbelievers. Boso responds that these beautiful pictures are not believable unless the "rational existence" of the truth that they represent precedes them.[2] What constitutes rational existence? This is an open question, for this prerequisite for adequate proof is not specified any further in *Cur Deus Homo*. One cannot anachronistically suppose that Anselm's idea of rational existence is the same as that of succeeding ages. Does Anselm's definition of rational existence compel him to choose theory or narrative? Recent interpreters take up a variety of positions in response to this question.

2. See Anselm, *Cur Deus Homo* 1.4.

When Gustaf Aulén undertook his outline of the history of sote-riology in *Christus Victor,* he classified Anselm as a firm advocate of a theoretical approach to soteriology. Aulén faulted Anselm both for not linking the incarnation of Christ to the atonement of Christ and for what Aulén saw as an unfortunate accent on the role of Christ's human nature in redemption. The greatest grievance that Aulén had with Anselm, however, was with the latter's attempt to construct a rational, juridical theory of Christian atonement. The so-called classical patristic idea of the atonement, which Aulén supported, did not try to construct a rational systematization of soteriology, and this was its strength according to Aulén. Luther, Aulén's soteriological hero, promulgated a soteriology that was superior to that of Anselm in large part because he shunned a theoretical solution to the atonement. Such a rationalistic endeavor explains away the oppositions that display God's transcendence over the orders of law and reason. Not simply *Cur Deus Homo* but all theoretical soteriology is misguided for Aulén.

Ted Peters, responding with a strong critique of Aulén's characterization of soteriological history, outlines what he understands as the essential moves in Anselm's theoretical argument in an article that compares the soteriologies of Anselm and Luther.[3] First, Anselm establishes a teleological starting point: God created humanity to enjoy perfect blessedness. Second, Anselm introduces a tension between what is and what should be. Sin has ruptured the relationship between God and humanity, frustrating God's plan. In reality, however, this plan cannot be frustrated since God is omnipotent. The third phase of the argument introduces the sinless God-human, whose reward for offering up his life to death for the sake of God's honor accrues to sinful humanity, thereby earning its redemption. According to Peters, there is a *reductio ad absurdum* that Anselm employs to safeguard the necessity of the third phase, which makes use of two sub-arguments. In the first place, forgiving humanity for its sin without any redemption would place the disobedient person in the same situation vis-à-vis God as the obedient one.[4] This would make the disobedient person like God, but that is unacceptable since only God is subject to no law. Next, such forgiveness would not repair the disfiguring of the universe that sin causes. These

---

3. See Ted Peters, "The Atonement in Anselm and Luther, Second Thoughts about Gustaf Aulen's *Christus Victor,*" *Lutheran Quarterly* 24 (August 1972) 301–14.

4. See Anselm, *Cur Deus Homo,* 1.12.

two outcomes are absurd; therefore the necessity of the God-human is secured.

Peters ends up denying that Luther and Anselm differ in that the former eschewed soteriological theory while the latter embraced it. For Peters, Anselm's apparently legalistic structure is "the means whereby God's mercy is shown to triumph," and one should not confuse the end with the means.[5] Luther, according to Peters, did not do away with the legal order, but posited it as the will of God, only to be done away with through Christ's satisfaction for human sins. Interpreting Luther differently would be to do away with his idea of justification, the forensic non-imputation of sin. For Peters, if there is a problem with Anselm, it is not with his use of theory.

Another writer who tries to explicate a foundational and theoretical approach in *Cur Deus Homo* is Alister McGrath. McGrath views rectitude as the moral foundation of Anselm's soteriology.[6] Like Peters he objects to a juridical or legalist reading of Anselm. *Rectitudo* is Anselm's description for the divine created order. Truth is a derived form of *rectitudo,* "a following of the right rules."[7] It can also mean conformity to the intended pattern of creation. McGrath offers an expanded schema treating the centrality of justice in *Cur Deus Homo*. *Iniustitia,* the human refusal to submit to God, characterizes the present human state. Humanity cannot get back to its original state of *iustitia* from its current state of *iniustitia*. Hence the need for the God-human, if indeed a redemptive sin offering is to be made.

Should it be made? At this point McGrath makes the provocative statement that "[f]rom a purely dialectical standpoint, the monograph could equally be entitled *Cur Deus non homo*."[8] God's justice, however, will not stand to see this option realized, for this would destroy the *rectitudo* of the universe, and so the God-human makes the necessary offering. McGrath makes the assumption that *Cur Deus Homo* can credibly yield a purely dialectical and theoretical reading. This is puzzling, as McGrath takes pains to show, although at times ambivalently, the interchangeability in Anselm's use of the terms *rectitudo, iustitia,*

5. Peters, "The Atonement in Anselm and Luther," 305.

6. See Alister E. McGrath, "Rectitude: The Moral Foundation of Anselm of Canterbury's Soteriology," *Downside Review* 99 (July 1981) 204–13.

7. Ibid., 206.

8. Ibid., 211.

and *veritas*—an interlocking and overlapping vocabulary that would appear to confound attempts at separating Anselm's dialectics from what could be called the moral *rectitudo* of *Cur Deus Homo*. A moral reading of Anselm appears to trump a metaphysical one at the close of McGrath's article, as McGrath locates the probable foundation for Anselm's discussion of satisfaction in the morality of penitential spirituality prevalent in Anselm's time.[9] It should be noted that Peters, following McIntyre, rejects such a penitential interpretation of satisfaction in *Cur Deus Homo,* noting that Anselm explicitly rejects this idea in the dialogue with Boso.[10]

Walter Kasper's *Jesus the Christ* follows Peters in his attempt to balance Anselm's use of *necessitas* with divine freedom.[11] Like Peters and unlike McGrath, Kasper concentrates his theoretical reading of Anselm on the theme of satisfaction in *Cur Deus Homo,* particularly as that intersects with the cosmological order. Christ as human cannot make satisfaction by mere obedience, since that obedience is obligatory for humans and there is nothing supererogatory in it to restore the honor of God. Honor for Anselm, as Kasper rightly points out, does not refer to a personal attribute of God. Instead honor refers to the cosmological and aesthetic order of creation. Honor is not an abstract legalism. Moreover, Kasper is careful to point out that it is God, and not anything else, who binds God's self to the order of justice and creation. Nevertheless, Kasper does not explicitly link the freedom of God to a recognition that Anselm may be doing something other than constructing a pure theory in *Cur Deus Homo,* for Kasper states his opinion that Aquinas corrected Anselm because "he turned into a pure suitability what Anselm intended as a proof that God *had* to act in that way."[12]

---

9. See ibid. For an explanation of *Cur Deus Homo* in light of the Benedictine Rule under which Anselm lived, see John R. Fortin, "*Satisfactio* in St. Benedict's *Regula* and St. Anselm's *Cur Deus Homo*," *The Modern Schoolman* 79/4 (May 2002) 305–11.

10. See Peters, "The Atonement in Anselm and Luther," 303–4. Symeon Rodger also notes the break between Anselm and the earlier penitential tradition on this point; see Rodger, "The Soteriology of Anselm of Canterbury, An Orthodox Perspective," *Greek Orthodox Theological Review* 34/1 (Spring 1989) 19–43.

11. See Walter Kasper, *Jesus the Christ*, trans. V. Green (New York: Paulist, 1976) 219–21.

12. Ibid., 220.

The summary of these interpretations points to a common theme in delineating the boundaries between theory and narrative in *Cur Deus Homo*—necessity. Aulén resisted Anselm in large part because he saw him as imprisoning God within the realm of necessity. For Aulén all theoretical talk that places God within the realms of law or reason is guilty on this score. Theoretical discourse and necessity here square off against narrative discourse and divine freedom. Peters disagrees with this methodological dichotomy pitting theory against narrative and necessity against freedom.

Gordon Watson moves away from this previous group of interpreters in emphasizing Anselm's methodological dependence on Christian revelation, steering the interpretation of *Cur Deus Homo* back toward its narrative qualities. Watson is helpful here because he draws upon Anselm's other works to make his argument, and refers the reader to the key distinction that Anselm made in his work *De Veritate* (*Concerning Truth*).[13] There Anselm noted that things do not participate in the truth in a Platonic sense. Rather a thing's truth is its right relation or state of affairs vis-à-vis the supreme truth, who is God.[14]

What Anselm developed in response to this idea was a construction of non-reciprocal likeness. The reality of being subsists in the Word, the essence of which exists so supremely that it alone exists in a certain sense. All other things are non-existent to a certain extent. They were created only in imitation of the Word, which is not like to any created thing since it suffers no gain or loss in relation to the mutability of its creatures. The Word is not the likeness of any created thing but the essence of created things, since created things do not possess their essences of their own accord. They only have likeness to the Word without sharing its essence. Unlike McGrath, Watson does not try to differentiate this likeness into moral categories on one hand, and metaphysical ones on the other.

Transposing this distinction from philosophy into the realm of soteriology, Watson argues that Anselm's philosophy of being preserves the freedom of the Word to create, since supreme truth outstrips creaturely truth, which does not share in the essence of the Word. Theological propositions are not the cause of supreme truth, which

13. See Gordon Watson, "A Study in St. Anselm's Soteriology and Karl Barth's Theological Method," *Scottish Journal of Theology* 42/4 (November 1989) 493–512.

14. See ibid., 499–500.

would indeed be rationalism. Rather, theological propositions are only true to the extent that they express the likeness of created things to God. Anselm's idea of theological truth, per Watson, was a relational one. Yet even this more modest formulation is problematic, because humans can never precisely determine the relationship to the infinite God since this relation originates from the side of God. With this framework in place, Watson succinctly notes that the incarnation in *Cur Deus Homo* "is no rational principle deduced from the nature of the Word, but its teleology, as its truth, is established through the lived life of the incarnate Word which presupposes a voluntary and therefore an ineffable condescension."[15] God deals with humanity freely in the incarnation and redemption, freely accommodating God's self to the created and relational truth present in the world, bringing beings back to the relationship of their creatureliness. This is not necessity at work but grace. More importantly for this argument, it is recognition that reason and the life of Christ may not necessarily be harmonized into a theoretical mode of discourse that supposedly offers an adequate interpretation of *Cur Deus Homo.*

Watson defends Anselm by noting, "the fittingness of which St. Anselm speaks is that of the way which God has actually taken in the act of atonement. The liberty of God and the creature is understood in terms of the way the Son of God has voluntarily assumed the creature's form for the creature's sake."[16] For Watson, because Jesus is freely obedient to God, this obedience serves as the measure for establishing what God can or cannot do in the order of law. This is not to say that the order of law transcends or encompasses God, but to claim that the relationship between God and creaturely truth, governed by law, is not founded upon an abstract theory but upon the narrative of Christ's free obedience to God. Here we have a different approach from that of McGrath, who attempts to found Anselm's theory of satisfaction on the supposed influence of the medieval penitential system. Where McGrath emphasizes *rectitudo* and penance, Watson chooses instead to point to Christ's obedience as the primary element in Anselm's soteriology. Where Kasper offers a reading that attempts to balance a theoretical approach with recognition of God's sovereignty, Watson explicitly

15. Ibid., 501.
16. Ibid., 511.

privileges the narrative of the incarnation over any theory that can be extricated from *Cur Deus Homo.*

William Loewe goes further and devotes an entire article to the question of the alleged rationalism in *Cur Deus Homo.*[17] Loewe probes the possibility that Anselm's actual performance in the treatise belies his methodological presuppositions. Implicit in this observation is the possible recognition that Anselm himself may be to blame for the differences among his interpreters. Anselm contrasted the *convenientiae* of the typological images of the church fathers with his own attempt to construct a soteriology based upon *ratio et necessitas.* As Loewe points out, however, Anselm was careful to characterize his *necessitas* as tentative, subject to correction by religious authority. In addition, Loewe argues that Anselm's statement that he will ascribe nothing unfitting to God, even something the slightest degree unseemly, collapses any distinction between *convenientia* and *necessitas.* Loewe notes, "[I]f 'even the slightest reason has the force of necessity,' if *ratio* and *necessitas* become practically synonymous, then no effective distinction between *necessitas* and *convenientia* remains."[18] Despite this, Loewe holds that *Cur Deus Homo* transcends the narrative of patristic soteriology.

For Anselm obedience to God fulfills humanity's purpose, which creates the good of order known as God's honor. Applied to God, honor is an analogical term drawn from the feudal order of Anselm's era. Simple forgiveness does not repair the breach to this order, which is God's will for humanity. Hence, Anselm understood the necessity for the God-human. Loewe sees this metaphysic as indicative of what he refers to as a "post-narrative mode of discourse," and credits Harnack and Ritschl with recognizing Anselm's significance in this area. René Roques offers what Loewe takes to be a better explanation of Anselm's place in soteriological history. Roques claims that Anselm wanted to bring an intelligible unity to the multiplicity of images in the intellect.

17. See William P. Loewe, "Method in *Cur Deus Homo*: Concept, Performance, and the Question of Rationalism," in *Ethnicity, Nationality, and Religious Experience,* ed. Peter C. Phan, Annual Publication of the College Theology Society 37 (Lanham, MD: University Press of America, 1995) 73–83.

18. See ibid., 75. For an older source that argues that modern interpretations of "necessity" in *Cur Deus Homo* are anachronistic, see A. M. Jacquin, "Le *Rationes Necessariae* de Saint Anselm," *Mélanges Mandonnet: Etudes d'Histoire Littéraire et Doctrinale du Moyen Age 2,* Bibliothèque Thomiste 14 (Paris: Librairie Philosophique J. Vrin, 1930) 67–78.

Nevertheless Anselm further limited his concept of *necessitas* by stating that this search for intelligible unity in soteriology was limited by God's transcendence and omnipotence: "Since, then, the will of God does nothing by any necessity, but of his own power, and the will of that man was the same as the will of God, he died not necessarily, but only of his own power."[19]

Loewe sides with those who view *Cur Deus Homo* as theoretical discourse, but is unwilling to grant it the title of "proof," much less the title of "rationalistic exercise." In his view Anselm fails to deliver a proof because of his precritical attachment to a philosophical idealism that confuses understanding and judgment, intelligibility and truth. For Anselm understanding something is the same as finding necessary reasons for it. This conflates systematics and apologetics. Loewe breaks new ground here with his recognition that *necessitas* and *convenientia* converge in *Cur Deus Homo*, and stakes out a unique position in the discussion, one that leaves open the possibility that a "convenient theory" could be the same thing as a "necessary theory," and that the former still qualifies as postnarrative discourse. A convenient theory can exist and still fall short of being a proof. Loewe is able to argue this consistently because he recognizes *Cur Deus Homo* "as marking the emergence of a systematic-theoretic mediation of the intelligibility of the Christian narrative."[20] Loewe's exposition differs from the earlier views in that he explicitly claims that the theory of *Cur Deus Homo* does not intend to negate the importance of the Christian narrative of salvation. One confidently deduces from his essay the recognition that post-narrative does not mean anti-narrative. The theory here mediates the narrative without replacing it. Loewe points the way toward a reading of Anselm that respects the distinction between narrative and theory while letting them peacefully coexist.

---

19. Anselm, *Cur Deus Homo* 2.17, in *Saint Anselm: Basic Writings*, trans. S. N. Deane, 2nd ed. (La Salle, IL: Open Court, 1962) 286.

20. Loewe, "Method in *Cur Deus Homo*," 79. For a comparison with Loewe's position regarding the relationship between the biblical narrative and Christian doctrine in *Cur Deus Homo*, see Stephen R. Holmes, "The Upholding of Beauty: A Reading of Anselm's *Cur Deus Homo*," *Scottish Journal of Theology* 54/2 (May 2001) 189–203.

Theory and Narrative in *Cur Deus Homo*

If Loewe is correct in his recognition that *Cur Deus Homo* contains
two different genres within the same text, where are the boundaries between theory and narrative in the text? In accord with the goals stated
at this essay's outset, one can address this question by moving to three
different authors, the first of whom disagrees with Anselm's construal.
Symeon Rodger criticizes Anselm from the perspective of Eastern
Orthodoxy.[21] Rodger states that Anselm made *iustitia* the theoretical
foundation of his soteriology, albeit an *iustitia* that attempts to partake
of the same cosmic grounding that McGrath sees in Anselm's use of *rectitudo*. Both authors reject a juridical interpretation of their respective
theoretical foundations on which to approach *Cur Deus Homo*. Thus
far Rodger is in line with most of the views already surveyed. Rodger
diverges sharply from the other views, however, in attacking Anselm's
grasp of the biblical narrative as it relates to sin and death. He claims
that to interpret Anselm's use of the honor of God as equivalent to God's
maintenance of the created order, as McIntyre, Kasper, and Loewe do,
is a tendentious reading.[22] Rodger holds that Anselm's language of punishment implies "that he who punishes equally had the option of not
punishing."[23] For Rodger this demonstrates that Anselm's understanding of death was that it is not "automatically" consequent to Adam's
sin, and hence "based exclusively on divine prerogative and therefore
is, properly speaking, a result of a juridical or external order," even if
Anselm understood *iustitia* in general in a non-juridical way.[24]

According to Rodger this runs counter to Genesis 2:18:

> Patristic tradition, by contrast, sees the death to which all
> men are subject precisely as the ontological result of the Fall.
> Illustrative of this fact is the wording of Genesis itself. God did
> not say to Adam, "If you eat of it (the tree of the knowledge of
> good and evil) I shall kill you," but rather, "in the day that you
> eat of it, you shall die."[25]

21. See Rodger, "The Soteriology of Anselm."
22. See ibid., 28.
23. Ibid.
24. Ibid.
25. Ibid., 29.

Rodger, unwilling to stray far from the narrative of Genesis, claims "death was an inescapable result of the fall, not only as far as man was concerned, but also, in a very real sense, as far as God was concerned as well."[26] Creation means that God submits to a voluntary helplessness. Anselm was mistaken then when he posited the choice of punishment or satisfaction as the only possible answers to human sin. Humanity's fall into death is not God's punishment but something that God permits to happen within the free order of creation. Rodger claims that sin and death are not "ontologically" connected for Anselm, but only linked by the juridical actions of God after the fact. Finally, hinting at his own interpretation of the relation between theory and narrative in *Cur Deus Homo,* Rodger offers the telling comment, "[A]n identical conclusion in doctrinal issues says nothing about the presupposition behind it or the route taken to arrive there."[27]

For Rodger, Anselm was wrong in understanding the human dilemma as one that is determined by the gravity of sin. Rodger names death as the real enemy of humanity. What reason is there for a distinction? The reason is that Rodger makes a sharp distinction between what he refers to as the ontological and metaphysical realm on one hand and the logical and legal realm on the other. The former is based upon the cosmological interdependence of created life with its loving obedience to God, while the latter aims to create a separation between a cosmological reality such as life and legal realities such as sin and law. Rodger dislikes Anselm's penchant for stressing the legal approach and the concomitant division it apparently posits between human nature and the punishment humanity suffers. Only the legal order could possibly envision the punishment/satisfaction dilemma as even a hypothetical possibility. Anselm phrases his discussion of the unrepentant sinner possibly being admitted to the kingdom of God in legal terms. This is insufficient for Rodger. Not only would divinity and justice be undermined, but human nature itself would not remain what it is if such a sinner were granted salvation.

Eventually Rodger gets around to linking the ontological and legal orders with the literary genres of narrative and theory, respectively. He notes, "Anselm's theory of redemption has no similarity to the patristic

26. Ibid.
27. Ibid., 29–30.

explanation."[28] Again, "The whole thrust of the patristic tradition has not been to construct a theory of the redemption but to render explicit the ontological realities behind it. Theories are only necessary when these are forgotten."[29] Is Rodger in agreement with Aulén's perspective that theoretical soteriology is inherently wrong-headed? No, because in the very same article Rodger critiques Aulén's legalist reading of Anselm. Rodger, unlike Aulén, does not hold that Anselm's soteriology is completely juridical and forensic, for Rodger knows that Anselm understood his soteriology in terms of cosmology and metaphysics, but thinks the juridical language Anselm employed was not adequate to convey the proper meaning of the narrative. Rodger holds that it is only a tendentious, though prevalent, reading that equates God's honor with the maintenance of the created order that could mistakenly try to bridge this gap.[30] Where the Lutheran Aulén contends that Anselm does not recognize God's proper omnipotence over creation, the Orthodox theologian Rodger claims that Anselm's performance overstates God's direct influence in creation by apparently demonstrating that God re-deems in a forensic and voluntarist way that undermines nature's in-tegrity, despite Anselm's actual intentions. For Rodger, God has truly given up power in creation. Aulén and Rodger criticize Anselm from opposite poles on this point. When summarizing Rodger's position on the acceptable boundary between theory and narrative in Anselm's so-teriology, one could claim that he holds that for a theory to mediate the Christian salvific narrative properly, one must not separate the orders of creation and redemption, as could happen with a predominantly fo-rensic or legal soteriology.

Others see this danger, but unlike Rodger they do not believe that Anselm has divided what cannot be separated. In the second volume of his *Herrlichkeit*, Hans Urs von Balthasar devoted a chapter to Anselm and his "perfectly balanced aesthetic reason," a possible analogue to Loewe's "convenient theory."[31] For Balthasar, Anselm did not reckon the merit of Christ's death to guilty humanity. He wrote of Anselm's

28. Ibid., 37.

29. Ibid., 38–39.

30. See ibid., 27–28.

31. See Hans Urs von Balthasar, *Studies in Theological Style: Clerical Styles*, vol. 2 of *The Glory of the Lord: A Theological Aesthetics*, ed. John Riches, trans. Andrew Louth, Francis McDonagh, Brian McNeil (San Francisco: Ignatius, 1984) 211–59.

understanding of satisfaction, contra the type of argument represented by Rodger, "It is not a matter of reckoning, but of inner, ontological union."[32] For sinful humanity to enter heaven would not be primarily an affront to God's justice, but to human destiny. Unlike Rodger, Balthasar claimed that Anselm's language of sin and redemption is inextricable from the reality of human blessedness. In effect, Balthasar denied Rodger's claim that Anselm had abandoned the patristic ontological link between sin and death. For an explicit link to soteriology here, one must recall Anselm's explanation to Boso:

> *Anselm:* But while man does not make payment, he either wishes to restore, or else he does not wish to. Now, if he wishes to do what he cannot, he will be needy, and if he does not wish to, he will be unjust. . . . But whether needy or unjust, he will not be happy. . . . So long, then, as he does not restore, he will not be happy.[33]

On this point Balthasar quoted Eadmer's claim that Anselm told his astonished associates that he himself would rather suffer hell sinlessly than attain heaven while a sinner, a statement that would be masochistically nonsensical if Anselm did indeed privilege sin over death in his soteriology as Rodger claims.[34] Of course the wish is an ironic one, and it provides a context that helps to defeat a juridical interpretation of satisfaction and redemption in *Cur Deus Homo.*

Balthasar wanted to give Anselm's soteriology a Trinitarian framework. If successful, this would appear to break the back of an argument such as Rodger's. For if God's plan of redemption is God's self-communication of the kenotic loving obedience of the Son toward the Father, how could one possibly claim that Anselm granted more weight to the absence of guilt than to divine life? Since Jesus is without sin, his obedience is not an attempt to gain additional merit on his own behalf. A juridical reading can only hold if the intra-Trinitarian relations are severed from the redemption. Rodger knows this and charges Anselm on this score. Balthasar made an opposing argument based upon Anselm's little-known work *On Similes.*

---

32. Ibid., 249.

33. Anselm, *Cur Deus Homo* 1.24, in *Anselm: Basic Writings*, 250.

34. See Balthasar, *Clerical Styles*, 249.

To begin this line of inquiry, one notes that toward the end of *Cur Deus Homo* Anselm directs his attention toward an elucidation of the word *debere* (to have to, to be obliged to) in the context of both celibacy and the Trinity.[35] A person is not bound to a celibate life, and should marry if he or she wants. There is no debt here if *debere* is understood as a legal or financial debt, but Anselm points out an important point:

> [W]e use the word *"debere"* precisely as we sometimes do the words *"posse,"* and *"non-posse,"* and also *"necessitas,"* when the ability, etc., is not in the things themselves, but in something else. When, for instance, we say that the poor ought to receive alms from the rich, we mean that the rich ought to bestow alms upon the poor. For this is a debt not owed by the poor but by the rich. We also say that God ought to be exalted over all, not because there is any obligation resting upon him, but because all things ought to be subject to him. And he wishes that all creatures should be what they ought; for what God wishes to be ought to be.[36]

While one could fruitfully set this excerpt within the attempt to understand necessity and convenience in Anselm's writings, one could also use this quote to question whether Anselm really promoted any separation between redemption and creation, as Rodger claims. God wills to be exalted over all. God creates with this intent. Christ obeys the Father because that is who he is as Son. His own obedience to the Father must be grounded in what Rodger calls the ontological and metaphysical realm, for Christ as member of the Trinity is complete and is under no legal obligation to the Father. Anselm noted that the honor of God is Christ's own honor, making the point even more firmly.

In *On Similes* Anselm wrote that when one makes a vow to live a celibate life, he or she provides a human example of this Christ-like obedience. Balthasar called this a model of the atonement.[37] Celibacy is not only a gift of good works, or a ritual or liturgical sacrifice, but also the gift of one's very person. The celibate person is improved (one hopes) so that he or she may genuinely belong to Christ, which sounds

35. See Anselm, *Cur Deus Homo* 2.18.

36. Ibid., in *Anselm: Basic Writings*, 296.

37. See Balthasar, *Clerical Styles*, 251–52; Glenn W. Olsen, "Hans Urs von Balthasar and the Rehabilitation of St. Anselm's Doctrine of the Atonement," *Scottish Journal of Theology* 34/1 (February 1981) 49–61.

quite patristic and hardly juridical. Hence, the celibate person models Christ's very transcendence of all legal obligations in the redemption, despite the fact that one could speak of religious vows in legal terms. In fairness to Rodger, Balthasar had to move outside *Cur Deus Homo* in order to make this last point, but his argument bolsters the link that Anselm made explicitly in *Cur Deus Homo* between payment, human need, and human happiness. It appears that Anselm grounded his argument in terms of the contrasts between divine union and human rupture, between eternal Trinitarian life and the human death that occurs outside that life, despite the use of juridical language to mediate this argument. The fundamental contrast in *Cur Deus Homo* is not between merit and sin, *pace* Rodger.

If Balthasar does not explicitly raise the issue of the genre of *Cur Deus Homo,* his concluding remarks on Anselm in *The Glory of the Lord* help to address my present concern with locating the boundaries between theory and narrative in Anselm's soteriology. In order to begin to understand this, one should note that Balthasar wrote that freedom is the constant companion of obedience to God. Christ's obedience is the fruit of his infinite freedom. In the same way, Christ-like obedience on the part of humanity redeems it, not in a juridical way but through liberation and solidarity. If one looks at Anselm's letter to Urban II on the incarnation, one finds that Anselm reiterates the patristic ideas of universal humanity and Christ's place in it, in contrast to those of his contemporaries, the "heretics of dialectic," who deny the reality of universal substances.[38] With the patristic solidarity between Christ and humanity reaffirmed, Balthasar is not far off base when he uses this idea to link Christ's freedom with human freedom. He noted:

> Man had indeed to become free for the convenant [*sic*] with God, that is, free for absolute freedom. . . . His [Anselm's] doctrine of redemption is conceived after this pattern. It is loving, creaturely freedom, which wholly gives itself up to eternal freedom, and on its side finds a model in the trinitarian freedom of the Son, whose spontaneous loving obedience to the Father is necessitated by nothing, but in the splendour of his absolute

---

38. See Anselm, "On the Incarnation of the Word," trans. Richard Regan, in Anselm *of Canterbury: The Major Works,* ed. Brian Davies and G. R. Evans, Oxford World's Classics (New York: Oxford University Press, 1998) 233–59.

freedom is that which is most acceptable to God, and, to that extent, most necessary.[39]

Balthasar's emphasis on freedom helps to reemphasize that Anselm's soteriological theory depends upon the Christian narrative. Anselm's *necessitas* is contingent upon the narrative of a theistic world within which God freely intends human salvation, a salvation that is accomplished by incorporating humanity into the divine life.

At this point one should ask, if the intra-divine life of the Trinity is ultimately indistinguishable from humanity's final destination in the order of redemption, are they indeed even distinguishable? Michael Root warily brings these questions to bear on his own reading of *Cur Deus Homo*.[40] Root traces Anselm's argument through its initial steps. First, the goal for which God created the universe has to be accomplished. Root makes the correct and trenchant comment that the elucidation of the divine teleology in *Cur Deus Homo* stems from Anselm's understanding of creation.

For Root *Cur Deus Homo* is static and not historical in its soteriology. He writes:

> Many have noted that in CDH redemption is conceived as restoration. While this restorationist character has been exaggerated by a failure to note the teleological character of Anselm's anthropology and the importance of life in Christ beyond satisfaction, the most important work of Christ for Anselm is the removing of obstacles so that the original creative intent may be fulfilled. The original situation in creation must play an absolutely determinative role for Anselm. While many criticisms of Anselm's depiction of God as wrathful, vindictive, and unforgiving miss the mark, they do point to the rigidity of Anselm's depiction of God once one moves beyond the first moment in the story. Anselm has no way of speaking about divine spontaneity and flexibility within the narrative.[41]

Root would prefer a soteriology that recognizes God's "diachronic freedom," claiming that such a concept would speak "about God's freedom

---

39. Balthasar, *Clerical Styles*, 250.

40. See Michael Root, "Necessity and Unfittingness in Anselm's *Cur Deus Homo*," *Scottish Journal of Theology* 40/2 (May 1987) 211–30.

41. Root, "Necessity and Unfittingness," 229–30.

today in relation to what God did or intended yesterday."[42] Root wants
a divine freedom that one can understand not simply *in se* but as existing within a sequence of divine acts. Such an approach would not
indicate a change in God's intentions, but would be a referent for the
unpredictably new ways in which God acts. In Root's opinion, Anselm's
discussion of divine freedom is too immutably synchronic to incorporate these qualities.

In regards to the question of theory and narrative in *Cur Deus
Homo,* Root apparently will not accept any soteriological narrative
governed from a synchronic pole outside history. Root points out that
the word "theory" itself is the contemporary translation of the patristic
term *theoria,* an experiential knowledge and intellectual vision of God
impregnated with divine love. *Theoria* and *contemplatio* are ideas originally formulated within the philosophical and theological outlines of a
classicist neoplatonic worldview, in which the eternal and immutable
governs the temporal and mutable. Conversely, the mutable mediates,
to use Loewe's term, the immutable. Anselm's attempt to found what
Loewe referred to as a "post-narrative mode of discourse" involves
subjugating the temporal narrative beneath the synchronic nature of
God. Root's rejection of Anselm's soteriology is also a rejection of this
neoplatonic theological and chronological horizon on one hand, and
any narrative that is governed by synchronic *theoria* on the other.

This exposition leads one to note that the dispute about narrative
and theory in *Cur Deus Homo* may not only be about the relationships
of creation to redemption and of the intra-divine life to human life. This
argument is also about the ordering of time itself. It is not difficult to
understand why those theologies that reject natural theology and any
attempt to argue from the analogy of being, as seen in creation, to God,
would in turn reject the neoplatonic chronology and soteriology that
Anselm promotes. If redemption is something other than the restoration of God's plan in creation, Anselm is wrong. If Christians cannot
found a soteriology upon God's teleological plan in creation, whether
because the created order has been radically corrupted or because God
has something truly new in mind with redemption, as Scotus for one
argued, than *Cur Deus Homo* fails in its attempt.

42. Ibid., 229.

Here, however, one has moved beyond simply arguing about the literary genre of *Cur Deus Homo*. Now the issue becomes one that highlights the different doctrinal and fundamental positions with which interpreters approach *Cur Deus Homo*. In the context of the contemporary discussion, it is not hard to understand why Anselm and his theology of creation are more favorable to a Roman Catholic view of soteriology than to a classic Reformed understanding of Christian redemption. One unwilling to support any mediations of the biblical narrative will find Anselm distasteful, while those who want to bring order to the different strands of biblical and patristic soteriologies can find *Cur Deus Homo* helpful. A process theologian will likely find Anselm's neoplatonism stifling, while a theologian specializing in interreligious dialogue with Hindu and Buddhist traditions could find Anselm's partiality to the synchronic element very promising. Theory and narrative are not univocal terms whose value is equivalent for all persons. They are elements within larger intellectual horizons and their value is determined by those horizons. The proper ratios of creation to redemption and of historical time to eternity are matters of fierce debate. It is not surprising that Anselm's work provokes reactions that begin to uncover these fault lines. What is disappointing is that so much of the interpretation of *Cur Deus Homo* takes place within a particular predetermined framework that remains dimly elucidated. This framework assumes that certain values, such as freedom (often understood in a voluntarist sense) and narrative theology, are superior to obedience, order, and necessity, and its defenders often make no serious attempt to defend this scale of values. They are silently assumed. Placing Anselm in context enables one to determine what differences are matters of interpretation and what differences are matters of systematic and foundational theology.

Conclusion

Cur Deus Homo marks a transitional moment in the history of Christian soteriology as it attempts to provide "necessary" reasons for the redemption offered by Christ. In the contemporary era, a new set of concerns has provoked a new discussion of Anselm's soteriology. While some might assume that Anselm posits too much as necessarily given in his "proof," all intellectual horizons assume certain factors as given. A comparison of today's contemporary givens with those of Anselm can help to clear away much of the misunderstanding surrounding *Cur Deus Homo*. One could even hope, ambitiously, that such an approach could promote new contemporary soteriologies that have the same influence that Anselm's has had throughout Christian history.

To conclude, I note that *Cur Deus Homo* represents not only a milestone in the history of Christian soteriology, but one of Christian history's most ambitious attempts to relate the central narrative of the Christian Scripture to a theoretical theology. Understood in this light, our approach to Anselm's work reveals not only our evaluation of his ideas, but also what we expect from and hope for theology itself.

PART 3

Lonergan and Theological Method

8

The Law of the Cross and Emergent Probability

CYNTHIA S. W. CRYSDALE

UNIVERSITY OF THE SOUTH

Bernard Lonergan is known for his work on epistemology and theological method.[1] He is less well known for his writings in Christology.[2] William Loewe is one of the scholars who has attended to this latter aspect of Lonergan's work, and has made questions of salvation—soteriology—his specialty. The centerpiece of Lonergan's approach to Christ's work of salvation lies in his appeal to the Law of the Cross, as explicated most extensively in one of his Latin textbooks, *De Verbo Incarnato*.[3]

---

1. Bernard Lonergan was a Canadian Roman Catholic philosopher and theologian. His early *magnum opus* on epistemology and scientific method, originally published in 1957, is *Insight: A Study of Human Understanding*, ed. Frederick Crowe and Robert Doran, The Collected Works of Bernard Lonergan 3 (Toronto: University of Toronto Press, 1992). His later work on theological method is *Method in Theology* (New York: Seabury, 1973).

2. These consist of three Latin works as follows: *De Constitutione Christi Ontologica et Psychologica*, *De Verbo Incarnato*, and *De Deo Trino*. These works were published by the Gregorian University Press in various editions from 1956 to 1964. See the discussion of these works in John Carmody, "Lonergan's Latin Theology: Résumé and Critique," *Princeton Seminary Bulletin* 68 (1975) 81–89.

3. See Bernard Lonergan, *De Verbo Incarnato* (Rome: Gregorian University Press, 1964). From here on this work will be cited as *DVI*, with page numbers corresponding to the Latin text. English quotations come from the English translation by Charles Hefling, which is vol. 9 of The Collected Works of Bernard Lonergan (forthcoming). This English translation is cited here by permission of the Lonergan Estate.

Loewe's work has aided other scholars in comprehending this notion and its significance for the transposition of classical Christology to the modern context.

Another of Lonergan's contributions to modern thought that remains less well known lies in his explication of "emergent probability." This regards the unfolding of world process, from the subatomic level to human decision and action, as an interaction of regularities and probabilities, invariant "laws" and chance occurrences. Lonergan's work on emergent probability lies in *Insight: A Study of Human Understanding*, as he elaborates on scientific method.[4] Nevertheless, the notion of emergent probability can be fruitfully expanded to include the transformation of human brokenness into a renewed human agency that can realign the distortions brought about by sin.

In this light, redemption unfolds not through direct cause and effect, nor as a transaction of divine justice. Rather, redemption involves shifts in human acts of meaning, whereby higher configurations of mind and heart increase the likelihood of the reversal of human decline. So, a Christian theology of salvation can establish its ground, not on a violent act yielding atonement, but on a process of emergence consistent with world process itself. Renewal of life in Christ is not about control and certainty but about creating conditions of possibility for transformation. The objective of this essay, thus, is to review Lonergan's notion of the Law of the Cross (as explicated by William Loewe) and connect it to the heuristic notion of emergent probability in an effort to clarify elements of a contemporary theology of salvation.

The Law of the Cross and Historical Consciousness

In 1977 William Loewe commented: "It has become fairly commonplace to draw a line between Bernard Lonergan's explorations in methodology and his more directly theological writings."[5] These theological writings have been inaccessible to many for a variety of reasons: not only are they composed in Latin, they are written in a style of scholastic

4 *Insight*, 144–62. This discussion of emergent probability is set within the larger discussion of scientific method presented in 33–139.

5. William P. Loewe, "Lonergan and the Law of the Cross: A Universalist View of Salvation," *Anglican Theological Review* 59/2 (1977) 162–74, at 162.

theology that is more propositional than constructive. They thus can be easily written off as outdated, with nothing new to offer to the contemporary theological climate.[6] In particular, Loewe indicates that classical soteriology of the kind that Lonergan practiced is no longer current in the modern era. However, in another early article Loewe makes two assertions. First, he believes that "despite the virtual disappearance of classical soteriology from the recent theological scene," soteriological questions remain of central importance to the Christian theological enterprise. Second, he argues that "the work of Bernard Lonergan provides elements of enormous value for the task of constructing a responsible contemporary soteriology."[7]

At present, though "classical soteriology of the kind Lonergan practiced" is rare, soteriological issues have resurfaced, mostly in relation to criticisms of Anselm's "satisfaction" theory of the atonement and its hybrid offspring. Christian feminists have unpacked the cult of suffering that ensues when the central narrative of the gospel is about a father figure God who wills the suffering and death of his son.[8] As more and more "theologies from the underside" come to the fore, theologians who speak for the oppressed have revealed the triumphalistic cruelty of the cross as an instrument of imperialism.[9] The work of René Girard on scapegoating has provided a new angle from which both to understand and to criticize the violence of many atonement theories.[10]

---

6. For an early review and critique of these works, see John Carmody, "The Biblical Foundation and Conclusion of Lonergan's *De Verbo Incarnato*," *Andover Newton Quarterly* (1974) 124–36; "Lonergan's Latin Theology: Resumé and Critique," *The Princeton Seminary Bulletin* 68/2 (1975) 81–89; and "Lonergan's Trinitarian Insight," *American Academy of Religion, Philosophy of Religion and Theology: 1975 Proceedings*, 161–76.

7. William P. Loewe, "Toward a Responsible Contemporary Soteriology," in *Creativity and Method: Essays in Honor of Bernard Lonergan, S.J.*, ed. Matthew L. Lamb (Milwaukee: Marquette University Press, 1981) 213–27, at 214.

8. See Joann Carlson Brown and Carole R. Bohn, eds., *Christianity, Patriarchy, and Abuse: A Feminist Critique* (Cleveland: Pilgrim, 1989).

9. See Yacob Tesfai, ed., *The Scandal of a Crucified World: Perspectives on the Cross and Suffering* (Maryknoll, NY: Orbis, 1994).

10. See René Girard, *Violence and the Sacred*, trans. Patrick Gregory (Baltimore: Johns Hopkins University Press, 1977); *Things Hidden Since the Foundation of the World*, trans. Stephen Bann and Michael Metteer (Stanford: Stanford University Press, 1987); *The Scapegoat*, trans. Yvonne Freccero (Baltimore: Johns Hopkins University Press, 1986); *The Girard Reader*, ed. James G. Williams (New York: Crossroad, 1996).

Most recently, theologians from the peace churches—Mennonites and Quakers—have raised the challenge again: How can a good God have instituted a transaction for the forgiveness of our sins that is primarily understood as a required act of violent sacrifice?[11] In this climate, the retrieval of key Lonerganian concepts such as the Law of the Cross may prove crucial to a theology of salvation for the postmodern world.

What precisely, then, is the Law of the Cross? It is formulated as Thesis 17, the last of the theses that form the nexus of *De Verbo Incarnato*:

> This is why the Son of God became man, suffered, died, and was raised again: because divine wisdom has ordained and divine goodness has willed, not to do away with the evils of the human race through power, but to convert those evils into a supreme good according to the just and mysterious Law of the Cross.[12]

Lonergan's objective here is to determine the "fittingness" of this way of resolving the problem of evil. He takes for granted the kerygmatic claims of the New Testament narrative, along with the theological development of these in subsequent patristic writings and church councils. His aim is to elucidate the "intrinsic intelligibility" of redemption. What is the "sense" that Jesus' work of salvation makes?

Initially, it is that evil is not the final word in human history. Evil can be transformed into a higher good. This process of transformation is what Lonergan calls the Law of the Cross. In Loewe's words: "According

---

See also Raymund Schwager, *Must There Be Scapegoats?* (San Francisco: Harper, 1987); and *Jesus in the Drama of Salvation* (New York: Herder, 1999). See also the review articles by Leo D. Lefebure: "Victims, Violence, and the Sacred: The Thought of René Girard," *The Christian Century* 113/36 (1996) 1226–29; and "Beyond Scapegoating: A Conversation with René Girard and Ewert Cousins," *The Christian Century* 115/11 (1998) 372–75. More recent works that deal with mimetic theory and the atonement include Anthony Bartlett, *Cross Purposes* (Harrisburg, PA: Trinity, 2001); and S. Mark Heim, *Saved from Sacrifice* (Grand Rapids: Eerdmans, 2006).

11. See J. Denny Weaver, *The Nonviolent Atonement* (Grand Rapids: Eerdmans, 2001); and Brad Jersak and Michael Hardin, eds., *Stricken by God?: Nonviolent Identification and the Victory of Christ* (Grand Rapids: Eerdmans, 2007). For other recent evaluations of traditional soteriologies see Stephen Finlan, *Problems with Atonement: The Origins of, and Controversy about, the Atonement Doctrine* (Collegeville, MN: Liturgical, 2005); and Robert Daly, "Images of God and the Imitation of God: Problems with Atonement," *Theological Studies* 68/1 (March 2007) 36–51.

12. *DVI*, 552. Loewe cites this thesis in his own translation in "Toward a Responsible Contemporary Soteriology," 216.

to this law, sin leads to death. Death, however, if accepted out of love, is transformed. Such transformed death receives the blessing of new life."[13] In *De Verbo Incarnato* Lonergan uses this quasi-biblical language, retaining the categories of sin, death, and redemption. Loewe undertakes to transpose this approach in light of Lonergan's other works on transcendental method and his efforts to draw historical consciousness into a theology for the modern world.[14]

Lonergan's account of human consciousness—his anthropology—is grounded in the upward dynamism of wonder. In *Insight* this is discussed as the "pure desire to know" and its objective is "being": the reach of wonder is unrestricted and human persons are oriented toward knowing everything about everything. Human finitude of course makes this ultimate objective impossible. Nevertheless, human persons do ask questions and attain answers to some if not all of their queries. Cognitive self-transcendence occurs when such answers are reached.[15] In subsequent years Lonergan recognized that this cognitive self-transcendence is only one step on the way to a fuller achievement that includes distinct questions for deliberation and action. So he expanded his account to include a distinct level of value, elucidating moral knowing and its terminus in action. Thus, "Lonergan locates the fulfillment of humanity beyond knowing in the activity which strives for the actualization of value."[16]

The starting point for Lonergan, then, is a *positive* view of human persons as oriented innately to truth and goodness. It is in light of this positive orientation that human failures and the perpetuation of evil can be delineated. Sin, the theological designation of this problem, involves a failure of self-transcendence, indeed at times it includes explicit

13. Loewe, "Law of the Cross," 164.

14. See Loewe's discussion of historical consciousness as the challenge for modern theology in "Toward a Responsible Contemporary Soteriology," 215–16. He states: "The soteriological question of Christian theology becomes a matter of hope for the course of history" (216).

15. This is the basis of Lonergan's critical realism: objective knowing is possible and does occur, but not, as naïve realists would assert, merely by "looking." Knowing is a task that involves a number of cognitive operations. Still there is implicit in human consciousness an exigence that not only spurs the questions on but indicates when enough data are available to fulfill the conditions for some proposition to be true. See the discussion of the *virtually unconditioned* in *Insight*, 279–318, esp. 305–8.

16. Loewe, "Toward a Responsible Contemporary Soteriology," 218–19.

choices to avoid or misdirect the eros of the human spirit towards one's own selfish ends. Sin, according to Lonergan, involves a flight from understanding, while bias entails asking questions only up to a point—the point at which questions would direct one away from answers that would serve one's own interests.[17] Furthermore, while basic sin is a privation of a positive, nevertheless it yields moral evils—consequences—that themselves generate further misunderstanding, misdirection, disorientation.[18] So the failure of self-transcendence accumulates over time to infect a community, such that the community in turn socializes its children into the errors of prejudice, oppression, and abuse. Loewe's summary is as follows:

> The real self-transcendence which presses cognition into the service of value cannot consist simply in the progressive actuation of human potential through a series of successively richer integrations. To be born into this world is to be born into an historical process which is, among other things, shot through with dehumanizing dynamics. The familial, social, and cultural situation into which one is born contains elements which concretize a previous history of the refusal of fidelity to the demands of self-transcendence. These elements constitute an objective surd; they embody human oversight, irrationality, unreasonableness, and irresponsibility. And they are sure to combine with the structural disequilibrium resulting from the complexity of the ordered systems which compose human nature to ensure the occurrence of bias and distortion in the individual's development.[19]

In light of this analysis of human potential and its failure, Lonergan's appeal in *De Verbo Incarnato* to sin and death can be transposed. Indeed, the wages of sin is death, however, as Loewe puts it:

> Death connotes the effects of man's failure to develop, of his infidelity to the exigences of self-transcendence. It connotes man's loss of his humanity on the individual and social levels. In this

17. "Bias" for Lonergan has negative connotations, unlike its use in common parlance in which alluding to a person's bias simply means their stance in the world—their perspective. Lonergan expands on four types of bias: psychic, egoistic, group, and general. See *Insight*, 242–51; and Loewe, "Toward a Responsible Contemporary Soteriology," 222–23.

18. See *Insight*, 689–98, on basic sin, moral evils, and physical evils.

19. Loewe, "Toward a Responsible Contemporary Soteriology," 219.

light the biblical connection of death with sin which the Law of
the Cross formulates in its first step becomes a clearly intrinsic
relationship, in no way the result of some arbitrary divine decree
imposed from without.[20]

Hence, sin and its resulting "death" is not only an individual matter,
nor merely a matter of life hereafter. "Death" indicates the moral evils
that impact entire systems of meaning, whereby an increasingly irrational social situation feeds back on itself to create new generations
who are confused and systems of injustice that perpetuate themselves.
Eventually, even those who think they are trying to fix moral evils
merely repeat them. "Thus are neutralized the sources of creative and
responsible change which might counter and reverse the process. At its
limit this anti-history results in moral impotence; in religious terms, it
constitutes the reign of sin."[21]

Is there a remedy to this situation? Yes, but the crucial step—the
second element of the Law of the Cross—seems counterintuitive.
Rather than contradicting or overcoming the forces of evil, the Law of
the Cross would have us submit in loving obedience to them. Liberation
comes through entering more deeply into death itself. "The cycle of
dehumanization can only be broken through the loving obedience of
which Lonergan's formula speaks, through a fidelity to the demands of
self-transcendence which crucifies what is biased, distorted, and closed
within oneself. Death of this sort turns out to be a liberation; it frees one
for the qualitatively new life which is the reward of authenticity."[22] If this
seems counterintuitive that is because on the natural level it is impossible. It involves a supernatural work. "It follows that strictly speaking
the achievement of authenticity lies beyond man's unaided grasp; all his
striving for it consists in fact in cooperation with a prior gift."[23]

So the third element of the Law of the Cross is the new life that it
yields. While Lonergan in *De Verbo Incarnato* speaks of the blessings
of God subsequent to the voluntary taking on of evil, his later writ-

---

20. Loewe, "Law of the Cross," 173. See Charles Hefling, "A Perhaps Permanently
Valid Achievement: Lonergan on Christ's Satisfaction," *Method: Journal of Lonergan
Studies* 10/1 (Spring 1992) 51–76, which elaborates on a similar point.

21. Loewe, "Toward a Responsible Contemporary Soteriology," 224.

22. Ibid., 219.

23. Ibid., 220.

ings elucidate the felt meaning experienced in religious conversion.[24] In religious conversion one experiences an "otherworldly falling in love" in which the aspirations of the eros of the human spirit are fulfilled. The deepest desires of the human heart are met, not through effort and achievement, but through grace. One gets a glimpse of God as pure being, ultimate goodness. That towards which human consciousness in its positive orientation is headed, is encountered as gift.

So the solution to the problem of evil involves a *metanoia*, a conversion that is at once an "other worldly falling in love" and a submission to death. Self-sacrificial love is both the occasion for and the consequence of such a conversion. The intrinsic intelligibility of redemption lies in the transformation of persons and communities through a self-sacrificing love that stops retaliation in its tracks, accepts unjust treatment, even to the point of death. In so doing, the possibility of new life emerges, and the "dead" (the damages consequent to basic sin) are raised to new life.

This self-sacrificing love has as its supreme instance the incarnation of God in Jesus, his execution on a Roman cross, and his resurrection to new life. So the Law of the Cross applies first and foremost to the historical person Jesus of Nazareth. The narrative of his life, death, and resurrection is the supreme instance in which submission to "sin" (its consequences) becomes an occasion for new life to emerge. This narrative, and the ongoing kerygma and sacraments that provide both the power of symbolic meaning and the need for cognitive understanding, reveals that the evil cycle in which violence is perpetuated has at least once come to a full stop.[25] The one pure victim in history—the one who most justifiably might have retaliated—chose to suffer evil rather than to do evil. In so doing he exposed the "myth of redemptive violence" and the limits of retaliatory vengeance.[26] In participating in this narrative we discover the false promise of redemptive violence; encountering ourselves as both perpetrators and victims of evil. The mystery of resurrection embodies for us the prospect of both forgiveness and healing:

24. See *DVI*, 570.

25. See Loewe "Law of the Cross," 167–69. See also Sebastian Moore, *The Crucified Is No Stranger* (London: Darton, Longman & Todd, 1977); and Cynthia Crysdale, *Embracing Travail: Retrieving the Cross Today* (New York: Crossroad, 2001), esp. 18–39.

26. See Walter Wink, *Engaging the Powers: Discernment and Resistance in a World of Power* (Minneapolis: Fortress, 1992); and Crysdale, *Embracing Travail*, 40–68.

our deep desire for God, so long distorted and entrapped by others' and our own self-occupation, is liberated for an otherworldly and an earthly falling in love.

Lest this sound as if evil is overcome merely through contemplation, through some solipsistic inner revelation, Lonergan insists that the Law of the Cross is, for us, first and foremost a *precept*. It has the force of a moral prescription: we are called to new life by *following* Jesus—even and especially in his refusal to retaliate.

> It is for us a precept. It is a precept of loving one's enemies (Mt. 5:28–48), of daily accepting one's cross (Mk 8:34; Mt 16: 24; Lk 9:23), of the wisdom of laying down one's life for Christ and the gospel so that one truly saves one's life (Mk 8:35; Mt 16:25; Lk 9:24). It appears in the parable of the seed that dies and bears fruit (Jn 12:24-25) and in the blessedness promised to those who suffer (Mt 5:11–12).[27]

So the Christian community follows Christ's example. By embracing the sufferings entailed in our distorted world, by refusing to return evil for evil, the cycle in which sin yields consequences that further distort moral agency, yielding more sin, can become instead a cycle of healing, forgiveness, and new life. So we follow his example not only in the death he accepted but in the resurrection life that follows: "For if we have been united with him [*symphytoi*] in a death like his, we shall certainly be united with him in a resurrection like his" (Rom 6:5).[28]

In fact, this kind of redemptive movement in human living is not merely a Christian phenomenon. Whenever evil and its consequences are turned around, it is because some new possibilities arise through the revival of healthy desire. These new possibilities most often arise because an agent or agents has engaged in the self-sacrificing work of love. So William Loewe insists that the Law of the Cross becomes a criterion of authenticity for any redemptive shift in human living. "Besides the Christian churches there are other world religions. Christians must be ready to recognize in them also the symbolic mediation of religious

---

27. *DVI*, 571.

28. On p. 573 of *DVI*, Lonergan has the heading, "But the example presented is no less an example of resurrection than of death," and then has a string of New Testament quotes, including the one from Romans cited here and 1 Pet 5:10; Rom 8:18; 2 Cor 4:17; 1 Cor 2:9; Rom 8:28.

conversion."[29] Even beyond an explicitly religious context, the Law of the Cross may be at work. "From this procedure it follows that wherever the Law of the Cross is operative, wherever men's activity flows from an authentic, self-sacrificing love, the redemptive process is occurring."[30]

Emergent Probability and World Process

Lonergan's Latin works were the product of his teaching at the Gregorian University in Rome in the 1950s.[31] At the same time that these works of a scholastic genre were unfolding, Lonergan was developing his epistemology of dynamic human consciousness, seeking to ground the modern enterprise of theology in the actual processes of any human mind trying to make sense of the world. His conviction was that one must begin with the fundamental operations of enquiry as a foundation for method, not only in theology but in any of the sciences, from natural science to human science to the quest for human meaning illustrated by the highest of cultural endeavors. His *magnum opus* in this regard was published in 1957 as *Insight: A Study in Human Understanding*. This was not a work of theology but a sort of preamble for theological thinking— the necessary epistemological grounding for any methodological enquiry. His term for this approach was "Generalized Empirical Method," and his starting point is stated early in the introduction: "*Thoroughly understand what it is to understand, and not only will you understand the broad lines of all there is to be understood but also you will possess a fixed base, an invariant pattern, opening upon all further developments of understanding.*"[32]

While Lonergan's starting point involves the unfolding of operations of human consciousness, he moves from his empirically grounded explication of human enquiry to draw out implications for the way in which the world has unfolded, and continues to unfold, in history. This process he calls "emergent probability," and the key to this explication involves grasping that there are two ways in which scientists make sense

29. Loewe, "Law of the Cross," 173.
30. Ibid., 174.
31. See Carmody, "Lonergan's Latin Theology," 81.
32. *Insight*, 22; emphasis original.

of the world, which correspond to two different types of intelligible relationships that interact to fuel the dynamism of an ever changing world.

The most basic thing to understand is the distinction between classical science and statistical science. Classical science seeks the laws by which we understand principles that work with regularity and universality across a wide range of circumstances, for example, the law of gravity. But there are also statistical laws that explain if and when something is likely to occur, or why a certain event rather than another has occurred in the past. These are laws of probability. They are attended to by meteorologists, casino owners, and quantum physicists alike. While such laws have always been operative in our world, Darwin's theory of natural selection has brought this aspect of the world into our cultural vision in the last two centuries.

In determining classical laws, scientists use a long series of instances of some phenomenon in order to discover the common principles governing such events. So Galileo sought to grasp the nature of the freefall by observing similar properties of numerous objects dropped from various heights. In doing so he discovered certain patterns. Eventually he was able to determine a differential equation whereby the relationship that held invariantly over all similar situations could be explained. This invariance is what is presumed by science of the classical type, which seeks to explain the systematic aspects of creation.[33]

In contrast, statistical science deals with the irregular, the variable aspects of the world. Classical laws are based on the proviso "all other things being equal," but statistical investigation recognizes first and foremost that all things are not always equal. The latter concerns itself, not with the *invariance* of certain phenomena, but with the *frequency of the occurrence* of such phenomena. Classical laws explain the laws of motion by which a coin tossed in the air moves through space, but statistical science deals with the probability of such a coin landing with heads up. Galileo explained the nature of a free-fall, but his theory could not determine whether or how often objects fall off buildings.

33. Note that "classical" as used here is to be distinguished from "classicist." The "classicist worldview" refers to a premodern understanding of both human nature and the world, and it is to be contrasted with the modern worldview which incorporates historical consciousness. While it can generally be said that the classicist worldview conceives of science as predominantly that of discovering classical laws, classical science continues within the purview of historical consciousness. What is new is the recognition of statistical as well as classical types of investigations.

Statistical science thus deals with the frequencies of events. Whereas classical investigation aims to understand *the nature of* a certain event (by comparing it with other events of a similar type), statistical scientists want to know *how often* an event of a given type occurs. Statisticians aim at generalizations, but in this case they are seeking ideal frequencies rather than principles of regularity. These may be events in the natural world, such as the number of polar bears living in a given year on a certain ice flow in the Arctic. Or it may involve human actions, such as calculating rates of cigarette smoking in a given city during a given year. The point is that one makes sense of these events not by discovering a systematic set of principles that explains them all, but by counting and calculating probabilities.

While it is important to grasp that these two endeavors are distinct, this does not mean that we live in a bifurcated world. It is not the case that some aspects of our lives can be explained by regular laws of the classical type while in other arenas we live by laws of probability. Rather, both are different ways of explaining the same world—by attending to different kinds of data and by asking different kinds of questions.

To give an example, the classical laws of biology explain what occurs when a sperm fertilizes an egg and conception takes place. But the biological definition and explanation of conception cannot, in and of themselves, determine fertility rates. To determine these one must count and calculate, considering a range of variables, such as age, education, health, and frequency of intercourse, among couples within a certain geographic location. So both classical and statistical laws attend to the same phenomena, seek to explain the same world. But they do so in very different but complimentary ways. How, then, do these two kinds of laws operate in the ongoing development of the world?

The first point to grasp in this case is the notion of a "scheme of recurrence." A scheme of recurrence occurs when a series of conditions for an event coil around in a circle, such that event A fulfills the conditions for the occurrence of event B, which in turn fulfills conditions for C to occur, which then satisfies the conditions for A to *recur*. A recurrent cycle emerges that has a certain stability to it. Further, defensive mechanisms can develop so that any intervening event that threatens the cycle is offset by a second cycle designed to eliminate the intruder. Examples of schemes of recurrence include the planetary system, the circulation of water over the face of the earth, the digestive system of mammals, the nitrogen cycle that keeps plants alive. Examples of defensive systems would be the body's immune system or the compensatory reactions of an environment when the ecological balance is disturbed.

Note that these schemes of recurrence are not permanent and inevitable. Thus, though the scheme itself is a combination of classical laws that function with regularity, "schemes begin, continue, and cease to function in accord with statistical probabilities."[34] Further, not only are there single schemes, there are conditioned *series* of schemes of recurrence. So it is that the circulation of water over the face of the earth is a scheme that itself is a condition for the possibility of the nitrogen cycle of plant life to occur. And the nitrogen cycle of plant life is a scheme that is itself a condition for the possibility of the digestive system of animal life to occur. So individual cycles themselves form a conditioned, recurrent series of schemes. In recent years the effects of climate change have highlighted the centrality of these conditioned series of schemes of recurrence.

At any stage of history, then, there are probabilities for the emergence and probabilities for the survival of various schemes of recurrence. The emergence of new schemes depends on a coincidental manifold of underlying events that produce the conditions for such an emergence. An example would be random genetic mutations. These do not directly cause new species or subspecies to emerge, but they set the conditions that make such emergence possible. The survival of new species and their schemes of recurrence depend on the continued survival of the underlying conditional schemes. Such is the ecosystem that, when changed, leads to the extinction of species.

Emergent probability, then, is a heuristic explanation of world process that contradicts a determinism by which all of creation is governed according to classical laws. While classical laws explain the systematic and recurrent aspects of the world, the emergence and survival of these systems depend on underlying conditions. And these underlying conditions occur according to schedules of probability.[35] This worldview incorporates an indeterminacy that is not "mere chance" and has its own intelligibility (that is, one can make sense of it), even though it is

34. *Insight*, 141.

35. Lonergan's definition of emergent probability is as follows: "Emergent probability is the successive realization in accord with successive schedules of probability of a conditioned series of schemes of recurrence" (*Insight*, 148–49).

not the intelligibility of automatic progress or of a totally determined system.[36]

What about human living? How do human actions, the stuff of history and culture, fit into this explanation of emergent probability?

What is true of atoms, bacteria, insects, plants and animals is all the more true of human life, relationships, and behavior. There are regularities—schemes of recurrence—that function according to a series of directly causal events; from individual habits of personal hygiene to the laws and practices governing traffic patterns. Generally we notice these patterns of recurrent behavior only if they break down, as when there is a snowstorm that leaves us stranded overnight in an airport. While there are many orderly patterns of human conduct and meaning that perpetuate themselves, these patterns are not inevitable but depend on the persistence of underlying conditions. As Lonergan puts it:

> The political machinery of agreement and decision is the permanent yet self-adapting source of an indefinite series of agreements and decisions. Clearly, schemes of recurrence exist and function. No less clearly, their functioning is not inevitable. A population can decline, dwindle, vanish. A vast technological expansion, robbed of its technicians, would become a monument more intricate but no more useful than the pyramids. An economy can falter, though resources and capital equipment abound, though skill cries for its opportunity and desire for skill's product, though labor asks for work and industry is eager to employ it; then one can prime the pumps and make X occur; but because the schemes are not functioning properly, X fails to recur.[37]

Furthermore, human affairs fall under emergent probability in a distinctive way. Though human schemes emerge and reach a stability whereby they function routinely, as human life develops, less and less importance becomes attached to mere circumstance and more and more importance is attached to the operation of human intelligence and choice. The significant probabilities become, not those of emerg-

---

36. The third section of ch. 4 of *Insight* (151–61) deals with a "Clarification by Contrast," in which Lonergan discusses the Aristotelian, the Galilean, and the Darwinian worldviews, as well as that of indeterminism. See also Kenneth R. Melchin, *History, Ethics and Emergent Probability: Ethics, Society, and History in the Work of Bernard Lonergan*, 2nd ed. (Ottawa, ON: Lonergan Web Site, 1999) 115–17.

37. *Insight*, 235.

ing physical, chemical, biological, or zoological systems, but those of the occurrence of insight, communication, persuasion, consensus, and action. Rather than being merely *conditioned by* our environments, humans are *conditioners of* our environments and, hence, of ourselves. While this is true of many, if not all, living species, it is true in an unprecedented way of humans, who are not only intelligible but intelligent, that is, we are agents who grasp meaning and transform our worlds through action.[38]

So "survival of the fittest" as it operates at the biological level takes a different turn with human life. Human life is not a matter merely of biological survival and reproduction but has to do with the meaning and values that we ascribe to our living. The schemes of recurrence that make our lives possible have to do with habits of meaning, regular choices of value, an antecedent willingness to opt for value when value and satisfaction conflict. "Survival" is about the survival of meaning, of purpose in life, of self-esteem and dignity, of communities of cooperative interaction. Such survival of meaning is dependent of course on the material resources that make physical survival possible but the presence of such material resources is itself dependent on systems of schemes of recurrence that have been created by human industry and intention. Thus, promoting life has to do with promoting the conditions for the possibility of meaning, value, community, loving intersubjectivity. To the degree that egoism, group bias, prejudice, or a quest for mere power distorts these underlying conditions to favor some to the exclusion of others, survival of the fittest means that some, literally, survive at the expense of others. Perhaps more profoundly, some claim personhood, meaning, and self-value at the expense of others' dignity. So we return, again, to the entrenched surd of human living, the schemes of recurrence that perpetuate injustice and inauthenticity.

38. The recognition of this, as applied to evolution, can be traced back to shortly after Darwin. "Sociobiology" has a long and varied history and has been tied to various eugenics movements over the last 150 years. For example see Walter T. Anderson, *To Govern Evolution: Further Adventures of the Political Animal* (New York: Harcourt, Brace, 1987); Howard L. Kaye, *The Social Meaning of Modern Biology: From Darwinism to Sociobiology* (New Brunswick, NJ: Transaction, 1997); and Michael Ruse, *From Monod to Man: The Concept of Progress in Evolutionary Biology* (Cambridge, MA: Harvard University Press, 1996).

Emergent Probability, the Law of the Cross,
and the Solution to the Problem of Evil

The Law of the Cross as the solution to the problem of evil is related
to emergent probability most obviously because it is about *emergence*.
In order to understand the implications for a postmodern theology of
salvation we need to grasp more clearly (1) the nature of emergence
and the higher integrations that result and (2) the means by which this
particular emergence—transformation from a life of sin and death to
new cycles of healing and forgiveness—takes place.

Note that schemes of recurrence form hierarchies in which higher
schemes depend on lower manifolds of events. So atoms move in their
own recurrent schemes but also provide the material that is systematized by molecules into chemical processes that sustain themselves
over time. Likewise, chemical processes, with their dependable recurrence, become the underlying manifold that makes organic processes
possible. Such biochemistry becomes the dependable manifold of
events that makes the neurological life of animals possible. The recurring cycles of neurosensitivity are then transformed to a new level in
the operations of human intelligence.

The point is to grasp the notion of a *higher integration*. Higher
integrations systematize recurrent schemes of lower processes that are
otherwise merely coincidental. They are at once dependent on these
lower manifolds of events yet form something altogether different.
When neurological processes break down, a person can no longer think
intelligently. Plant life ceases to exist when the chemistry of photosyn-
thesis fails. Still, the human mind is more than and other than animal
sensitivity writ large: what emerges with human consciousness is constituted by neurological sensitivity but is something entirely distinct.
Likewise, plant life, while utterly dependent on chemical processes, is
a new differentiation that integrates yet goes beyond mere chemical
reactions.

Thus *emergence* needs to be distinguished from mere *change*.
Changes of state can occur because probabilities shift, for example,
when cases of the H1N1 virus are more prevalent in Texas than they
were two months ago. But when this virus itself shifts to become a
new virus, perhaps one immune to current vaccines, something else

has emerged. Lonergan uses human insight as his prime example of emergence:

> The prototype of emergence is the insight that arises with re-
> spect to an appropriate image: without the insight, the image is a
> coincidental manifold; by the insight the elements of the image
> become intelligibly united and related; moreover, accumulations
> of insights unify and relate ever greater and more diversified
> ranges of images, and what remains merely coincidental from
> a lower viewpoint becomes systematic from the accumulation if
> insights in a higher viewpoint.[39]

Perhaps the best illustration of this involves "getting" or "not getting" a joke. When one is "out of the loop" and doesn't get the joke, one
merely has a series of words and phrases that make sense in themselves
but don't add up to anything else. Once you "get" the joke, some new
configuration has occurred—an insight—in which all the pieces cohere
into a new sense—a higher integration.

As this example of an insight shows, in humans higher integrations
are most often higher *viewpoints*—human consciousness constitutes
a *dynamic* integration whereby acts of intellect and will continually
move a person forward to new questions that spark new integrations—
viewpoints—which can, in turn, yield decisions that constitute a new
situation. So the coincidental underlying manifolds involve previous
insights and judgments, actions of self, others, the community and
its narrative of meaning, all of which set the stage for further insights,
judgments, and decisions to take place. So, as noted above, the relevant
probabilities include the likelihood of authentic questioning, genuine
discovery, integrity of values, and consistent living.

Note, however, that while emergent probability involves higher integrations of otherwise coincidental events, which in humans become
higher viewpoints setting the stage for the integrity of action, emergent
probability is *not* automatic progress. In addition to development there
are breakdowns. Lower manifolds can remain merely coincidental or
higher integrations with their schemes of recurrence can become unstable or degenerate into their component parts. Alternately, schemes
of recurrence can become so stable as to become static—not allowing
for new integrations to emerge. At the level of human meaning there

---

39. *Insight*, 506.

is the failure of insight, the bias that refuses to ask the requisite questions, the selfish stubbornness that resists doing the good even when it is recognized. So in addition to progress in history, there is decline. Abnormalities, maladies, and, at the level of meaning, prejudice and hatred, can become entrenched in their own schemes of recurrence.

So the solution to the problem of evil will involve some kind of higher viewpoint in human persons that will open up the possibility of grasping truth that had otherwise been distorted, of willing and acting for justice that has been perverted. But according to the Law of the Cross, this will not be the result of actions of power but will occur through embracing the consequences of the distortions themselves. The Son of God became man, suffered, died, and was raised again: "because divine wisdom has ordained and divine goodness has willed, not to do away with the evils of the human race through power, but to convert those evils into a supreme good according to the just and mysterious Law of the Cross."[40] In other words, because moral evils are established into recurrent schemes of irrationality, disvalue, and systemic injustice, these need to break down, to exhaust their faulty expectations, in order for some new set of habits and practices to emerge. Just as the instability or the breakdown of geological or organic systems (biological mutations, environmental catastrophes) can become the occasion not only for new events to occur, but for these to become recurrent as newly emergent integrations, so the failure of "progress" can become the occasion for a decline that begs for its own reversal.

The key point here, which is so counterintuitive as to become a stumbling block for many who encounter the Christian gospel, is that solutions to the problem of evil that remain at the same level as the problem itself—that involve merely a "change of state"—will result only in shifts of power.[41] In order for real transformation to occur, the system itself, the distorted schemes of recurrence, need to be dismantled. And it is precisely through *allowing* the evil embedded in them to be exposed for what it is that this dismantling can occur.[42] The life of the Incarnate One, who did not retaliate but let evil run its course, was the occasion for the moral evil embedded in human selfishness and

40. *DVI*, 552.

41. See Wink, *Engaging the Powers*, and the discussion in Crysdale, *Embracing Travail*, 40–68.

42. See Moore, *The Crucified Is No Stranger*, esp. ch. 4.

oversight to be revealed for what it was. This death of distorted human aspiration became, as well, the opportunity for something radically new and different to emerge. What emerged was a new set of meanings and values embedded in healing and forgiveness. The earliest disciples experienced this and established new "schemes of recurrence" in which truth, fellowship, sharing, forgiveness, authentic worship, and healing perpetuated themselves. Thus the ongoing work of the Holy Spirit in church and sacrament sets the conditions of possibility for further redemption. To the degree that the worshipping community continues to embody self-sacrificing love, recurrent schemes of new life continue to emerge and survive.

Implications for a Contemporary Soteriology

A few implications of salvation as emergence can be drawn out. First, this is not a matter of cause and effect. It is not the case that some event in history served as an efficient cause with a determinate outcome, as when a fire burns down a house or cooks a stew or gives warmth to a home. Salvation is not like the law of gravity in which determinate processes ensure regular outcomes. Rather, redemption unfolds as an interaction of probabilities and regularities. Consistent with an emergently probable world process, underlying manifolds of events set the conditions of possibility for new higher integrations to emerge. Such emergence is not inevitable but is subject to probabilities. *To the degree that* persons open themselves to the forgiveness and healing of God's love, healing and forgiveness, new insights, judgments, decisions, and actions, will establish themselves as redemptive habits and practices, in individuals and in communities.

Thus, redemption as emergence contradicts assumptions that underlie a cult of suffering. The cult of suffering finds its ground in the notion that suffering *produces* redemption. Thus, the more you suffer, the more you are redeemed. Alternately, the more sinful you are, the more you need to suffer. In times and cultures where women and minorities are assumed to be especially deprived or sinful, such direct causality—suffering = redemption—becomes an agent of oppression. Not only does this lead to gross injustices, it is startlingly erroneous in its oversight of the probability-shaped nature of world process and, hence, of renewed life in Christ.

Thus, secondly, redemption ought not to be understood as a transaction of some sort, before which persons were "damned" and after which (some) persons are "saved." Soteriologies that conceive of the problem of evil as a zero-sum game—that we were bound to lose if Jesus had not come and taken our part—lend themselves to distortions, not only of human redemption but of the very nature of God himself.

While it is unfair to lay a faulty transaction view of atonement solely on Anselm's shoulders, the metaphor that he adopted in his elaboration of the "satisfaction" owed to God due to human sin laid the ground for a theological conception of righteousness as a zero-sum endeavor. Stephen Finlan summarizes the contemporary concern over the implications of such a straightforward exchange as the basis of God's forgiveness:

> The agenda is largely set by the widespread dismay regarding the received doctrines of atonement, for instance, such notions as these:
>
> - God's honor was damaged by human sin;
> - God demanded a bloody victim—innocent or guilty—to pay for human sin;
> - God was persuaded to alter God's verdict against humanity when the Son of God offered to endure humanity's punishment;
> - The death of the Son thus functioned as a payoff; salvation was purchased.[43]

Robert Daly, SJ, in reference to this quote from Finlan, says:

> If this, or this kind of, atonement theory is central to our idea of God and of salvation, we are in deep trouble. In effect, this notion turns God into some combination of a great and fearsome judge, or offended lord, or temperamental spirit. It calls into question God's free will, or justice, or sanity."[44]

43. Finlan, *Problems with Atonement*, 1; here Finlan argues, "Most strategies for dealing with objections to these doctrines involve separating the objectionable from the biblical, either showing that the objectionable doctrines do not occur in the Bible, or that they do occur but are not objectionable when properly explained."

44. Daly, "Images of God," 41. He refers here to Finlan, *Problems with Atonement*, 97–98.

Overlooking the dynamic unfolding of world process, and its tentative nature, some continue to functionally accept a mechanical determinism in which justice operates as a mathematical equation, which God resolved by offering his Son to equal the balance left by sin's deficit. Not only does this ignore the way the world actually works, it ultimately places such justice over above God and incorporates violence into God's very nature.

Third, because the surd of sin is so well embedded in human communities, reversing the cycle of sin is not an accomplishment one can achieve through self-effort. Some new element needs to enter in; some new unifying higher integration (in this case a higher viewpoint) needs to be established. In other words, it is not enough to show up moral evil for what it is, to dismantle unjust orders. Emergence occurs when some new viewpoint unfolds that incorporates underlying meanings and values but transforms them. Christians name this *agape* and proclaim that such pure love is divine and has been revealed to human persons in the incarnation, death, and resurrection of Jesus of Nazareth. But whether cloaked in Christian language or not, the reversal of moral evil always occurs when the current situation is transcended by an encounter with extra-ordinary love, which in turn is incorporated into new habits of meaning and value.[45] Thus, self-sacrificing love is both the *occasion for* and the *consequence of* an "otherworldly falling in love" that transforms both intellect and will through the revelation of new truths and values and the establishment of reformed desires that issue in concrete habits and practices.

Fourth, because salvation emerges in this dynamic way, it is never a sure thing. Just as the laws of classical science establish regularities but are nonetheless subject to probabilities, so the new life that emerges and reconstitutes self-transcendent habits and practices on a stable basis is ever subject to further development or, alternatively, breakdown. This means that salvation is not a *state* of being but an ongoing *process* of purgation and conversion. It means, further, that we are not in control of either our own redemption or others'. Just as we cannot coerce others into having insights, so we can contrive neither our own nor others' *metanoia*. All we can and ought to do is to set the conditions of possibil-

---

45. See Loewe's point about the universality of redemption in "Law of the Cross," 173–74.

ity whereby the probability of conversion, of an otherworldly falling in love, is heightened.

This instability contradicts theories of atonement that rely on models of direct causality or transactions between God's justice and human sinfulness, which often incorporate a desire for certainty about salvation. But the quest for control or certainty in matters of salvation overlooks the dynamic nature of human meaning. Just as organisms, no matter how well adapted to an environment, must continually cope with new developments in their contexts, so redemption means different things at different times for different people. Just as stasis in an organism's development can doom it to extinction, a static view of salvation can close off new channels for the manifestations of God's grace.

Finally, this approach sheds new light on the *already*-but-*not-yet* nature of Christian eschatology. There *is* a sense in which redemption and new life are secured for us through the life, death, and resurrection of Jesus the Christ. But what have been established are the new *conditions of possibility* for healing and renewal. The full *actuation* of such possibilities remains an elusive objective. Nonetheless, our current glimpses of a higher viewpoint experienced in transcendent loving relations with a triune God are sufficient to ground our hope in a final and complete fulfillment. Thus we have the distinction between *hope* in an unknown future and *expectation* oriented toward specified outcomes. With a cloud of witnesses we walk by faith not by sight, accepting the suffering at the heart of the cross, not as the quick fix of redemptive violence, but as the condition of possibility from which new life can and will emerge.[46]

---

46. For more on this approach to redemption, see Cynthia Crysdale, "Jesus Died for Our Sins: Redemption as an Ethic of Risk," in *From Logos to Christos: Essays in Honour of Joanne McWilliam*, ed. Ellen M. Leonard and Kate Merriman (Waterloo, ON: Wilfrid Laurier, 2010) 209–28.

9

Finding the Ground: Method, Universality, and Ethical Discourse

DAVID M. HAMMOND
HIGH POINT UNIVERSITY

The global situation today is in need of basic ethical agreement among peoples of different cultures and religions. From genocide to environmental degradation to multinational economic exploitation, the lack of moral cooperation spells disaster for many peoples throughout the world. If philosophy and Christian theology are to be authentic and not escapist, they must encourage moral collaboration among the peoples of the world. With this concern I would like to take a few cues from my teacher and friend William Loewe, whom we celebrate in this *Festschrift*. It was my great good fortune to learn many things from him, both in graduate school and afterward from his own exemplary theological performance. In particular, he taught me the value of struggling with the writings of Bernard Lonergan, the philosopher and theologian whose foundational work in the twentieth century possesses great potential for philosophical and theological progress in the twenty-first.[1]

Let me introduce the topic by referring to a few of Loewe's comments in his evaluation of John Milbank's *Theology and Social Theory*. As is characteristic of his open and fair readings of those with whom

---

1. I am grateful to the editors of this volume and to Professor Dennis Doyle for their comments, which helped me to clarify my meaning at certain points in the essay.

he has fundamental disagreements, Loewe found Milbank's book "to be a valuable critique of the positivism that undergirds much modern theory; the social sciences' commonly uncritical acceptance of modern practice, shot through with bias and sin."[2] Loewe ended his review by commending Milbank's appeal to Blondel and Balthasar as thinkers whose work might aid in recognizing, in Loewe's words, "the priority of praxis in intellectual performance" (Blondel) and "the transformative role of aesthetic form in effectively orienting human feeling to the genuinely good and true" (Balthasar).[3] On Milbank's foundations, however, Loewe found an undifferentiated return to myth and rhetoric. The bias against theoretic consciousness is manifest in Milbank's retreat to a neoplatonic version of the Christian story in opposition to "any apologetic use of universal human reason."[4]

As a follow-up to Loewe's insistence that it is a mistake to rule out of court any and all notions of "universal human reason," I would like to suggest the urgency of coming to agreement on what can be called "universalist" grounds for ethical thought and action. More precisely, the focus of this essay is on the need for verifiable foundations in "universal human reason" and ethics, and the help that Lonergan's heuristic can give to meet that exigence. As we shall see, that universalist position is far from the isolated individualist rationalism that is often the target of recent theological reaction.[5]

Lonergan's work provides a critical method for affirming the concrete social and historical specificity of human living, including the vital role of belief that carries particular traditions and practices forward.

2. William P. Loewe, "Beyond Secular Reason? Reflections in Response to John Milbank's *Theology and Social Theory,*" *Philosophy and Theology* 9 (1996) 447–54, at 449. See John Milbank, *Theology and Social Theory: Beyond Secular Reason* (Oxford: Blackwell, 1990).

3. Loewe, "Beyond Secular Reason?," 454.

4. Ibid., 450.

5. For a recent critique of the particularist perspective of postliberal and Radical Orthodox theology, see Francis Schüssler Fiorenza, "The Cosmopolitanism of Roman Catholic Theology and the Challenge of Cultural Particularity," *Horizons* 35/2 (Fall 2008) 298–320. The Radical Orthodox position is represented by John Milbank, and the postliberal by George Lindbeck in his book *The Nature of Doctrine: Religion and Theology in a Postliberal Age* (Philadelphia: Westminster, 1984). For a critique of Lindbeck's interpretation of Lonergan, see Dennis M. Doyle, "Lindbeck's Appropriation of Lonergan," *Method: A Journal of Lonergan Studies* 4/1 (March 1986) 18–28.

The method, however, does not yield to the temptation to end the conversation about reason with a mere acknowledgement of incommensurable worldviews.[6] Lonergan's major achievement was to find in the subject the ground of all modes of inquiry, and by extension, all mentalities and forms of common sense. His turn to the subject, far from collapsing into a subjectivism, actually provides a way of acknowledging particularity while locating the source of all diverse constructions of meaning in a set of universal operations that constitute the human subject as originating value. That self-transcending ground, however, is not the full story. Lonergan's position is no individualist or relativist rationalism. His "Generalized Empirical Method" is a heuristic both utterly personal and thoroughly social and historical. The method is "generalized" because the basic operations of human thinking are at work in any particular example of human intelligence. It is "empirical" in the sense that it is not a matter of adopting a theory but of experiencing one's own intelligent and rational operations. And finally, it is a method that is identical with the operator and not a technique recipe for some particular form of inquiry.

The first part of this essay briefly outlines Lonergan's notion of redemption as God's solution to the problem of evil. The source of the problem of evil is located in the failure of the self-transcending subject. Its solution is in the ongoing process of healing that failure and the consequent evil. Such healing promotes a creative and intelligent response that wills the good. Such willing is the concrete form of the love of God: God's love for us revealed in our love for God. Concretely, the theological virtues of love, hope, and faith are operative not as supplying moral content but as promoting and sustaining the drive toward the true and the good. The second (and longer) part is a presentation of the foundations of ethics in the subject's dynamic desire for what is true and good. Ethics is understood as putting into practice the redemptive movements of God's grace operative in human living. Such practice requires the cooperation of large numbers of people of good

6. In a lecture from 1962, for example, Lonergan set out to incorporate diverse forms of meaning while moving beyond what he called an "archipelago of islands" of meaning—the acceptance of multiple cultures or mentalities as the last word. See "Time and Meaning," in *Philosophical and Theological Papers, 1958–1964, Collected Works of Bernard Lonergan 6*, ed. Robert C. Croken and Frederick E. Crowe (Toronto: University of Toronto Press, 1996) 94–95. Hereafter *Collected Works of Bernard Lonergan* will be abbreviated as *CWL*.

will over long periods of time for the maintenance of recurrent schemes or structures necessary for providing the various needs of the human race. Ethical practice also requires that the biases that distort structures and inhibit progress toward the fulfilling of human needs be rooted out to allow for the emergence of new structures. The third section turns to the issue of ethics and Christian dialogue with the world's religions and with other men and women who may not be explicitly religious. Within this understanding of Christian redemption dialogue takes on the character of moral necessity because the progressive transformation of the world cannot occur without significant collaboration among the religions and others who are all part of the emergently probable universe. The theology of redemption requires collaboration and openness, both necessary for the progressive transformation of the world. The conclusion of the argument is that there are religious and moral as well as intellectual warrants for maintaining a universalist position in philosophy and theology today.

Redemption as the Solution to the Problem of Evil

Lonergan understands Christian redemption from sin within the context of a theology of God and creation transposed into categories that incorporate modern historical and scientific consciousness. Salvation, in other words, involves the perfection of an emergently probable universe through the progressive increase in human control of history through intelligence, decision, and action.[7] Evil then is understood as a problem, not a mystery to be accepted in faith. (The traditional term *mysterium iniquitatis* simply means that evil as nothingness—nonbeing—is not open to understanding because it makes no sense.) The cross of Christ functions as the mysterious transformative symbol of God's solution to the problem of evil, while the resurrection certifies the solution as authentically divine. Flowing as benefits from the divine love communicated through the Christ event are the three theological virtues, infused into the concrete human being as transformed living.

Theology is obviously not the complete science of human living.[8] There are many further relevant questions that theology has no capacity

7. See Lonergan, *Insight: A Study of Human Understanding*, CWL 3 (1992) 228.
8. See Lonergan, *Method in Theology* (New York: Seabury, 1972) 364.

to answer. And yet, without the root motivation in living faith that theology seeks to understand, the love and hope necessary for sustaining cooperative moral effort over the long term will be always vulnerable to despair. The temptation to resign oneself to the myth of the way things are will be powerful indeed. Such resignation can only make matters worse. The three theological virtues enable and encourage ethical striving in the face of massive decline, the anticipation of failures, and the impotence of individual efforts.

Without faith or hope, commitment to ethical struggle might falter. But love provides a start. Love calls forth the disinterested desire to know, which in turn calls into question the intelligibility of the social surd. Only faith can walk the fine line between despair ("sin reigns supreme—nothing will ever change—progress is impossible") and naïve optimism ("random acts of good will and kindness will convert the world"). There is of course a kind of religious despair of the world that is manifest when the appeal to the next life functions as an escape from this one. Despair reduces Christianity to a series of earthly tests for entrance into heaven. Despair neutralizes the New Testament's eschatological vision of a new heaven and a new earth, with its concomitant call to Christian responsibility for the transformation of the world. What remains is the status quo myth: the surd is simply understood as part and parcel of reality. A religious worldview burdened by this myth then encourages retreat from the problem of evil and the meaning of Christianity's doctrines and practices shrinks. But authentic Christian hope resists despair and promotes moral perseverance in love even while acknowledging and indeed anticipating the multiple and pervasive distortions that result from the reign of sin.[9]

Grace operates universally and in mysterious ways through the instrumentality of universal history for the purpose of transformation. What follows is a chastened theory of progress that will require the recurrence of many structures and the involvement of many people over a long period of time. With that exceedingly brief summary of key elements in Lonergan's theory of redemption, we now ask how that response might be understood structurally and historically.

9. See William Loewe, "Lonergan and the Law of the Cross: A Universalist View of Salvation," *Anglican Theological Review* 59/2 (1977) 162–74.

Originating Value, Structure and Trajectory

Rather than as a set of rules that enter at a moment in history, Lonergan locates the foundations of moral action in the self-transcending subject. Although it is of vital importance to understand that ideas have histories within communities, the fact remains that the foundation is the subject herself or himself, not a set of doctrines. While inherited beliefs and practices are an essential component in the socially and historically mediated solution to the problem of evil, doctrines and their developments are the products of human subjects. But human subjects are within social and historical forms of mediation. An ethics that seeks to maintain what is good, to heal what has been wounded and to create the new and better in society and history, requires intelligent reflection on the structures emergent within human history.[10]

The origin of all ethical response is the subject's own rational and responsible self-consciousness.[11] Just as the assembled operations of human cognition head toward knowledge, so do the further questions of value and decision find their term in action for the good. And just as cognition is not reducible to logical deduction or conceptualization, so is ethical response never a simple matter of applying rules or performing one's preestablished duty. Inherited principles, rules, and moral strategies are formulated by human beings, and so have their root in the human desire for the true and the good. In the process of making a moral decision, one consults one's moral heritage the way one might consult any aspect of the accumulated wisdom of the past. The principles, rules, and moral strategies into which one is socialized or educated are of enormous significance and value (about which more below). But no matter how well formulated, these do not think or decide for us. We can verify this from an intelligent reflection on our own experience. It is only when we try to explain our moral behavior that we resort to images of the "application" of principles or "seeing the good or evil quality in an action," as if the rule had a ready-made answer to one's inquiry about what might bring about some concrete good. Images of application and quality distract from what is actually going on: one

---

10. See Lonergan, *Understanding and Being,* CWL 5 (1990) 376–81.

11. See Lonergan, *Insight,* 604.

thinks, judges fact and value, and decides and acts in response to what one knows (or thinks one knows) and values.[12]

One more component in ethical response should be noted. In addition to many people's ideas, judgments, decisions, and actions collaborating to maintain a structure, there are also feelings. Because feelings can carry meaning by signaling the values that are operative in the subject, we need to attend to them. Spontaneity, however, can also discourage questions that seek the meaning of those feelings. The post-Hobbesian reduction of ethics to feelings—a move that segregates thinking and judging to the realm of science—is an exaggeration of a truth: the turn to the subject must value feeling and the symbols that evoke affective response, but the subject inquires as well as feels. As data, feelings are to be understood, not naïvely obeyed. Value-laden feelings (not mere transitory emotions) direct us to the kinds of questions that the drive toward moral self-transcendence requires. To ignore feelings would be to lose important meaning—something would then be missing or repressed.[13] Conversion to the good sometimes will require the transformation of affectivity. My summary of these elements of Lonergan's heuristic structure of ethics has been brief because, rather than focus on moral conversion, I want to focus on the structures of the good and the need for cooperation today among all people of good will.

As an example of how intelligent moral action goes beyond obedience to rules or strategies, imagine a typical parent. She wants her very young child to obey her and heed her advice as the child develops into adolescence. She teaches the child the wise moral strategies that he will need for an authentic life. But she also wants that child to do more than follow orders: she wants him to grow up by learning to think and to decide, even if that means the possibility of making mistakes and suffering from them. There is simply no authority or recipe or regulation that can obviate the need to think and decide and act. What finally

12. For more on these themes, see the excellent popular discussion of the ethical challenge today—especially in its presentation of structure, recurrence and emergence—in Kenneth Melchin's *Living with Other People: An Introduction to Christian Ethics Based on Bernard Lonergan* (Collegeville, MN: Liturgical, 1998).

13. For a clear presentation of moral conversion, see Walter Conn, "The Desire for Authenticity" in *The Desires of the Human Heart: An Introduction to the Theology of Bernard Lonergan*, ed. Vernon Gregson (Mahwah, NJ: Paulist, 1988) 36–56.

determines the moral question is the intelligent and reasonable grasp of and response to the concrete situation.

Moral action, however, is rarely an isolated event; we usually think and decide within a context of structures that need to be maintained if the goods they produce are to flow out of them. And just as there are no laws that relieve us of thinking and deciding, so our responsibilities within structures are not reducible to mere obedience to regulations. A high school is an example of a social structure, and the recurrent performance of duties by the members of that community of learning insures its regular functioning. The teacher, who is only one of the actors in the structure, must regularly prepare lessons, show up at the classroom at the right times, communicate knowledge to students (a task that we could break down into many sub-skills, having to do with understanding the content of the lessons as well as the concrete insights needed to promote that understanding in the students), correct students' errors, encourage the perseverance and humility that learning requires, empathize with those who are having problems of various kinds, and so on. Now, imagine an actual teacher in a particular school—how will he perform his duties? There are so many things he must know already, learn more about in the process of his work, and decide upon. Knowing the explicitly stated duties as set forth in the teacher handbook or contract provides only a general direction. A good teacher, in other words, is not simply one who performs according to the handbook; a good teacher is an intelligent, reasonable, and responsible teacher. Ultimately decisions and the acts that follow them emerge not from duty or obedience or authority but from the moral response of the originating value, the subject, in the ever changing concrete situations of that particular school.

If we shift the focus onto the responsible student, we find the same structure operative. There is the student handbook, which one might profitably consult, but learning only happens when one pays attention, reads, asks questions of the readings, imagines possible implications of the ideas encountered in those books, asks more questions of teachers and other serious students, etc. Even then there is no guarantee of learning but the probabilities of success are dramatically increased when these things happen. And yet, the school is more than teacher and student, who are but two factors in the recurrent structure. The building and maintenance, the salaries, the library books, the bus system, and a host of other things function to maintain the structure, and citizens' taxes pay for it all. The coordination of efforts is a delicate and often vulnerable reality; stupidity or irresponsibility at any point could reduce its effectiveness or close it down altogether.

We have seen that an individual's moral response alone is not effective in bringing about the good or order. The best student will benefit little in an unsafe school with incompetent teachers. Progress requires the maintenance of recurrent structures as well as the emergence of new structures to reform or replace earlier ones found to be inadequate. The dynamic sense of the human good "is a history, a concrete cumulative process resulting from developing human apprehensions and choices that may be good or evil. And that concrete, developing process is what the human good in this life is."[14] The world process that Lonergan calls "emergent probability" not only structures physical, chemical and biological evolution but human history as well:

> The advent of man does not abrogate the rule of emergent probability. Human actions are recurrent; their recurrence is regular; and the regularity is the functioning of a scheme, of a patterned set of relations that yields conclusions of a type: If X occurs, then X will recur.[15]

There is, however, an important difference between emergent probability on the physical, chemical or biological levels and emergent probability on the human level:

> But as human intelligence develops, there is a significant change of roles. Less and less importance attaches to the probabilities of appropriate constellations of circumstances. More and more importance attaches to the probabilities of the occurrence of insight, communication, agreement, decision. Man does not have to wait for his environment to make him.[16]

The products of human creativity such as tools, techniques, the economy, political structures, etc., result from "insight, communication, agreement, decision." Therefore, assumptions usefully made in the natural sciences become less reliable when attempting to anticipate what will emerge from human intelligence. In other words, in the analysis of human history, "the analogy of natural process becomes less

14. Lonergan, *Topics in Education, CWL* 10 (1993) 33.
15. Lonergan, *Insight*, 235.
16. Ibid., 235–36.

and less relevant."[17] Both mechanistic thinking and natural selection are to be sublated in favor of an understanding of emergence that takes into account the decisive factor of human intelligence.

Just as a scientific law explains relations in an ideal situation, so moral law explains what is objectively good about the relations among the elements in moral experience.[18] Abstractly, the moral precept is infallible, but the good "always is concrete," hence Lonergan's emphasis on the need for social policy in ethical reflection and not mere abstract condemnations.[19] As we have noted, precepts do not determine or decide. They are judgments based on human experience and they are of inestimable value but they cannot replace the subject's engagement with the concrete situation while intending the concrete good. No mere application of rule to situation can deduce a decision because one who decides needs to know what the situation is, whether or in what way the rule may be useful in one's deliberations in that concrete situation and finally, what historical trajectory is likely to result from the possible courses of action. One must intend knowledge as well as the good. Good intentions are no substitute for responsible intentionality.

Two points need to be emphasized here: first, the progress that heads toward the good of order is beyond the control of the individual; second, that which is beyond individual control (structures and trajectories) is open to understanding. When human beings begin to understand those recurring and emergent structures, something significant enters into the "manifold" of data to be understood. Simply knowing that human structures are human products increases the effective freedom to alter those products. In other words, knowing that intelligence is part of the manifold can give rise to new insights and thus to new forms of organization, structure, etc. The circumstances set by human history at any given point—what has been going forward through human intelligence or its lack—is both beyond the control of the individual and at the same time open to human understanding, criticism and change.

17. Ibid., 236.

18. Here I am following Kenneth Melchin, *History, Ethics, and Emergent Probability: Ethics, History and Society in the Work of Bernard Lonergan* (Lanham, MD: University Press of America, 1987), chs. 5–6. See also his *Living with Other People* (see n. 12 above), ch. 2, "The Social Structure of Moral Knowledge."

19. See Lonergan, *Method*, 27; *Topics in Education*, 65.

We have noted that progress is beyond the capacity of any individual, but that does not mean that it is beyond human control. Insight is a new component in the manifold that reveals as mistaken any deterministic understanding of history. Included in the intelligible universe is our own knowing and acting, which is a factor within world process as emergently probable. Our understanding can be "the fulfilling conditions for the occurrence of something new, something that has not yet occurred."[20] Insight itself becomes a key condition that can make possible the emergence of much greater human control over the direction of history. But only through the recurrent collaboration of many people over a long period of time can that control be exercised. And collaboration requires common meanings and values.

How, then, do structures and recurrent patterns change? In any potential insight into data, there is data left over; in the manifold of data to be understood, that empirical residue is not systematized. On the level of social structures there is also a "left-over," something not included or systematized within the structure, and this structural residue poses opportunities for insights into the limitations and inadequacies of the structure, and thus opportunities for changing it.

As a simple example of a recurrent structure and the ways in which structures reveal both stability and potential for change, let's go back to our imaginary high school. If many of the students are graduating but cannot read above a fifth grade level of competency, a further question—why aren't these students learning how to read—must be asked. What is obstructing the learning process? If the problem is widespread in the school, then it is possible that the structure intended to bring about some good is not succeeding with the frequency necessary to meet its purpose. Problems outside of the school can scuttle the school's success; perhaps the questioning will lead beyond the resources of the school, and so the context for understanding necessarily expands beyond the recurrent structure.

Progress depends on successful structures. When one becomes aware of the limitations of a structure, then an inverse insight is possible: the present structure does not account for all the data.

---

20. Melchin, *History, Ethics, and Emergent Probability*, 112.

Global Ethics and Religious Dialogue

In world process, new structures or schemes of recurrence can emerge when the manifold of data to be understood gives rise to new insights, which in turn urge the questioners toward higher viewpoints. As more voices are added to the call for moral dialogue among the religions there will be efforts to build new recurrent structures of cooperation.[21] When the response involves a large enough population and establishes the conditions for its own recurrence, progress can occur. A religious philosophy that acknowledges ever higher viewpoints will ground and encourage the movement toward religious cooperation that is so needed in today's global crisis. Conversely, religious or philosophical perspectives that obscure what human beings have in common, or deny the human ability to know whether there is any commonality among human beings across cultural differences, will not be predisposed to search for cultural or doctrinal agreement. The assumption that an already existing way of understanding things is sufficient for dialogue—the common sense of a particular society need not turn to a higher viewpoint in order to understand and judge the meanings and values of the other—undercuts the fundamental drive toward ever higher viewpoints that is the dynamic and universal élan of human being.

As illustration of the value of the turn to interiority as the ground of dialogue, consider the task of what has recently been termed "comparative theology." It is no doubt a valuable and necessary moment in the process of dialogue. Comparative theology, however, proceeds with the (at least implicit) assumption that religious people receive and communicate meanings that they judge to be true; there is the further assumption that believing those truths and acting accordingly is a valuable thing to do. So, any approach to comparative theology that includes in its basic method an explicit acknowledgement of these facts of universal human intentionality will be more likely to meet with greater insight than those that do not. To illustrate the importance of this foundational element, consider the Muslim's affirmation of the One God. This most basic pillar of Islamic faith also often carries with it the rejection of any being that might be placed alongside God or intimately associated with God. Such a being is an idol. The Christian belief in the divinity

21. On globalization see Neil Ormerod, "Theology, History, and Globalization," *Gregorianum* 88/1 (2007) 23–48.

of Christ, therefore, is easily rejected as being just that. The Christian theologian, of course, will be quick to correct that misunderstanding: Christ is not associated with God or compared to God or even (pictorially) the son of God in the way that any son is a distinct being from his father. Rather, Christ is the very Word of God, expressed in history. How do Christian and Muslim dialogue partners eliminate this misunderstanding? Minimally, they must be attentive to and understand the fact that both parties are united in a quest for understanding; their differing religions and cultural locations do not alter that fact, which is universal: all human beings desire to understand what is true. Might there be blindness or even ill will that interferes with the correction of that misunderstanding? No doubt about it.

As a further clarification of Lonergan's universalist position, let us note that it differs from what is often named "secular reason." As I understand the use of this phrase among many of its recent critics, "secular reason" points to a foreshortened and self-contradictory version of the human spirit that is controlled by an a priori dismissal of questions that transcend the narrowly empirical concerns of the natural sciences. In contrast to this stunted version of reason, Lonergan's account of reason invites us to discover in ourselves the fact that inquiry does not stop short of transcendental questions. The dynamism of intelligent questioning is not to be artificially restrained within a pluralistic society's secular common denominator. Intelligence heads toward the understanding of the universe of being, which is intelligible. To criticize defects and distortions in modern conceptions of reason as do postliberal and Radical Orthodoxy theologians requires some ground in human reason itself. There is no unbridgeable chasm between secular and religious reason and the turn to the subject provides verification of this critical ground. Loewe's critique of Milbank makes the point clearly: "Simply put, there exists a contradiction between what Milbank says about the radical limits of human rationality and its inability to negotiate difference, on the one hand, and the appeal to human rationality implicit in his saying it."[22] In other words, in his critique of "secular reason" Milbank's reasonable performance reveals the opposite of what he says about reason: his theory denies what he does.

22. Loewe, "Beyond Secular Reason," 452.

As Loewe has persuasively argued in his study of the parallels in Lonergan and Max Horkheimer on the nature of basic sin, the problem with mass culture today is not the Enlightenment apotheosis of the subject freed from particularity and tradition, but rather its opposite. In its distorted communication (think of the half-truths of so much of the advertizing that floods our *sensorium*) modern mass culture might exalt the free individual (an image taken from the first or classical eighteenth century phase of the enlightenment) but in practice such distorted communication represses freedom and creativity. Both Lonergan and Horkheimer understood that the demand for practicality in mass culture today, justified by pseudo-theory, issues in less, not more, freedom.[23] The result is the loss of human creativity and insight into the vast social problems that need to be solved. If the way things happen to be at any given time is absolutized as reality, conformity is the "rational" response. The challenge is to be liberated from that dehumanizing mentality. Loewe appreciates Horkheimer as an example of what Lonergan identified as a growing critique of sin developed by social theorists and philosophers such as Marx and Nietzsche.[24]

As an apologetic category employed by certain Christian theologians, the category "secular reason" has been used to differentiate Christian reason from the (admittedly serious and obdurate) antireligious biases abroad in modern and postmodern culture. But the critique of any form of distorted reason should not be at the expense of the ongoing collaboration that is called for in the progressive redemption of the world.[25] Any critique of positivist assumptions about reason must not repress the questioning that moves toward greater integration. If there is no universal ground for asking and answering questions of fact and value, then the Christian church isolates itself from the good will and serious moral efforts being made by men and women throughout the many cultures and religions of the world.

23. See Loewe, "Dialectics of Sin: Lonergan's *Insight* and the Critical Theory of Max Horkheimer," *Anglican Theological Review* 61 (1979) 224–45, at 243.

24. See ibid., 235; Lonergan, *Topics in Education*, 69.

25. In one sense, of course, Christian theology understands redemption to have been delivered once and for all in Christ; in another sense, that redemption must be appropriated by individuals and thus by communities, which thus promotes a progressive redemption that is socially and historically realized. Christ has conquered sin and death but the theological problem of evil remains and its solution must be pursued in history and society.

Without an adequate and verifiable account of human intelligence in its concrete operations, there is the likelihood of a drift toward less and less comprehensive solutions to the problem of evil. Biased common sense refuses the drive toward higher viewpoints and so idealizes absurdities that should be challenged rather than accepted as reality. The world today needs greater, not lesser, syntheses, higher, not lower, viewpoints.[26] Higher viewpoints become more likely when the unrestricted desire to know and decide and love is liberated from the myth that those absurdities are real and to be known when in fact they are unintelligible. A method grounded in human subjectivity that moves away from the myth is not a doctrine, but a dynamic questioning that heads for an ever higher viewpoint.

From his earliest work, Lonergan has consistently identified the fact of universal human solidarity. Given the fact of human solidarity and the capacity for self-transcendence, there is the possibility of some degree of shared meanings and values across cultures and worldviews. In the present situation increasing numbers of Christians have become aware of their responsibility to engage in dialogue with the other. If we extend the notion of recurrent structures to this situation of dialogue, we might observe that for most Christians, the other religions are still closed books, yet if the church is a redemptive process it cannot isolate itself from other movements. Just as theology needs the sciences, so the church needs other religions.[27] Indeed, as part of the world, the church understands itself and makes itself in relation to the world, which includes the world's religions. This fact does not demand the reduction of Christian doctrines as a way of making the faith acceptable to others, but it does suggest that until Christians learn more about the other religions, the reasonable Christian stance will usually be the one that Loewe has recommended more than once: the Socratic wisdom of the *via ignorantia*, an honest and humble acknowledgement of our lack of knowledge of the other and an encouragement for further learning through dialogue.[28] As parts of the emergent universe of being, other

---

26. See Lonergan, *Insight*, 690–93.

27. See Lonergan, *Method*, 364.

28. See, for example, Loewe, "Encountering the Crucified God: The Soteriology of Sebastian Moore" *Horizons* 9/2 (Fall 1982) 216–36; Loewe, Review Symposium for Paul Knitter's *No Other Name?*, *Horizons* 13/1 (1986) 123–26.

traditions are to be known, and that potential knowledge would now seem to be morally and religiously required.

Today, a globalized world sets the moral and theological task of dialogue, mutual understanding and cooperation. In the process of responding to this exigence, there must be no waiting until all of the questions made available through the dialogue are answered before beginning concrete steps toward moral cooperation. The fact of ongoing dialogue and frequent intersubjective exchanges of meaning will make such cooperation more likely. The motive for dialogue, beyond the desire to avoid the threats of short-term violence and chaos, is the desire to avoid a trajectory of decline that is very likely to occur if we fail to seize the opportunity. The structures that supply the goods needed for decent living cannot be maintained without cooperation, which requires shared meanings and values. In an increasingly small world, there is an urgent need for widespread inclusion within the ambit of moral discourse, deliberation and collaborative action.

Objections have been raised, of course, to universalist positions. It is sometimes suggested that an assumption of basic equality must be made: the world's religions are different paths to the same salvation. Such an assumption is certainly ahistorical and uncritical, but not because of any commitment to universal reason. If the foundational reality is the human subject rather than a set of doctrines or practices, there is at once a universal base for dialogue and moral cooperation that does not pivot on doctrines. As Loewe has intimated, any dialogue among the religions that depends for its success on the relativization of doctrines as a way of reaching common ground can "suggest a reduction of theology to an exercise of instrumental rationality . . . [whereby] the reality of the world's religions is subordinated to the logical control of an increasingly formalized set of categories. Such a procedure promotes, not the encounter of religions, but a relativizing rationalism."[29] The foundational reality is not on the level of doctrine but on the level of the subject.

A method grounded in the empirically verifiable operations of the human subject is universal in the sense of being fully generalized: no particular inquiry or science will circumvent these operations. Only when all methods and modes of inquiry are thus grounded in a grasp

---

29. Loewe, Review Symposium for Paul Knitter's *No Other Name*, 126.

of the human subject in her historically dynamic and self-correcting process of living can this verifiable critique of the Enlightenment bias against religion and tradition hope to receive a hearing. As human subjects, members of the wisdom traditions of the world might have practical and recurrent ways of effecting that liberation. Dialogue is not infallible; we should expect dialogue to issue in mistakes but mistakes are facts that can be known and thus corrected. A dynamic movement to ever higher viewpoints, a movement that possesses its own sanctions for self-correction, will reverse any anti-religious short-circuiting of reason that would insist on a terminus of self-transcendence less than God. Other worldviews can indeed encourage progress *so long as* they are promoting intelligent, reasonable, responsible action.

Besides the religions of the world there are humanist traditions as well. Loewe's universalist approach encourages engagement with all such intellectual traditions, even those distorted by "rationalism and positivism" because these traditions caution "against any lazily triumphalistic fideism" and so deserve "not easy dismissal but measured response from a faithful reason capable of vindicating itself in face of modernity's diminution of reason's scope and power."[30] One is reminded of the three "publics" that David Tracy identifies as possible audiences of theological discourse. Tracy's insistence on the public nature of hermeneutics and thus the religious classic as open to interpretation by any serious inquirer can provide an entry point for the universalist position. Religious classics can function even for non-believers not only as a compelling statement of the human condition but also as a worldview in which things might be other than they are.[31] Because the Christian church has as a central responsibility the extension of the gospel's liberating and healing message, it necessarily must reject the myth of the way things are, and that includes the way the human family is fragmented into what Lonergan has called "an archipelago of islands of meaning."[32] Tracy's responsible evaluation of the role of tradition opposes any standard of orthodoxy set by narrowly traditionalist approaches closed to higher viewpoints.

---

30. William Loewe, review of *Beyond Resurrection* by A. J. M. Wedderburn, *Theological Studies* 62/2 (June 2001) 390–91.

31. See David Tracy, *The Analogical Imagination* (New York: Crossroad, 1981).

32. See n. 6 above.

Writing about the three theological virtues that figure so importantly in the Law of the Cross, Loewe notes that "charity and hope rest
upon some grasp of the truth concerning God's existence and man's
existence before God. While a philosopher might attain that truth,
many philosophers do not, and most men do not become philosophers
at all; hence belief comes in to make the truth about God and man
generally available."[33] I want to elaborate on that last, very significant
phrase: "belief comes in." Any universalism worthy of the name cannot, of course, neglect belief and tradition as essential elements in an
adequate account of self-transcendence and the trajectory of progress.
Belief does not function merely within religion; any theory of human
reason must integrate the empirically verifiable fact that belief plays a
critical role in human development. Belief, in other words, is part of
the foundations of universal reason as grounded in the human subject.
As carriers of meanings and values through history, beliefs are as important in science as in religion. Examples are everywhere to be found,
so I will simply identify one: The chemistry student does not verify the
periodic table inside the front cover of her textbook. To do so would
be impossible not because it is unverifiable but because the student has
not the skill, knowledge or time. Believing it, the student can go on to
learn chemistry; not believing it, the student is condemned to chemical
ignorance.

Whether in science, common sense or religion, belief stabilizes
structures and makes available the content of human learning through
the generations. Structures recur because belief maintains them, but

> believing can be too helpful. It can help one to see what is not
> there. . . . The investigator needs a well-stocked mind, else he
> will see but not perceive; but the mind needs to be well-stocked
> more with questions than with answers, else it will be closed and
> unable to learn.[34]

While belief serves progress by extending the elements of the solution
to the problem of evil to those who have faith, there is also the need for
openness to new questions as they arise when the redemptive intention
is not being fully achieved. Inheritance can be a mixture of authentic

33. Loewe, "Lonergan and the Law of the Cross," 167.

34. Lonergan, "Method: Trend and Variations," in *Third Collection: Papers by
Bernard J. F. Lonergan, S.J.*, ed. Frederick Crowe (New York: Paulist, 1985) 17.

meanings and values as well as nonsense and disvalue. What is going forward by way of these new questions keeps the inheritance attentive to its own limitations and opportunities for expansion and growth. The great value and inescapability of tradition and belief does not alter the fact that traditions are generated and maintained in human subjects. One believes for reasons and when one understands that fact, from the perspective of the higher viewpoint of interiority, one can then account for the development of tradition and the role of belief as well as their distortions and need for purification.

Lest there be misunderstanding here, let me clarify the phrase "higher viewpoint of interiority." The turn to the subject is not a question of selecting a model or theory to apply to a situation, just as making a moral decision is not a matter of applying a rule to a situation, as if the rule has the answer to the questions "What's going on?" and "What should I do about it?" If "interiority" were simply application of theory, then successful dialogue would be a matter of parties in the conversation having selected a theory they prefer, one that they have decided to privilege. The title of this essay is "Finding the Ground," not "Choosing a Model." The Buddhist and the Christian in dialogue, for example, have not decided that humans are curious beings who want to know what is true and how to achieve some good. On the contrary, the turn to interiority as the ground from which one thinks, decides, and acts is the correct understanding of a fact. The fact is not chosen but understood. The Buddhist or the Christian who has made the turn to the subject has understood that she and her dialogue partner are in fact oriented toward the true and the good, and when that orientation is scuttled, it is because of blindness, "attachments," irrationality—in a word, sin.

The aberrant trajectories of undeveloped traditions and cultures will mean lack of ability to oppose evil. Dialogue with secular thinkers and non-Christians can be an appeal to men and women of good will who, from the resources of their own traditions and cultures, share with Christians a commitment to the self-correcting process of learning. The awareness of human historicity and its concomitant plurality of cultures need not obscure the fact that there is also something permanent in human living. That permanence need not be confused with an image of stasis or unchanging universality, as was the assumption of classicist culture or in some versions of reason that we find in the pre-Kantian continental rationalist philosophies. One of Lonergan's recurrent phrases is "system on the move." What a historically conscious mentality understands as universal is precisely the need for development directed by the permanent transcendental precepts. Those same precepts, when made actual in concrete living, aim at complete self-knowledge and thereby gradually eliminate misunderstandings and mistaken judgments concerning many things, including what is permanent and what can be developed in human life. The position does not assume that there is only accidental change in cultures or mentalities or people. Nor, at the other extreme, is it the free-floating relativism of certain postmodern accounts of reason. Rather, the universal element is ever "on the move" because it is the inquiring operator of normative human subjectivity.

> There is a responsibility to intelligence or reasonableness, and it is neglected when one overlooks the inadequacy of answers and, no less, when one withholds a qualified assent when further relevant questions are not made available.[35]

The further relevant questions sometimes lead to radical change, to the leap of conversion. In the present situation, those further relevant questions sometimes arise out of dialogue with other religions. For example, dialogue with Muslims can help Christians to eliminate inadequate or misleading images regarding the doctrine of the Trinity. The persons of the Trinity are not three in the arithmetic sense of that word since God is not to be counted in that way. Attending to the obstacle that Muslims have with their understanding of the Trinity can help to purify the Christian's own understanding of that doctrine. Moreover, as the Muslim connection between the two Islamic "pillars" of God's Oneness and the responsibility to the poor is better understood by the Christian in dialogue—only God is God, and one's wealth is not to be worshipped—Christians might rediscover the theological ground for their own responsibility for the poor and the impossibility of serving two masters.

The opportunity to enter more deeply into one's own religion through dialogue can be understood within this dynamic framework of the questioning subject. Religions are responses to questions of ulti-

35. Lonergan, "A Post-Hegelian Philosophy of Religion," in *Third Collection*, 206–7. See also in the same volume "Natural Right and Historical Mindedness," 169–83.

macy; they are therefore generated by unrestricted desire and thus head toward the unique solution to the problem of evil. When distorted, they are directed by restricted and interested desire and head toward fragmentation in the human family. As religious encounter and dialogue proceed, one recognizes the good in the other because of the shared foundation in human self-transcendence. If one's own tradition, at a given time and cultural manifestation, happens to be weak on a particular element of the solution to the problem of evil, then it could be that, encountering that element in another tradition, one's own tradition is strengthened and aided in its self-purification. Buddhist meditation, for example, might aid in the recovery of forms of Christian prayer that have lain dormant. The more this happens, and the more people engage in it, the greater the possibility that cooperation in promoting the good will occur.[36]

On the benefit of Christian dialogue with other religions, one can do no better than Loewe's succinct judgment:

> . . . the solution to the problem of evil will be one, and it is possible that the dynamic of the Law of the Cross may be found in more than one set of religious symbols. At any rate, a dialogue situation with other world religions constitutes a new experience for Christianity. Openness to dialogue implies the possibility, not of a loss of identity, but of a revised and enriched self-understanding for all participants.[37]

Dialogue enhances the images and ideas that constitute the manifold out of which new insights might emerge. One cannot understand what is not available to think about. Dialogue and the anticipation of new insights enhance the probability that such insights might occur. If moral response requires knowledge (including judgments of fact and not merely value judgments and decisions), then knowledge of the other traditions is a moral need. A universalist view increases one's effective freedom to cooperate with others while the long-term and widespread dialogue of many peoples responding to the transcendental precepts work to recover human solidarity in promoting the good.

---

36. For a concise summary of recent strategies for interreligious dialogue with the intention of promoting reconciliation and liberation, see Peter C. Phan, "Global Healing and Reconciliation: The Gift and Task of Religion, a Buddhist-Christian Perspective," *Buddhist-Christian Studies* 26 (2006) 89–108.

37. Loewe, "Lonergan and the Law of the Cross," 174.

In an emergently probable universe there is a chance that certain elements of the random manifold will give rise to something new. Today, globalization has delivered a manifold that makes collaboration among peoples of different cultures, traditions and religions more likely. This development, it seems to me, presents an opportunity to make concrete the call of Vatican II's "Declaration on Non-Christian Religions" (*Nostra Aetate*) for moral cooperation among the religions. In other words, a widely held belief in the possibility of progress that depends on the responsible human subject will make progress more likely.

From the perspective of Christian theology, the world's religions can agree to explore the experience of desire given by the Spirit to all. Lonergan has noted that

> [t]here is to Christianity an aspiration to universalism, *e.g. I Tim.* 2:4. Perhaps the simplest explanation of this universalism would be that (1) salvation of the Christian is in and through charity, and (2) this gift as infrastructure can be the Christian account of religious experience in any and all men.[38]

Charity, in those outside Christian discourse, may be conscious but not known, and so as the Christian religion names the content in its historically and culturally conditioned practices and doctrines, it is at least worth asking whether other traditions have done the same thing within their own historically and culturally conditioned ways. It is a question to be answered, not an assumption to be taken for granted. The moral demands of our time would seem to suggest such a working hypothesis.[39]

I have argued that there are intellectual, moral, and religious reasons for affirming a universalist position, grounded in the human subject. William Loewe has often reminded us that ideal structures, from the self-generated knowledge of individuals to multinational corporations and every structure in between, is in the concrete always to

38. Lonergan, "Prolegomena to the Study of the Emerging Religious Consciousness of Our Time," in *Third Collection*, 71.

39. In the past hundred years there have been indications of convergence. Lonergan pointed to Robley Whitson's book, *The Coming Convergence of World Religions* (New York: Newman, 1971), and to William Johnston's work in Christian-Zen dialogue. See for example William Johnston, *Silent Music: The Science of Meditation* (New York: Harper, 1974).

some extent distorted by sin. We must anticipate failure and decline. Naïve optimism is not a philosophy that promotes progress, and it can easily make matters worse. My claim that interreligious cooperation is an intellectual, moral, and religious exigence is certainly not meant to be taken as a simplistic formula for progress. But assumptions that deny the ideal structure and withdraw to an ecclesiocentric theology will not contribute to the universal trajectory toward which Christian eschatological hope resolutely points.

10

"Irrational Exuberance" at the Foot of the Cross: Redeeming the Rhythms of Economic Life

STEPHEN L. MARTIN

IMMACULATA UNIVERSITY

In the late 1970s and early 80s, William Loewe published several groundbreaking essays extending Bernard Lonergan's accounts of sin and soteriology to address the field of economic life.[1] Since then, several important developments have taken place that highlight both the timeliness of Loewe's work and its applicability in a new theological context. I will focus my attention in this essay on the economic consequences of the contrasting theological approaches to social-scientific mediation in the writings of selected theologians in the Radical Orthodoxy movement and in the work of Bernard Lonergan.[2] Amidst these developments

---

1. See the following works by William P. Loewe: *Toward the Critical Mediation of Theology: A Development of the Soteriological Theme in the Work of Bernard Lonergan* (PhD diss., Marquette University, 1974); "Dialectics of Sin: Lonergan's *Insight* and the Critical Theory of Max Horkheimer," *Anglican Theological Review* 61 (1979) 224–45; "Lonergan and the Law of the Cross: A Universalist View of Salvation," *Anglican Theological Review* 59/2 (1977) 162–74; "Toward a Responsible Contemporary Soteriology," in *Creativity and Method: Essays in Honor of Bernard Lonergan, S.J.*, ed. Matthew L. Lamb (Milwaukee: Marquette University Press, 1981) 213–27; "Encountering the Crucified God: The Soteriology of Sebastian Moore," *Horizons* 9/2 (Fall 1982) 216–36.

2. Daniel Bell, D. Stephen Long, and William Cavanaugh have published books and/ or articles in the Routledge Radical Orthodoxy series edited partially by John Milbank,

Loewe's work continues to be an important resource in the conjunction of grace and economic flourishing. In fact, he seems to foreshadow the present state of affairs among theologians when he writes:

> If for example an economic system proves unjust, the Christian community must offer more than anathema; it falls within the community's redemptive task to promote the theoretical research which might discover how the system could be corrected or transformed. In far broader terms, the Christian community, with its commitment to the objectivity of truth and value, surely has a contribution of crucial importance to make to the scientific world in an age dominated by neopositivism and relativism. That contribution can, of course, only come through those who possess the necessary scientific expertise.[3]

Loewe signals that, contrary to John Milbank's eschewal of social-scientific theory in his influential *Theology and Social Theory: Beyond Secular Reason*, Christian ethics needs to cultivate and incorporate economic expertise if it is to promote redemptive recovery. After all, Lonergan insists that "if you want to give moral advice to an economist, you have to know how the economy runs."[4]

This may seem to accept the primacy of economics over theology that Milbank and others have set their program against. Milbank is upfront; in the first paragraph of *Theology and Social Theory* he declares his intention to "demonstrate that all the most important governing assumptions of [modern, secular] social theory are bound up with the

---

whose monumental and influential *Theology and Social Theory: Beyond Secular Reason* (London: Blackwell, 1990) can be said to be Radical Orthodoxy's founding document. See Daniel Bell Jr., *Liberation Theology after the End of History: The Refusal to Cease Suffering* (London: Routledge, 2001); D. Stephen Long, *Divine Economy: Theology and the Market* (London: Routledge, 2000) and "Catholic Social Teaching and the Global Market," in *Wealth, Poverty, and Human Destiny*, ed. Doug Bandow and David L. Schindler (Wilmington, DE: ISI, 2003) 77–102; William Cavanaugh, *Theopolitical Imagination: Discovering the Liturgy as Political Act in an Age of Global Consumerism* (London: T. & T. Clark, 2002); "The Unfreedom of the Free Market," in *Wealth, Poverty and Human Destiny*, 103–28; and "The City: Beyond Secular Parodies," in *Radical Orthodoxy: A New Theology*, ed. John Milbank, Catherine Pickstock, and Graham Ward (London: Routledge, 1998) 182–200.

3. Loewe, "Toward a Responsible Contemporary Soteriology," 226.

4. Bernard Lonergan, *Caring about Meaning: Patterns in the Life of Bernard Lonergan*, ed. Pierrot Lambert, Charlotte Tansey, and Cathleen Going (Montreal: Thomas More Institute, 1982) 225.

modification or the rejection of orthodox Christian positions."[5] For D. Stephen Long, in a time when "the triumph of capitalism is heralded as the end of history," the proper theological question is not, "Which global economic system should the Church, its theologians, and its philosophers support?" Instead, Christians should be asking, "How are we to be faithful in these times, which we must discern by the gift of dogma and doctrine handed down to us?"[6] William Cavanaugh, though not as methodologically allergic to social science as Milbank and Long, is against dialoguing with those outside the church through "concrete practices that do not need translation into some putatively 'neutral' language to be understood."[7] Daniel Bell Jr., while not directly criticizing economic theorizing, urges us to realize that "capitalism's victory is not simply economic; it is, more insidiously ontological."[8]

Dissenting from Radical Orthodoxy on these points does not mean that one has to minimize the importance of Christian orthodoxy, the responsibility to be faithful to it, to isolate Christian thinking on the economy from strictly theological understanding, or to underestimate the importance of ontology or conversion in overcoming the defects of capitalism. The full context of Lonergan's economic thought, however, is the church's responsibility to both heal human alienation and misery, and to help create, through theory and practice, alternative ecclesial and "secular" social structures that exemplify the reign of God in this world. I argue that the elements of the "reign of sin" in political economy as identified by Lonergan, Radical Orthodoxy theologians, and others can only be redeemed on this side of heaven by first identifying and understanding the rhythms of economic life. It is to this broader context that I believe Lonergan refers when he claims, belying the Radical Orthodoxy critique of his thought as secularist and humanist, that "a good economics needs Christianity."[9] I will use recent economic history to illustrate a theological response that creatively mediates economic healing. I offer a brief summary of Lonergan's economic thought alongside Loewe's and others' explications of Lonergan's Law of the Cross. Lonergan takes

5. Milbank, *Theology and Social Theory*, 1.
6. D. Stephen Long, "Catholic Social Teaching," 77–78.
7. Cavanaugh, *Theopolitical Imagination*, 94.
8. Bell, *Liberation Theology*, 3.
9. Lonergan, *Caring About Meaning*, 225.

as seriously as Radical Orthodoxy does the failings of "secular reason," but his theology can function better than Radical Orthodoxy as an adequate economic soteriology.

Irrational Exuberance and the Clinton "Boom"

Though the recent burst of the housing bubble has begun to tarnish his reputation, former Federal Reserve Chairman Alan Greenspan (1987–2006) is generally credited with managing what President Clinton in his 1999 State of the Union address called "the longest peacetime economic expansion in our history, with nearly 18 million new jobs, wages rising at more than twice the rate of inflation, the highest home ownership in history, the smallest welfare rolls in 30 years, and the lowest peacetime unemployment since 1957."[10] Greenspan was lauded for "taming" the waves that threaten to turn every boom into bust, thereby avoiding in this period the serious recession that according to business cycle theory inevitably occurs as a result of economic growth.

A self-described "inflation hawk," considered by many on the right and left to be overly worried about inflation, Greenspan was not afraid to refrain from raising interest rates even when unemployment fell below the "natural" or "structural" rate, viewed by most economists at that time to be 6.5 percent.[11] Most economists held that below this threshold tight labor markets would give workers leverage to demand wage increases, though some worried that this could bring back the runaway inflation of the late 1970s and early 80s. Nonetheless, when the specter of inflation arose, held to be signaled by wage growth due to lower unemployment from economic expansion, Greenspan was willing to slow the growth of the "overheating" economy by raising interest rates.

While some of Clinton's bipartisan economic policies such as welfare reform and entitlement reductions exemplified a certain political "turn to the right," the general belief was that the tides of the country's deficit reduction and economic growth had "raised all boats." However,

---

10. William J. Clinton, "Address before a Joint Session of the Congress on the State of the Union," January 19, 1999, online: http://frwebgate.access.gpo.gov/cgi-bin/get doc.cgi?dbname=1999_public_papers_vol1_text&docid=pap_text-44.pdf.

11. See Alan Greenspan, *The Age of Turbulence: Adventures in a New World* (New York: Penguin, 2007) 170.

as data indicate, Clinton's "middle-way" politics and Federal monetary policy together skewed this growth to the upper income classes and maybe even made the lot of the middle and poor income classes worse. Although, to be fair, this was generally the case under the two previous Republican administrations served by Greenspan, the 1990s presented two opportunities that tend, though not always, to raise the lot of poorer income classes: (1) a sustained economic expansion and (2) a Democratic president. As Robert Pollin argued in a 1999 article in *New Left Review* (which typically takes a negative view of capitalism pursuant to its roots in critical theory), despite higher unemployment and lower inflation, "the overall conditions of life for America's most destitute households may have worsened during the Clinton Administration."[12] Though Clinton was able to get through an increase in the minimum wage, it still was 40 percent below its buying power in 1968,[13] and his 1997 tax cuts reduced taxes for the top 60 percent of the population with the great bulk of the cuts going to the top 20 percent of wage earners.[14] Meanwhile expenditures on food stamps and other nutritional assistance dropped by $4.3 billion.[15]

Overall, despite rosy reflections about the Clinton "boom," workers experienced more thorns than petals. Despite record corporate profits in the underlying economy, under the Federal Reserve's watch the average wage for non-supervisory workers as a whole dropped 60 cents per hour when comparing the periods of 1980–90 to 1991–98, and the earnings of those in the lowest tenth percentile of wage distribution over those same two periods dropped 19 cents per hour.[16] Moreover, wage inequality measured by the ratio of the highest tenth percentile to the lowest tenth percentile increased sharply, even more than under Reagan and Bush.[17] Only at the end of a stock market boom during 1998–2000 did wages rise above the inflation rate.[18]

12. Robert Pollin, "Anatomy of Clintonomics," *New Left Review* 3 (May–June 2000) 27.

13. See ibid., 21.

14. See ibid., 22.

15. See ibid., 26.

16. Bureau of Labor Statistics, cited in Pollin, "Anatomy of Clintonomics," 36.

17. See ibid., 35.

18. See Lawrence Mishel, Jared Bernstein, and John Schmitt, *The State of Working America 1996–97* (Armonk, NY: M. E. Sharpe, 1997) 144.

As Greenspan himself recognized and even in a sense exploited, the combination of low inflation and high employment in the Clinton era was not primarily due to the breakdown of the natural law of unemployment, which supposedly let him repeatedly lower interest rates to keep the economy growing without high inflation. In a striking juxtaposition of good news and bad news marking this period, Greenspan, celebrating what he viewed as the "'extraordinary' and 'exceptional'" economic performance for 1997, remarked that a major contributing factor was "a heightened sense of job insecurity," which inhibited workers from seeking higher wages and prevented the wage and price inflation that is supposed to occur at low unemployment.[19] Indeed, Pollin cites Federal Reserve Bank statistics showing that between 1990 and 1995 the "stagnation of wages and benefits itself fully explains the lack of inflationary pressure"[20] that engendered the bipartisan support of Fed policies that did achieve low unemployment and low inflation, though conservatives like Steven Forbes bemoaned Greenspan's periodic brakes on the economy.[21]

At the height of his persuasive power in December 1996, Greenspan posed the rhetorical question, "How do we know when irrational exuberance has unduly escalated asset values, which then become subject to unexpected and prolonged contractions as they have in Japan over the past decade?"[22] This goes far beyond fear of investors acting upon the reading of tea leaves. For Lonergan, basic sin *is* the irrational: "If there is a reason there would not be sin. There may be excuses; there may be extenuating circumstances; but there cannot be a reason, for basic sin consists, not in yielding to reasons and reasonableness, but in failing to yield to them; it consists not in inadvertent failure but in advertence to and in acknowledgment of obligation that nonetheless is not followed by reasonable response."[23]

---

19. Quoted in Pollin, "Anatomy of Clintonomics," 39.

20. Ibid., 38.

21. See Steve Chapman, "Steve Forbes, Prairie Populist," *Chicago Tribune*, September 12, 1999, online: http://articles.chicagotribune.com/1999–09–12/news/9909120192_1_inflation-rate-low-prices-deflation.

22. Quoted in Bob Woodward, *Maestro: Greenspan's Fed and the American Boom* (New York: Simon & Schuster, 2000) 179.

23. Bernard Lonergan, *Insight: A Study of Human Understanding*, vol. 3 of *Collected Works of Bernard Lonergan*, ed. Frederick Crowe and Robert Doran (Toronto: University of Toronto Press, 1993) 690.

Irrational exuberance in this context is thus a compound sin—the enthusiastic disregarding of rationality in pursuit of self-interest without regard to the consequences. Further, this goes beyond individual sin, as the growth in the gap between classes in the midst of a boom usually considered to lift all boats is the result not just of investors seeking above-normal profits, but is instead the consequence of sinful social structures that concentrate government power and economic wealth. These structures call forth a religious response. In Christian terms, irrational exuberance is a metaphor and an instantiation of evil as not only intentional malice but also the "unplanned moral disorder that may not be intended."[24] Thus in order to identify unplanned moral disorder, we need to examine two competing accounts of economic malaise and its origins: the Radical Orthodoxy analysis of how capitalism replaces charity with self-interest, and Bernard Lonergan's macroeconomics, in which he examines what constitutes an intelligently, reasonably, and responsibly guided moral economic order. As Lonergan writes, "when the system that is needed for our collective survival does not exist, then it is futile to excoriate what does exist while blissfully ignoring the task of constructing a technically viable system to put in its place."[25]

Radical Orthodoxy and Economics

John Milbank notes that political economy as delineated by Adam Smith was "founded specifically on that area of morality having to do with self-interest"—pure benevolence belonging only to God—and is thus not a justice foremost concerned with the common good.[26] Benevolence and charity are confined to the private and the familial world. Milbank notes the less benign, Machiavellian dimension of Scottish Enlightenment economics, characterizing James Stewart's view of the marketplace as a "self-regulating agon," "marked and constantly redrawn by arbitrary political violence."[27] Therefore, for Milbank, capitalism is not founded

24. Kenneth Melchin, *Living with Other People: An Introduction to Christian Ethics Based on Bernard Lonergan* (Collegeville, MN: Liturgical, 1998) 131.

25. Bernard Lonergan, "Healing and Creating in History," in *Third Collection*, ed. Frederick Crowe (Mahwah, NJ: Paulist, 1985) 108.

26. See Milbank, *Theology and Social Theory*, 31.

27. Ibid., 36

by the spontaneous activity of supposedly free subjects as Smith maintained, but rather as "depending upon class struggle and initial confinement of the majority of the population; a removal of their freedom and their talents."[28] In other words, like most sinful social structures, the game is already fixed by those in power against and at the expense of those without. William Cavanaugh writes that this freedom, so long as it is not directed toward a common end or a common good, becomes "the aggrandizement of power and the manipulation of will and desire."[29] Economists such as Milton Friedman and theologians like Michael Novak defend capitalism for liberating freedom, but Radical Orthodoxy thinkers, relying on Augustine, rightly point out that the freedom that is liberated is the *libido dominandi* of the powerful. In the context of Greenspan's comment, the libido of irrational exuberance enables prosperity through the state's manipulation of economic expansion through political tools. Daniel Bell Jr. cites Gilles Deleuze, displaying Radical Orthodoxy's reliance upon postmodern thinkers as well as Augustine, in claiming that "the state is not an emancipatory agent but a repressive instrument of the capitalist order."[30] Loewe too cites the critical theorist view of Max Horkheimer that "reason in its modern form functions as a blind servant of the vested interests which determine the status quo."[31]

D. Stephen Long indicts most of modern theological economic ethics in its celebration of human freedom in line with market values, since theology has adopted essentially the same anthropology described above: a freedom granted with no content, no telos. Long argues that modern anthropology is "the inevitable result of a moral theology that first seeks to be relevant to the dominant social order when that order is defined by theologians."[32] Any alliance with social science as a product of that dominant social order thus taints theological economic ethics, so long as it is divorced from the witness of the church and the testimony of Scripture.

It is not the case that the relationship between social science and Christian ethics outside Radical Orthodoxy has been unproblematic.

28. Ibid.
29. Cavanaugh, "Unfreedom of the Free Market," 103–4.
30. Bell, *Liberation Theology after the End of History*, 19.
31. Loewe, "Dialectics of Sin," 237.
32. Long, *Divine Economy*, 68.

Even those who do not spurn the use of social science as completely as does Radical Orthodoxy are wary of making particular social theories normative in their theologies. For example, Neil Ormerod notes at least six competing strands within sociology (the functionalist, etc.), with the result that "engagement with social sciences by ecclesiologists has been eclectic, sporadic, intermittent and secondary to what they view as their primary task."[33] Lonergan summarizes the problem as follows: "The human science is itself open to suspicion. Its representatives are divided ideologically. They advocate contrary courses of action, all of which have their respective good points, but none is without very serious defects. The notorious case at the present time is economics."[34] The solution is not to jettison economics, but to reorient it by making it empirical, critical, and normative.[35]

Radical Orthodoxy seeks to resolve this problematic relationship by ending it—there is no place in Christian ethical reflection for dialogue with social science because all social science is inherently anti-theological and secularist, and rooted in metanarratives of violence and conflict incongruent with the metanarratives of Christianity. For Radical Orthodoxy, even the reliance of traditional Catholic social teaching upon natural law tends not to be sufficiently theological and confessional, because it ultimately still grants determination of the "facts" to a non-theological analysis. For Long and Milbank, Christian economic practice does not result from attempting to deduce a "universally normative human society . . . from metaphysical or theological first principles."[36] Rather it is a creative, *poetic*, open-ended practice, much like building on to a Gothic cathedral, which seeks and creates truth, goodness, and beauty in practical implementations.[37] This results in Christian socialism, by which Milbank means that market exchanges are determined not by impersonal contract nor central planning, but

---

33. Neil Ormerod, "A Dialectical Engagement with the Social Sciences in an Ecclesiological Context," *Theological Studies* 66/4 (December 2005) 816.

34. Bernard Lonergan, "Moral Theology and the Human Sciences," in *Philosophical and Theological Papers, 1965–1980, Collected Works of Bernard Lonergan* 17 (2004) 302.

35. See Lonergan, *Insight*, 261.

36. John Milbank, "On Complex Space," in *The Word Made Strange: Theology, Language, Culture* (Oxford: Blackwell, 1997) 270.

37. See ibid., 276–78.

by democratic, "freely assented-to transactions—the outcomes of processes of free and equal negotiation."[38]

This freedom is not a liberal freedom for freedom itself, nor does this freedom preserve an essentially unjust status quo, but this freedom has a teleological goal to "repeatedly seek to preserve or extend a distribution of resources held to be just." Milbank makes the important distinction that this is not a "market socialism" that still gives free reign to "*pure* market forces of supply and demand," which are indifferent to the "collective and individual unconstrained agreement" in the pursuit of justice that marks authentic socialism. Against a "free" market–shaped society then, whatever shape it ends up taking, authentic socialism rules out "exploitation of scarcity and necessity for profit."[39] While recognizing legitimate and beneficial "needs," it does not grant "automatic legitimacy" to all expressed needs as the "free" market does. This critique must be a religious critique: "Only [with an] invocation of transcendence can there be a critique of capitalist order whose secularity is its primary character."[40]

Radical Orthodoxy, while offering necessary correctives to simple secularistic variants of social science, does not lead to viable ways of achieving that vision, and by denying the possibility of any social-scientific mediation to understand reality Radical Orthodoxy may actually undermine its own vision.[41] As Colin Gunton writes in his critique of Radical Orthodoxy,

> [T]heology has a responsibility for the healing of the disastrous modern breach between the worlds of the true, the beautiful and the good. But to leave it there, and particularly to leave the ethical dimensions as little more than implicit, is to run the danger, intrinsic in much English theology, of an apparently frivolous aestheticism (fiddling while Rome burns, perhaps). Unless more is done, one cannot develop the theological criteria with which to distinguish between that which is Christian in scientific and secular rationality and that which participates in mod-

38. Ibid., 271.

39. Ibid.

40. Milbank, *Theology and Social Theory*, 199.

41. See Stephen Martin, "John Paul II, Milbank and Lonergan," *Lonergan Review* 2/1 (Spring 2010) 315–27.

ern apostasy. Without them, however, are not polemics against secularization likely to be mainly reactionary?[42]

While adding an essential stress on the importance of religious traditions for mediating truth, Radical Orthodoxy can also serve to undermine efforts like Lonergan's to develop relatively autonomous economic theories helpful to both religious communities and economic science. Dismissing approaches to economics that are not strictly theologically originated leaves a void of substantive alternatives to truly secularistic economics such as orthodox and Marxist theory. Though Long offers valuable critiques of the impersonal contractual market system of exchange, the only concrete alternative he offers is the example of how churches hosting small farmers markets transform the "anonymous and impersonal exchanges that usually characterize the supermarket" into interactions characterized by "friendship and personal relations."[43] The Catholic social ethicist and economist Daniel Finn takes Radical Orthodoxy strongly to task:

> Neither Long nor Milbank seems to have a scientific bone in his body. Scientists attempt to understand how the world works, separate from any preconceived notions of how it ought to work. . . . Neither exhibits anything of what theologian Paul Tillich once called "humility before the fact," a trait of empiricist science that Tillich appreciated in spite of his critique of the movement. Long begins his book by declaring that he has never been able to "get inside" economics as a science. Perhaps as a result, the novel elements of his critique will be persuasive only for others similarly situated. As the 19th century economist Heinrich Pesch said, "Theology does not grow wheat."[44]

Lonergan's New Economic Paradigm

Contra the strictures of Radical Orthodoxy, the application of Lonergan's thought to these events and the management of the economy is not de-

---

42. Colin Gunton, "Editorial," *International Journal of Systematic Theology* 1/2 (July 1999) 117.

43. Long, *Divine Economy*, 269.

44. Daniel Rush, "Catholic Social Thought and Contemporary Economic Thinking," *Commonweal* Spring 2002 Colloquium, New York, April 19–21, 2002, online: http://www.catholicsinpublicsquare.org/papers/spring2002commonweal/finnpaper/finnpaper.htm.

rived from revelation, doctrine, and specific church teachings, at least in the explicit terms of his analysis. His macroeconomics does not focus on greed or sin, nor on the rate of inflation or the level of employment at particular moments, but seeks primarily to understand and guide the economy in terms of significant variables more complex than those recognized by orthodox economics. As Fred Lawrence points out, "the lack of ultimacy that Lonergan ascribes to price and price theory can scarcely be overemphasized."[45] This does not leave out other ultimate concerns; Lonergan once remarked to Patrick Byrne that all his writings were in response to the Deuteronomic command that "the widows and the orphans won't starve"—a salient point that is still accessible to those outside the Judeo-Christian tradition.[46]

Instead of trying to "tame the waves" of economic growth, Lonergan argues that waves of economic expansion do not lead inevitably to recession and depression but have exigencies of their own that cannot be sublimated to other concerns, whether these be profit maximization or government intervention.[47] Instead of allowing irrational exuberance to head economic expansion off to economic ruin, we can read economic signals reasonably and responsibly. This points ahead to more religious emphases in Lonergan's economics that demonstrate that our thinking, theorizing, and precepts are directed by our ultimate concerns.

Instead of explicating Lonergan's macroeconomics in a rudimentary fashion, I wish to briefly sketch how Lonergan's pure cycle differs from the familiar business cycle in practice and in the theory that guided Greenspan's understanding and manipulation of monetary policy. This occurs in a context that both Greenspan and Lonergan view as crucial: the changes to an economy resulting from a major technological advance, in this case the computer revolution. In Lonergan's general theory of economic expansion the computer revolution contained a major surplus expansion that nonetheless did not result in its proper

45. Frederick Lawrence, "Editor's Introduction," in *Macroeconomic Dynamics*, ed. Frederick Lawrence, Charles Hefling, and Patrick Byrne, *Collected Works of Bernard Lonergan* 15 (Toronto: University of Toronto Press, 1999) xlvi.

46. Patrick H. Byrne, "*Ressentiment* and the Preferential Option for the Poor," *Theological Studies* 54/2 (June 1993) 241.

47. See Lonergan, *Macroeconomic Dynamics*, 7–9.

end—a major basic expansion that would have raised the standard of living for all.

Lonergan's *For a New Political Economy* and *Macroeconomic Dynamics: Essay in Circulation Analysis* were both written from 1930–44 in response to the misery arising from, and inadequate economics that gave rise to, the Great Depression.[48] As he wrote sometime in the mid to late 1930s, he wanted to avoid the "asinine confidence in political economy that has landed this century in an earthly hell."[49] He returned to his economics making some revisions and new inroads in the late 1970s until his death in 1984.[50] This renewed attention was occasioned by the stagflation and recessions of these years and also by the failure of political and liberation theology to make good use of economics in their sociopolitical analyses.[51]

Lonergan's functional analysis, which he differentiates from ortho-dox economics' more descriptive and predictive analysis, divides goods into basic and surplus goods.[52] Basic goods make up our standard of living, while surplus goods go into producing the tools and providing the services that either produce the tools that make basic goods or produce tools to make other surplus goods. An example of a basic good would be toothpaste, while a surplus good would be a cash register to ring up that purchase—the customer desires to consume the former and not the latter. Other examples of basic goods are shelter, food, household furniture, televisions, vacations, lawnmowers, college tuition, magazine subscriptions, internet access, etc., as long as these are used to augment one's standard of living. The list could go on almost indefinitely, espe-

48. See Bernard Lonergan, *For a New Political Economy*, ed. Philip McShane, *Collected Works of Bernard Lonergan* 21 (1998); and *Macroeconomic Dynamics*.

49. Bernard Lonergan, "Philosophy of History," 4, unpublished manuscript quoted in Lawrence, introduction to Lonergan, *Macroeconomic Dynamics*, iii.

50. For other biographical details concerning Lonergan's return to studying and teaching economics see Frederick E. Crowe, *Lonergan*, in Outstanding Christian Thinkers Series, ed. Brian Davies (Collegeville, MN: Liturgical, 1992) 133.

51. For example, Fred Lawrence reports that "Lonergan took part in a round-table conference in 1974 at which Gustavo Gutierrez stated that the real problem with lib-eration theology was that none of the liberation theologians of the day had a serious knowledge of economics." Lonergan himself considered that reflections such as Johann Baptist Metz's on economic injustice "lacked anything on economics" and needed to be "taken out of the context of the family wage and put into that of inadequate eco-nomic theory" (Lawrence, introduction to Lonergan, *Macroeconomic Dynamics*, xl).

52. See Lonergan, *Macroeconomic Dynamics*, 26–35.

cially as new basic goods such as iPads are developed constantly. These goods are paid for typically out of wages (either present wages or future wages, as when bought on credit), therefore there exists a basic circuit between supply of basic goods and demand for basic goods that gets its purchasing power at least partly from wages paid by basic suppliers (a worker at *Newsweek* stops at McDonalds on the way home for work or puts aside part of his or her paycheck to pay the mortgage).[53]

Examples of surplus goods are the cash register that rings up the hamburger purchase, the computer within the cash register, the technology used to make the computer chips within that computer; or a bulldozer that clears the land for the worker's house, the machine tools such as robotics used to manufacture the bulldozer, the computer technology that designs and controls the robotics, and so forth. Surplus goods are thus produced in tiers—a higher level of the surplus circuit produces the computer controls inside a cash register, the next highest level produces computer chips that help make up the computer controls, the next highest level of the surplus circuit provides silicon to make the chips, and so on. These companies creating surplus goods make up the surplus circuit—they supply each other with both tools and machines but also with funds to run their business. Following the economist Michael Kalecki, Lonergan points out that "not each individual capitalist but capitalists as a group get what they spend," in that surplus enterprises purchase goods from each other in this roundabout fashion.[54] In this way, the surplus circuit contributes only indirectly to someone's standard of living (unless Caterpillar employs them) while the basic circuit makes and consumes our standard of living. Because they are two distinct circuits, each circuit has its own price level, level of investment, gross product, employment level, and so forth.

Despite their distinct nature, almost constituting two different economies, there are crucial crossovers between the distinct circuits: (1) wages paid by surplus firms such as Caterpillar that are spent on the "consumer goods" of the basic circuit, and (2) money that flows from basic enterprises into the surplus circuit to maintain or purchase new equipment, such as a grocery store purchasing new cash registers.[55]

53. See ibid., 48–53.

54. See ibid., 70.

55. There is also a "redistributive function" that does not produce good per se, into which category fall banks, governments, insurance companies, pension funds, etc.

The importance of identifying these two circuits and their relationship to each other is that these forces need to be kept in balance for the economy to flourish and not to break down. Their dynamic, mutual conditioning of each other, especially during a major expansion (which usually begins within the surplus circuit, then moves outward to the entire economy), constitutes for Lonergan the significant variables of economic analysis.

Dynamics of Authentic Development vs. Dynamics of Growth and Decline

Neither the rudimentary analysis of recent US economic history above nor this very brief summary of Lonergan's economics is meant to approximate the breadth of economic theory and practice involved in economic expansion.[56] What can be done in this instance, however, is to show how a more effective outcome might have been achieved than what took place during and since the Clinton "boom." A major problem for anyone completing this analysis is the lack of statistics that would allow economists to determine the level and tendencies of basic and surplus goods, employment, price level, etc., and thus what stage of economic expansion the economy is in. In a major surplus expansion, what Lonergan terms "pure surplus income" (over and above the "normal profits" needed to stay in business) accelerates due to the increases in production, the expectations of sales, and the high number of surplus circuit businesses involved in the transformation of the economy

These take money from one circuit to another—moving money out of basic demand, in favor of investment in the surplus circuit, for example. See ibid., 48–60.

56. For far more extensive dissection, discussion,and development of Lonergan's economic thought, I list here only the current book-length treatments: Bruce Anderson and Philip McShane, *Beyond Establishment Economics: No Thank-You Mankiw* (Halifax, NS: Axial, 2002); Paul Hoyt-O'Connor, *Bernard Lonergan's Macroeconomic Dynamics* (Lewiston, NY: E. Mellen, 2004); Philip McShane, *Economics for Everyone: Das Just Kapital* (Halifax, NS: Axial, 1998) and *Pastkeynes, Pastmodern Economics: A Fresh Pragmatism* (Halifax, NS: Axial, 2002); and Elaine de Neeve, *Decoding the Economy: Understanding Change with Bernard Lonergan* (Montreal: Thomas More Institute, 2008); plus "Forging a New Economic Paradigm: Perspectives from Bernard Lonergan," a very helpful special issue of *The Lonergan Review* (2/1; Spring 2010), ed. Richard Liddy, containing twenty-nine essays and responses to Lonergan's economics from within several different economic, methodological, theological, and political perspectives, taking into account the current economic crises.

through different and increased technologies. Besides being saved or used to pay down debt and for other day-to-day operating expenses, a portion of these rising profits goes back into the company to fund further expansion, another portion is spent for the personal income of executives, another portion is paid to stockholders, and another portion pays more workers higher wages in the surplus circuit. This is one "crossover" between the surplus and basic circuits.

This tremendous increase of basic demand causes prices to rise, because the supply of basic goods has not risen significantly. In contrast to Greenspan's analysis, for Lonergan the increase in the basic price spread is positive because it discourages basic spending in favor of investment in surplus expansion, a practice termed by economists "forced savings." For example, if the economy in the 1990s had been in a surplus expansion, Greenspan's decision to raise interest rates would have slowed economic growth by increasing spending within the basic circuit when funds should have been allocated to further surplus expansion. Though sounding suspiciously like "trickle-down" economics at this point, Lonergan had good reason to call this stage "inegalitarian" because at this stage it is beneficial that surplus income go to higher-income workers since they are less likely than lower-income workers to spend any increased income on basic goods, since upper-income groups have them already.

Nevertheless, as a surplus expansion proceeds more and more lower-income workers are employed in the surplus circuit. There is the chance that the crossover of wages paid by the surplus circuit that is spent purchasing basic goods will not be offset by basic enterprises that invest these windfall profits caused by higher demand back into the surplus circuit. Such reintroduction of funds into the surplus circuit can take place through financial investment or through purchasing additional surplus goods. If such an offset does not occur, not only will the surplus circuit (and thus the standard of living of the economy as a whole) not grow to its fullest potential, but the surplus economic circuit will begin to shrink. Orders within the surplus circuit will falter, newly built factories will be closed, workers will be laid off, prices for surplus goods will fall—in other words, the surplus circuit economy will enter a recession, which eventually will lead the basic circuit to shrink as well through the fall-off of basic demand.[57] The "pure cycle" of economic growth will then be short-circuited into the familiar business cycle.

Part of the problem is the tendency endemic to cultural and economic theories (whether capitalist or Marxist) to regard surplus income in a proprietary way. In capitalist economic theories, surplus profits are "mine" and should be used to maximize my self-interest, which will coincidentally contribute to the common good through the economic workings described in Adam Smith's famous metaphor of the invisible hand.[58] In Marxism, surplus profits belong to workers to ensure that the fruits of the proletariat's labor are not being stolen by capitalists for their own benefit. By contrast, but in alignment with the emphasis on the common good in Catholic social teaching, in Lonergan's analysis surplus income is not to be treated proprietarily.[59] Rather surplus income is a "social dividend" to be spent or saved intelligently, reasonably, and responsibly according to which stage of the economic expansion the economy is in. For example, if the economy was in a surplus expansion, Greenspan's policies would not only cut off further growth that should have eventually benefited all rungs of the economy, but also would have preserved the incomes of wealthier classes by stifling the wage growth of lower classes.

As surplus income and high profits diminish as the surplus expansion peters out, in order for the transition from the surplus expansion to a basic expansion to be successful both surplus and basic firms should maintain or increase production instead of downsizing to preserve high profits. The surplus circuit should be trying to maintain production and employment as high as possible to take advantage of the increased demand from the basic circuit, as new technology increasingly becomes incorporated into the production and nature of basic goods. On the basic side, if desire for continuous high profits can be sublimated to the common good firms should continue to increase production to take

57. See Lonergan, *Macroeconomic Dynamics*, 69.

58. "[Every individual] generally, indeed, neither intends to promote the public interest, nor knows how much he is promoting it . . . he intends only his own gain; and he is in this case, as in many other cases, led by an invisible hand to promote an end which was no part of his own intention. . . . I have known much good done by those who affected to trade for the public good." Adam Smith, *An Inquiry into the Nature and Cause of the Wealth of Nations*, ed. Edwin Cannan (New York: Modern Library, 1994; orig. ed. 1776) 572.

59. See Lonergan, *Macroeconomic Dynamics*, 26.

advantage of better ways to produce better goods. Though rates of return would fall, overall profit would increase and more and more goods would become available to consumers. The basic expansion would continue as lower-income workers who spend most of their income on basic goods would receive more and more of the pie, which in turn would spur the basic demand that brings higher employment, higher real wages due to the increase in wages and a decrease in inflation. If the Federal Reserve Board, fearing inflation, were instead to raise interest rates at this egalitarian stage this would have the effect of direct starvation of the economy.

To sum up, economic problems result when a culture fails to distinguish a normal profit from surplus income: "every bias away from human authenticity brings about a situation ever more inhuman and intractable."[60] As Lonergan wrote,

> In equity [the basic expansion] should be directed to raising the standard of living of the whole society. The reason why it does not is not the simple-minded moralist's reason: greed, but the prime cause is ignorance. . . . When people do not understand what is happening and why, they cannot be expected to act intelligently. When intelligence is a blank, the first law of nature takes over: self-preservation. It is not primarily greed but frantic efforts at self-preservation that turns recession into depression, and depression into crash.[61]

If the transcendental precepts to "be observant, intelligent, reasonable and responsible"[62] were able to be complemented by an understanding of the dynamics of basic surplus and production, and surplus and basic expansions, the final phase of a major economic expansion would be marked by increases in demand for labor in the basic sector, which would in turn take up the slack from decreased demand for labor in the surplus sector. Wages would rise so that even people on fixed incomes would benefit. Per capita production would increase due to better technology and the number of basic enterprises would increase. There would be a boost in the standard of living for the entire economy. Situated within Lonergan's wider conceptions of the human good, the

60. Ibid., 94.

61. Ibid., 82.

62. Lonergan, *Method in Theology* (Toronto: University of Toronto Press, 1994) 20.

pure cycle shows that, contrary to proprietorial views of economic process,

> The human good then is at once individual and social. Individuals do not just operate to meet their needs but cooperate to meet one another's needs. As the community develops its institutions to facilitate cooperation, so individuals develop skills to fulfill the roles and perform the tasks set by the institutional frame-work. Though the roles are fulfilled and the tasks are performed that the needs be met, still all is done not blindly but knowingly, not necessarily but freely. The process is not merely the service of man; it is above all the making of man, his advance in authenticity, the fulfillment of his affectivity, and the direction of his work to the particular goods and a good of order that are worth while.[63]

Lonergan's "Divine Economy"

Lonergan's economics, while scientifically autonomous, is integral with the larger project of religious teaching and discipleship. Therefore, while "secular" as opposed to "theological," it is not secularistic, humanistic, or fully autonomous from religion as is the social theory critiqued by Radical Orthodoxy. As Lonergan writes, if science and values are not integrated, with economic values subordinated to higher ones, "The better educated become a class closed in upon themselves with no task proportionate to their training . . . the meaning and values of human living are impoverished. The will to achieve both slackens and narrows. Where once there were joys and sorrows, now there are just pleasures and pains. The culture has become a slum."[64]

While religious and moral conversion are necessary in a just economic order, Lonergan's economic analysis itself does not mention Scripture, doctrine, or church tradition, and also does not require conversion to Christianity to mediate economic reality, in the manner prescribed by Radical Orthodoxy. However, the explicitly Christian Law of the Cross, along with the universalist dimensions pointed out by Loewe, does provide an integral connection between Christian narrative, belief, practice, and economic decision making. In the last sec-

63. Ibid., 52.
64. Ibid., 99.

tion of *Macroeconomic Dynamics*, entitled "The Position of the Essay," appended in 1980 to his macroeconomic analysis finished thirty-six years earlier, Lonergan enters into theological critiques of economics similar to those Radical Orthodoxy theologians would later place front and center. After a discussion of individual, group, and general bias, he writes of the possibility of a solution:

> Now it is important to grasp that we are touching upon a very large issue. In its *fundamental form* it is the tension between grace and sin (Romans 7 and 8). It its *theological* form it is the thought of Augustine and his commentators and continuators. . . . In its *secularist* form it is the affirmation of the perfectibility of man by man. . . . Economists move under this secularist mantle when they conceive economics on the analogy of natural science, or when that fails, hand the management of the economy over to the welfare state . . . [L]ike [Machiavelli] they have no taste for imagined commonwealths and principalities which never were, because they look at how men in fact do live and not at such stuff as how men ought to live.[65]

The implication is that the "imagined commonwealth and principalities which never were" are analogous to a successful transition of the surplus expansion to the basic expansion, which can only be occasioned by understanding these dynamics and through grace.

Lonergan's more general interpretation of the solution to the problem of bias and inauthenticity incorporated into our individual lives and socioeconomic systems that become "facts" of human existence, follows his general presentation of the "fact" of the Law of the Cross, found in the last three theses of his yet-untranslated Gregorian University textbook, *De Verbo Incarnato*.[66] As discussed by Loewe, it involves three basic principles, one following upon the other: (1) sin leads to death; (2) if accepted out of love, death is transformed; (3) this transformed death receives "the blessing of new life."[67] Taken up into the context of Jesus Christ's mission, life, death, and resurrection, this law holds that "The Son of God thus became man, suffered, died and was raised, because the divine wisdom ordained and the divine good-

65. Lonergan, *Macroeconomic Dynamics*, 94–95.

66. See Lonergan, *De Verbo Incarnato* (Rome: Gregorian University Press, 1964) 552–93.

67. Loewe, "Lonergan and the Law of the Cross," 164.

ness willed, not to take away the evils of the human race by an exercise of power, but to convert those evils into a certain highest good through the just and mysterious Law of the Cross."[68]

Lonergan's Law of the Cross lays out a framework of redemption familiar in modern Christian soteriology: our moral incapacity leads to alienation and dehumanization; compounded by sinful social structures, this leads to moral impotence when it deprives persons of hope; this is only one form of death caused by sin; instead of fighting evil with evil, we can choose to accept and follow Jesus' example of accepting this death out of religious love, as Jesus did in order to transform it. When compared to Radical Orthodoxy, however, Lonergan and those besides Loewe who have developed further his Law of the Cross emphasize (1) the force of operative and cooperative grace in human transformation; and (2) the concurrent role of insight and understanding that can result from grace and that can lead to social transformation as well—"the blessing of new life" and new goods of order.[69] As Cynthia Crysdale notes, this "intervention of grace into distorted cycles of alienation" occurs through our ordinary insights and choices that "do not circumvent our natural ways of knowing, deciding and being in the world."[70] Since God does exist, Lonergan affirms the possibility of progress, in that through the intervention of grace, distortions of bias need not prevent the accumulations of insights that can transform the original situation. The "wheel of progress moves forward," despite the probability that it

68. Lonergan, *Dei Verbo Incarnato*, 552; quoted in Loewe, "Lonergan and the Law of the Cross," 163–64.

69. Besides Loewe's works cited herein, see Sebastian Moore, *The Crucified Is No Stranger* (New York: Seabury, 1977); *The Fire and the Rose Are One* (New York: Seabury, 1981); *Jesus the Liberator of Desire* (New York: Crossroad, 1987); and Cynthia Crysdale, *Embracing Travail: Retrieving the Cross Today* (New York: Continuum, 2001).

70. Crysdale, *Embracing Travail*, 131. Although Crysdale is linking Lonergan's epistemology with cooperation with divine grace, this stress on the immanent process of knowledge seems to be the reason for Milbank's inclusion of Lonergan's *Insight* in the foundationalist, modernist, "secular humanist attempt to confine critical reason to the Kantian level, to hold onto the notion of a 'reality' with which propositions made in discourse can be compared and so confirmed or disconfirmed, and to defend the noumenal subject as a *locus* for certain constant, universal, predilections and dispositions" (Milbank, *Theology and Social Theory*, 294).

becomes instead a "wheel of decline when this process is distorted by bias."[71]

When Patrick Byrne asked Lonergan what theology has to do with religious conversion, Lonergan replied cryptically, "Well, the dialectic." Byrne took this to mean that "the dysfunctions of contemporary structures have so trodden the spirits of human beings that the word of God has a difficulty finding root in our hearts, let alone bearing fruit a hundred-fold." Thus, "the transformation of economies can occur concretely only insofar as injustice is not repaid with hatred and violence. Sacrifices and suffering accepted now for the good of those members of the human-divine community to come is the most concrete condition for the emergence of the well-adapted economy."[72] Otherwise, as Matthew Lamb puts it, "social policies are formulated and violence and sin become structured in to society and culture" as people are socialized into alienating patterns of living.[73] These structures in turn limit our horizons through emphasis on self-interest which encourages egoism, through group bias which resists fruitful change, and through general bias which restricts understanding either to common-sense or to pseudo-theory, resulting in governing economic forces, such as irrational exuberance, which result from this flight from understanding.

It is not relatively difficult to move needed capital into a surplus expansion, especially when surplus income is going into the hands of the wealthier class who are most likely to reinvest it (if executives, unions, governments and others can avoid using this surplus income for conspicuous or increased consumption). As Fred Lawrence points out, however, there are no mechanisms for the exigency to meet the requirements of the movement to the egalitarian stage: even if understood, these requirements "will still make constant demands for further correct understandings and ever increasing moral choices."[74]

71. Lonergan, "Healing and Creating in History," 105.

72. Patrick Byrne, "Economic Transformations: The Role of Conversions and Culture in the Transformation of Economics," in *Religion in Context: Recent Studies in Lonergan*, ed. Timothy J. Fallon and Philip B. Riley (Lanham, MD: University Press of America, 1988) 342.

73. Matthew Lamb, "Nature, History and Redemption," in *Jesus Crucified and Risen: Essays in Spirituality and Theology in Honor of Dom Sebastian Moore*, ed. William P. Loewe and Vernon J. Gregson (Collegeville, MN: Liturgical, 1998) 131.

74. Frederick Lawrence, "Between Capitalism and Marxism: Introducing Lonergan's Economics," *Revista Portuguesa de Filosofia* 63/4 (2007) 941–59, at 959.

I believe that this difficulty, combined with the problems of bias in restricting human understanding reveal, *contra* Radical Orthodoxy, the possibility of an economics being secular without being secularist, which Radical Orthodoxy and Lonergan resist equally in the defense of economic justice. In correspondence with the brief discussion above of Lonergan's views on bias, sin, social sin, and the necessity of grace, Lawrence points out that Lonergan believed that the intellectual and moral demands of making the transition from the surplus expansion to the basic are still possible. Further, there is no inherent reason why such understanding and avenues of correct action cannot be communicated in ways accessible to those outside the Christian community, even if the desire for such understanding is partially formed by Scripture (Lonergan's desire to help the "widows and the orphans"). This is why, as Lawrence states, "whenever it should occur, the willingness of human beings to learn what the exigencies of the pure cycle are, to understand their specific concrete dynamisms, and to act habitually in accord with that correct understanding will not be due to a Christian economics, but to God's healing grace."[75]

Conclusion

After a doctor had done major surgery to both of a patient's hands, the patient asked, excitedly holding up her heavily bandaged hands, "Doctor, will I be able to play the piano when these bandages come off?" "I don't see why not," answered the doctor. "That's strange," says the patient. "I wasn't able to play it before." This old joke still expresses well the common distinction between "freedom from" and "freedom to" central to William Cavanaugh's argument; but a teleological freedom, however, involves knowing what to do. Although the patient's hands can be healed, she will not be free to play the piano as well as possible without the necessary desire, knowledge, and practice, and without patiently learning to adapt old skills to new situations through the aegis of some understanding of music theory.

In response to modern economics' denial of charity, John Milbank and Radical Orthodoxy propose "the endless construction of charity," to the point of transforming the economy itself into a "gift economy"

75. Ibid.

through Christian socialism.[76] Somewhat similarly, part of the task of Lonergan's economics is to help Christians and non-Christians alike to know how and when to "channel benevolence" in economic exchange. For Lonergan, "channeling benevolence" has a very concrete, almost technical meaning—one that can be formulated, tested, communicated, and put into action. In other words, "Moral precepts that are not technically specific turn out to be quite ineffectual."[77]

Regarding the Law of the Cross, even Long maintains that Milbank tends to "eviscerate Christological content" and thus collapse Christology into soteriology.[78] This move calls into question the transformation at the level of thinking and loving of individual subjects operative in Lonergan's concept of salvation. Milbank's "gnostic apriorism"/"illuminism" also goes hand in hand with Milbank's collapsing of church and economic ethics.[79] Further, this concurs with Loewe's questioning of a refusal in Milbank of a "realm of meaning beyond the symbolism and rhetoric of religious common sense,"[80] needed for the "often incremental transformation of economic understanding and practice"[81] involved in helping society as a whole decide how and where our "exuberance" should be placed—either at the service of irrationally compounding economic inequality or toward a more just, flourishing and democratic society.

---

76. See Jennifer A. Herdt, "The Endless Construction of Charity: On Milbank's Critique of Political Economy," *Journal of Religious Ethics* 32/2 (Summer 2004) 301–24.

77. Lonergan, "Healing and Creating in History," 109n14.

78. See Long, *Divine Economy*, 251–353. Milbank's claim that "The gospels can be read, not as the story of Jesus, but as the story of the (re)foundation of a new city ("On Complex Space," 150) is in turn read by Michael Horton as "ecclesiology swallows Christology." See Michael Horton, "Participation and Covenant," in *Radical Orthodoxy and the Reformed Tradition*, ed. James K. A. Smith and James Oltuis (Grand Rapids: Baker, 2005) 129; quoted in Stephen Finlan, *Options on Atonement in Christian Thought* (Collegeville, MN: Liturgical, 2007) 93.

79. See Carl Raschke, "A-dieu to Derrida," in *Secular Theology: American Radical Theological Thought*, ed. Clayton Crockett (New York: Routledge, 2001) 44.

80. William P. Loewe, "Beyond Secular Reason? Reflections in Response to John Milbank's *Theology and Social Theory*," *Philosophy and Theology* 9 (1996) 450–51.

81. Hoyt-O'Connor, *Lonergan's Macroeconomic Dynamics*, 290.

PART 4

Finding Salvation in a Pluralistic World

11

Woundedness and Redemption in the Feminine Body of Christ

KATHLEEN A. MCMANUS, OP
UNIVERSITY OF PORTLAND

Introduction

Christology is arguably the most dynamically controversial discipline in Catholic systematic theology today. At the beginning of the third millennium, William P. Loewe analyzed the then recent but long-emerging paradigm shift in Christology through a critique of a 1984 debate between David Tracy and Elizabeth A. Johnson over the under-standing of the category "the historical Jesus" and its uses in theology.[1] He proceeded to note that the christological consensus that had pro-vided the common ground for that debate subsequently disappeared in the wake of the 1985 publication of E. P. Sanders's *Jesus and Judaism*, and the parallel eruption in that year of The Jesus Seminar.[2] The year 1985, Loewe suggested, was a turning point equal in significance to Ernst Käsemann's launching of the "New Quest" in 1953.[3] Loewe de-

1. See William P. Loewe, "From the Humanity of Christ to the Historical Jesus," *Theological Studies* 61/2 (June 2000) 314–31.

2. See Ed P. Sanders, *Jesus and Judaism* (Philadelphia: Fortress, 1985).

3. See Loewe, "From the Humanity of Christ," 324; see also Ernst Käsemann,

veloped his own argument regarding the limits of the paradigm shift by differentiating elements in Johnson's definition of "the historical Jesus" vis-à-vis Tracy's. Loewe's analysis led him to conclude:

> "The historical Jesus" and "the Christ of Faith" differ as episte-
> mological categories, not substantively, and this state of affairs
> grounds the positive theological functions that both Tracy and
> Johnson assign "the historical Jesus." When historical-Jesus con-
> structs are drawn into the horizon of faith and illumined by the
> light of faith, the coherence of these historical images and nar-
> ratives with the transformative values appropriated in the tra-
> dition's confession of Jesus as the Christ may be grasped. Thus
> endowed with religious significance, in a fashion analogous to
> the original formation of the christological tradition, these his-
> torical images and narratives may provide the material for new
> christological symbols and post-critical narratives disclosive of
> both Jesus' status as God's self-presence in the present and of the
> values inherent in the faith response to this Jesus the Christ.[4]

Indeed, "new christological symbols and post-critical narratives disclosive of both Jesus' status as God's self-presence in the present and of the values inherent in the faith response to this Jesus the Christ" abound today, and nowhere more so than in the diverse narratives arising from women's experience in intercultural contexts through-out the globe. Consider these scenarios: In diverse Asian feminist Christologies, images emerge of Jesus as Mother, Symbolic Woman Messiah, and Wisdom Incarnate.[5] Jesus is imaged as Worker in solidar-ity with those who labor, and Grain nourishing those who are hungry.[6] Jesus is the [feminine] Shaman who releases *han*, the pervasive suffer-

---

"The Problem of the Historical Jesus," in *Essays on New Testament Themes*, trans. W. J. Montague (London: SCM, 1964) 15–47. Loewe cites Sanders's work as a watershed revealing the distortions of the post-Bultmannians, the reality of pluralism charac-terizing Second Temple Judaism, and opening the way to studies focusing on the Jewishness of Jesus.

4. Loewe, "From the Humanity of Christ," 330.

5. See Muriel Orevillo-Montenegro, *The Jesus of Asian Women*, Women from the Margins (Maryknoll, NY: Orbis, 2006) 104–11. Elizabeth Johnson and others have provided extensive commentaries on early Christian renderings of Jesus as Wisdom/Sophia. See Elizabeth A. Johnson, *She Who Is: The Mystery of God in Feminist Theological Discourse* (New York: Crossroad, 1992).

6. See Chung Hyun-Kyung, *Struggle to Be the Sun Again* (Maryknoll, NY: Orbis, 1990) 71–73.

ing of Korean women, restoring them to healing and wholeness.[7] In the Philippines, some women image Jesus as the Fully Liberated One who labors within their struggle for liberation; others, imbued with a matriarchal indigenous memory, see Jesus as a many-breasted Mother giving and nurturing communal life.[8] Reflection on the power of blood leads some African and Asian feminist theologians to associate the blood of Jesus which births new life with women's menstrual flow.[9] Womanist theologians similarly speak of the power of blood to give life.[10] In Mexico, faith in Christ took hold through the encounter of an indigenous peasant with the Mother of God arrayed as an Aztec goddess.[11] And the contemporary theologizing of Latin American women reveals that St. Rose of Lima's visions of Christ as a stonemason bear a profound relationship to her solidarity with the plight of indigenous miners.[12] What these merely representative scenarios have in common is their rootedness in ancient Christian Tradition permeated by still more ancient indigenous sacred experience, and expressed through the prism of women's theological imaginations. It is at the intersection of such diverse cultures and traditions that ecofeminist theologians struggle to articulate the meaning of faith in Jesus as the Christ for women who suffer oppression, poverty, and diminishment. Engaging an ecofeminist epistemology, we will contemplate the basis and need for new christological images as we explore the meaning of woundedness and redemption in the Feminine Body of Christ.

---

7. See ibid. See also Orevillo-Montenegro, *Jesus of Asian Women*, 102–3.

8. See Orevillo-Montenegro, *Jesus of Asian Women*, 155–56.

9. See Elizabeth Joy, "The Meaning and Origin of Dalit Theology" (ThM thesis, South Asia Theological Research Institute, 1998), cited in Orevillo-Montenegro, *Jesus of Asian Women*, 72; see also Gabriele Dietrich, *One day i shall be like a banyan tree*; quoted in Chung, *Struggle to Be the Sun*, 66–71.

10. See JoAnne Marie Terrell, *Power in the Blood?: The Cross in the African American Experience* (Maryknoll, NY: Orbis, 1998) 125, cited in Orevillo-Montenegro, *Jesus of Asian Women*, 73.

11. See Gabriela Zengarini, "Mary of Guadalupe: Receive and Announce the Word," online: http://www.domlife.org/LatinAmerica/LAIndex.htm; see also Virgil Elizondo, *Guadalupe: Mother of the New Creation* (Maryknoll, NY: Orbis, 2007).

12. See Gabriela Zengarini, "Bartolomé De Las Casas and Saint Rose of Lima Doing Theology in Latin America," online: http://www.domlife.org/LatinAmerica/LAIndex.htm.

An ecofeminist epistemology is a way of knowing that gives primacy to the experiences of women in the context of creation.[13] It is a fundamentally phenomenological epistemology—that is, it is concerned with
phenomena, or what manifests itself to us as embodied subjects in the
world. In short, it takes concrete experience in and of the created world
seriously as the starting point of theology. Phenomenology emerged
as a tool of some male theologians, such as Edward Schillebeeckx, in
the twentieth century. It made embodied encounter in the world a
primary category for theology.[14] Since then, feminist and ecofeminist
theologians have embraced this method as natural to their concretely
engaged, relational approach to theology in the Tradition that is above
all incarnational. Because of who they are, where they are, and because
of the people among whom they live and work in diverse parts of the
world, women who engage this method are raising challenging new
questions and directions for theology, and especially for Christology.
These questions and directions are not abstract or purely theoretical,
but rooted in the very stuff of life and of death. It is on this basis that I
venture to reflect upon "woundedness and redemption in the Feminine
Body of Christ." I will structure my reflections around concrete images
drawn from the Christian Tradition as experienced and articulated by
women in diverse cultures and distinct moments in history; in the process, the parameters of each term of my title will emerge. The spiraling
hermeneutic of suffering, resistance, and hope will guide my movement, and I will conclude by contemplating what hope the Feminine
Body of Christ might bear for the healing and full flourishing of the
Body of Christ in the world.

Body of Christ

Most Christians take for granted that we know what we mean when we
speak of the Body of Christ. Perhaps, though, its easy usage in some

13. Ivone Gebara elaborates an ecofeminist epistemology over against traditional
patriarchal epistemology in the first chapter of *Longing for Running Water: Ecofeminism
and Liberation* (Minneapolis: Fortress, 1999) 19–66.

14. The contribution of phenomenology to Edward Schillebeeckx's theology is
commonly noted; see for example William J. Hill, "A Theology in Transition," in *The
Praxis of the Reign of God: An Introduction to the Theology of Edward Schillebeeckx*,
ed. Mary Catherine Hilkert and Robert J. Schreiter, 2nd ed. (New York: Fordham
University Press, 2002) 1–18.

churches is such that the symbol's rich multivalence is in the minds of many reduced to flat definitions and correspondences limited by clearly identifiable boundaries. I begin by probing those limits and pushing those boundaries. What/who is the Body of Christ? The physical, human body of the historical Jesus of Nazareth. The bread and wine consecrated in Eucharist: *This is my Body.* The gathered assembly participating in this eucharistic liturgy. Other such assemblies throughout the world. The global Roman Catholic Church. *We are the Body of Christ.* Other Christian churches? Yes. Sadly, we are divided, but still all members of the Body of Christ. The whole human race? By extension, yes—Christ gave his body, poured out his blood of the covenant *for the many—for all.* "The Synoptic Gospels say that the blood of the covenant will be shed for 'the many' (Mark, Matthew), for 'you' (Luke). In both, the reference is to Israel. The hope for Israel is in these texts, as in other Jewish texts, to be interpreted simultaneously as a hope for all nations."[15] *Lumen Gentium* underscores the universal scope of Christ's grace in a plan of salvation which includes not only all who acknowledge the Creator, but also "those who, without blame on their part, have not yet arrived at an explicit knowledge of God . . ."[16] Even more, God's covenant is a covenant in and with the whole creation, a covenant renewed, sealed, and fulfilled in the bodily living, dying, and rising of Jesus Christ. And yet, with Paul, we recognize that "all creation is groaning in labor pains even until now; and not only that, but we ourselves, who have the firstfruits of the Spirit, we also groan within ourselves as we wait for adoption, the redemption of our bodies" (Romans 8:22–23 NAB). These firstfruits of the Spirit, the fruits of the resurrection in which we share, make us the Body of Christ, although a Body still in the process of growth, a growth in communion. J-M Tillard points out that Paul first employed this image to characterize the communion in the unity of life which comes from the Spirit; to be in Christ, to be this Body, is to be in the Spirit.[17]

15. Andrea Bieler and Luise Schotroff, *Bodies, Bread, and Resurrection* (Minneapolis: Fortress, 2007) 60.

16. Dogmatic Constitution on the Church (*Lumen Gentium*) 16, in Austin Flannery, ed., *Vatican Council II: The Basic Sixteen Documents* (Dublin: Dominican, 1996).

17. Jean-Marie Roger Tillard, *Flesh of the Church, Flesh of Christ: At the Source of the Ecclesiology of Communion*, trans. Madeline Beaumont (Collegeville, MN: Pueblo/Liturgical, 2001) 5.

At the very beginning of the recorded Christian Tradition, Paul provides language and imagery that forbids us to reduce the symbol of the Body of Christ to something pat and measurable, something that might function in exclusionary ways. At the very beginning of the Christian Tradition, Paul insists upon a Mystery that holds life in the flesh together with cosmic forces of creation and promises to be the universal fulfillment of each particular desire. Inverting conventional wisdom about life and death, power and weakness, Paul engages the social metaphor of the body in his time precisely to shatter its oppressive function. Nathan Mitchell offers this analysis:

> To the power elite within the Roman empire, the metaphor of the body bespoke coercion, the power to subjugate others and to enforce the will of an absolutist state. The body was the site of subjugation or (for the privileged few) of sovereignty. In contrast, Paul's master metaphor of "body" became the icon of power *emptied*, erased—of powerlessness, *kenosis*, self-surrendering love that lets go to give others life.[18]

Kenosis, the act by which God took flesh in history and accepted the constriction of finite human life, is also the act by which Jesus freely and painfully relinquished his human life on the cross. In other words, incarnation set Jesus on the path of limitless, non-exclusionary loving, which brought down upon him the crushing force of the sinful world's violence. Herbert McCabe asserts that Jesus' obedience to the Father was to be totally and completely human, which for him meant simply to love. "[H]e shows the humanity that lies more hidden in us—the humanity of which we are afraid. He is the human being that we dare not be. He takes the risks of love which we recognize as risks and therefore for the most part do not take."[19] This humanity that lies hidden in us is, according to Edward Schillebeeckx, the humanity of God:

> Therefore the cross is also a judgment on our own views: a judgment on our ways of living out the meaning of being human and of being God. Here is revealed ultimately and definitively the humanity of God, the nucleus of Jesus' message of the kingdom

18. Nathan D. Mitchell, *Meeting Mystery: Liturgy, Worship, and Sacraments* (Maryknoll, NY: Orbis, 2006) 182.

19. Herbert McCabe, "Good Friday: The Mystery of the Cross," in *God Matters* (New York: Continuum, 2005 [1987]) 93.

of God: God who comes into his own *in* the world of human
beings for their healing and happiness, even through suffering.[20]

What the world requires for salvation then, is more humanity, and
that requires of human beings willingness to risk the vulnerability of
God—God who vulnerably risked entrusting creation to us, God who
risked sending the Son into the world, God in whose image we are
made.[21] To be the Body of Christ, to be in the Spirit who orchestrates
communion, is to mirror together the mutually overflowing, self-giving
love of the triune God, Creator, Son, and Spirit. What Jesus reveals in
his fleshly existence is that the working out of that communion in our
earthly lives entails suffering.

Feminine Body of Christ

Suffering, woundedness—in the Feminine Body of Christ—is really our
subject. But what, exactly, *is* the "*Feminine* Body of Christ?" Does it signify the bodies of women, taken individually and collectively? Might it
signify the body of the more inclusive "other"—those who are displaced,
marginalized, subjugated, *including* diverse communities of women, as
their experiences are witnessed, reflected upon, and responded to by
women through a feminine and feminist hermeneutical lens? I suggest
that the Feminine Body of Christ of which we speak here entails all of
this—and perhaps more.

A *mystical* feminist lens perceives the historical, concrete embod-
iedness of women as revelation in the world. Interpreting women's body
as the site of embodied contemplation, Beverly Lanzetta writes,

> Women's bodies function not simply at the biological or mate-
> rial level, but as the site in which and through which women
> experience the presence of truth and awe. The body is always
> seeking to communicate its divine origins through the multiple
> textuality that *is* women's full presence. . . . To imagine women's
> body as a mystical text implies the full embodiment that con-
> stitutes their presence—biological, psychological, emotional,

20. Edward Schillebeeckx, *Church: The Human Story of God*, trans. John Bowden
(New York: Crossroad, 1990 [1989]) 126.

21. The vulnerability of God in risking creation is a theme in Schillebeeckx; see
Philip Kennedy's analysis in "God and Creation," in *Praxis of the Reign of God*, 37–58.

spiritual and so forth—is the act of inscribing women's revelation in the world. Every day, women write the body of divinity
through the text of their bodies.[22]

Lanzetta speaks of women's body as *hierophany*, but at the same time
cautions that "every hierophany, by virtue of expressing the sacred
through a concrete form, ceases to be absolute." This is not an attempt
to deify women. "Rather, it is a way to approach and understand the
integral, undivided, and holistic plurality that constitutes women's lived
experience. It involves an interpretive shift in which women recognize
their potential to become transparent vessels of sacred power in and
through their bodies."[23]

Why is this necessary, and why does it entail an interpretive shift?
The incarnation reveals the holiness and divine capacity of *all* human
bodies, but centuries of patriarchy have obscured and denigrated the
divine image in women's bodies. As Wendy Farley writes, "it is an excruciating reality of Christian history that this extravagant unveiling
of the availability of human form to Good Beyond Being became yet
another occasion for the triumph of patriarchy and its logic of violent
exclusion."[24] The historical obscuring and denigrating of women has
infiltrated the deepest recesses of women's souls and psyches, making
it difficult—for some, impossible—to truly see and claim their equal
dignity as bearers of the divine. Lanzetta discerns a "continual and
subtle form of violence" against women that is difficult to name precisely because it oppresses and wounds them in the vulnerable depths
of their most intimate interiority.[25] Speaking again of women's body as
a mystical text that cannot be explained or determined away, as something luminous and elusive, Lanzetta notes that "[i]t is not understood
by those outside or afraid of the circle of vulnerability. . . . [W]omen's
body, its 'otherness'—*is* a mark of holiness. But, in anti-body cultures,
women represent the rejected closeness of God."[26]

---

22. Beverly Lanzetta, *Radical Wisdom: A Feminist Mystical Theology* (Minneapolis:
Fortress, 2005) 160–61.

23. Ibid., 164.

24. Wendy Farley, *The Wounding and Healing of Desire: Weaving Heaven and Earth*
(Louisville: Westminster John Knox, 2005) 104.

25. Lanzetta, *Radical Wisdom*, 9.

26. Ibid., 164–65.

It is precisely this "otherness" that embodies vulnerability, the very vulnerability of God in a crucifying world, which is signified by the Feminine Body of Christ. Thus, the Feminine Body of Christ is comprised of all women, of all colors, nations, sexual orientations, and socioeconomic backgrounds, including women who exercise leadership in all sectors of society as well as within the Church. It is comprised most particularly of those who suffer, interiorly and exteriorly, the wounds of patriarchy—invisible soul wounds and glaring physical wounds. The Feminine Body of Christ includes the children of women in poverty throughout the globe, and it most especially includes the children who have lost their mothers to violence or trafficking—or who are violated and trafficked themselves. By extension, it includes men deemed "other" by patriarchy for various reasons, but most especially reasons of sexual orientation.[27] It is becoming all too clear that to begin to speak of the Feminine Body of Christ is necessarily to begin to speak of woundedness, a woundedness that springs from "the rejected closeness of God."

Woundedness

"Woundedness" connotes excruciating physicality; it equally connotes an injury of the flesh that sears the soul, and an affliction of the soul that sears the body with pain. The point is that woundedness is always *embodied.* In the context of Christian Tradition, it evokes the wounds inflicted on Christ's body during his passion. In the immediate contemporary context, it brings to mind the myriad forms of suffering experienced by human beings and, in fact, by our planet, itself a living organism threatened with death. Contemplation of the suffering that plagues our world compels contemplation of its kinds, causes, and effects. Many kinds of suffering stem from wars and from catastrophic natural disasters such as earthquakes, floods, and tsunamis; other kinds of suffering stem from quieter, but perduring "natural disasters," such as the starvation resulting from famine and drought, widespread illness resulting from plagues such as AIDS, or the seemingly individual

27. M. Shawn Copeland asserts, "Church teaching repels gay and lesbian bodies to the periphery of the ecclesial body and may well disclose just how afraid the church may be of the body of Jesus of Nazareth." Copeland, *Enfleshing Freedom: Body, Race, and Being* (Minneapolis: Fortress, 2009) 76.

sufferings of illness from the diverse forms of cancer that afflict people in almost epidemic proportions. I say *seemingly* individual because, in fact, increasing evidence suggests that human poisoning of the earth is at the root of the proliferation of cancers.[28] When the earth is ravaged and poisoned, women's bodies and the bodies of their yet-to-be-born children bear the most profound scars. Like so many other ills, toxic illness is a corporate and global issue resulting from what Thomas Berry has called the "turn away from the earth."[29] This turning away from the earth is a turning away from the earth's most vulnerable people, especially women and the children who depend upon them.

The suffering and well-being of women and nature are inextricably entwined; it is no secret that corporate wealth and the increasing demands of consumer lifestyles increase poverty and further the exploitation of the earth, women, and children in the Two-Thirds World.[30] While there are many positive aspects to the "world without borders" that globalization has produced, this "world" also allows for the globalization of organized crime, drug trafficking, and the sex trafficking of women and children. While a "world without borders" connotes increased communication and a sense of relationship as a global community, it paradoxically fragments relational structures. One of many examples is the system of "care chains" that allows women to make a bare living while separating them from their children. For instance, women from the Philippines and other struggling nations come to the US to work as nannies caring for other people's children. While their families at home gain a minimal economic benefit, they suffer the emotional deprivation of their mothers' absence. Meanwhile, this system sets up a servant class in countries like ours, proliferating the

28. See, for example, D. Belpomme et al., "The Multitude and Diversity of Environmental Carcinogens," *Environmental Research* 105/3 (November 2007) 414–29, and Marilena Kampa and Elias Castanas, "The Human Health Effects of Air Pollution," *Environmental Pollution* 151/2 (January 2008) 362–67.

29. Thomas Berry, *The Great Work: Our Way into the Future* (New York: Bell Tower, 1999), cited in Mary C. Grey, *Sacred Longings: The Ecological Spirit and Global Culture* (Minneapolis: Fortress, 2004) 11.

30. 2008 World Bank Development indicators show that in 2005 the world's richest 20% consumed 76.6% of the world's goods, the middle 60% consumed 21.9%, and the poorest 20% consumed 1.5%. The poorest 10% accounted for just 0.5% and the wealthiest 10% accounted for 59% of all consumption. See Anup Shah, "Poverty Facts and Stats," *Global Issues*, http://www.globalissues.org/article/26/poverty-facts-and-stats#src3.

diminishment and degradation of women even within a culture where women have achieved the highest degrees of professional success and autonomy.[31] Such relational fracturing is in stark negative contrast to the communal extensions of maternal care to other people's children at home in the Philippines. There, amidst poverty and oppression, women offer succor and sustenance from their own bodies not only to their own children, but to the children of other women as well. Their sense of being the Feminine Body of Christ is perhaps subliminally inspired by ancient indigenous memories of the many-breasted goddess Mebuyan. When we turn to an exploration of redemption in and through the Feminine Body of Christ, we will examine potential sources of healing and nourishment in contemporary evocations of Jesus as "many-breasted Mother."

Beyond relational fracturing, M. Shawn Copeland graphically asserts that globalization "cannibalizes the bodies, the labor and creativity, the sexuality and generativity of global 'others.'"[32] Red, yellow, brown, white, black, and poor bodies are handed over to the consuming forces of the market. Further, those whose bodies are disabled are of little or no value in labor-based cultures shaped by a market-driven economy, nor are they valued in corporate Western cultures that so prize autonomy and physical "perfection." Worse still, they are often marginalized, if not rendered invisible, in many Christian communities.[33]

This is a mere glimpse of woundedness—a fragmentary picture of the woundedness and brokenness of our world etched in the flesh of the most vulnerable members of the Body of Christ. Woundedness wrought by individual and corporate human choice and action is the tangible effect of sin, and thus begins in the distortion of desire—the pervasive disease of our global culture. British theologian Mary Grey suggests that globalization depends upon the fracturing of relatedness and a corporate failure of compassion.[34] She and others also argue that the dark side of globalization is sustained by entrenched patriarchy in our society and in our Church. We will be especially concerned here

---

31. See Grey, *Sacred Longings*, 32–33.

32. Copeland, *Enfleshing Freedom*, 66.

33. Nancy L. Eisland constructs a transformed perception of physical disability in society and in the Eucharistic community in *The Disabled God: Toward a Liberatory Theology of Disability* (Nashville: Abingdon, 1994).

34. See Grey, *Sacred Longings*, 21.

to examine how the Church, the "official" Body of Christ in the world, is a source of woundedness in its feminine members. Above all, I will attend to the spiritual, psychic, and emotional dimensions of woundedness in women who are thus afflicted.

I have been speaking of woundedness as suffering, especially as suffering afflicts the Feminine Body of Christ. Simone Weil speaks of affliction as being within the realm of suffering, but in some sense "apart, specific, and irreducible. . . . It takes possession of the soul and marks it through and through with its own particular mark, the mark of slavery. . . . Affliction is an uprooting of life, a more or less attenuated equivalent of death, made irresistibly present to the soul by the attack or immediate apprehension of physical pain."[35] Weil's point is that affliction, or what we are addressing as woundedness, entails pain that is simultaneously of body and soul. Further, it marks the soul "with the mark of slavery."

Bodies marked by literal slavery constitute the subject of M. Shawn Copeland's *Enfleshing Freedom: Body, Race, and Being*. At the center of this work focused on the suffering bodies of black women is Copeland's reflection on the Body of Jesus as "marked." Acknowledging the implicitly metaphysical character of Christianity, Copeland asserts,

> The body of Jesus of Nazareth presents a formidable entry point for the scandal of particularity in theological anthropology: formidable because of the marks of that body (gender, race, sex, culture); because of that body's openness to, turn toward, and solidarity with even radically different others (Matt. 15:26–27); and because of that body's pledge to be given and poured out for *all* others across time and space.[36]

Black slavery and its continuing mark upon the bodies, souls, and psyches of black women holds a sorrowfully distinct and unparalleled place in the annals of human suffering; it occupies its own tragic terrain. Even as we acknowledge this, it is evident that diverse forms of slavery stain the contours of our globe even unto the present, and the Church historically has been directly and indirectly implicated. From the fifteenth century onward, chattel slavery was a reality not only in

---

35. Simone Weil, *Waiting for God*, trans. Emma Crawford (San Francisco: Harper Colophon, 1951) 117–18.

36. Copeland, *Enfleshing Freedom*, 5.

the "New World" of both North and South America and the Caribbean, but also in Spain, Portugal, Italy, Holland, Germany, and England. And, as Copeland notes, "from early on, slavery in the Atlantic world was deeply entangled with Christianity."[37] This well-documented entanglement has left its mark not only on the suffering body of the Church, but also on its institutional and magisterial psyche.

At the root of the Church's entanglement with slavery is its patriarchal character. Critical assessment of Western patriarchy makes it clear that systems of male dominance impact not only women, but also all who are deemed rationally or morally inferior, all who are "other." No more dramatic example exists than the related events of the African slave trade and the conquest of the New World, beginning in the fifteenth century on the island of Hispaniola, today's Haiti and Dominican Republic. Gustavo Gutiérrez writes,

> We mean the encounter (or collision), unexpected on both sides, not only between the peoples of the territory today called America and those who lived in Europe, but including Africa as well—a third continent promptly and violently incorporated into the process of which we speak. This event is regarded as a *discovery* by those who see history from the old continent (as they themselves call it). A *covering*, others call it—referring to a history written in blatant disregard of the viewpoint of the so-called inhabitants of the New World. The "conquista" it was dubbed in the old history books; "invasion" some prefer to call it today.[38]

Reflecting on the social and ecclesial reasoning that rendered slavery acceptable and legal for centuries, reasoning ratified by the fathers of the Church and the great scholastics, including Thomas Aquinas, Gutiérrez notes that by the Middle Ages slavery was no longer practiced as extensively as in the ancient world. However, this inherited juridical and theological position set the stage for the exploitation of the Indies in the sixteenth century and, prior to that, the inception in the middle of the fifteenth century of "a phenomenon that would become one of the most wicked and shameful deeds of the human race: the traffic in African slaves." This practice begun by the Portuguese was justified on

37. Ibid., 26.

38. Gustavo Gutiérrez, *Las Casas: In Search of the Poor of Jesus Christ*, trans. Robert R. Barr (Maryknoll, NY: Orbis, 1993 [1992]) 321.

the grounds that these captured Africans were Muslims, with whom Christians were at war.[39] Then as now, graced streams of resistance within the ecclesial body worked to oppose and undo official ecclesial collusion in violent and oppressive movements of domination.[40] Such streams of resistance flowed from the wounds of the risen Body of Christ subversively alive within a sinful institution. They flowed in the public resistance to oppression that marked the life of Bartolomé de las Casas. They flowed in the positive relational ministries of healing, prayer, and solidarity with outcasts that marked the life of Rose of Lima. Later, I will turn to the divine visions that nourished Rose's dream of a Feminine Body of Christ.

The woundedness of the Feminine Body of Christ encompasses the diverse forms of slavery past and present, overt and hidden, resulting in the continuing marginalization and subjugation of the other. Moreover, as indicated earlier in this essay, the earth itself shares in this woundedness. The literal slavery we have just reflected on is related to the complex web of dynamics constituting the "turn from the earth." Thomas Berry writes: "As Christians, we lost our intimacy with the natural world . . . in three phases. The first phase came about during the meeting of early Christian spirituality with Greek humanism to form the basis of a strong anthropocentrism."[41] Biblical revelation overwhelmed the revelation of the natural world, focusing on the divine-human relation to the exclusion of the community of creation, placing the natural world at the bottom of a hierarchy of values. The result was a model of domination rather than participation.

"The second phase in the alienation of humans from the natural world came about when the Black Death ravaged Europe from 1347 to 1349."[42] The devastating loss of a third of the continent's population rendered nature a terrifying threat to be feared, and the plague a

---

39. See ibid., 320–21.

40. Such resistance is exemplified by the preaching of Anton Montesino, OP, in the name of the missionary Dominican friars in Hispaniola. The communal exhortation defending the human rights of Indians and declaring the Spaniards who enslaved them to be in mortal sin led to reprisals from King Ferdinand and the friars' Dominican superiors in Spain. See ibid., 28–37, 42, 93, 280.

41. Thomas Berry, *The Christian Future and the Fate of the Earth*, ed. Mary Evelyn Tucker and John Grim (Maryknoll, NY: Orbis, 2009) 60.

42. Ibid., 61.

divine punishment. The Christian, Catholic response was to intensify devotions and seek redemption outside of this world, thus entrenching dualism more deeply in the Western religious psyche. Mary Grey notes that this ecclesial pessimism has continued right up to the present: "'escape from the world' as a precondition for sanctity has made it almost impossible to see intrinsic value in embodied relationships with people and with earth's creatures, particularly in their appropriate physical and sexual expressions."[43] The second moment of this second phase entails the development of science during the sixteenth and seventeenth centuries deployed through a model of male domination graphically represented by Francis Bacon's "The Masculine Birth of Time." "In Bacon's thought . . . not only is the link between domination of nature and domination of women clearly displayed, but also the religious justification for the exploitation of nature. Conquering nature was seen through the metaphor of heterosexual conquest."[44] "A third moment in our loss of intimacy with the natural world occurred at the end of the nineteenth century when we abandoned our role in an ever-renewing, organic, agricultural economy in favor of an industrial, extractive economy."[45] The middle to the end of the nineteenth century saw the emergence of the corporations that now rule the world.[46]

Two interrelated approaches to redemption emerge from this broad analysis of patriarchy: escape from embodiment in the world, and domination of the other. Both are sinfully skewed, both serve to exacerbate woundedness and suffering; moreover, despite all our human and theological advances, both are woefully ingrained in our current ecclesial reality. Patriarchal fear of embodiment and domination of the inferior other have wrought extensive wounds in the Feminine Body of Christ. There is little need to elaborate in detail a most obvious and emblematic source of this woundedness: the denial of women's full and equal participation at the altar as sacramental ministers and in the institution as decision-making leaders in the Roman Catholic Church has ongoing ramifications for women's self-image and self-understanding as created fully and equally *imago Christi*. While claiming that a new

43. Grey, *Sacred Longings*, 13–14.

44. Ibid., 14.

45. Berry, *The Christian Future*, 63.

46. See Grey, *Sacred Longings*, 15.

season of women's ownership of the *imago Dei* doctrine is in bloom, Elizabeth Johnson acknowledges that, "because of the androcentric nature of the traditioning process, the understanding that women are likewise christomorphic has been more difficult to grasp." She explains,

> A mentality centered on the priority of men has taken identifi-
> cation with Christ as its own exclusive prerogative, aided by a
> naïve physicalism that collapses the totality of the Christ into
> the bodily form of Jesus. . . . If the model for sharing in the im-
> age of Christ be one of exact duplication . . . and if Christ be
> reduced to the historical individual Jesus of Nazareth, and if the
> salient feature about Jesus as the Christ be his male sex, then
> women are obviously excluded from sharing that image in full.
> But every one of those presuppositions falls short and twists
> the central testimony of biblical and doctrinal traditions. The
> guiding model for the *imago Christi* is not replication of sexual
> features but participation in the life of Christ, which is founded
> on communion in the Spirit.[47]

In its "androcentric traditioning process," however, the Church has steadfastly maintained the priority of Jesus' maleness in its argu-ment that, as instrument and sacramental sign, the priest stands *in per-sona Christi*. Theological analysis of the ban on women's ordination is well beyond the scope of this essay.[48] My point here is to make clear the wounding and denigrating impact on women of this very public eccle-sial reality. The pain of women who are called to priestly, sacramental ministry, who know that call in the depths of their spirits and who have heard it confirmed by the communities in which they minister, cannot be underestimated. Nor can the impoverishing impact of women's ab-sence from sacramental ministry on the lives and christological imagi-nations of women and men be overstated. The official ecclesial denial of authentic feminine priestly vocation wounds the whole ecclesial body.

We have held up a central, salient example of how the "official" Body of Christ can be an instrument of woundedness in its feminine members. It encapsulates both of the flawed patriarchal approaches to redemption mentioned above: escape from embodiment and domina-

47. Johnson, *She Who Is*, 71–72.

48. For a very recent and thorough analysis of the ecclesial evolution of this issue, see Elizabeth Groppe, "Women and the *Persona* of Christ," in *Frontiers in Catholic Feminist Theology: Shoulder to Shoulder*, ed. Elena Procario-Foley and Susan Abraham (Minneapolis: Fortress, 2009) 153–71.

tion of the other. At the same time, the best resources of the Catholic and Christian Tradition, from the New Testament to the writings of medieval mystics to the documents of the Second Vatican Council and beyond, celebrate an incarnate Christ whose Body historically and at present is *in* and *for* the world. How, despite its historically wounding contradictions, can the Church fulfill its self-proclaimed mission to be the "official" and efficacious Body of Christ in the world, sanctifying and drawing all into One Divine Body? How might the Feminine Body of Christ be an agent in this process?

Redemption

To be redeemed is to live from the resurrection, which comes through the cross of Christ. With Edward Schillebeeckx, I want to focus on the ultimacy of resurrection as the triumph of God's reign inaugurated in Jesus' life, a life lived faithfully unto death, a self-emptying death in love. Schillebeeckx repeatedly emphasizes that we can only attribute meaning to Jesus' suffering and death in the context of the meaning and message of his life vindicated in the resurrection.[49] This is a consoling caveat for women and all marginalized persons for whom overemphasis on the cross has justified lives of subjugation and imposed sacrifice.[50] The passion of Christ has been disturbing to feminists, womanists, and others who are appalled by efforts to understand redemption by bloody sacrifice.[51] Yet, the risen glorified Body of Christ heralding our redemption does remain marked by wounds. Blood and sacrifice of themselves do not effect redemption; rather, the other-centered love that gives rise to blood and sacrifice is what redeems. This is the meaning of the passion, in which we are meant to share.

Approaches to redemption that provide healing, rectifying alternatives arise from the depths of the Christian Tradition and are being newly configured by feminist and ecofeminist theologians in our day. Predominant among them is a critical reclaiming of kenosis together

---

49. See Edward Schillebeeckx, *Christ: The Experience of Jesus as Lord*, trans. John Bowden (New York: Crossroad, 1980 [1977]) 793–801.

50. Cynthia S. W. Crysdale addresses the negative impact of such theologies of the cross on women and constructs a healing alternative in *Embracing Travail: Retrieving the Cross Today* (New York: Continuum, 1999).

51. See Farley, *Wounding and Healing of Desire*, 111.

with a renewed reflection on the divine eros as the context of the passion. Ancient and contemporary poets of the divine "reach into the logic of desire for images that display the efficacy and creativity of the divine emptiness."[52] The language of medieval women mystics, language often imbued with feminine divine and christic imagery drawn from early church fathers, is a resource for reclaiming a liberating mysticism of desire.[53] Such language arises from an experience of human longing that reveals the Divine longing for her creatures. Eros is the power of love in the form of desire. As desire, Holy Mystery is constant, ecstatic, kenotic movement outside of itself, toward the objects of its yearning, leading to union. "It is the bond that holds creation in existence. . . . It is also the luminous and 'precious oneing' of the divine and human in each soul."[54]

God's desire activates the soul's desiring response, which requires the discipline of contemplation. For women mystics in the Church, the contemplative path has been a subversive path, often forged through suffering terrain. The social and spiritual devastation of Europe's Black Death discussed earlier was also the context in which the contributions of such women mystics as Catherine of Siena flourished. The Black Death swept through Europe during Catherine's infancy, leaving in its wake a devastated social infrastructure and economy. Amidst poverty, conflict, and war Catherine carried out a very public ministry rooted in a very intense practice of contemplative prayer. The images of God that both sustained her and shaped her preaching were images that merged the power of both kenosis and the divine eros noted above. Her frequently feminine and maternal language rendered the passion and wounds of Christ as expressions of a life-giving, rather than punishing, sacrifice. Mary Catherine Hilkert notes,

> In a single passage in her *Dialogue* she could refer to God as "the Father" and "the Son" and speak of "nursing at the breast of the crucified." In other passages she speaks of the Spirit, too, as a mother who nurses us at the breast of divine charity and writes of Christ as our "foster mother."[55]

52. Ibid., 101.

53. Lanzetta elaborates on this in *Radical Wisdom*, 49–60.

54. Farley, *Wounding and Healing of Desire*, 102.

55. Mary Catherine Hilkert, *Speaking with Authority: Catherine of Siena and the Voices of Women Today* (Mahwah, NJ: Paulist, 2001) 70.

Catherine's reflections on the cross and on the blood of Jesus must, Hilkert stresses, be seen in the context of her emphasis on God's love and life poured out for humanity. The undergirding experience of resurrection is Catherine's starting point; only from this vivifying experience of divine love does she speak of suffering and cross. Not only the cross, but also the incarnation is redemptive and motivated fundamentally by love. [56] While Catherine, like others, spoke of Christ's blood in terms of washing away sin, most often "her emphasis was on blood as food or life."[57] Her maternal and eucharistic images reflect the other-centered, communal character of the ministry that flowed from Catherine's mystical contemplation. Catherine speaks of the "table of the cross" and "envisions the Trinity as both feeding us and deepening our hunger for the salvation of others . . ."[58] Further, Catherine often alternates the image of drinking from Christ's breast with that of immersing oneself in the wound in his side, "which she identifies with both his heart and his breast. Just as love of God and love of neighbor were inseparable for Catherine, so too was plunging oneself into the side of Jesus inseparable from embracing the suffering of the world."[59]

As a lay Dominican and public, itinerant preacher in the fourteenth century, Catherine drew her share of clerical and patriarchal criticism. A century later, monastic Carmelite Teresa of Avila was critiqued and persecuted by patriarchal authority for teaching her sisters to pray in "formless" ways. In *The Interior Castle*, Teresa writes of the spiritual union in which the soul dies with the greatest joy because its life is now in Christ, and Christ is the "Someone" at the center of the soul giving life. "[T]here is a Sun in the interior of the soul from which a brilliant light proceeds and is sent to the faculties. The soul does not move . . . from that center nor is its peace lost; for the very One who gave peace to the apostles when they were together can give it to the soul."[60] Such prayer apart from ecclesially approved formulas was considered suspect. It suggested that women and others had experiential access

---

56. See ibid., 112–13.

57. Ibid., 115.

58. Ibid., 116.

59. Ibid., 117.

60. Teresa of Avila, *The Interior Castle* (7.2.7), in vol. 2 of *The Collected Works*, trans. Otilio Rodriguez and Kieran Kavanaugh (Washington, DC: Institute of Carmelite Studies, 1980) 435.

to Divinity without institutional mediation—a concept threatening to patriarchy both then and now. Nevertheless, it was the means of Teresa's great Carmelite reform, and for her sisters it became the path of interior freedom in an age of external constriction. At the same time, it must be emphasized that, like Catherine, Teresa and other women mystics were not withdrawn from the world. "More than any other legacy, it is their ability to integrate the highest states of mystic contemplation with the pastoral needs of their sisters, neighbors, and friends that sets apart women's mystical legacy."[61]

The path of contemplative mysticism is intrinsically bound up with the suffering of the world; it has power to heal and restore the wounds of the Feminine Body of Christ by making of its practitioners channels of the divine desire for the world. Teresa writes, "that (the soul's) life is Christ is understood better, with the passing of time, by the effects this life has. . . . For from those divine breasts where it seems God is always sustaining the soul there flow streams of milk bringing comfort to all the people of the castle."[62] Thus Teresa also evokes the maternal image of a breastfeeding God who is a source of sustenance not only during intentional prayer, and not only for the one who prays. Teresa's image is of a God who abundantly pours forth the divine milk at all times—lavishly and indiscriminately. Teresa's mission, it seems, is to teach others how to orient themselves, dispose themselves receptively to this abundance—so that they may be healed and made whole, so that they, too, may be a source of healing for others. The suffering body of Christ requires more than material justice and physical healing. It requires the deep spiritual healing that makes whole. This body hungers for the divine life as much as it hungers for food—and this is the hunger that concerns Teresa. So, too, it is the hunger, the poverty, and the suffering of the Feminine body of Christ that concerns women and women-identified men today.

Starting with the suffering world, Mary Grey speaks of the kenosis of the divine eros in the context of an ecofeminist vision of global justice. The movement from kenosis to flourishing is, she asserts, theology's true task. Juxtaposing the image of Jesus obediently taking the form of a slave (Phil 2:5–11) with the reality of global capitalism's production of multiple forms of slavery today leads her to pose a question

61. Lanzetta, *Radical Wisdom*, 81.
62. Teresa, *Interior Castle*, 435.

for theology and for the Christian church: What are we willing to let go of for the sake of justice and peace? On the one hand, the kenotic Christ is revealed in the crushed and broken of our world, painfully enfleshed in the constancy of suffering and oppression experienced by the Dalit people of India, the *Sudras* or Untouchables, especially the Dalit women. On the other hand, this incarnate, self-emptying Christ paradoxically reveals the fullness of God: "[C]lassical trinitarian theology tells us as Jesus was, so God is. This means that the Three Persons of God, united within in the ceaseless loving relationship or movement known as *perichoresis*, are also united without, in a sacrificial movement of identification with humanity and earth."[63]

Grey cautions against an uncritical embrace of the kenotic path, noting that the theological theme of self-emptying has long been enmeshed in a "patriarchal framework that sees pain, sacrifice, and degrading forms of subordination as the rightful lot of women."[64] She proposes situating the process of self-emptying in a revisioned, non-dualistic universe where "*vulnerability* could hold central stage as the divine quality linking God/humanity and earth."[65] This vulnerability that entails suffering is the vulnerability embodied in Christ as God's superior, redeeming power.[66] Grey asserts the importance of the witness of voluntary, chosen suffering for the process of redemption. At the same time, she notes that this is challenging for feminist liberation theology given the weight of the patriarchal tradition in women's suffering. Nevertheless, "the kenosis of God leads divine activity into the ambiguity and tragedy of the human condition."[67] What feminist liberation theologians have to offer here is their emphasis on the value of transcending the self to enter into relationship with the new and different other. "This meaning of divine transcendence is reflected in the discovery of meaningful connection and the movement into deep, sustaining relationships of justice."[68] Communities capable of the kenotic path will be needed to sustain such boundary-crossing relationships of

63. Grey, *Sacred Longings*, 73.

64. Ibid., 75.

65. Ibid., 76; emphasis in original.

66. This is a pervasive theme in the writings of Edward Schillebeeckx; see for example *Church: The Human Story of God*, 128 and 131.

67. Grey, *Sacred Longings*, 79.

68. Ibid., 80.

justice in a newly envisioned world where vulnerability holds center stage.

Vulnerability—the vulnerability revealed in Jesus' relationships of inclusivity and love, the vulnerability exemplified in the cross—would seem to be the hallmark of the Feminine Body of Christ. The vulnerability of the kenotic path might seem to contemporary feminists like passivity and surrender. Women mystics past and present, however, remind us that the practice of surrender entails determination and courage; "it is an empowering recognition of what it means to commit to inner fidelity—to a truth that takes away women's subordination and restores their equality."[69] The vulnerability that Jesus embodied was his courageous and determined surrender in love to the God who desires our full flourishing. Such vulnerability is God's superior power in the world, and this is the power embodied today in the Feminine Body of Christ.

When the passion of Christ is understood within the context of the mutually shared passion of the divine Intimacy, the kenotic path is revealed as redemption. Grey wonders aloud if the Christian church has the humility to embrace the kenotic way.[70] It may be that we need the humble in our world, those who bear the wounds of the Feminine Body of Christ, to teach us this way of redemption. Women of diverse cultures in our world who suffer oppression and poverty, who live their lives at the edge of death, know this passion, this way of redemption, in the depths of their experience. They know it as suffering in and for love. They bleed and they sacrifice to sustain their children, their families, and their communities in being. Somehow, the power to endure in love is made available to them. Those who seek that power in Christ approach the source of redemption from the place of their need, and the shape of their suffering and desire reveals the shape of the Christ. Thus is Christ named and redemption experienced. Christ is recognized and named according to the marks of the Body revealing the divine in the world today.

At the beginning of this essay, we sketched scenarios of christological images emerging from the experiences of women in diverse cultures. In Asian cultures, some Christians remain immersed in the

69. Lanzetta, *Radical Wisdom*, 89.
70. See Grey, *Sacred Longings*, 80.

atmosphere of indigenous traditions whose memory is kept alive in the practice of their neighbors. As noted above, Christianity, and especially Catholicism, has a tragic history of repressing ancient cultures and indigenous spiritualities in the process of evangelization. Today, intercultural feminist theologians attend to the vestiges of such spiritualities that continue to have meaning in the lives of Christians. Such sacred memories and images can become the means by which many are able to enter into relationship with the Christ revealed in Jesus of Nazareth. And they can also be the means by which ancient repressed images within the Christian Tradition are unearthed for the healing and restoration of the Feminine Body of Christ and, through it, the Body of Christ in the world. Feminine images of Christ abound in ancient Christian literature, and may provide saving correspondences for women consoled by lingering indigenous feminine images. I will briefly consider representative examples from our introduction—St. Rose of Lima's indigenous-inspired vision of Christ, and the image of Christ as a many-breasted Mother in relation to the power of blood and birthing.

St. Rose of Lima was a lay Dominican mystic born of Spanish-Indian parents. In seventeenth-century Peru, she witnessed the continuing degradation of the indigenous people through the colonial forces of church and state. She lived in a society undergirded by the enforced labor of miners, all of whom were impoverished peasants, most of whom were indigenous. Their plight in Rose's eyes was true slavery. Rose embodied the path of kenotic mysticism, patterning her life on the passion of Jesus not in a cloister, but in a tiny cell of prayer from which she went out to minister to the poor in the streets of Lima even as she helped support her family through needlework. She visited the socially segregated hospitals for blacks, for Indians, and for lepers. She visited the sick in their homes, and created her own infirmary where she nursed the sick and suffering who came in from the streets. Her ascetic spiritual practices were harsh—an intentional participation in the wounds of Christ. However, contemporary feminist theologians in Latin America now see her penances as acts of solidarity with the suffering of the Indians in the mines and the pain of the Indian women who saw their husbands and sons die. This is the background of Rose's vision of Christ orchestrating the foundation of a new Church built by women.[71]

Bartolomé de Las Casas had prophesied that the Church would be restored to the Indies free of colonial domination. St. Rose of Lima is purported to have had dreams and visions of a utopia for the Church in Latin America—a utopia of a renewed Church in a society that honors the yearnings and the labor of all its members. Among Rose's visions, witnesses at her canonization note one in which Christ appears as a master stonecutter and leads her to a quarry which he himself supervises. In Rosa's day, this was the scene of the enforced labor of peasant men, mostly Indians. In her dream, however, this labor was in the hands of finely and festively dressed young women. "They dug out mountains, they sawed marble, polished jasper, smoothed stones, and so that the tools could conquer the hardness of the marbles, they were softening them with repeated rains of tears."[72]

Latin American feminist theologians contemplating the ongoing pain of their people at the intersection of patriarchal Catholicism, indigenous experience, globalization, and the cries of women find in Rose's dream a vision of "a church where it is women who prepare the foundation stones for a new Christian community."[73] It is a vision of the Feminine Body of Christ redeemed precisely in and through the place of its woundedness.

The Church in the Philippines is similarly haunted by the specter of colonialism past and present, including historical repression of indigenous culture. Underlying Filipino Christianity, Muriel Orevillo-Montenegro explains, is an indigenous goddess tradition strongly imbued with the myth of Mebuyan, the many-breasted Mother. While there are multiple variations on this myth, the image in all cases symbolizes the Divine as one who is life-giving and life-sustaining. Orevillo-

---

71. For this account of Rose's relationship to the indigenous and her vision I am relying on the text of a talk given by Gabriela Zengarini at an international gathering of Latin American Dominican women ("Bartolomé de Las Casas and Rose of Lima Doing Theology in Latin America," cited above). General biographical information is from Mary Jean Dorcy, *St. Dominic's Family* (Washington, DC: Dominicana, 1983) 364–67.

72. Zengarini, "Bartolomé de Las Casas and Rose of Lima."

73. Ibid.

Montenegro acknowledges the hesitance of some theologians to dip into the goddess tradition. "But," she asks,

> if Jesus the Christ reveals the God who carried the people in her womb, who gave them birth (Is 46:3–4), who nursed them as her child (Is 49: 10-15), and, "as a mother, comforts her child" (Is 66:13), is it so difficult to explore the view that the Christ is a many-breasted Nanay or Ina (mother)? It would be helpful for theologians to lift up the concepts of some early church fathers who understood the close connection of flesh, body, and blood when it comes to nurturing an infant. Clement of Alexandria associates milk with Christ, and Ambrose calls Christ the Virgin who "fed us with her own milk."[74]

Filipino women frequently nurse and breastfeed the children of other mothers who cannot. Where mothering is a communal respon- sibility, might it not be appropriate to metaphorically envision Christ as a many-breasted Mother? Moreover, theologians need not limit this exploration of Christ to the image of Mebuyan. Orevillo-Montenegro holds up the scriptural image of Christ as the Wisdom-Mother who nurtures and nourishes her children in the eucharistic discourse of John's Gospel.[75]

Ancient sources are rich in feminine imagery concerning Christ. Janet Martin-Soskice notes that medieval art frequently depicted the crucifixion as childbirth, with the church being pulled from Christ's wounded side. Medieval stylizations of Jesus as Mother were explicitly physical, and date back to still more ancient texts. Martin-Soskice cites John Chrysostom's referencing of John 19:34 in his *Third Baptismal Instruction*: "'Just as a woman nourishes her offspring with her own blood and milk, so also Christ continuously nurtures with His own blood those whom He has begotten.'"[76] Verna Harrison draws upon Clement of Alexandria's imaging of Christ not only as nursing with milk, but as Mother "who gives birth to the new Christian people 'in labor pains of the flesh,' . . . Christ's death has become his childbearing. He transformed the destruction of life into an outpouring of new and

---

74. Orevillo-Montenegro, *Jesus of Asian Women*, 155.

75. See ibid., 156.

76. Janet Martin-Soskice, "Blood and Defilement," in *Feminism and Theology*, ed. Janet-Martin-Soskice and Diana Lipton (Oxford: Oxford University Press, 2003) 333–41, at 335.

eternal life."[77] In Clement's vision, Christ "combines in himself every aspect of the nurture, upbringing and education of his children and fulfills all the adult caregiving roles: 'father and mother and paedagogos and nourisher.'"[78]

The breastfeeding Christ is likewise a healing image in the reflections of North American feminist theologians seeking solidarity with women and others across the globe who suffer. Jeannine Hill-Fletcher draws on images from Scripture as well as early and medieval Christian writings in relation to her own mothering experience to envision a Christology "on behalf of a world in need."[79] She compares the sacrifice required to tend this world in need with the birthing, lactating, self-sacrificing experience of motherhood:

> As a mother, I act on behalf all the time. And while at first I feared that this meant the loss of me, it is an invitation to a dynamic evolvement of myself. In the parallel language of Christian theology, God was not fearful of becoming less in the person of Jesus, but lives in and through Jesus of Nazareth as a way of dynamically involving Godself in the world, because behalfing/halfing does not diminish, but calls something particular into being.[80]

In immanently concrete, particularized language, Hill-Fletcher is giving voice to what we have here spoken of as the kenotic path. The kenotic path is always a participation in the divine self-emptying fuelled by divine desire, a self-emptying that paradoxically leads to fullness; it is a going out to the other in love that leads to communion. Where solidarity with suffering others across the globe is concerned, it entails the sacrifice of comfortable constructs and the difficult crossing of safe boundaries that leads to redemption in very concrete, particular, enfleshed ways.

77. Verna Harrison, "The Breast of the Father," in *Feminism and Theology*, 327–32, at 330.

78. Ibid.

79. Jeannine Hill-Fletcher, "Christology between Identity and Difference: On Behalf of a World in Need," in *Frontiers in Catholic Feminist Theology*, 79–96.

80. Ibid., 95.

Conclusion

Women who theologize on behalf of suffering global communities recognize in their experience "the material for new christological symbols and post-critical narratives disclosive of Jesus' status as God's self-present in the present."[81] While William Loewe's statement refers to historical images and narratives of Jesus of Nazareth, theologians must engage these from the starting point of the lived Paschal Mystery enfleshed today. The kenotic way for the Christian churches just might entail surrender of rigid dogmatic confines in faith that the living Paschal Mystery expressed in new cultural contexts will always find its correspondences in the narrative of Jesus of Nazareth.

81. Loewe, "From the Humanity of Christ to the Historical Jesus," 324.

12

Marriage Practices and the Redemption of the World

JASON E. KING
SAINT VINCENT COLLEGE

In its recent pastoral letter, *Marriage: Love and Life in the Divine Plan*, the United States Conference of Catholic Bishops (USCCB) said that marriage should not be viewed "as a mostly private matter, an individualistic project not related to the common good" (4).[1] Rather, marriage reaches "beyond the home to the extended family, the neighborhood, and the larger community" (48), "out in hospitality to the poor and to anyone in need" (52) in order to "contribute to the unity of humanity and humanity's communion with God" (55). In his apostolic exhortation, *On the Family*, Pope John Paul II also emphasized the role of the family in shaping and affecting the social sphere. While he wove this theme throughout the document, a section of the USCCB's letter focuses specifically on the participation of the family "in the development of society" (42–43). In the March 2003 issue of *Theological Studies*, Lisa Sowle Cahill notes in her overview of recent scholarship on marriage that one of the emerging trends among contemporary theologians is a

---

1. USCCB, *Marriage: Love and Life in the Divine Plan*, available online at: http://www.usccb.org/laity/loveandlife/MarriageFINAL.pdf. Subsequent references to pages of this pastoral letter are indicated by parenthetical citations in the text.

focus on the role families can have in promoting social justice concerns and changing culture for the better.[2]

In urging that marriage should contribute to the good of society, John Paul II, the USCCB, and Cahill did not provide a theory explaining *how* a family can impact the world around them for the better. This essay will suggest just such a theory by situating marriage within the theological project of Bernard Lonergan, particularly his understanding of history and redemption as expounded by William Loewe. Lonergan's theory of history—building on the notion of world process as emergent probability—uncovers the dynamic of progress and decline. Loewe's work explores this prospective recovery from decline through the law of the cross. Situating marriage in this context provides the framework for understanding the complex ways in which marriages can further progress, cause decline, and promote redemptive recovery in history.

Two qualifications must be made at the outset, one about what this essay does not do and one about what it does do. First, this essay is not about what a marriage is but rather what it can do. While the debates over the form or definition of marriage are by no means minor, the argument here does not presuppose a particular position in these debates. Instead, the focus is how a home can affect redemption and, as such, includes all homes that can respond to sin and decline with loving obedience. Second, because marriages are complex phenomena and their interactions with culture are multitudinous, this paper focuses on the economic effects of marriages as a way of indicating how marriages contribute to progress and decline and promote redemptive recovery. In doing so, the fruitfulness of Lonergan's perspective for understanding the various social dimensions of marriage should become apparent.[3]

2. See Lisa Sowle Cahill, "Marriage: Developments in Catholic Theology and Ethics," *Theological Studies* 64/1 (March 2003) 78–105.

3. Lonergan's most extended treatment of marriage is found in his "Finality, Love, Marriage," *Theological Studies* 4 (1943) 477–510. The critical edition is found in *Collection*, ed. Frederick Crowe and Robert Doran, *Collected Works of Bernard Lonergan* 4 (Toronto: University of Toronto Press, 1988) 17–52. Lonergan addresses the then current issue of how to rank the ends of marriage by situating marriage in the context of history. The value of this essay does not come from its argument on the ends of marriage or its scheme of history but rather in the idea of situating marriage in history. Thus, I draw little directly from "Finality, Love, Marriage" but follow its form by attempting to map out the implications of emergent probability for understanding marriage.

Bernard Lonergan's Theory of History

Lonergan's theory of history centers on what he terms "emergent probability." Emergent probability is a view of the world in terms of (1) schemes of recurrence, (2) conditioned series of schemes of recurrence, and (3) progress and decline. Lonergan's definition of a scheme of recurrence can be quite daunting: "[T]he scheme might be represented by the series of conditionals: If A occurs, B will occur; if B occurs, C will occur; if C occurs . . . A will recur."[4] The scheme is a connected series of conditions that form a circle of causality, a sequence of events that sustain the existence of something. The respiratory system provides a good illustration of these series of connected conditions: The brain sends messages to the heart to beat, the heart sends blood to the lungs for oxygenation and then to the brain to receive the oxygen to continue sending signals to the heart. A person's character is also an example: Individuals encounter situations and respond to them. The responses then dispose them to act in a similar way when similar situations arise. The more this response is repeated the more dominant it becomes. The dispositions become habits, virtues if they are good habits, vices if they are bad habits. Character is the conglomeration of these habits that make it easy for people to respond similarly in similar circumstances and harder to respond differently.

Obviously, to become a virtuous person requires more than just correct decisions. Each scheme is actually built upon several other schemes, and this dependence is the second point in Lonergan's idea of emergent probability: conditioned series of schemes of recurrence. The two qualifiers "conditioned" and "series" are key. "Series" is used to indicate that any scheme of recurrence depends upon the emergence and continuation of earlier schemes. This series of schemes is "conditioned" because the continuation of these earlier schemes, and thus the continuation of the later schemes, is not guaranteed. It depends upon certain conditions being met, conditions that are determined by statistical law, by probabilities. Thus, the formation of an individual's character depends in part on a functioning respiratory system, which depends in part upon the intake of food and air, which depends upon a functioning ecosystem generating healthy plants and animals. None

4. Bernard Lonergan, *Insight: A Study of Human Understanding, Collected Works of Bernard Lonergan* 3 (1992) 141.

of these schemes are guaranteed. Heart attacks and global warming are but two examples of possible disruptions that indicate the series is conditioned, governed by the law of probabilities.

While these two ideas—schemes of recurrence and conditioned series of schemes of recurrence—are the basic ideas of emergent probability, they leave open the question of whether what is emerging is progress or decline, the third set of terms in understanding Lonergan's theory of history.[5] Progress is the accumulation of successive series of schemes of recurrence that better and more efficiently address the needs and demands of a situation. Or, as Lonergan says,

> For concrete situations give rise to insights which issue into policies and courses of action. Action transforms the existing situation to give rise to further insights, better policies, more effective courses of action. It follows that if insight occurs, it keeps recurring; and at each recurrence knowledge develops, action increases its scope, and situations improve.[6]

Still, despite the real achievements of individuals and communities, history is not a simple succession of better and better situations. Decline sets in when there is a breakdown in a scheme of recurrence such that it ceases to exist. And with the collapse of one scheme, the probability that other schemes will collapse is raised. Whole series of schemes can come cascading down. Lonergan describes decline as follows:

> For the flight from understanding blocks the insights that concrete situations demand. There follow unintelligent policies and inept courses of action. The situation deteriorates to demand still further insights, and as they are blocked, policies become more unintelligent and action more inept.[7]

Lonergan argues that bias is what leads to decline. Individual bias is the subordination of the demands of truth and goodness to the capricious demands of self-interest. Group bias is operative when a group organizes and achieves what is good for it over and against the good of others. General bias renders the decaying situation normative, de-

5. For Lonergan's discussion of these terms see *Insight*, ch. 7, and *Method in Theology* (Toronto: University of Toronto Press, 1994), chap. 2.

6. Lonergan, *Insight*, 8.

7. Ibid.

manding a practical response to "the way things really are."[8] Efforts are put into accommodating the decline, often cropping up in the form of one ideology or another, and attempts at rethinking the problem are labeled "idealistic" and "impractical." This general bias both encourages the decline and hinders attempts to reverse it. In the end, decline can take over and seem beyond redemption. The collapse of schemes generates worse situations, more collapse, and more irrational and unhelpful situations. The rise of schemes sustaining progress is replaced by an ever-calcifying situation of decline. Sin reigns.

Redemptive Recovery and the Law of the Cross

Lonergan's notion of redemptive recovery is the way out of seemingly intractable decline. William Loewe's work on Lonergan's Law of the Cross develops this notion of redemptive recovery. Loewe summarizes the Law this way: (1) sin incurs the penalty of death, (2) dying can be transformed if accepted in loving obedience; (3) this transformed dying receives the blessing of new life.[9] This statement can be explained by focusing on three points: (1) the reign of sin, (2) accepting dying in loving obedience, and (3) redemptive recovery.

First, the reign of sin embraces two realities: sin leads to death and people are born into a situation of sin. Bias limits understanding. Individual, group, and general bias stultify the desire to know by attempting to restrict questions, hinder insights, and thwart action—all in the interest of an ego, a group, or narrow practical concerns. The only response to the resulting disordered situation seems to be an attempt to dominate others and impose one's perspectives on them. The result is a constriction of human flourishing and a propensity toward destructive conflict. As Loewe summarizes it, "Once the surd element

8. See ibid., 244–51, for Lonergan's presentation of individual, group, and general bias.

9. This summary is based on William Loewe's appropriation of Lonergan's thought. See Loewe: "Lonergan and the Law of the Cross: A Universalist View of Salvation," *Anglican Theological Review* 59/2 (1977) 162–74; "Dialectics of Sin: Lonergan's *Insight* and the Critical Theory of Max Horkheimer," *Anglican Theological Review* 61 (1979) 224–45; "Toward a Responsible Contemporary Soteriology," in *Creativity and Method: Essays in Honor of Bernard Lonergan, S.J.*, ed. Matthew Lamb (Milwaukee: Marquette University Press, 1981) 213–28.

penetrates and pervades the cultural dimension of society, man is left morally impotent. The history which he forges closes in to become, not a thrust toward God, but a reign of sin."[10] This reign of sin is the term to which decline heads.

Decline, as already noted, infects a historical situation where problems are increasingly met with obtuseness and ineptness. All humans are born into the reality where sometimes situations are improved by insights and sometimes they are exacerbated by bias. As Loewe writes, "To be born into this world is to be born into an historical process which is, among other things, shot through with dehumanizing dynamics."[11] People thus find themselves being shaped by a partially destructive history and perpetuating it through their actions.

Second, accepting dying in loving obedience is the way to overcome this decline. As Loewe indicates, this is the "essence" and "intrinsic intelligibility" of the gospel message. Jesus responds to his betrayal, trial, and death with loving obedience to God's will. The biases that gave rise to the irrational and violent response to Jesus' ministry are met with Jesus' forgiveness, a response that rejects the pseudo-practicality of the reign of sin. The gospel presents loving obedience as a precept of human action.[12] People are called and empowered to respond to sin in the way Jesus responded. Lonergan transposes the biblical language of obedience to God's will into "fidelity to the demands of self-transcendence."[13] People must be attentive, intelligent, reasonable, and responsible. This achievement should not be understood individualistically. Rather, people are working within worldviews that are shaped by both progress and decline, they are limited by their own biases and those that they have inherited, and they must move beyond these limits to a new and expanded worldview through the wisdom of others, their own pursuit of the good and the true, and the grace of God.[14] Loving obedience is a commitment to self-transcendence that "crucifies what is biased, distorted, and closed within oneself" and "frees one for the

---

10. Loewe, "Dialectics of Sin," 235.

11. Loewe, "Toward a Responsible Contemporary Soteriology," 219.

12. See ibid.

13. Ibid.

14. See ibid., 220.

qualitatively new life," a way of living set in opposition to decline and promoting recovery.[15]

Third, as the intrinsic intelligibility of the gospel and a precept of human action, the Law of the Cross can be and is to be carried out by others, thereby creating a process of redemptive recovery. As Loewe contends, Lonergan's soteriology is not "purely contemplative" but has "a practical intention which finds fulfillment not in understanding but in action."[16] The Law of the Cross shows how to overcome sin, and people living the law of the cross in their lives is the means by which a situation of decline is halted and a process of redemptive recovery emerges in history. In Loewe's words, the "Law of the Cross formulates a principle of transformation required for the attainment of human authenticity under the concrete conditions of existence in a sinful world."[17]

This section highlighted three aspects of Loewe's understanding of the Law of the Cross. First, it is a response to the reality that humans live in a history that is a mixture of progress and decline. Second, it calls for dying to the power of sin and responding in loving obedience. In other words, people must accede to the demands of self-transcendence, and in doing so they will overcome bias and open up new ways of living. Third, if lived, this response will affect a redemptive recovery for society. As marriage and its relationship to society is complex, what follows focuses on the economic implications of marriage and understanding these implications in light of these three aspects of the law of the cross.

Marriage, Progress, and Decline

Marriages tend to accumulate wealth, and this statistical reality is a mixture of progress and decline. Those who marry generate more income and wealth than cohabitators and more than those who are single, somewhere between 10 and 50 percent more.[18] It is easy to see the ways

15. Ibid., 219.

16. Ibid., 218.

17. Ibid., 219.

18. See Kate Antonovics and Robert Town, "Are All the Good Men Married? Uncovering the Sources of the Marital Wage Premium," *The American Economic Review* 94/2 (May 2004) 317–21; Avner Ahituv and Robert I. Lerman, "How Do Marital Status, Work Effort, and Wage Rates Interact?" *Demography* 44/3 (August 2007) 623–47; David Popenoe and Barbara Whitehead, "Ten Important Research

in which these statistics could be understood as progress. Money is necessary to function in the United States in the twenty-first century. People need it to provide the basic necessities like food, clothing, shelter, security, and education. Money, usually stemming from work, enables people to get insurance for health care and plan for retirement. The wealth that is accumulated also affects the ability to raise and educate children as well as take care of elderly parents and extended family that might need assistance. It is hard to imagine how any of these goods are bad, how having more money for families cannot but help people to respond better to their situations, and how this is not, at least in part, progress.

This same reality, though, is mixed up with decline. Why do marriages generate wealth? While some argue that marriage causes the wage increase by promoting better work and health habits, or by a division of labor in the home, others such as John Kavanaugh cite studies that argue that wage increases are the result of a bias by employers in favor of those who are married. Beyond the causes of wealth are the ways people use wealth. In his *Following Christ in a Consumer Culture*, Kavanaugh contrasts the consumer culture with gospel values.[19] He argues that consumer culture views people as competitors instead of neighbors. Children are an economic drain, not a gift. Marriages are seen more and more as privately contracted affairs instead of communal and vowed endeavors. Products are viewed as status symbols, and success is determined by the money you make and the items you possess. The Christian virtue of poverty seems incoherent, irresponsible, and impractical. Fame and physical beauty are valued over ordinary life and charity.

In his *Consuming Religion*, Vincent Miller characterizes the tension between the gospel and consumer culture differently.[20] Miller's

---

Findings on Marriage and Choosing a Marriage Partner," available online at: http://www.virginia.edu/marriageproject/pdfs/pubTenThingsYoungAdults.pdf. All of these studies indicate that the "marriage effect" on wealth accumulation benefits white males more than female heads of households and African Americans. Despite these differences, women and African Americans accumulate more wealth in marriages than outside of marriages.

19. See John F. Kavanaugh, *Following Christ in a Consumer Culture: The Spirituality of Cultural Resistance* (Maryknoll, NY: Orbis, 1991) specifically chaps. 10–11.

20. See Vincent J. Miller, *Consuming Religion: Christian Faith and Practice in a Consumer Culture* (New York: Continuum: 2005) specifically chap. 3.

perspective differs from Kavanaugh's in that Kavanaugh argues that the market economy offers a set of values that are in tension with Christian values whereas Miller argues that the market economy offers several value systems for sale, even Christian ones. For Miller, when people adopt Christian values, they have adopted them through the market system, thereby making the market system the foundation of their identity and beliefs. People may buy and display Christian symbols to indicate their faith but in the end they have done so through the market. Their identity as Christians is strengthened not by their loves but by what they have bought. In the same way, people might buy Ché Guevara or USSR or John Paul II T-shirts to indicate their dislike of a consumerist culture, but, in the end, they have forged their anti-consumerist identity by buying into and participating in a consumerist society.

Together, these two perspectives indicate the ways the wealth families generate can perpetuate and further decline. Kavanaugh's analysis indicates how consumer values turn other people into competitors and thus threats. Family members can easily value their goods over and against each other, an example of individual bias, or wealthier families can look down on poorer families, an example of group bias. Hence marriages face difficulties in staying together in our culture and families face enormous economic pressure to buy bigger houses and cars and send their kids to better schools. Miller adds to this understanding by indicating the ways in which the consumer mentality becomes the default horizon in understanding the world. Any problems or solutions are viewed in terms of their economic implications, and questions about the good, the true, the real, and the beautiful are reconfigured so that they are thought about as mainly preferences in a consumerist worldview. The situation is a case of general bias.

Families, though, can function differently. They can live in a culture saturated by consumer values and ubiquitous commodifying and can still replicate the law of the cross in their households. They can respond in love to the current situation. In Loewe's understanding, loving obedience is responding to the demands of self-transcendence, and this brings about an overcoming of biases and an emergence of a new way of living. Julie Rubio's work on the dual vocation of parents and David McCarthy's notion of the open household exemplify how families can respond to the reign of sin in society with a loving obedience that overcomes it.

Acceptance and Loving in the Dual Vocation of Parents

Given the situation described above—families generating wealth that often nourishes values at odds with Christian values—work often becomes something that feeds into this decline. In her essay "The Dual Vocation of Christian Parents," Julie Rubio suggests an alternative. She contends that parents have a "dual vocation."[21] The work of parents need not be done to pursue consumer values or to further one's own or the family's identity. Work can be understood as part of the call of discipleship and part of the parental responsibility toward children.

Rubio contends that parents have a public vocation, one outside of the home. She notes that early Christians were suspicious of families because families often looked after their own and neglected neighbors and strangers. The early Christians were often exhorted to leave the family behind for the sake of the kingdom. This call was not, Rubio writes, a dismissal of the importance of the family and parenting but a realization that the Christian call requires people to love and work for the good beyond the family. Rubio states, "[O]ne cannot, I would argue, fully realize the demands of discipleship to Jesus of Nazareth unless one also has a public vocation."[22] This public vocation entails the work the parents do outside of the home.

This work, though, is not at odds with parenting. The work relates to the rearing of children in two ways. First, being a parent and loving a child calls one to love other children, and thereby inspires one to change the world and not abandon it.[23] It is the love that one lives and learns in the family that leads one outside of the home to work for the good of others. This love is not just the family going out to help others, however, as the work of the parents outside the home is brought in so that the family learns love of others. Rubio gives an example of how her father's discussion of his work as an attorney for the government-funded Legal Services at the dinner table shaped both her family's commitment to justice in the world and their understanding of what it meant to be Christian.

---

21. See Julie Hanlon Rubio, *A Christian Theology of Marriage and Family* (New York: Paulist, 2003) 89–110.

22. Rubio, *Christian Theology of Marriage*, 99.

23. See ibid., 108.

The understanding of work that Rubio proffers reflects not just loving obedience but also an acceptance of what Loewe describes as the dying required by the reign of sin. As Rubio says about the way her family lived, "The relatively low pay [of my father's work] meant that we did not enjoy some of the luxuries many of our friends did. The political nature of the work meant that our conversations frequently centered on politics. The public nature of the work meant that we often had to defend our values to neighbors and friends."[24] Meeting the demands of self-transcendence in the family meant living in a new way, but this new way was not outside the world but enmeshed in an environment that was both progress and decline. Her family rejected the sinful situation surrounding work and the family: the existence of work that replicates what Kavanaugh called "consumer values," work that is for an "individualistic pursuit of self-fulfillment or monetary gain."[25] The acceptance entailed suffering in pursuit of the new way of living envisioned by the dual vocation of her parents.

Acceptance and Loving in the Open Household

In his *Sex and Love in the Home*, David McCarthy articulates another example of the Law of the Cross as lived out in family life. In chapter 5, McCarthy describes two types of households, open and closed. The closed household is what is typically held up as the ideal in our society. "The closed family understands its health and well-being in terms of emotional and financial independence."[26] People seek to find jobs that provide a kind of sufficiency where they do not have to depend upon others. Work in and for the family—child care, lawn care, maintenance work, house work—is contracted out. The family does not need to depend upon grandparents, aunts and uncles, friends, or neighbors. Interactions with these people are thus leisure activities and not necessary ones. Children are optional. They are merely one way in which a couple can invest their time and money and emotions.

McCarthy's closed household, where the "economic strategy is structure outside the home" and is "product-oriented," is the family

24. Ibid., 189.

25. Ibid., 189.

26. David Matzko McCarthy, *Sex and Love in the Home* (London: SCM, 2001), 93.

understood in light of Miller's consumer culture. The closed family is defined by buying and consuming outside of the home and not by the activities within it. Families buy certain kinds of houses in certain neighborhoods and certain kinds of cars to drive to certain kinds of work and, if they have kids, to certain kinds of schools. The money earned outside the home is used "for the family" in the sense of buying those products that help the family identify itself within a whole range of life options, all available from and whose meaning is mediated through the market economy.

McCarthy contends that this decline, to use Lonergan's terminology, can be overcome through an open household. An open household is one that depends for its well being upon family, friends, neighbors and kin, and operates in part through a gift economy. McCarthy provides two examples of an open household. The first comes from a family that needed to take in a tenant after a divorce.[27] The family needed the money and had an extra room and large garage, and the tenant, a friend of a friend, needed a cheap place to live and a garage to build up his upholstery business. Over time, the line between the tenant and the family blurred. They mutually helped one another out in ways that went beyond their contractual arrangement. The tenant helped out with repairs around the house that the husband used to do, and the family welcomed strangers into their home who were customers for the upholstery business. These gift-exchanges altered the contractual nature of the relationship and made it closer to kinship, "persons with whom we feel a bond of long-term commitment."[28] The second example comes from one of McCarthy's neighbors using his snow blower after a winter storm. The neighbor used the machine to clear everyone's sidewalks. This created a situation where nobody quite knew how to respond. When a lighter snow came, another neighbor used his leaf blower to clear the sidewalks. When another light snow came, one family sent their kids out to shovel everyone's drive. Another family made cookies for the snow-blower neighbor. There was no one way to respond, yet these responses are keys, according to McCarthy,

> . . . to a basic pattern of household exchange between kinfolk, friends, and neighbors. No one responded to our good neigh-

27. See ibid., 97.
28. Ibid., 98.

bor by writing him a check or by dashing out of the house to help him. In either case, he rightfully would be offended. If he were obviously struggling with a shovel, that would be a different matter. Given his mastery of his task, our duty as neighbors was to accept and appreciate his kindness. . . . in one sense, his benevolent use of his snow-blower will always be understood as a gift; yet in another, it would become part of a pattern of reciprocity, part of the neighborhood equilibrium whereby we sustain a certain status among others and exchange benefits.[29]

The gift economy not only entails the family's dependence upon others but also, through the exchange, strengthens the relationship with others. The gift economy does not view openness as a failure of the family to be self-sufficient but rather understands openness as how a neighborhood both sustains and understands itself. The network of relationships creates an economy not based on consumption but rather on meeting mutual needs. The economy is not contractual—where the arrangement ends when the work is done—but rather relational. It turns neighbors and strangers into kin.[30]

McCarthy's open household is an example of the unfolding of the Law of the Cross. The closed household is recognized as part of the problem. It is contributing to the process of decline that Miller described in that the closed household replicates the pattern of finding one's identity in and through the marketplace. The open household overcomes this situation by conceiving of the identity of families differently. Families understand who they are not by what they buy in a market economy but by their relationship to others—friends, families, neighbors, kin—through the gift economy.

As in Rubio's case, this response to overcome general bias entails an acceptance of suffering. It is almost scandalous in our society to have to take in a tenant to get by or to have your neighbors involved in the care of your own family. Yet, this is part of the accepting dying in loving obedience that is called for in the law of the cross. Families who

29. Ibid., 102–3.

30. What is implicit in this understanding of marriage is that marriage becomes a domestic church: a marriage that embodies the Law of the Cross is carrying out the redemptive work of Christ that the church is called to do. For more extensive work on how families function as a domestic church, see John Paul II, *Familiaris consortio*, 48; and Florence Caffrey Bourg, *Where Two or Three Are Gathered: Christian Families as Domestic Churches* (Notre Dame: University of Notre Dame Press, 2004).

attempt to embody an open household will often suffer the appearance of foolishness or impracticality though it is something like the open household that enables the family not to participate in decline and contribute to recovery.

Marriage and Redemptive Recovery

McCarthy's open household and Rubio's understanding of work and family are both ways in which the law of the cross can be embodied in family life. For these practices to turn back the deleterious effects of the economy and thereby foster redemptive recovery, however, they must spread from family to family. McCarthy's and Rubio's proposed responses to the biases in the economy participate in recovery because they have the potential to draw families in.

McCarthy's gift economy is not practiced by a family in isolation. It requires a family to relate to others, not in some money-making pyramid scheme but in order to care for one another. This meeting of mutual needs and relationships between homes makes the open household resistant to being coopted by the market economy. A gift economy that works through meeting each other's needs contrasts with a consumer economy built on contracts. The former unites families in open-ended relationships where meeting a need perpetuates and strengthens the relationship, while the latter binds people together in a limited endeavor that ends as soon as the need is met. To the degree that families can build and sustain an open household, they are reworking the commodification of the family in our culture and contributing to recovery.

Rubio's understanding of the dual vocation of parents also implies a connectedness of the families to others. It reconfigures the understanding and work of the family so that it can be understood as the historical unfolding of the law of the cross. Families carry the love learned between themselves to their work and workplace and learn from this work and workplace how to love those outside the family. Rubio makes this point in her discussion of how Jack Nelson-Pallmeyer, author of *Families Valued*, realized that when his daughter's tricycle was destroyed by neighborhood children, he not only had to care for his daughter's needs but also the needs of the other children that did the destroying if he was truly to love other children as he loved his own.[31] Living the Law of the Cross such that it flows from one family to another entails responding to destroyed property, low pay, and disagreements with love. Otherwise, retaliation, climbing the pay scale, or excluding those who differ will become the family's response, and the cycle of decline will be perpetuated.

Conclusion

The foregoing attempt to understand marriage in terms of progress, decline, and recovery has two major benefits. First, it provides a framework for analyzing the effects of marriage on the broader society—some good, some bad, and some potentially redemptive. By focusing on the economic dimension of marriage, the hope has been to show how the claims of the USCCB, John Paul II, and Cahill that the family has an important social dimension is strengthened by understanding the dynamics of this interaction both in theory (Lonergan's theory of history) and in practice (McCarthy's open household and Rubio's dual vocation of parents). Second, by drawing on Loewe's work on the Law of the Cross, the hope is to have shown not just a theory about *how* the family can carry out its Christian mission but also provide *hope* that it can do so. Even in times of rampant decline, the Law of the Cross can be lived, impact history, and contribute to the redemption of the world.

31. See Rubio, *Christian Theology of Marriage*, 108; Jack Nelson-Pallmeyer, *Families Valued: Parenting and Politics for the Good of All Children* (New York: Friendship, 1996).

13

Christ in the Many and Diverse Religions: An Interreligious Christology

PETER C. PHAN
GEORGETOWN UNIVERSITY

Given Professor William Loewe's signal contribution to Christology it would be appropriate to honor him with an essay on how this theological theme can be developed further to meet the challenges of contemporary religious pluralism. By religious pluralism is meant not merely religious *diversity*, that is, the sociological fact that today, thanks especially to migration and globalization, most religions are no longer confined to their places of origin but have spread far and wide, and consequently, believers must learn how to live in harmony and collaborate with people of different faiths for the common good.[1] By contrast, religious *pluralism* refers to the philosophical and theological issues arising from the fact that postmodernity has rendered it extremely problematic for any religion—Christianity included—to claim that it alone possesses the fullness of truth and goodness.[2] Postmodernity's

---

1 For the United States, see Diana Eck, *A New Religious America: How a "Christian Country" Has Become the World's Most Religiously Diverse Nation* (San Francisco: HarperSanFrancisco, 2001).

2. There is no point in presenting here even an essential bibliography on religious pluralism as a philosophical and theological problem. The popular and scholarly literature on this theme has grown by leaps and bounds, and it is a rare theologian who can keep up with it! Suffice it to note that a new doctoral program with a focus on religious pluralism was recently founded at Georgetown University.

theory of knowledge, not to mention its dismissal of metaphysics, may lead to relativism and skepticism.[3] On the other hand, there are those who, though acknowledging the validity of the postmodern emphasis on the contextuality and partiality of all human knowledge, still defend the possibility of a certain, albeit ever provisional, knowledge of reality when the manifold and varied insights of different traditions are brought together in a common quest for knowledge. As a result, a consensus has been emerging among many religious communities regarding the necessity and usefulness of interfaith dialogue in which one religion's beliefs and practices can be corrected, complemented and enriched by those of others.

The question under consideration here is whether the Christian understanding of who Jesus is (Christology) and what he has done (soteriology) as has been formulated in the Bible and the tradition can be broadened by this interfaith dialogue. At first sight, "interfaith Christology" is an oxymoron since by definition Christology is a faith-based reflection on the *Christian* confession in Jesus as the Christ. Yet, in a globalized age such as ours and within the contemporary context of religious pluralism, it would seem that such theological reflection can no longer be done only intraconfessionally. Hence, there arises question of the possibility and desirability of an "interfaith Christology." By this expression I do not mean simply a Christology undertaken by Christians on the basis of the Christian faith in dialogue with the beliefs of other religions; such Christology might be termed "dialogical Christology."[4] Rather, I would like to consider the possibility and desirability (and perhaps even necessity, at least for today) of a Christology constructed by Christians and non-Christians alike, ideally in collaboration with one another, on the common beliefs and practices of different religious traditions. Such a Christology replaces neither the classical Christology based solely on the Bible and the Christian tradition, which still retains its necessity and validity, nor the "dialogical Christology," which considers the Christian beliefs in Jesus as normative and seeks to enrich itself from the insights of non-Christian religions.

---

3. For a helpful collection of postmodern writings, see *From Modernism to Postmodernism: An Anthology*, ed. Lawrence Cahoone (Cambridge: Blackwell, 2007).

4. The majority of Christologies written by Christians in dialogue with other religions falls within this category, for example, comparing Jesus to Krishna, the Buddha, the Qur'an, or Confucius.

Within the narrow space allotted to it and given its highly experimental nature, this brief essay is more a programmatic manifesto than a systematic elaboration of a complete interfaith Christology.[5] I begin with reflections on the conditions of possibility for such a Christology, its limitations, and its desirability. Next I outline its main features. Finally, I refer to some salient pioneering works, especially those of Raimon Panikkar, pointing toward an interfaith Christology.

Interfaith Christology: Possibility, Limits, Desirability

The possibility of interfaith Christology of necessity rests on the kind of interreligious dialogue in which participants genuinely respect differences and try to understand religions other than one's own as they present themselves on their terms, and avoid interpreting them through the lens of one's categories and belief system.[6] These differences do not of course preclude commonalities, or at least analogues, among religions, but they must not be papered over or minimized, much less homogenized, as simply various ways of talking about God, or the Ultimate, or the Real. In other words, religions must not be taken simply as various paths leading to the same religious summit (e.g., God) or merely diverse cultural expressions of the same core religious experience.[7]

Concerning the possibility of interfaith Christology, it will be objected at once that Christology is by definition a *Christian* category and therefore calling the projected interfaith theology a "Christology" already violates the above-mentioned hermeneutical principle. The point is well taken. However, the objection can be obviated by the following considerations. First, "Christ," both as a term and a concept, is per se not restricted to Christianity; it is found in Judaism (the *māšîaḥ*)[8] and

5. Some of the ideas developed here have been presented in my "An Interfaith Christology: A Possibility and a Desideratum?" in *Negotiating Borders: Theological Explorations in the Global Era*, ed. Patrick Ghanaprasagam and Elisabeth Schüssler Fiorenza (Dehli: ISPCK, 2008) 379–85.

6. For a recent reflection on the nature of interreligious dialogue, see Catherine Cornille, *The Im-Possibility of Interreligious Dialogue* (New York: Crossroad, 2008).

7. On this point, see Stephen Kaplan, *Different Paths, Different Summits: A Model for Religious Pluralism* (Lanham, MD: Rowman & Littlefield, 2002).

8. The Hebrew term, which means "anointed," is applied primarily to the king, and later to priests and prophets. When the ideals of kingship were not realized in the Davidic monarchy, there arose a hope of a future king who would bring a kingdom of

the figure of Jesus is also present in Islam.[9] Consequently, at least as far as Judaism and Islam are concerned, an interfaith Christology is legitimate and not a prima facie impossibility.

Secondly, it is possible to speak of "Christology" without making the Christian claims regarding Christ's divinity, resurrection, unique and universal role as savior and other beliefs about him the starting point and basis of the interreligious discourse, even though these claims must not be dissimulated by the Christian partners-in-dialogue. In other words, it is possible to discuss the *meaning* of a statement (which concerns *understanding*) and thereby enriching our understanding of it without affirming its *truth* at the same time (which is an exercise of *judgment*). In this kind of interfaith Christology, which is, to use Bernard Lonergan's distinction of functional specialties in theology, "systematics" and not "doctrines," the Christian claims about Christ are not denied a priori.[10] Rather they are theologically assumed by the Christians but methodologically bracketed with the goal to arrive at a richer and pluralistic understanding of what constitutes Jesus as the Christ on the basis of what Christianity and other religions say about the "Christ."

Thirdly, strictly speaking, just as Christians speak of an interfaith Christology, Buddhists can rightfully speak of an interfaith "Buddhology," Hindus an interfaith "Krishnology," Muslims an interfaith "Qur'anology" and perhaps "Muhammadology," Sikhs an interfaith "Gurology," and so on, without demanding that others accept as true claims about the Buddha, Krishna, the Qur'an, or Muhammad. The point of interfaith Christology is not to demonstrate, much less to convert others to, the belief that the Christ of the Christians is unique, universal, and superior to all other religious figures, or vice versa. In principle, a *rational* demonstration of such a claim is not logically possible since it is essentially an affirmation of faith. At best a believer can

---

justice and peace and the idea that God would intervene in history by sending a savior, possibly as a priestly or prophetic figure. Finally, there is also the idea that this savior would deliver his people from suffering and injustice by means of his own suffering (the "Suffering Servant").

9. For the figure of Jesus as the messiah in Islam, see Tarif Khaladi, *The Muslim Jesus: Sayings and Stories in Islamic Literature* (Cambridge, MA: Harvard University Press, 2001).

10. On Lonergan's distinction, see his *Method in Theology* (New York: Seabury, 1972) 132–33.

only show why his or her belief is not absurd or self-contradictory. The purpose of interreligious dialogue is to obtain as profound and diverse an understanding as possible of the Christ on the basis of the most varied and even contradictory affirmations of different religions on what makes a particular being (e.g., Siddhārtha Gautama, Jesus of Nazareth, the Qur'an, or any religious founder) the Christ.

Thus conceived, interfaith Christology no doubt has several limitations. The most obvious one is that it is not a "dogmatic Christology" and hence would be judged by those seeking an orthodox Christology as theologically inappropriate and even heterodox in the light of, for instance, Chalcedonian Christology. Nor is it a "historical Christology," a "Christology from below," or an "ascending Christology" insofar as it is not based primarily on the Gospels' account of Jesus' life and ministry and is not designed to show that Jesus is the Word of God made flesh. In this respect it lacks the historical specificity characteristic of, for example, liberation Christology of various stripes (e.g., Black, Latin American, Asian, feminist, ecological, etc.). Finally, it does not perform the apologetic function of a "transcendental Christology" such as that proposed by Karl Rahner, intended to explicate the conditions of possibility for the faith in Jesus as the Christ on the basis of a metaphysics of human knowledge and love.

Nevertheless, interfaith Christology, while distinct from the three above-mentioned Christologies, does not exclude them but rather helps clarify some of their key concepts, one of which is of course that of "Christ." Given the religiously pluralistic situation of our time and the urgent need for mutual understanding and collaboration among followers of different religions, such interfaith Christology is arguably a legitimate desideratum and a pressing necessity for contemporary theology. Whether it is feasible or not cannot be settled a priori nor should it be rejected out of hand simply because of potential errors and weaknesses. At least an outline of its general features may be attempted.

Contour of an Interfaith Christology

The central concept to be elaborated in interfaith Christology is of course the"Christ." Here an apparently insurmountable challenge immediately surfaces. The term, and more crucially the concept, of the

"Christ"—at least as it is understood in Christianity—are not espoused by all religious traditions, and even where the concept is used, it is far from univocal. Hence, a major task of an interfaith Christology is to determine the meaning of the "Christ" and its place, if any, in a particular religion. In this conceptual elaboration of the "Christ," the Christian understanding of Jesus as the Christ, as pointed out above, can play a heuristic role but not a normative one. It must be correlated with concepts and images present in other religions that exhibit significant similarities or functional analogies with it. A new and enlarged understanding of the "Christ" may thus be construed out of these critically correlated concepts and images, and the result may be termed a "comparative" or "interfaith" Christology.[11]

Which are, to begin with, the main features of the Christian concept of the Christ? A straightforward answer to this question is impossible since it is universally acknowledged that the Jesus of the Gospels fits no single description. He is, yet is not—in the usual sense of the words—a priest, a prophet, an apocalyptic seer, a rabbi, a teacher of wisdom, a miracle worker, a political leader, to cite just the main titles that have been attributed to him. In the eyes of New Testament scholars, as Colin Greene notes, Jesus was variously a Cynic, a mystic, a healer, a *ḥasîd*, a prophet or the eschatological prophet, a reformer, a sage, personified Wisdom, and a/the Messiah.[12] Greene goes on to show that until modernity Christology emphasized Jesus as the eternal Logos made flesh (cosmological Christology), as "Lord of lords and King of kings" (political Christology), and as the New Adam (anthropological Christology).[13] Here, my interest is not to show how these three traditional Christologies have been challenged and emended in modernity and postmodernity, but to use them as a launching pad for outlining an interfaith Christology.[14]

11. On comparative theology, see Francis X. Clooney, *Theology after Vedanta: An Experiment in Comparative Theology* (Albany: SUNY Press, 1993) esp. 153–208. Another relevant work by Clooney, soon to be published by T. & T. Clark/Continuum, is *Comparative Theology: Thinking Interreligiously in the 21st Century.*

12. See Colin J. D. Greene, *Christology in Cultural Perspective: Marking Out the Horizons* (Grand Rapids: Eerdmans, 2003) 6–15.

13. Ibid., 30–71.

14. For this, see Greene's study cited above. Of course, contemporary studies of Christology are legion! For our purposes, the following are especially useful: Anton Wessels, *Images of Jesus: How Jesus Is Perceived and Portrayed in Non-European*

Underlying these divergent Christologies, I suggest, is the notion that somehow in Jesus, however his historical role is interpreted, humans are given the possibility of fulfilling their nature and reaching their ultimate goal, referred to in theistic language as union with God and in non-theistic language as self-transcendence (e.g., liberation, enlightenment, salvation, redemption, transformation, etc). This is central to the notion of the "Christ," apart from the concrete and historical way(s) in which such possibility of self-realization is realized. The basic question then is whether such a notion is found in religions other than Christianity (the answer to which is of course affirmative), and how they can be used to construct an interfaith Christology.

Concomitant with the notion of the Christ is that of a supernatural or superhuman (even divine) power by which the Christ achieves his or her mission of bringing humans and the cosmos to fulfillment. The Christian faith confesses that this superhuman power is a gift of the risen Christ and that together with the Father and the Son, this personal power, who is named by Christians as the "Holy Spirit," constitutes the Trinity. Various symbols and images such as breath, wind, fire, water, and dove have been used to describe the Spirit's transformative power. Since the Spirit is the power by which both the Christ himself/herself and all humans achieve their goals, it is theologically proper to preface interfaith Christology with pneumatology.[15] In fact, methodologically, from the Christian point of view, Christology, especially an interfaith one, makes more sense if we begin with the Spirit, then move to the Son, and end with the Father.[16]

Cultures (Grand Rapids: Eerdmans, 1990); Volker Küster, *The Many Faces of Jesus Christ: Intercultural Christology*, trans. John Bowden (Maryknoll, NY: Orbis, 2001); Clinton Bennet, *In Search of Jesus: Insider and Outsider Images* (London: Continuum, 2001); Veli-Matti Kärkkäinen, *Christology: A Global Introduction* (Grand Rapids, MI: Baker, 2003); Gregory A. Barker, ed., *Jesus in the World's Faiths: Leading Thinkers from Five Religions Reflect on His Meaning* (Maryknoll, NY: Orbis, 2005); and Michael Amaladoss, *The Asian Jesus* (Maryknoll, NY: Orbis, 2006).

15. One of the best studies of contemporary theologies of the Holy Spirit is Kirsteen Kim, *The Holy Spirit in the World: A Global Conversation* (Maryknoll, NY: Orbis, 2007).

16. I wrote in 1988: "With regard to the structure of the treatise of the Trinity, I suggest that we reverse the traditional order. Rather than beginning with the Father, then moving to the Son, and ending with the Holy Spirit, given the principle that we should root our trinitarian theology in our experiences of salvation, we should begin with our present-day experiences of the Holy Spirit, and then show how this

Since the Spirit is not embodied in any particular historical person, it is easier to find analogies—not identical entities—for the Christian concept of Spirit in non-Christian religions, such as *atman/brahman* in *advaita* Hinduism, *shakti* in classical Hinduism, *antaryamin* in *bhakti* Hinduism, *ch'i* in Daoism and Confucianism, the *yin* of the *yin-yang* polarity, and spirits in many religious traditions. Nor should an interfaith pneumatology limit itself to religious and philosophical sources. Since the Spirit is associated with freedom, she has often functioned as the source and inspiration for revolution and the struggle for personal and national independence.[17]

Forerunners of Interfaith Christology

An interfaith Christology is essentially a Spirit or pneumatological Christology consisting in an elaboration on the work of Jesus as the Christ by virtue of the Spirit in bringing about humanity's union of God and/or human self-realization. With pneumatology as its prolegomenon, interfaith Christology can move forward to consider the many titles that have been ascribed to the Christ in the Christian tradition and inquire whether similar titles are also found in non-Christian religions, not to establish their conceptual equivalence, much less their truth, but in order to obtain a richer understanding of what the Christ means.

Mention has already been made of the figure of the Christ in Judaism and Islam, and studies on this theme are plentiful.[18] In addition, comparative studies between Jesus and Krishna, between Jesus

Spirit is the Spirit of Jesus, and end with Jesus' revelation of the mystery of God the Father" (Peter C. Phan, *Being Religious Interreligiously: Asian Perspectives on Interfaith Dialogue* [Maryknoll, NY: Orbis, 2004] 38). It is gratifying to note that Kim writes in a similar vein: "We may be able to put the gospel message across more meaningfully if we begin from the Spirit, rather than the historical Jesus. And after all, it is the role of the prevenient Spirit to prepare the world to receive Christ" (*The Holy Spirit in the World*, vi).

17. This is particularly true of Korea. See Kim, *The Holy Spirit in the World*, 112–21.

18. The literature is immense. On Jesus in Judaism, see the comprehensive articles by Susannah Heschel, "Jewish Views of Jesus" and Jacob Neusner, "Why Jesus Has No Meaning to Judaism," in *Jesus in the World's Faith*, 149–60 and 166–73 respectively. On Jesus in Islam, see Muhammad Ata ur-Rahim, *Jesus Prophet of Islam* (Elmhurst, NY: Tahrike Tarsile Qur'an, 1991); and Tarif Khalidi, *The Muslim Jesus: Sayings and Stories in Islamic Literature* (Cambridge, MA: Harvard University Press, 2001).

and Confucius, and between Jesus and other religious figures abound.[19] An irony in the development of such interfaith Christology is that its most significant pioneers were not Christians but Hindus. The writings of Sri Ramakrishna, Swami Vivekananda, Keshub Chunder Sen, Mohandas Gandhi, Swami Akhiananda, and Sarvepalli Radhakrishnan are well-known. Among Christian Indians, Manilal C. Parekh and Bhawami Charan Banerji (also known as Brahmabandhab Upadhyaya) were influential.[20] Among contemporary Buddhist leaders, the works of the Dalai Lama and the Zen Vietnamese Buddhist monk Thich Nhat Hanh should be noted.[21]

Among contemporary Christian theologians M. M. Thomas, Stanley Samartha, George M. Soares-Prabhu, Raimon Panikkar, Samuel Ryan, Michael Amaladoss, Aloysius Pieris, Roger Haight, Thomas Thangaraj, *Minjung* theologians, and Asian women theologians, to cite only a few, have offered valuable insights into how an interfaith Christology can be constructed. [22] In the final part of this essay I would like to draw attention to one theologian in particular who has pioneered this kind of interfaith Christology.[23]

19. For an overview, see Bennet, *In Search of Jesus*, 292–344.

20. See the studies by M. M. Thomas, *The Acknowledged Christ of the Indian Renaissance* (Madras: Christian Literature Society, 1970); and Stanley Samartha, *The Hindu Response to the Unbound Christ* (Bangalore: IISRS, 1974).

21. See the Dalai Lama, *The Good Heart: A Buddhist Perspective on the Teachings of Jesus* (Somerville, MA: Wisdom, 1996); Thich Nhat Hanh, *Living Buddha, Living Christ* (New York: Riverhead, 1995); *Going Home: Jesus and Buddha as Brothers* (New York: Riverhead, 1999). See also Marcus Borg, *Jesus and Buddha: The Parallel Stories* (Berkeley, CA: Ulysses, 1997).

22. See Thomas, *Acknowledged Christ of the Indian Renaissance*; Samartha, *Hindu Response to the Unbound Christ*; George M. Soares-Prabhu, *The Dharma of Jesus* (Maryknoll, NY: Orbis, 2003); Raimon Panikkar, *A Dwelling Place for Wisdom* (Louisville: Westminster John Knox, 1993); Samuel Ryan, *The Holy Spirit: Heart of the Gospel and Christian Hope* (Maryknoll, NY: Orbis, 1978); Michael Amaladoss, *The Asian Jesus* (Maryknoll, NY: Orbis, 2006); Aloysius Pieris, *Love Meets Wisdom: A Christian Experience of Buddhism* (Maryknoll, NY: Orbis, 1988); Roger Haight, *Jesus Symbol of God* (Maryknoll, NY: Orbis, 1999); Thomas Thangaraj, *The Crucified Guru: An Experiment in Cross-Cultural Christology* (Nashville: Abingdon, 1994); Muriel Orevillo-Montenegro, *The Jesus of Asian Women* (Maryknoll, NY: Orbis, 2006). My own contributions may be found in my trilogy *Christianity with an Asian Face* (Maryknoll, NY: Orbis, 2003); *In Our Own Tongues* (Maryknoll, NY: Orbis, 2004); and *Being Religious Interreligiously* (Maryknoll, NY: Orbis, 2004).

23. All the above reflections had been written before I came to read Panikkar's book discussed in the next section of the essay. I am immensely gratified that some of

Raimon Panikkar: "Christophany" Born out of Interreligious Dialogue

Among Panikkar's immense theological corpus, his *Christophany: The Fullness of Man* is no doubt the most explicit and detailed essay on interfaith Christology.[24] Panikkar intentionally eschews the word "Christology" (by which he means the Western theology of Christ) and coins the word "christophany" to characterize his theological proposal. Panikkar does not pretend that his christophany is a universal paradigm or that it should be adopted by historical Christianity. He simply wishes to "offer an image of Christ that all people are capable of believing in, especially those contemporaries who, while wishing to remain open and tolerant, think they have no need of either diluting their 'Christianity' or of damaging their fidelity to Christ."[25]

While not ignoring or abolishing the christological teachings of the last two millennia, Panikkar's christophany intends to build an interfaith Christology by privileging the active presence (the *phania*) of the Holy Spirit in all human cultures and especially in all religious traditions:

> Christology has been, in general, a reflection pursued by Christians who, except in its first period of formation, have virtually ignored the world's other traditions. Christophany, on the other hand, is open to both a dialogue with other religions and an interpretation of that same tradition on the basis of a scenario that embraces the past (including the pre-Christian) as well as the present (even what is called the secular).[26]

Central to Panikkar's christophany is his belief that every being, in particular every human being (he prefers to use the word "Man") is a

---

my ideas find echo in Panikkar's work.

24. Raimon Panikkar, *Christophany: The Fullness of Man*, trans. Alfred DiLacia, Faith Meets Faith (Maryknoll, NY: Orbis, 2004). The Italian original *La pienezza dell'uomo: una cristofania* appeared in 1999 (Milan: Jaca). My intention is not to present here Panikkar's theology as a whole or his Christology in particular, but only to highlight his pointers toward an interfaith Christology as I have proposed. Panikkar's theology has been the subject of numerous dissertations and critical studies. For a helpful evaluation of Panikkar, see *The Intercultural Challenge of Raimon Panikkar*, ed. Joseph Prabhu (Maryknoll, NY: Orbis, 1997).

25. Panikkar, *Christophany*, 9.

26. Ibid., 11.

christophany, that is, the divinization of humanity, which is the other side of the humanization of God: "Christophany bears a double meaning: the humanization of God corresponds to the divinization of Man. Christ is the revelation of God (in Man) as much as the revelation of man (in God)."[27]

In light of this dual reality, christophany is built on what Panikkar calls a "cosmovision," that is, a vision of the world with the "third eye," in which the divine and the human are experienced as "theandric," not as one (either human or divine) or two (both human and divine) but "non-dualistic." In other words "it is an *advaita* experience," distilled in the upanishadic dictum on the identity between *brahman* and *atman*: *tat tvam asi* (that thou art).[28] Panikkar illustrates this non-dualistic experience with an insightful commentary on Saint Theresa of Avila's famous poem containing Christ's words to her: *"Teresa, búscate en mí, búscame en tí"* (Seek for thyself in me, seek for me in thyself). As Panikkar puts it: "The *seek me* cannot be divided from the *seek thyself*, for the *me* and the *thou* are correlative. The *metron* is human and divine, theandric—indeed, cosmotheandric."[29]

What is the nature of this *advaita* christophany that Panikkar claims is shared by Jesus and all human beings? Panikkar describes it by commenting on three New Testament texts, the three *mahāvākya* (great sayings): Mark 14:36; John 10:30; and John 16:7. These texts express not three different religious experiences of Jesus but rather one experience, that of the non-dualistic identity between God and Jesus (and between God and us). This experience, which is universal, is made possible only by the Spirit. Ultimately, therefore, the *advaitic* experience is a trinitarian experience.

Panikkar defends his christophany against charges of gnosticism, ahistoricism, and relativism in nine *sūtra*.[30] Whether his answers are fully satisfactory to his critics is for the reader to judge, and space does not permit me to examine each of them in detail here, but no one can say that Panikkar is not fully aware of all the possible errors to which his christophany may lead. Furthermore, no one can gainsay Panikkar's following statement: "If Christ is to have any meaning for Hindus,

27. Ibid., 17.

28. Ibid., 21.

29. Ibid., 27, 35; emphasis in original.

30. See ibid., 144–84.

Andines, Ibos, Vietnamese, and others who do not belong to the Abrahamic lineage, this meaning can no longer be offered in the garb of Western philosophies."[31] In other words, in addition to (not in place of) "Christology from above" and "Christology from below," there is the need of what Panikkar terms "Christology from within" or "christophany from the center," or what I call an "interreligious Christology."[32] No doubt, interreligious Christology is still in its infancy, but its future, in the hands of Panikkar and many others, is bright.

31. Ibid., 185.
32. Ibid.

Epilogue:
Continuing Conversations

WILLIAM P. LOEWE

THE CATHOLIC UNIVERSITY OF AMERICA

That students become both peers and friends has counted among the foremost pleasures of academic life for me. I am deeply grateful to Christopher Denny and Christopher McMahon for conceiving and bringing this book to fruition, and to the other friends and colleagues who have contributed to it. They honor and humble me.

Academic life also privileges one to participate in the ongoing conversations that constitute traditions. However abstruse they may appear to become, those conversations ought not readily meet dismissal as merely academic. Opportunities for distortion may and obviously do abound, but when they remain faithful to the wonder that calls forth their various disciplines, humanists and scientists alike advance and enrich the common good of the *humanum*. Theologians join in pursuing a further goal as well, namely, to promote the redemptive mission that confers on the Christian Church its reason for being. By that mission the Church seeks nothing less than to collaborate with God in rendering the divine solution to the problem of evil effective in history. A holy passion for that mission clearly animates each of the essays in the present volume and adds a further dimension to the bonds of collegial affection that exist among its authors.

By dint of the diligent digging through dusty archives that is his *forte*, Patrick Hayes evokes the world that formed me, the Catholicism of a New York suburb in the 1940s and 1950s. The ministrations of Dominican sisters and Irish Christian Brothers planted me firmly in that world, but, on the other hand, it was not my whole world. My father only came into the Church after I had left home, and I was the only Catholic child on our block. Hayes mentions my paternal grandfather, an assimilated German Jewish professor of pharmacology for whom, like many of his generation and since, Comte had got it right; science had succeeded to philosophy and religion. I sometimes wonder if what animates my theology is not an impulse to mediate between the worlds of my grandparents. Visits to my mother's parents in Syracuse featured kneeling with my grandmother to recite the rosary during thunderstorms, and my maternal grandfather regularly took the 3 AM slot for adoration of the Blessed Sacrament.

Hayes also delves into my youthful sojourn at the Jesuit philosophate at Shrub Oak, New York. Contrary to rumors abroad in other Jesuit houses of formation, we did not smuggle Heidegger into the chapel beneath our missal covers. Still, even as the stable world of Jesuit formation was coming undone in the early 1960s, at great human cost, the superb faculty of the philosophate impressed upon me that philosophy was first of all something to be done, with verve and excitement, not something found ready-made in books—and certainly not in those official neoscholastic textbooks that never left the seminary librarian's closet.

Dennis Doyle generously credits me with having prodded him to a discovery (always a self-discovery) of the relevance of Lonergan's articulation of generalized empirical method, specified as theological by religious conversion, for his own subsequent outstanding work in ecclesiology. Specifically, Doyle's essay wields Lonergan's construal of the relationship between faith and beliefs in order to exhibit the possibility of reconceiving the Catholic doctrine of the foundation of the Church by Jesus Christ. Doyle seeks to do so in a manner both responsive to the challenge of historical consciousness and capable of promoting Christian ecumenism. Operating from the same Lonerganian base, David Hammond addresses the broad front established by contemporary globalization and the need it generates for a macroethic (Schillebeeckx) or *Weltethik* (Küng). Dialogue and collaborative praxis across cultural and religious traditions require common ground, and Hammond locates that ground, not in any set of propositions or first principles, but in the concrete reality of human persons ineluctably negotiating the exigencies of cognitive, moral, and religious self-transcendence. In this manner he succeeds in rehabilitating the notion of "universal reason" in a non-rationalist, non-foundationalist manner.

Gerard Sloyan and Peter Phan consider the christological tradition from either end, as it were, Sloyan revisiting the period of its classical formation and Phan gazing adventurously forward. Sloyan mounts a vigorous defense of Nestorius that by implication absolves both the unlucky fifth-century patriarch of Constantinople and today's Nestorian churches of the heretical "Nestorianism" constructed, not without ulterior motive, by Cyril of Alexandria. Notable, and typical of Sloyan's scholarship, is Sloyan's appeal to liturgical sources that informed Nestorius's faith. With the absolution for which he calls I entirely agree. Cyril and Nestorius embraced the same faith, and their insistence on reading one another in the worst possible light, for whatever reasons, had an unnecessary and tragic outcome. At the same time I find that some questions linger about the relative adequacy of their respective formulations as Sloyan presents them. So, for example, Sloyan finds the key to Cyril's argument to lie in a univocal use of the non-biblical term *hypostasis* for both the divine and the human. Univocity, of course, was the flaw Schleiermacher thought to detect in the Chalcedonian formula, and so I would ask whether Sloyan wants to subject Cyril to the same criticism. Or again, Sloyan has Nestorius charge that Cyril's notion of hypostatic union militates against the fullness of Christ's human personhood—a charge leveled against Chalcedon by both Schleiermacher and in contemporary revisionist proposals like those of Piet Schoonenberg and Roger Haight. Does Sloyan himself endorse the charge? Further, given the ultimate inadequacy of all human efforts to conceptualize divine mystery, should Nestorius's notion of prosoponic union merit indulgence or does it, ironically, reduce to the idea of natural union that Nestorius found so abhorrent? I suspect that the fifth-century debate has not really ended.

Phan finds in the contemporary practice of interfaith dialogue an opportunity to complement and enrich Christian understanding of who Jesus is with a collaboratively constructed "interfaith Christology." In a move I find important and promising, he stipulates the construction of a pneumatology as the prolegomenon for this effort. For all its novelty, Phan's project can claim very traditional antecedents and analogues, from the Logos Christologies of the patristic era to the reimaginings of Christ and Mary in indigenous settings to which Kathleen McManus's

essay in the present volume draws our attention. As did they, he anticipates that his project will enhance the intelligibility of belief in Christ in
non-Western and non-Abrahamic contexts. His project becomes provocative, as he readily admits, when he pursues a dialogical reconstruction of the term "Christ," while bracketing the issue of the relationship
of the reality intended by that term to Jesus of Nazareth.

Continuing the theme of Christology, Christopher McMahon
addresses a position I have taken on the theological relevance of historical-Jesus constructs, and Anthony Godzieba challenges the way I
have approached the question of the origin of Christian belief in the
resurrection of Jesus. As it happens, Godzieba figures in McMahon's
essay as well. With regard to that essay, the position I took reflected my
sense at the time that a number of my Catholic colleagues seemed to
be hastening to catch up with what I regarded as a nineteenth-century
Protestant liberal mistake, exemplified by Adolf von Harnack when he
appealed to "Jesus and his simple message" as the norm for Christian
belief and practice. This maneuver I took to be a mistake for two reasons. Viewed formally, it represented an exercise in the foundationalism
so widely and rightfully criticized of late. Terrence Tilley has made this
point about the misuse of historical-Jesus constructs cogently.[1] Second,
it advanced a simplistic identification between the "real Jesus" and a
contingent and unstable historical construct. Hence I took the position
that historical-Jesus constructs were by no means the basis or norm of
Christian faith, although they could suitably provide grist for the religious imagination engaged in retelling the story of Jesus at particular
times and under particular circumstances.

McMahon responds with a complex argument that invokes
Godzieba's contention for continuity between precritical and postcritical readings of the Gospels and for the permanent theological necessity of assigning criteriological value to the life of Jesus. On this basis
McMahon wants to suggest that, at the hands of John P. Meier and N.
T. Wright, historical-Jesus research displays both the exercise of that
criteriological function and further ecclesial-kerygmatic dimensions as
well. With regard to Godzieba, I fully agree that a medieval like Ludolf
of Saxony is likely to have a more accurate grasp on the truth about Jesus
than does a contemporary scholar like, say, John Dominic Crossan. The

1. See Terrence W. Tilley, *History, Theology and Faith: Dissolving the Modern Problematic* (Maryknoll, NY: Orbis, 2004).

truth in question I take to be that of Christian faith in Jesus' divine identity and redemptive agency. On the other hand, where historical questions about Jesus in his first century context are in play, I would not grant the advantage to Ludolf. Indeed, his concern for trustworthy witnesses is precisely what defines his notion of history as precritical. More generally, where Godzieba brings to the issue something like a hermeneutics of continuity, I confess to wielding a hermeneutics of disruption. (Enter the voice of my grandfather?) I find great value in Paul Ricoeur's analysis of the first naïveté that informed the world of someone like Ludolf and that critical history serves to shatter. Having grown up in the security of that first naïveté, I find compelling the challenge of forging a postcritical mediation of the faith—a mediation to which Godzieba, in his appropriation of certain strands of postmodern philosophy, himself contributes admirably.

Restricting myself to McMahon's comments on John P. Meier, I find that McMahon cogently demonstrates why Meier's performance as historian is superior to his articulation of his methodology. Meier lays out the criteria wherewith he sifts the relevant data—largely the four Gospels—to extract from those data a set of variously probable historical facts representing what Jesus said, did, and underwent. The criteria do not, of course, operate automatically, and so already Meier's keen intellect, vast learning, and judicious discernment come into play. More importantly, however, that set of varyingly probable facts does not interpret itself, and so they furnish the data for a second set of operations in which Meier also engages but which he does not thematize. Besides establishing the facts, he entertains the further question of what they amount to, and by so doing, he moves beyond the purview of his method as he has articulated it. Still, I would note that in conversation Meier has expressed admiration for the methodological section, if not the results, of Ben Meyer's *The Aims of Jesus*, in which this further dimension of the historian's task receives attention.[2] Be that as it may, I find it something of a leap in McMahon's argument, when, having demonstrated that Meier, like any good historian, does more than assemble a set of facts, he concludes that Meier's performance exemplifies "the theological character of historical Jesus research," or that Meier, along with Wright, has effected "the construction of a saving narrative."

2. See Ben F. Meyer, *The Aims of Jesus* (London: SCM, 1979).

Others may employ Meier's results to that end, and McMahon even suggests how they might do so, but I remain unpersuaded that that is the task that so strenuously engages Meier.

Space constrains me to one final comment. McMahon invokes Latin American liberation theology as paradigmatic for the criteriological function of historical-Jesus research. I would ask, however, whether the term "historical Jesus" does not bear different, even equivocal meanings when employed by someone like John Meier on the one hand and the Latin Americans on the other. For Meier the term clearly means Jesus in so far as his earthly career can be reconstructed by historical-critical procedures. For the Latin Americans, however, the term stands in contrast to Christ viewed solely, and hence "dangerously," through the dogmas of the patristic era. For the liberation theologians the term primarily designates Jesus as narrated especially in the Synoptic Gospels, even if they also engage in a loose, at most incidental, and perhaps rhetorically unfortunate appeal to Meier's sense of the term.

In the copious literature on the question of the origin of Christian belief in the resurrection of Jesus I have discerned three distinct positions represented by believing Christian authors. All agree that a real encounter with the risen Christ initiated that belief, but they differ on how that encounter was mediated. Some authors postulate that it involved an experience of really seeing what was objectively out there to be seen, although given the eschatological character of that reality, the seeing is unique and mysterious. Others are content to attribute the element of sight in the encounter to a visionary experience, while the reality of the encounter is safeguarded by a sacramental analogy. In a third category I located the position advocated by Edward Schillebeeckx in his *Jesus: An Experiment in Christology*.[3] On that account the origin of the belief lay in a conversion experience on the part of Peter and the disciples regathered around him, while the language of sight derived from a literary convention. It struck me that the underlying issue at stake lay in differences among proponents of the three positions on the relations among experience, objectivity, and the real.

I would offer two minor refinements to Godzieba's presentation of my account. First, I find his observation that I placed the third position between the first two simply puzzling. The first two took the element of

3. See Edward Schillebeeckx, *Jesus: An Experiment in Christology*, trans. Hubert Hoskins (New York: Crossroad, 1979).

seeing as a historical fact (over the explanation of which they differed) while Schillebeeckx did not. As for my explication of Schillebeeckx, I did not have him arguing that the disciples' experience of grace resulted from a real encounter; rather, I saw him as identifying the two. Parenthetically, I regarded this aspect of his argument as a strength because it served to highlight the fact, also emphasized by Walter Kasper, that at the origin of belief in Christ's resurrection lay a faith experience attributable, in faith, to divine initiative. By no means, then, did I join those critics who found in Schillebeeckx grounds for a charge of subjectivism.

Godzieba would relocate Schillebeeckx. His argument requires that one (1) prescind from the speculative narrative of conversion postulated in Schillebeeckx's *Jesus*; (2) advert to emendations that Schillebeeckx made subsequently in response to his critics; and, most importantly, (3) give full weight to Schillebeeckx's wielding of a phenomenological epistemology and ontology of experience. By this route Godzieba would discover in Schillebeeckx a "strong" theory of the origin of belief in the resurrection that, in terms of the three positions I outlined, would move him into the first while at the same time offering an adequate solution to the issue of objectivity.

With Godzieba's insistence that the objectivity in question is the objectivity of divine revelation and that revelation cannot but be mediated by experience I agree. A preliminary question I would raise is whether, in the course of his masterful exposition of the phenomenological tradition, Godzieba's dismissal of "realism" *tout court* is not too sweeping. Granting the inadequacy of the dogmatic realism of modern scholasticism, I would urge the value of a critical realism—Bernard Lonergan's—for which objectivity is the fruit of authentic subjectivity. This is a realism that, like Godzieba's phenomenologists, gives full weight to the notion of constituted experience. And like them, Lonergan exhibits as illusory the subject-object dichotomy that plagues modern thought.

Godzieba's "strong" theory insists on the reality of God's act in raising Jesus, an act by which God eschatologically transformed Jesus in his corporeal identity. That act is distinct from and prior to the disciples' faith experience in and through which the resurrection is manifest. With these two elements of Godzieba's "strong" theory I concur. To them he adds a third. Godzieba riffs on Schillebeeckx's terminology

("Jesus' personal-cum-bodily resurrection") to propose Jesus' transformed corporeality as the "objective" component of the disciples' faith experience, its "not-I catalyst," and he appeals to the New Testament testimony to argue that only the language of body and vision is appropriate to an experience of this "objective" component. On this basis he postulates the third component of his theory, namely, that it regards the appearance narratives and empty tomb narratives as interlocking, inseparable evidence.

The sophistication of Godzieba's argument and constraints of space allow me only the following questions, which, I would note, I intend as genuine inquiries, open-ended. First, does he conceive the outcome of God's act in raising Jesus, the "spiritual body" of which Paul speaks, as a still material and hence literally imaginable reality? There exist phenomenological analyses of corporeality that would allow a negative response to this question, but when, in a companion piece to the present article, Godzieba applies the fourfold medieval hermeneutic of Scripture to Jesus' risen bodiliness, he seems to incline to the positive.[4] If that is the case, second, does not the modern subject-object dichotomy still underlie his account of the rise of belief in the resurrection when he locates Jesus' transformed corporeality precisely as the "not-I catalyst"? Does this "catalyst" function as an instance of what Lonergan would call an "already out there now real" object to be known, finally, by taking a good, if constituted, look? Finally, does his promotion of empty tomb and appearance narratives to the status of "interlocking and inseparable evidence" establish them as the kind of proof that entails a supernaturalist dualism and its crudely modern sense of "miracle"?

Anselm of Canterbury's *Cur Deus Homo* dominated Western soteriological reflection for the better part of a millennium. As both Thomas Schärtl and Christopher Denny attest, however, in recent years his satisfaction theory has met vigorous critique. Schärtl ingeniously suggests that an advance may be made if one substitutes the notions of virtue and paradigm for Anselm's central metaphors of debt and payment while retaining the basic "grammar" of Anselm's argument,

---

4. See Anthony J. Godzieba, "Bodies and Persons, Resurrected and Postmodern: Towards a Relational Eschatology," in *Theology and Conversation: Towards a Relational Theology*, ed. Jacques Haers and Peter De Mey, Bibliotheca Ephemeridum Theologicarum Lovaniensium 172 (Leuven: Leuven University Press, 2003) 211–25.

a move, I would note, with interesting consequences for the modern debate between proponents of "objective" and liberal "subjective" theories of the atonement. Still, Schärtl concurs with Peter Hünermann that the Anselmian grammar itself is conceived in legal terms that hopelessly compromise it. Hence a fresh start is in order, and Schärtl builds from the New Testament grammar of reconciliation and participation toward a Trinitarian theology of salvation that relates the cross to both Jesus' ministry and the resurrection. In that context the cross functions as the revelation of both the depth of sin and violence and of the divine forgiveness that initiates a counter-history to the reign of sin.

On the one hand I would ask whether Anselm's text is fairly characterized as legalistic, a point contested by several of the authors whom Denny surveys. The Latin *debitum* is, of course, ambiguous, and I believe a case can be made that what controls Anselm's usage is a Platonic-Augustinian metaphysics wherein human beings achieve their humanity by corresponding to the divine will for them, namely, by loving God as the Highest Good, so that his construal of both sin and its remedy acquires relational and existential depth beyond the merely legal realm. This is not, however, to claim that Anselm's satisfaction theory can serve as an adequate contemporary soteriology, nor that it is flawless on its own terms. With regard to the latter point, what Hans Kessler identified as *Äquivalenzdenken* plays a distracting, if not commanding, role in Anselm, and it reappears in Aquinas as well.[5]

Christopher Denny continues the discussion of Anselm with a richly textured, wide-ranging survey of contemporary interpretations and evaluations of the *Cur Deus Homo*. Differences continue to abound in construing what Anselm means to say, what he is doing when he says it, and how well his performance passes muster as Christian theology, and Denny nimbly draws them into an ordered conversation. My own view has been that Anselm opens up the realm of theory in soteriology, theory understood as the realm of meaning one enters by proceeding from a descriptive existentially compelling grasp of things as they relate to us to a systematically explanatory grasp of things in their relations to one another, from the *priora quoad nos* to the *priora quoad se*, as Aquinas might put it. If this notion of theory derives from Aristotle, it also needs to be adjusted in three directions. First, *pace* Aristotle,

---

5. See Hans Kessler, *Die theologische Bedeutung des Todes Jesu. Eine traditionsgeschichtliche Untersuchung* (Düsseldorf: Patmos, 1970) 130.

explanation is not tied to necessity, and this is as true of theology as it is of natural science. Both seek the intelligibility of the contingent matter of fact. Second, in theology theory is not an end in itself but finds completion in service to the praxis generated by the primary narrative. Third, given the divine incomprehensibility, theology will always resort to analogy in forging the nest of terms and relations that renders it systematic. This latter claim serves to highlight one of Denny's most significant findings, namely, that a fault line runs along roughly confessional lines dividing those amenable to a theoretic mediation of the intelligibility of biblical narrative from those for whom narrative temporality is not only primary but also normative.

Among our authors Thomas Schärtl has already broached the topic of a contemporary theology of salvation, and I find myself in agreement with his suggestion that salvation refers at least in part to a process in history "kick-started" by the Christ event. Our understanding of both the event and the process has been enriched greatly in recent years by the emergence of feminist, womanist, and mujerista theologians, and in Kathleen McManus's essay the voices of all three eloquently converge. Operating phenomenologically, McManus draws us into the overwhelming history of innocent suffering, past and present, which for Edward Schillebeeckx constitutes the hermeneutical a priori for contemporary theology. In a move similar to Jon Sobrino's when he wrote of the "crucified people" of Latin America, McManus would have us recognize in suffering humanity and ravaged earth the Feminine Wounded Body of Christ. She finds that a path to redemption lies in appropriating from medieval women mystics a liberating mysticism of desire. This mysticism discovers in the passion of Christ a path of self-transcendence through *kenosis*, and McManus identifies the self-sacrificing love that animates this path as the key to redemption even in the face of the damage inflicted on women by misuse of the notion. Her essay honors the Dominican ideal of *contemplata tradere*; it also inspires gratitude for the rising generation of feminist theologians.

Self-sacrificing love and the heart's desire for God are also central to the transposition of soteriology that Lonergan tucked away in the final thesis of his *De Verbo Incarnato*.[6] Having reviewed the New Testament affirmations of redemption in Christ and clarified the tra-

6. See Bernard Lonergan, *De Verbo Incarnato* (Rome: Gregorian University Press, 1964).

ditional notion of satisfaction, in that final thesis Lonergan transposed those *vetera* into the further realm of meaning—interiority, beyond common sense and theory—differentiated with the appropriation of the operations of human consciousness. In that context he proposed a principle of transformation, what he called the Law of the Cross, as the intrinsic intelligibility of the economy of incarnation, cross, and resurrection. I have long been persuaded that with the Law of the Cross Lonergan articulates the dynamics of the *metanoia* effected by the gift of the Spirit as pledge of a share in the resurrection of Christ. For this reason it can stand as my candidate for the "essence" of Christianity.

Lonergan also elaborated a theology of history in which he posited redemption as the third "vector." Cynthia Crysdale first lays out the Law of the Cross and then helpfully relates it to the larger context of the worldview—"emergent probability"—that Lonergan found implicit in the complementarity of classical and statistical methods in the empirical sciences and that underlies his understanding of history. One point about the Law of the Cross deserves emphasis. When its second step prescribes that the effect of sin, death, be accepted out of love, misunderstandings easily ensue. Nietzsche famously dismissed Christianity as a religion for the world's doormats, and, as both McManus and Crysdale recognize, women have particularly suffered from the ideological perversion of the ideal of self-sacrifice. Crysdale astutely deflects this misconstrual. As she notes, the Law of the Cross counsels not passivity but active resistance in the face of evil. In his passion Jesus actively refused to descend to the level of his persecutors and thus to further the spiral of dehumanization—death in the larger sense—that sin engenders. That refusal to meet violence with violence, malice with malice, flowed from the love for his Father and for his fellow human beings; it transformed the reality of his dying into an expression of that love. His acceptance of death asserts the worthwhileness of fidelity to the exigencies of self-transcendence unto God even, in extreme circumstances, at the cost of one's physical life. In all circumstances for those who, unlike Jesus, are not wholly innocent, that fidelity entails a dying to one's own sinfulness, to the hold that the dehumanizing dynamics of the society and culture into which one has been initiated have over one. This is the kenotic path, to use McManus's term, toward the fullness of human authenticity. In a world marked by sin the anticipatory experience of risen life cannot but be cruciform.

For most people marriage and parenthood are probably the most immediate occasion for the exercise of self-sacrificing love, the ordinary means of salvation, and Jason King gives the discussion a concrete turn by exploring the family as a potentially redemptive agent. Drawing on the critical analyses of the consumer society offered by John Kavanaugh and Vincent Miller, he searches out resources for countering the disvalues on which that society is founded. Julie Rubio's suggestion of dual vocation renders participating in the world of work a matter of loving collaboration in the common good rather than unbridled competition in pursuit of self-satisfaction. David McCarthy in turn elaborates the notion of the open household in which the operative value is community rather than self-sufficiency, a community constituted by the sharing of gifts in a pattern of reciprocity. As countercultural, both suggestions set the family at odds with the normative ideals of the larger society, and the price of such dissonance, King contends, validates the Law of the Cross.

The consumer society, however, takes as gospel a specific understanding of the economy, namely, the classical liberal theory according to which the dynamics of supply and demand coupled with free competition cannot but guarantee a healthy, self-regulating economic sector. Very early in his career, under the shadow of the Great Depression, Lonergan discerned that mere denunciation of the evils of the dominant economic ideology was insufficient and, in the long run, vain. The solution of economic problems required a correct understanding of the dynamics of the economy. Having begun to address this task in the 1930s and 40s, he returned to it in his retirement.

Stephen Martin opens up the results at which Lonergan arrived in a manner most helpful to theologians like me who run the risk of becoming *Fachidioten*, locked up in the discipline that defines their comfort zone. Given Lonergan's theology of history, of course, such self-limitation becomes self-contradictory. As a force within history redemption heals the ravages of sin in a manner that also frees the creativity of human intelligence and so promotes progress in the achievement of the human good. It is that holistic redemptive process that both Church, and within the Church, theology, exist to serve. Neither is an end in itself.

Besides unveiling the *arcana* of Lonergan's understanding of surplus and basic goods and cycles and the relations between them Martin also contrasts Lonergan's critical and creative appropriation of the modern differentiation of the social sciences to their deconstruction and dismissal at the hands of various participants in the Radical Orthodoxy movement. If the latter seek to obviate the dangers of scientific reductionism, their response seems to swing to the opposite extreme, what might be fairly called a theological reductionism. But beyond noting the profound contrast between Lonergan and the Radical Orthodoxy proponents one might also raise the further question of what generates that contrast. Martin offers an important clue, I think, when he cites a 1980 piece in which, reflecting on the biases that distort history and the possibility of a solution, Lonergan notes that the theological form of the issue lies in Augustine and his commentators. Certainly the Radical Orthodoxy figures take Augustine as their hero, and their rejection of secular thought seizes upon Augustine's portrayal of the corruption of reason consequent upon sin. Lonergan, on the other hand, stands squarely in the tradition of Aristotle and Aquinas, with the latter's recognition of the integrity and relative autonomy of the order of creation and confidence in the power of grace to heal and restore the power of reason. For Lonergan religious conversion can generate both moral and intellectual conversion, and it is from within the horizon generated by those conversions that he can set about the task of figuring out the workings of the economic order on its own terms. His economic theory thus counts as secular, as Martin notes, without being secularistic.

I would reiterate my humble gratitude to the editors and contributors to this volume for the honor they do me and for the opportunity for conversation they afford. In closing, I would like to acknowledge one more debt of gratitude. Had Patrick Hayes extended his narrative beyond New York, across the Hudson and all the way to Milwaukee, he would have surely have devoted some pages to the influence of Professor Quentin Quesnell. It was he who both introduced me to the thought of Bernard Lonergan and inspired me with a model of free, fiercely relentless, and totally committed theological inquiry. To him, and to all those—students, colleagues, and friends—who have taught me over the years and continue to do so, thank you.